TRADITIONAL RITUAL AS CHRISTIAN WORSHIP

The American Society of Missiology Series, published in collaboration with Orbis Books, seeks to publish scholarly works of high merit and wide interest on numerous aspects of missiology—the study of Christian mission in its historical, social, and theological dimensions. Able presentations on new and creative approaches to the practice and understanding of mission will receive close attention from the ASM Series Committee.

About the Cover

The cover is a photograph of an 84- by 79-centimeter storyboard titled "The Last Supper," and is a vivid example of the hybridization that our book revolves around. The artist, Peter Dambui, is from Kambot on the Sepik River of Papua New Guinea, a place that has a long tradition of carving the wooden masks used in the Spirit Houses (*Haus Tambaran* in Melanesian Pidgin) that were the center of traditional ancestor veneration in the East Sepik district.

The storyboard was brought to Stephen Reichert, OFM Cap, Catholic archbishop of Madang by Mr. Dambui's wife. Archbishop Reichert immediately liked it and hung it (temporarily, he thought) behind the tabernacle of the Madang Cathedral. The bishop received so many positive comments that he decided to purchase it and make it a permanent part of the cathedral.

"The Last Supper" storyboard is interesting for the Melanesian features given to Jesus and his disciples but also the juncture it makes between Jesus opening the scroll of the prophet Isaiah in the synagogue of Nazareth, where he began his public ministry (Luke 4:16, 18–21ff). The artist links the beginning of his ministry (of the Word) with the Last Supper (Luke 22:7–20) and the ministry of the Sacrament, the two bringing together the Old Testament and the New to be sealed in his blood.

The storyboard reminds one of the fresco by Taddeo Gaddi, who painted the Baroncelli Chapel in the Franciscan church of Santa Croce in Florence, commonly known as *The Last Supper*, *Tree of Life*, and *Four Miracle Scenes* (early fourteenth century). That famous fresco brings together figures from the Old Testament and the new, as well as contemporary figures, grouped around both the crucifixion of Jesus and the Last Supper. The works of both Gaddi and Dambui are allegorical, products of a religious imagination that teaches the meaning of Christ and his presence today in terms that conflate and collapse history, as salvation is an ever-recurring dimension that unites time and eternity. Their art speaks of the life of faith at a different level than exegetical exactitude. Dare we call it the fruit of "hybridization" using traditional techniques to convey meanings deeper than words can yield?

American Society of Missiology Series, No. 56

TRADITIONAL RITUAL AS CHRISTIAN WORSHIP

Dangerous Syncretism or Necessary Hybridity?

Edited by

R. Daniel Shaw and William R. Burrows

ORBIS BOOKS
Maryknoll, New York 10545

ORBIS BOOKS
Maryknoll, New York 10545

Fathers and Brothers MARYKNOLL

Founded in 1970, Orbis Books endeavors to publish works that enlighten the mind, nourish the spirit, and challenge the conscience. The publishing arm of the Maryknoll Fathers and Brothers, Orbis seeks to explore the global dimensions of the Christian faith and mission, to invite dialogue with diverse cultures and religious traditions, and to serve the cause of reconciliation and peace. The books published reflect the views of their authors and do not represent the official position of the Maryknoll Society. To learn more about Maryknoll and Orbis Books, please visit our website at www.maryknollsociety.org.

Published by Orbis Books, Maryknoll, New York 10545-0302.
Manufactured in the United States of America.

Library of Congress Cataloging-in-Publication Data

Names: Shaw, R. Daniel (Robert Daniel), 1943– editor.
Title: Traditional ritual as Christian worship : dangerous syncretism or necessary hybridity? / edited By R. Daniel Shaw and William R. Burrows.
Description: Maryknoll : Orbis Books, 2018. | Series: The American Society of Missiology series ; No. 56 | Includes bibliographical references and index.
Identifiers: LCCN 2017035658 (print) | LCCN 2017048114 (ebook) | ISBN 9781608337279 (e-book) | ISBN 9781626982628 (pbk.)
Subjects: LCSH: Public worship. | Worship. | Ritual. | Rites and ceremonies. | Ritualism. | Christianity and culture. | Missions.
Classification: LCC BV15 (ebook) | LCC BV15 .T73 2018 (print) | DDC 264—dc23
LC record available at https://lccn.loc.gov/2017035658

To the members of the American Society of Missiology;
source of so many insights—
our colleagues and conversation partners for many years

"Jesus does not replace the messengers Creator sent to our peoples, He completes the messages they brought. He does not take away the ceremonies, He restores and strengthens them. His path is not that of assimilation, nor of destruction, but of peace, healing, restoration, and walking humbly with the Creator as the people He made us to be. I am in no way bound or oppressed by following Jesus, but free to follow Him on the Red Road, and take my place dancing before the Sacred Fire."

—One Hot Mama, Native American artist

Contents

Preface to the American Society of Missiology Series

The purpose of the American Society of Missiology Series is to publish—without regard for disciplinary, national, or denominational boundaries—scholarly works of high quality and wide interest on missiological themes from the entire spectrum of scholarly pursuits relevant to Christian mission, which is always the focus of books in the Series.

By mission is meant the effort to effect passage over the boundary between faith in Jesus Christ and its absence. In this understanding of mission, the basic functions of Christian proclamation, dialogue, witness, service, worship, liberation, and nurture are of special concern. And in that context questions arise, including how does the transition from one cultural context to another influence the shape and interaction between these dynamic functions, especially in regard to the cultural and religious plurality that comprises the global context of Christian life and mission.

The promotion of scholarly dialogue among missiologists, and among missiologists and scholars in other fields of inquiry, may involve the publication of views that some missiologists cannot accept, and with which members of the Editorial Committee themselves do not agree. Manuscripts published in the Series, accordingly, reflect the opinions of their authors and are not understood to represent the position of the American Society of Missiology or of the Editorial Committee. Selection is guided by such criteria as intrinsic worth, readability, coherence, and accessibility to a range of interested persons and not merely to experts or specialists.

The ASM Series, in collaboration with Orbis Books, seeks to publish scholarly works of high merit and wide interest on numerous aspects of missiology—the scholarly study of mission. Able presentations on new and creative approaches to the practice and understanding of mission will receive close attention.

Acknowledgments

We are grateful to the presidents and annual meeting organizers of the American Society of Missiology: Craig Van Gelder, Robert Priest, Stanley Skreslet, Greg Leffel, Patricia Fenrick, and Allison Fitchett. All have offered their help in enabling us to discuss the concepts presented in this book at four different meetings of the ASM. We also owe a debt of gratitude to Robert Hunt and the ASM Series Committee for their support in making this book a reality. Their work with the editors at Orbis Books to bring this volume to publication is deeply valued.

We are also grateful to Stephen Bevans, Justin Barrett, Ennio Mantovani, and Darrell Whiteman, who have read and critiqued our work. We appreciate the encouragement offered by colleagues in our respective academic institutions: Fuller Graduate School of Intercultural Studies and New York Theological Seminary. Lunch conversations, lectures, and critiques have all contributed to our thinking. Our students also loom large as they process our ideas in their contexts, many represented in the chapters of this book. Their feedback and excitement demonstrated we were on the right track. Finally, we acknowledge the John Templeton Foundation for funding the research project (ID: 59142). This has enabled Dan Shaw to confirm his ideas by gathering data that reflects how people think about God, which in turn affects relevant godly worship.

As the project that eventuated in the book you hold in hand went into overtime, we are especially grateful to our wives, Georgia Grimes Shaw and Linda Burrows, who persevered through belabored discussions and encouraged us through the process. Thanks!

Contributors

Cheryl Bear is a multiple-award-winning singer/songwriter who shares stories of Indigenous life—the joy, sorrow, faith, and journey. She has a BA from Pacific Life Bible College in Surrey, British Columbia, Canada; an MDiv from Regent College in Vancouver, BC; and a DMin from The King's University in Los Angeles, California. She is from the Nadleh Whut'en First Nations community (Bear Clan) in northern British Columbia. She travels to First Nations communities around North America, sharing songs of healing and songs to the Creator. Dr. Bear is the author of *Introduction to First Nations Ministry* (Cherohala Press, 2013). She makes her home in Vancouver and Prince George, British Columbia, Canada.

William R. (Bill) Burrows is research professor of missiology at New York Theological Seminary and Senior Fellow in the Andrew F. Walls Center for the Study of Christianity in Africa and Asia at Liverpool Hope University. He became a student for the Society of the Divine Word (SVD) in 1958 and was ordained in Rome in 1971. He holds the STL from the Gregorian University in Rome and a PhD from the University of Chicago Divinity School. From 1972 to 1977 he worked as a theology teacher and rural pastor in Papua New Guinea and left the SVD to marry Linda Williams Fyfe in 1985. Dr. Burrows became managing editor of Orbis Books in 1989 and supervised acquisition and publishing of over three hundred volumes. He has served the American Society of Missiology as president and received the ASM's lifetime achievement award in 2016. He and Linda make their home in Cortlandt Manor, New York.

Joshua Kurung Daimoi is Principal Emeritus of Christian Leaders Training College (CLTC) in Papua New Guinea (PNG). He took his theological training at Baptist Theological College in Sydney, Australia and earned an LTh from Melbourne College of Divinity; a BA from the University of Papua New Guinea; a ThM from Fuller Graduate School of World Mission, Pasadena, California; and a PhD from the University of Sydney. Dr. Daimoi served as principal of CLTC for twenty-two years and was senior pastor of Boroko Baptist Church in the National Capitol District (NCD) for seven years. He is an Officer of the Order of Logohu awarded by the PNG government for his leadership development in the community and his service to the Baptist Church. He is married to Mone, and they have three children and six grandchildren. They make their home in Boroko, NCD, PNG.

Stuart Dauermann is director of Interfaithfulness, a think tank dedicated to interfaith futurist thinking. He earned an MA and PhD in intercultural studies from Fuller Graduate School of Intercultural Studies, Pasadena, California. He is committed to understanding spirituality and relationships between Christians and Jews, as well as raising up households for Yeshua within the House of Israel. He is an ordained rabbi under the auspices of the Union of Messianic Jewish Congregations and the Messianic Jewish Rabbinical Council and served as rabbi at Ahavat Zion Messianic Synagogue in Beverly Hills, California. Dr. Dauermann's publications include *The Rabbi as a Surrogate Prie*st (Pickwick, 2009) and several monographs. He and his wife, Naomi, have three grown children and make their home in Altadena, California.

Chinaka S. DomNwachukwu is professor of multicultural education and associate dean for diversity and values at Azusa Pacific University School of Education in Azusa, California. He earned a BTh degree from the Nigerian Baptist Theological Seminary; an MA in educational leadership from National University, San Diego, California; and an MA and PhD in intercultural studies from the Fuller Graduate School of Intercultural Studies, Pasadena, California. Dr. DomNwaChukwu is an ordained Baptist minister and has published journal articles and several books, including *Multiculturalism: A Shalom Motif for the Christian Community* (Wipf and Stock, 2014) and *An Introduction to Multicultural Education* (Rowman and Littlefield, 2010). He is married to Nkechi; they have four children and make their home in Azusa, California.

John Sanjeevakumar Gupta died unexpectedly before this book went to press. His legacy lives on and inspires other Indian leaders to follow his example in developing ways to train Indians to reach India, as developed by his father, N. Paul V. Gupta, who was the founder of Hindustan Bible College in what is now Chennai, Tamil Nadu. John was a graduate of the University of Madras and the UCLA Graduate School of Management. He was awarded a doctor of divinity degree by the Institute for Leadership Development in Hyderabad, India. Expanding on his business experience, Dr. Gupta's focus for the past twenty years had been on training over five hundred cross-cultural communicators to serve in India. He applied an Indian approach for training village pastors to take the gospel message to their rural communities using methods and language that relates to their context. This made him a frequent conference speaker as well as a respected, mission leader and teacher, both in India and the United States. Until his untimely death, he lived in San Pedro, California, and is survived by four adult children.

Bradford Haami is a well-established Māori author and screenwriter focusing most recently on Māori biography. He is currently studying in a diploma graduate program on *Wairuatanga: Māori and Christianity* at Laidlaw College, Auckland, New Zealand. He was an elder with Victory Christian Church, Auckland, and has been a leader in the British-Māori repentance journey throughout New Zealand for the past four years. His latest book, *A Biography of Ihaka Samuels* (2016), tells the story of a Māori missionary who applied authentic indigenous ways to reach the hearts of the Kukukuku people of the Watut Valley, Papua New Guinea, in the 1970s. He and his wife, Salina, make their home in Henderson on the North Island of New Zealand.

Dan Hopkins is a bivocational pastor who serves the Exit 59 Downtown Church in Marion, Indiana, while also working on staff at Indiana Wesleyan University. He holds an MDiv degree from Grand Rapids Theological Seminary. Following seminary he and his wife, Cindi, served as missionaries for ten years, primarily in Recife, Brazil. His primary areas of interest are discipleship, ancient Christianity, and spiritual direction. He and Cindi make their home in Indianapolis, Indiana.

Paul Mantae Kim is the director for the Global Church Mission Institute in Los Angeles, California. He earned a BA in English language and literature from Yonsei University, South Korea, and has a ThM and PhD in intercultural studies from the Fuller Graduate School of Intercultural Studies, Pasadena, California. He was a missionary in Sri Lanka and now serves as an adjunct at Fuller and other seminaries in Southern California. Dr. Kim's publications include *The Puberty Ritual in Sri Lanka: A Comparative Exploration of Perceptions and Attitudes between Buddhists and Christians* (Peter Lang, 2011) and several articles on mission. He is married to Esther, and they live with their two children in Chino Hills, California.

Gabriel Kuman is a case worker and consultant to the government of Papua New Guinea (PNG) on Manus Island. He holds a BTh from the Catholic Theological Institute in Port Moresby, PNG; a postgraduate diploma in education from the Divine Word University in Madang, PNG; and an MA in international public health (MIPH) from the University of New South Wales, Australia. He has served as research and campaign manager for Transparency International, research officer with the Melanesian Institute in Goroka, and research project coordinator for the PNG Institute of Medical Research in Goroka. He has authored many research articles and chapters in books published by the Melanesian Institute and the research journal of the Divine Word University. He makes his home in the highlands of PNG.

Petros G. Malakyan is the founding president/CEO of Christian Leadership International Inc. (California) and National Leadership Institute (Armenia). He is currently serving as head of the department of organizational leadership at Robert Morris University. He holds dual master's degrees and a PhD in intercultural studies, with leadership concentration, from Fuller Graduate School of Intercultural Studies, Pasadena, California. Upon completing the PhD in 1998, he returned with his family in Armenia, where he has been engaged in grassroots leadership development. He has also had teaching and administrative posts at Azusa Pacific University and Indiana Wesleyan University, where he taught international leadership courses and oversaw leadership programs. Dr. Malakyan has authored journal articles and book chapters both in Armenia and the United States. He and his wife, Anahit, have two adult children and currently make their home in Pittsburgh, Pennsylvania.

Yoshiyuki Billy Nishioka is senior pastor of Kawagoe Church in Saitama, Japan, and the dean of Tokyo Biblical Seminary. Following graduation from Tokyo Biblical Seminary, he engaged in church planting for three years. He then went to America where he earned a BA and MDiv from Azusa Pacific University, a ThM in missiology, and a PhD in intercultural studies from the Fuller Graduate School of Intercultural Studies, Pasadena, California. While studying in the United States, he served as an assistant pastor at West Los Angeles Japanese Holiness Church. Dr. Nishioka's publications include *The Time a Person Considers God* (in Japanese), and "Worldview Methodology in Mission Theology" (*Missiology* 26, no. 4 [1996]). He is married to Mariko, and with their three daughters, they make their home in Saitama, Japan.

Emmanuel Obaro Obasare is a businessman and mission strategist with primary focus on Jamaica, Ghana, and Nigeria. He qualified as a Chartered Certified Accountant in London; earned an MDiv from the Caribbean Graduate School of Theology, Kingston, Jamaica; and earned the PhD in intercultural studies from Fuller Graduate School of Intercultural Studies, Pasadena, California. He currently serves as liaison officer for the Jamaica Maroon Secretariat as well as serving as a guest lecturer in mission theology at the Caribbean Graduate School of Theology. Dr. Obasare's publications include *Implications of Jamaican Maroon Understanding of Ancestors: An Interpretation* (UMI, 2005) and articles on Jamaican Maroon culture and other contexts where the power and influence of ancestors are prevalent. He and his wife, Carol, have five adult children and make their home in Kingston, Jamaica.

Osias Segura-Guzman serves as regional coordinator of curriculum and small group leadership development for the General Board of Global Ministries of the United Methodist Church in Nicaragua and Honduras. He earned a BA in sociology from Universidad de Costa Rica. He then earned an MDiv, ThM, and DMiss from Asbury Seminary, Wilmore, KY, and received an MA in organizational leadership from Eastern University, Philadelphia, Pennsylvania. He has been a missionary in the Caribbean and

Central America for the United Methodist Church and has served as affiliate faculty at Fuller Theological Seminary as well as other institutions. Dr. Segura-Guzman's publications include essays on contextualization, emerging churches, discipleship, evangelism, and general missiology. Together with his wife, Dr. Desiree Segura-April, and son, they make their home in Nicaragua and Costa Rica.

R. Daniel Shaw is senior professor of anthropology and translation at the Fuller Graduate School of Intercultural Studies, where he has served since 1982. He grew up the son of missionary parents in India and the Philippines. An interest in Native peoples led to a BA and MA in anthropology from the University of Arizona in 1967–68 and a PhD from the University of Papua New Guinea in 1975. He served with Wycliffe as a Bible translator among the Samo from 1969 to 1981. In 1982 he was invited to join the faculty of the then School of World Mission at Fuller Theological Seminary, Pasadena, California. He regularly consults and teaches around the world regarding cultural issues in translation and cross-cultural research and serves as an international anthropology consultant with SILInternational. Dr. Shaw has authored, coauthored, or edited numerous books, including two Samo ethnographies, as well as many chapters in books and numerous articles. He has three adult sons and six grandchildren. He and his wife, Georgia, make their home in Altadena, California.

Prologue

As Christianity increasingly encompasses the Global South, the face and expressions of Christianity in today's world are changing. Missionaries coming from Global South nations currently outpace those coming from the so-called Global North. Migration brings the mission field to countries that once sent out missionaries, and increasingly, former sending nations are themselves becoming mission fields. Yet Western theological concerns, worship styles, and approaches to Christian piety still dominate Christian expressions everywhere. The impact of Western control still affects how churches are run, what people hear from the pulpit, and how they worship God. The net result is what Robert Schreiter called "dual religion"—an underground traditional structure with its manifestations of deep beliefs and values, appearing to accept Christianity but without true understanding (Schreiter 1985). All over the world, people struggle with a power vacuum precipitated by Western views of spirituality.

In spite of efforts to train Western missionaries in things anthropological, a lack of appreciation remains for the conceptual clash that takes place when missionaries, from whatever country, interact with local people around the globe. The way Christianity has been portrayed still emanates from Western assumptions and theological systematics reflecting how people are presumed to respond to God. Christianity around the world remains, for the most part, a Western perspective on God rather than allowing people to determine God's intent in their local context and realize God's presence in their midst (Lev 26:12–13). The way people relate to God through recognition of Christ's death and resurrection in the power of the Holy Spirit must be manifest in ways that reflect local patterns of worship.

What is at stake is whether apparent biblical condemnations of traditional, non-Jewish and Christian rituals are the hermeneutic key with which to understand the meaning of *solus Christus* (Christ alone) in an intensely multicultural world. Historically these words, retrieved from the Protestant Reformation of the sixteenth century, formed the basis of missionary exhortations to abandon rituals that were performed to please, placate, and gain favor from superhuman beings, including ancestors. Such a removal of ritual from spiritual engagement in the church resulted in an impoverished understanding of God's presence. Traditional, largely actor-oriented communal engagement demonstrated active spirituality: leaving food for the spiritual presence, placing sacred rocks in the corners of a new garden, solemnly retelling how the ancestors taught a people's forebears to live abundant lives. These practices were replaced by individual-oriented patterns that reduced the relevance of spiritual expression and demeaned the one being worshiped. What then can contemporary Christians around the world do to restore what has been lost by virtue of misguided cultural readings of biblical and contemporary spiritual expressions? When God's intent (as expressed in biblical content) is responsibly joined with cultural expressions of spirituality in a hybrid mix, a new excitement and relevance emerge.

Working through these essays, we have come to realize that, while hybridity is a current hot topic with implications for postmodernism (Bhabha 1985; 1994), it is really just a new name for what always occurs when faith crosses cultural boundaries. Anthropological studies demonstrate that, in a globalizing world where change reflects sociocultural adjustments from precolonial, to colonial, and now postcolonial, no culture is static (Robbins 2004, 327ff.). More concretely, as reflected in recent presentations at the annual meetings of the American Society of Missiology (P. Lee, Weerakoon), we realize that we are really giving voice to a more general recognition of the cross-pollination or grafting that results in something new. We use the concept of hybridity to denote the space that is new by virtue of interaction between very different contributors. It implies an excitement and beauty of new expressions of worship that bring Scripture into the human context—the impact of God's presence in the midst of every people (Rev 7:9). This book reflects our desire to make the biblical and cultural interconnection positive rather than the negativity implied by using the term "syncretism." Using hybridity as we do creates a need to understand the dynamics and synthesis that create the new experience, thereby giving syncretism a positive focus rather than the typical negativity so often associated with native or Indigenous expressions of spirituality.

We begin by reflecting on the dynamic nature of ritual and ceremony from anthropological and personal (Shaw, chapter 1), as well as biblical, historical, and personal (Burrows, chapter 2) perspectives. In chapter 1, Shaw considers the importance of ritual and ceremony in people's lives. What is their rationale for engaging in ritual and ceremony? What can anthropological awareness and contemporary cognitive models tell us about the role of ritual and ceremony? As an anthropologist, Shaw must account for the recent development of an "Anthropology of Christianity" as a new subdiscipline that requires missiologists to account for the impact Christianity has on human socioreligious expression. The presence of Christianity must be accounted for, not ignored both culturally and missionally. Its impact on and relevance to the human condition bring renewed interest in change dynamics and the role of religious expression (Robbins 2004). If the use of locally understood rituals and ceremonies, long recognized as crucial to a people's well-being by anthropologists but largely ignored by missionaries, can be redirected to worshiping God, people may view Christianity as more than a "religion" and, rather, as a way of life centered on a relationship with Jesus. If ritual and ceremony can be reconceptualized to serve as a means for people to rethink their ancient wisdom in relationship to God's intent for them, Christianity may be seen as less foreign. A recent special edition of *Current Anthropology* makes the point that anthropologists can no longer ignore Christian presence (Robbins and Haynes 2014). In this volume, we seek to redeem culturally appropriate spiritual manifestations so that people can responsibly honor God by using their traditional rituals as a means for Christian worship.

In chapter 2, Burrows presents a biblically oriented reflection on God's perspective of ritual that contrasts how Catholics and Protestants have responded both positively and negatively from their respective hermeneutical positions. His insights in this area come from studies of the way in which St. Paul translated Hebrew and Aramaic terminology coming from the Old Testament and oral traditions of what Jesus said in his teaching. The work of N. T. Wright (passim, but most accessibly see 2008) and Paul Bradshaw (2002; 2004) helped lead Burrows to realize that the earliest documents of the New Testament are a profound translation of Semitic theological and cultural concepts into a form of Greek that was universal in the Mediterranean world of the time.

The origins of Christian worship and the Eucharist emerge from diaspora Judaism as well as Greek and Roman mystery cults, all profoundly transformed or converted to celebrate the "mystery" of the life, death, and resurrection of Jesus as the Christ and the power of the Holy Spirit in each community. Mystery cults such as Mithras, with origins in Persia, influenced the celebration of the Eucharist as a "making present" in the worshiping community of the entire saving dynamic of Jesus's *paschal transitus* to the Father (Casel 1962). Burrows proposes an alternative reading of early Christian history that encourages readers to consider whether (1) "hybridization" names what occurs when the Christian message encounters a people in a new socioreligious context and (2) this process is a necessary and legitimate part of a people giving voice in symbol and ritual to their new understanding of relationship with God.

Together we bring our respective field experience as well as lifetimes of professional research and writing, informed by academic teaching and insights from students who span the globe. Historically, Western missionaries have adamantly rejected local religious expressions. Sadly, colonial and mission history reveals the imposition of Western notions of power and authority in judging what was to be considered right and wrong, sacred and secular. We seek to avoid this externally induced "syncretism" and choose rather to reflect on the interaction that comes when God makes himself known. How can the use of familiar, culture-based ritual and ceremony, directed to God, rekindle spirituality and generate meaningful, godly worship? *Our intent is to encourage communities of believers to eschew dangerous syncretism while recognizing their culturally based spirituality that reflects necessary hybridity.*

The contributors to this volume are the true authors of the book and have impacted our thinking about this vital topic. They come from around the world to discuss the perspective of their own people. Each reflects, in their culturally induced ways, how the concept of hybridity can be applied to appreciating the role of traditional dances, recitals of ancient lore, celebrations, and exchanges between the visible world and the world beyond. Each brings God's Word into their context to demonstrate incarnation—God with us. In this way they clearly demonstrate how Scripture makes sense to their people. Through their experiences with worship forms that were often rejected by outsiders, they demonstrate how God's people bring their love for God into meaningful daily life. They show how people they know and love express their passion for Christ and through the power of the Holy Spirit present their honor and respect to God. They thereby present traditional rituals as a means of effective, meaningful Christian worship that shuns dangerous syncretism and celebrates necessary hybridity. The amazing people who emerge from these chapters bring their praise and worship to *Creator* and give thanks for all the blessings *Yahweh* (the almighty God above all other gods), *Chukwu* (the Igbo creator), the *Dema* (ancient ancestors of the Simbu), *Yenkipon* (the transplanted Ghanaian god of the Maroons), or *Rongo* (the Māori god of peace) has bestowed on them. Truly God was there before missionaries arrived.

STRUCTURE OF THE BOOK

We have structured the book on the basis of the title: *Ritual*, what human beings do to worship God, and *Worship*, a celebration of who God is and what God has done for human beings through Christ. Within each of these major parts, authors tend to emphasize the nature of ritual and worship, or focus more on the context in which those rites make sense. We, therefore, further divide each part into subsections reflective of the authors' foci. These are, of course, "fuzzy sets" as Paul Hiebert would call them (2008), as the authors present their material to reflect the interests and concerns of the people they represent. We, in turn, organize them to both reflect that interest and at the same time relate to our objective to reduce "dual religion" by encouraging people to connect Indigenous spiritual belief and practice to the observance of their faith.

The first two chapters provide a thoughtful introduction, using cultural and theological frameworks to empower those who have been impacted by Western missionaries and enlightenment ideology. The chapters in part one all reflect on use of traditional (i.e., pre- or non-Christian) rituals in Christian worship. They demonstrate how pre-Christian socioreligious traditions can be adapted to enable people to praise and give thanks to God who lives among them, who has revealed God's love in Jesus, and who wants them to live fulfilled lives. In part two, the focus shifts to Christian worship, which the authors show is a portrayal of Christianity among their people and not just an artificial, imposed religion. The respective expressions of God's presence among them clearly demonstrate their desire to give honor to God in culturally meaningful ways that express Christian worship. To be sure, these two emphases overlap, but together they provide an awareness of how people use ritual in the context of Christian worship.

In chapter 3, Osias Segura-Guzman tells how he helped a village pastor appreciate the theological implications of valuing a folk enactment of a Catholic myth while himself discovering reconciliation between Protestants and Catholics, not just in Costa Rica, but throughout Latin America. Next we experience a Simbu pig-kill through the eyes of Gabriel Kuman, who unites the traditional Dema myth with both the Passover and paschal mystery as a way to realize the powerful Melanesian theme of abundant life. Emmanuel Obasare then takes us to the interior of Jamaica to help us appreciate the personal struggle Maroon shamans experience as they seek to relinquish their "rights" of association with the Kromante Spirit in order to develop a dependence on the Holy Spirit.

The next three chapters emphasize the context in which ritual takes place. Paul Mantae Kim illustrates the value of ancestors in his own family experience and warns the Korean church that this strong element of Korean identity dare not be ignored. Bradford Haami appropriates traditional Māori protocol to encourage reconciliation between today's inhabitants of Aotearoa (contemporary New Zealand) so that they may once again experience wholeness and enjoy the peace for which they all long. In chapter 8, Petros Malakyan and his protégé, Dan Hopkins, tell a story spanning seventeen centuries of sensory worship that creates Armenian orthodoxy as experienced today. They conclude with a personal tale of identification with the prayers of St. Gregory that span the ages to ensure meaningful worship, despite being far removed from the context of their original expression.

As in part one, the chapters in part two loosely divide into a strong emphasis on relevant Christian worship per se or on the context in which that worship makes sense. Chinaka DomNwachukwu builds on Igbo cosmology to deftly demonstrate how an Igbo cultural hermeneutic shapes Igbo dynamics of worship and reflects their understanding of cosmic reality. In chapter 10, rural Japan comes alive in Billy Nishioka's empathetic description of a Christian ossuary designed to provide a place of honor and memory that enables Japanese pastors to use ancestral remembrance as a bridge to God. Messianic rabbi Stuart Dauermann closes this section of the book by bringing a long, scriptural-focused history to bear on contemporary Jewish family worship in the most sacred of Jewish religious expressions—Shabbat. He demonstrates that culture matters when he draws attention to Yeshua as the Messiah, who incorporates history and tradition while living in the reality of now.

The final three chapters place an emphasis on the context of Christian worship. Cheryl Bear connects the context of Indigenous North Americans with their spirituality through the spiritual cleansing that takes place during the smudging ceremony in its many manifestations. In chapter 13 Joshua Daimoi exegetes the Epistle to the Hebrews in light of Melanesian expectations. He presents Jesus as the "great ancestor" who is the object of Sentani faith recognized through both social and physical engagement. Finally, the late John Sanjeevakumar Gupta takes a narrative approach to help us recognize we dare not confuse culture and religion. He acknowledges that the story of God's presence has cultural roots common to the Hebrews and the people of India. Expressing biblical content should, he argues, reflect that common heritage.

The underlying question is this: how do the peoples who populate this volume utilize their religious experience to reflect contemporary Christian identity and self-understanding? Lurking behind this question is an issue of discernment that has bedeviled the church since Paul was confronted by Jesus on his way to Damascus (Ac 9:1–22) and the Holy Spirit challenged Peter about releasing non-Jewish converts from the requirement of obeying Israel's ritual laws (Ac 15). This book revolves around using traditional elements from a society's pre-Christian past and present and finding ways to incorporate these elements into meaningful Christian worship in a biblically responsible way. The contributors bring into relief ways to reflect through worship, prayer, and daily life the principle that Jesus is the Messiah, the *Christos*. As Christ-followers are added to his body, the church, from among all the peoples of earth, and as they mature in their identities as disciples, their worship and prayer must be suffused with elements that arise from wrestling with how they find the Spirit of Christ dwelling among them.

Let it be said that most of the contributing authors have kindly moved out of their interactive realm, with its focus on relationship, into our Western, academic realm with its didactic, propositional emphasis. We thank them. Sadly, colonialism still prevails. Writing for such a volume forces them to play by our rules. As you will see, they have entered our realm while we have also encouraged them to highlight their context so that we might benefit. We give these authors voice in the anthropological sense—license to reflect on what is important to them and the people they represent. We have encouraged culturally stylized introductions and leave-takings: genealogies, blessings, songs, and emotive reflection that echo the authors' perspective and context. It is interesting that many of these authors have positions in Western academic and ecclesial contexts that recognize their strengths and seek to bring them alongside Westerners who can benefit from that exposure.

We conclude the book with an Epilogue in which we organize collective insight, clarify ideas, and respond in a manner consistent with a cultural and biblical—that is, missiological—approach to the dynamic role of ritual and ceremony in worship.

William R. Burrows
R. Daniel Shaw

Introduction

1

The Dynamics of Ritual and Ceremony

Transforming Traditional Rites to Their Intended Purpose

R. Daniel Shaw

"Something is happening in the village—wake up." It was about 3 AM and Karen was trying to rouse me. "Something is going on in the village." As I struggled to wake up, I could hear singing coming from one of the longhouses. The sound rose and fell and was clearly different than anything I had heard before, so I went to check it out. The sound drew me to the Homamaku longhouse. A few people were roaming about carrying flaming torches to penetrate the dark, moonless night. But the focus of attention was clearly in the house. As I stepped across the threshold of the doorway a wave of sound engulfed me. I passed through the cook-area with its open fires tended by women busy ensuring guests were adequately fed. As I navigated up the notched log to the main house platform, I heard a lone voice singing and was nearly knocked off the log by the force of the crowd repeating the same phrase. Then the voice again, alone, plaintive and weak followed by the crowd repeating the phrase with gusto.

Huddled in a dark corner of the main room sat a soot-blackened figure wearing a cassowary headdress. This was the shaman and the source of the song—a message from the ancestors. As people responded to my questions, I learned the community had spent the night drumming and singing to coax the shaman's spirit out of his body. Once he entered a trance, his spirit sought for the cause of a recent death: flying across the forest looking for evidence

> of sorcery or spirit activity and finally going to the home of the ancestors to seek advice. Those gathered around the shaman heard glossolalic vocalizations as a portent of answers to come. Later, the shaman's spirit repossessed his body and he began to sing an interpretive song. As the shaman sang each phrase those gathered around him repeated it, thereby reinforcing the message into the collective memory of the group. This was the source of our reveille. (Personal journal, 1972)

Ritual and ceremony have long been associated with religious experience. From ancient cave paintings to contemporary healing rituals around the world, human beings have recognized the relationship between spiritual power and physical need. God introduced ritual in the Garden of Eden and instructed the Israelites to use ritual as a way to demonstrate obedience exemplified in their worship patterns. Ritual served as a means of worshiping the creator and recognizing relationship with God. This vertical relationship, in turn, reflected horizontal interaction patterns with human beings, as Jesus pointed out when discussing the relationship between the first and second commandments (Mk 12:28–34). Relationship was based on the realization of the interaction between spiritual and physical reality, which sets the tone for the role of ritual and ceremony. One way of thinking about this is realizing that the vertical relationship with God is reflected in horizontal relationships through kinship and other social patterns of interaction with human beings. The use of kinship terms serves to identify dyadic relationships, each with its attendant cultural expectations of behavior acted out in the reality of life (Goodenough 1965). I believe that we can apply this same principle to derive the expected interaction patterns implied in terminology used for God and other spiritual entities. Throughout the biblical record, God provided elaborate rituals to help people, in largely oral societies, understand God's ways and encourage an appropriate response in obedience to God (e.g., Lev 9:22–25).

UNDERSTANDING RITUAL AND CEREMONY

Historically, people have acted on the stored information encased in myths and repeated experiences with "superhuman agents." Thomas Lawson and Robert McCauley develop a theory of "religious ritual competence" in which they hypothesize that interaction in the spiritual realm operates on the same set of categories and behavior patterns as activity in the physical realm. Furthermore, human agents in the form of shamans, priests, prophets, and teachers understand superhuman agency and assist people through ritual and ceremony; human beings need assistance in their involvement with spiritual influences (Lawson and McCauley 1990, 5).

We could say that God provided rituals that capitalize on ordinary experience, which is to say that God met humans in their createdness. In this sense, incarnation is manifest throughout Scripture. How do people act out their beliefs and values through the rites that are familiar to them and that have impacted their awareness of spiritual influence in their socioreligious context? As Paul Hiebert, together with Tite Tiénou and myself, noted, it is "by means of the tabernacle, priestly robes, blood sacrifices, washings, taboos, offerings of bread and incense, marching, shouting, chanting, singing, and a hundred other ways the people expressed their faith in God" (Hiebert, Shaw, and Tiénou 1999, 319).

The objective was to give honor to God and recognize God's provision and care (Prov 3:9–10). This is manifest among peoples throughout the world today. A myriad of religious expressions are designed to demonstrate piety, virtue, and reverence, as Lori Nicholson notes in her contrast of daily religious practices of village Hindus and Christian converts from Hinduism. The primary difference is who they worship, not how they worship (Nicholson 2015).

All this, and so much more, demonstrates God's desire for relationship as well as providing protection for people in the context of a dangerous spiritual and physical environment. Societies reflected in the chapters of this book, like so many others around the world, continue to utilize ritual and ceremony as a means of tapping spiritual power for human benefit, personal and collective.

AN EPISTEMOLOGICAL DILEMMA

In a book published at the turn of the twenty-first century, Hiebert laid out an epistemological perspective designed to help cross-cultural workers understand the epistemological shifts impacting mission (Hiebert 1999a). Hiebert contrasted "instrumentalism" (a subjective focus that emphasizes experience) with "positivism" (an objective focus on dogmatic understanding that emphasizes knowledge). He maintained that the very nature of their discipline forced anthropologists to emphasize cultural diversity and celebrate relativism. Missionaries, by contrast, approached their cross-cultural experience from a knowledge-based perspective. In effect, missionary dogmatism blinded them to the relevance of what may have been God's more tolerant view of behavior patterns within societies different from their own. While anthropologists reveled in the diversity of traditional rites, the missionary focus on theological issues predisposed them to discount the role of ritual and ceremony in ministry contexts.

Hiebert mediated these polar perspectives by suggesting the need for a position he called "critical realism." This perspective presented the importance of recognizing multiple realities with a pluralism of experience while acknowledging the presence of ultimate reality. Critical realism, in Hiebert's view,

> strikes a middle ground between positivism, with its emphasis on objective truth, and instrumentalism, with its stress on the subjective nature of human knowledge. It affirms the presence of objective truth but recognizes that this is subjectively apprehended. On another level, as Laudin points out (Laudin 1996), it challenges the definition of "rationality" in both positivism and instrumentalism that limits rationality to algorithmic logic. In so doing, critical realism offers a third, far more nuanced, epistemic position. (Hiebert 1999a, 69)

Typically, Western missionary training was focused on knowledge about God, rather than on the impact of God on the human condition. Restoring harmony, bringing reconciliation and ensuring human well-being are all themes that run deep in both cultural phenomenology and biblical ontology; together they are the stuff of theology. Anthropologists, however, emphasized the need for grasping the specificity of each context, studying the diversity of human experience that reflects beliefs and their corresponding behavior patterns. Missionaries, for their part, emphasized biblical knowledge and stressed the view from above. From a contemporary point of view, I believe that each approach is inadequate; although both look at the same material, they approach it from a limited perspective. It is essential, then, to understand more broadly what we are looking at when we seek to understand ritual and ceremony.

THE NATURE OF RITUAL AND CEREMONY

Despite the work of early anthropologists like E. B. Tylor (1871), James Frazer (1894), Arnold van Gennep (1960 [1909]), and their contemporary followers, there has been little consensus on definitions of ritual and ceremony—most anthropologists describe rather than define it (Moro and Myers 2012). Edmund Leach (1964) notes that rituals are actions that communicate meanings or embody those meanings to reflect sacred or profane patterns that can be compared cross-culturally. Victor Turner (1970) utilized ritual as a means to analyze and interpret cultural symbols that are subsumed in religious activity. Roy Rappaport defined ritual as "the performance of more or less invariant sequences of formal acts and utterances not entirely encoded by the performers" (Rappaport 1999, 24ff.). David Hicks, in turn, characterized ritual as a "stereotyped, repetitive behavior or set of behaviors that uses symbols to communicate meaning" (Hicks 2010, 94).

More recently, cognitive anthropologists have come to appreciate that aspects of religious thought and behavior are a natural part of the way the human mind works. If this theory is correct, it means that religious thought and behavior around the world are rooted in cognitive processes common to all human beings. For cognitive science of religion (CSR) purposes, researchers define "ritual" very specifically as "someone acts in some observable way upon some object to prompt the gods (or use a god's power) to bring about some sort of change" (Barrett 2011, 120). By this definition, crossing oneself with holy water when entering a cathedral for Mass is an example of a "ritual": someone (a parishioner) acts in an observable way (crosses oneself) to prompt God to take action (because of the holy water) in order to bring about a change (cleanse/prepare the person for Mass). Rituals could have positive consequences (as in blessings) or negative effects (curses), and need not be part of a formal religious system or setting (Barrett 2011, 119ff.).

Most of yesterday's missionaries and today's "message bearers" (a term being popularized to avoid the negativity of colonialism—cf. Ryan Shaw 2006, 8) simply do not know how to deal with ritual and ceremony. McCauley and Lawson have postulated two primary characteristics of ritual: "performance frequency" and "sensory pageantry" (2002, 6). Both aspects enhance memory, which in turn impacts cultural transmission. These two dynamic properties are affected by what they call "culturally postulated superhuman agents"—gods and other culturally defined spiritual entities. These spiritual beings, in turn, interact with human agents (religious practitioners) who perform ritual on behalf of human patients (the recipients of spiritual action), often using religious paraphernalia (sacred objects). Simply put, ritual involves observable, repetitive practices, often mediated by spiritual practitioners using special instruments to connect spiritual beings with human beings.

In Figure 1-1, I depict two types of rituals: Type 1 based on frequency and Type 2 based on sensory pageantry. Because of frequency and lack of emotional impact, Type 1 (exemplified by communion, daily *puja*, or performing *salat* five times a day) is remembered by virtue of sheer repetition. Though memorable and easily reproducible, the net effect of such repetition is a high potential for what McCauley and Lawson call a "tedium effect" that often leads to indifference and boredom, which precipitates nominalism. I use "nominalism" here in the sense of people making little or no connection between a religious expression and its relevance to their lives. Thus, excessive repetition leads to a focus on the form rather than the intended meaning of repeated chants, mantras, recitations and liturgies common in religious experience (as illustrated on the lower right in Figure 1-1). By contrast, making superhuman expressions relevant to the reality of living life provides the focus of faith. Type 2 rituals are relatively infrequent but have high emotional impact on those involved due to the accompanying pageantry (events like initiation, weddings and funerals—what anthropologists typically call "rites of passage"). Specific episodes from life trigger "episodic memory" (McCauley and Lawson 2002, 43, 87).

To this typology McCauley and Lawson add "ritual form," which represents behaviors pursuant to either the role of agents or patients. When patients are the focus of ritual, simple forms of greater frequency create memorable, though somewhat mundane, religious experience. In contrast, when agents are in focus, the level of emotion increases and the form becomes increasingly elaborate, thus enhancing memory (see Figure 1-2).

Figure 1-1: The Nature of Ritual and Ceremony

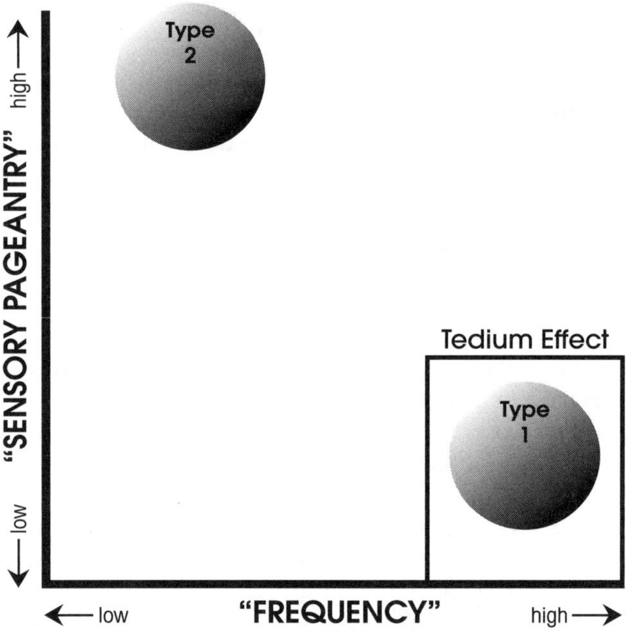

(From McCauley and Lawson 2002, 51)

In my own work, I have distinguished between ritual and ceremony on the basis of social issues: small-scale, individual expressions in contrast to large-scale, group-oriented events (Shaw 1990, 8). When overlaid on McCauley and Lawson's model, individually focused religious experience tends to engage either agent or patient in relatively small-scale, personalized activity I prefer to call "ritual." In contrast, "ceremony" reflects group-oriented experience that engages participants in collective religious activity. As frequency of these experiences increases, so does the tedium effect, while increased sensory pageantry enhances the mystery and perceived effect of spiritual activity.

As the introductory ancestor-singing event demonstrates, a Samo shaman communicating with the ancestors serves as a mediator between the people and a source of knowledge. The religious agent can be observed communing with superhuman agents on behalf of patients for the purpose of obtaining knowledge expressed through the power of soul flight and glossolalia. The answers, in turn, are presented to the Samo through sensory pageantry that imprints the message on all who are present—the message can be acted upon and understood. In the context of a relatively large number of people, excitement builds as the silent figure in the corner of the "dance floor" bursts into unintelligible bird calls and staccato speech, revealing superhuman agency working on their behalf. When the shaman emerges from the trance and begins to sing, everyone is alert to the message that is reinforced through repetition. The resulting refrain and response strengthen a message that people remember because it is important to their well-being. The ritual of individual glossolalia is reinforced for the public through a group liturgy; people receive "superhuman" information not normally available to them.

Figure 1-2: Ritual Form Impacts the Nature of Religious Experience

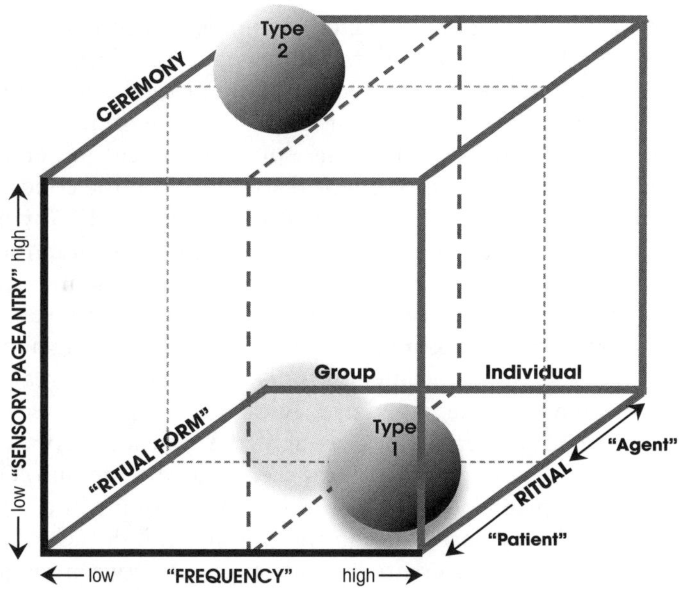

(Adapted from McCauley and Lawson 2002, 139)

It should not escape our attention that all this is not unlike God's communication with people in the Bible. The revelation to people gathered for the feast of Pentecost in Acts 2 is one in which all heard God's message in their own tongue, after which Peter interpreted the experience into the trade language that, in turn, they all spoke. While this is the reverse of the Samo experience, the principle is the same; people receive spiritual guidance and explanation through supernatural means. Ritual and ceremony, in other words, can be aligned to enable worshipers to focus on God. The process for accomplishing that goal will be specific to each worshiping community. It may reflect frequent, more-or-less tedious repetition of ritual and ceremony (for example, the stable structure of liturgy in Roman Catholicism or Anglicanism) or it may reflect "sensory pageantry" that is much more event-specific and enhances memory through individual or collective experience (as when a new monarch is anointed by the archbishop of Canterbury and crowned in Westminster Abbey). When worship reflects the nature of obedience to God's command as perceived by faithful communicants who are committed, loyal, and sincere, spirituality is dynamically engaged, whether frequent or highly emotional, patient- or agent-focused, or group-oriented or individual in nature.

A MISSIOLOGICAL RESPONSE TO RITUAL AND CEREMONY

In his classic naming of the excluded middle, Hiebert (1982) developed a model to help Western missionaries understand the clash they experience when interacting with people who assume the spiritual world interacts with and is a dynamic part of the physical reality of this world.

Hiebert based this model on his epistemological understanding to help Christians in all parts of the world struggle with the conceptual clash between the West and much of the rest of the world. Following Greco-Roman logic, Westerners tend to contrast what can be seen in the empirical and physical realm with what cannot be seen in the transemperical or spiritual realm. From this point of view, that which cannot be seen is doubted and often considered nonexistent on an a priori basis. Long ago the scientific method developed experimental tools to ascertain the reality of what could not be seen with the naked eye. Telescopes helped us see other parts of the universe, and microscopes brought the tiniest microbes into view. But what about God whom we cannot see? An elaborate ontology derived from apologetics provided a means to develop theology in a world where science was gradually becoming, in the popular mind, the sole arbiter of what is real and true. This created a wide contrast between religion, which dealt with the mystery of God by focus on personal choice and faith, on the one hand, and science, which dealt with quantifiable reality, on the other. The result was what Hiebert called the "excluded middle." Science and religion were completely separate, with little or nothing to connect them; there was little interaction between God and life, which was largely controlled by science (see Figure 1-3).

In contrast, people in the non-Western world tend to follow the Hebrew perspective, with its emphasis on a creator over and against everything that was created. Though God is not part of this creation, he cares very much about it; God's first instruction to Adam was to name everything and care for it (Gen 2:18). This approach to caring for the world is a common theme in many religions. It incorporates spiritual presence, created by God, into the very fabric of human life.

Given this contrast of cultural expectations, it is no wonder that Western missionaries considered the many practices people use to interact with and manipulate spiritual power inappropriate. We need, I believe, to be aware that both of these systems are ruled by epistemological assumptions and, from a biblical perspective, have shifted from God's original intention. The two systems in themselves are logical and depend on certain assumptions about reality. Based on Hiebert (1999a, 112ff.), I use the contrast between them to develop my focus on using ritual and ceremony as a means to worship God. When science rejects subjective value (considering meaningful and effective religious activities to be subjective and irrelevant to what is "true" and "reliable"), it becomes "faith" resting on its own indemonstrable premises. Similarly, Western missionaries working in a religious context embodied a scientific disdain for rituals and ceremonies, removing the peoples' "faith" in their primary source of power. Figure 1-3 helps to appreciate these differences and demonstrates the results of this socioreligious dichotomy.

Figure 1-3: Contrastive Religious Understanding

WESTERN CONTEXTS (Based on Greek Philosophy) Seen vs Unseen	**NONWESTERN CONTEXTS** (Reflective of Hebrew World view) Other World/Creator vs This World/Created
Religion (When all else fails)	**Ultimate Reality** Origins/Purpose Destiny of Universe Spirituality
Excluded Middle	**Socio-Religious Reality** Ancestors Spiritual Beings Handle Crises Explain the Unexplainable Deal with Success/Failure
Science (Solves all problems)	**Lived Reality** Controlling Nature Handling Human Relationships

(Adapted from Hiebert 1982)

Hiebert's excluded middle coincides with insights from McCauley and Lawson's (2002) depiction of the nature of ritual in Figure 1-1. Missionaries often exchanged ritual and ceremony filled with pageantry and spiritual influence in "this world," with repetitious religious experience that emphasized what others perceived as a distant and irrelevant "other world." Religious experience manifested in the socioreligious reality of people grappling with the vagaries of "this world" was replaced with an emphasis on the "other world" with little or no connection to the reality of their lived experience. Thus when people followed the outsiders' instruction and eliminated meaningful ritual and ceremony, they lost touch with the superhuman agency associated with those rites. The trade-off was for frequent, foreign rituals that had little efficacy for local spirituality.

In his novel *Things Fall Apart*, Chinua Achebe chronicles the collision of Nigerian and Western beliefs and values. Through the first half of the book, Achebe builds an appreciation for life in a lively Igbo village where community went beyond the bounds of what could be seen, with much activity focused on how humans were being affected by the blending of the spiritual and physical worlds, as DomNwuchukwu notes in chapter 9 on ancestors. Achebe then introduced the missionaries with their Western focus on what can be seen with minimal acknowledgment of unseen, spiritual beings. These two perspectives clashed, and missionaries quickly banned many of the rituals that enabled the Igbo to live in harmony with each other and with the spiritual "presences" they felt surrounding them. Paradoxically, many Nigerian presuppositions relating to spiritual manifestations and presences are closer to those of the people populating both the Old and New Testament worlds than people like the theologically trained but culturally uninformed Rev. James Smith, who "saw things in black and white . . . and . . . believed in slaying the prophets of Baal" (Achebe 1959, 169). Unfortunately, with local variations, Achebe's story was repeated around the globe. The typical missionary response to local spiritual practices was to reject them out of hand and to replace them with practices derived from a Western understanding of God's activity. The result? Nominalism—a lack of understanding and confusion about the reality of God's plan in the context of human behavior.

Following Bulatao (1966), Hiebert called this "split-level" Christianity—a separation of God and life that had once been integrated. From a Nigerian or Papua New Guinean or Asian perspective, eliminating Indigenous rituals and ceremonies resulted in a relatively powerless Christianity that was largely irrelevant for important matters such as recognizing the ancestors, the fertility of gardens, or warding off the influence of magical power perpetrated by sorcerers. While many people initially accepted Christianity (often seen as a first step to the broader world), they continued their use of emotive (type 2) rituals and ceremonies, which were often performed in secret so as not to "disappoint" the foreigners. Ironically, people adapted a dualistic approach to religion in order to maintain their own spiritual survival, thereby mimicking the split realities of the missionaries. Had missionaries studied local ritual and ceremony, they would have realized the importance of Hiebert's excluded middle expressions and could have sought to apply a deeper understanding of the biblical-era cultural contexts to better communicate the gospel in similar circumstances. Missionaries translated the Bible, but in many cases those who received it understood biblical assumptions regarding spiritual matters better than the translators. Scripture fits non-

Western assumptions about how the universe works better than it connects with the dualistic Enlightenment perspective assumed by missionaries from the West.

As it turned out, missionaries unwittingly ensured that Christianity would be considered irrelevant for the daily spiritual concerns of their converts. A church without power in a culture with a strong middle zone is not able to help people cope with their spiritual surroundings. People thus felt compelled to supplement Christianity with ritual and ceremony that manifested spiritual power. The veteran Indian missionary and missiologist Lesslie Newbigin noted trenchantly that Western missionaries inadvertently brought Enlightenment principles and ended up creating secular societies rather than communicating the gospel (Newbigin 1995, 5, 9).

Furthermore, sad to say, missionaries did not know how to communicate the role of Jesus Christ as the mediator between God and all of creation. And we must not be afraid to remember other dimensions of nonmaterial reality, such as angels and demons, which dropped out of the equation in much of missionary teaching. As Charles Kraft has written, the power of the Holy Spirit that energizes the creation was lost from sight, in part because the Spirit and spirits were not part of the missionaries' conceptualization (Kraft 2002). In fact, Jesus relied on the Holy Spirit, not his own deity, as he performed miracles, interacted with spiritual powers, and argued with the spiritual leaders who had come to focus on their self-interested interpretations of God's Word, rather than on God's intended message. Christ's reliance on the power of the Holy Spirit gives human beings confidence to depend on the same power for their survival (Brown 1984, 299). The contrast of what populates the middle zone has, accordingly, resulted in an epistemological clash that continues to affect the way people understand what God desires them to know about themselves, the world in which they live, and their relationship with a God who cares about everything in all three zones of reality (see Figure 1-3).

Upon removing ritual and ceremony from people's Christian experience, missionaries inadvertently drove these practices underground, thereby perpetuating Satan's twisted focus on the result of the experience—human well-being. Recognizing the importance of spiritual power, people maintained the observances with an emphasis on practical life issues. If, however, ritual and ceremony can be restored to God's intended focus, God's power can be brought to bear on the issues of daily life. In this way, the people's desire for human well-being will be realized. In Melanesian Tok Pisin, this is *gutpela sindaun* (literally, that people may sit/be well); in chapter 2 Burrows calls this "the good life," and Daimoi calls it "salvation" in chapter 13. Salvation that brings true transformation (the "good life" from God's perspective) should be part of what people process as they consider the role of ritual in the worship of God. The shift from Satan's lie with its focus on self-centered human objectives to God's intention for worship comes when people accept Jesus Christ as God's presence energized by the power of the

Holy Spirit. Ancient rituals and ceremonies, I suggest, can be adjusted to come into line with God's plan for the whole of creation—that all may be well upon the earth (Gen 2:25). Realizing God's desire to bestow infinite blessings will transform ritual into worship that enables a church to grow in ways that reflect the socioreligious expectations of people in that context, as several authors in this book make clear.

CONTEXTUAL TRANSFORMATION OF RITUAL AND CEREMONY

As a symbolic anthropologist, Hiebert understood the importance of connecting behavior to the rationale for that behavior. To this end he developed the sequenced steps for what he called "critical contextualization." Figure 1-4 is an adaptation of Hiebert's model.

FIGURE 1-4: Research Appropriate for Critical Contextualization

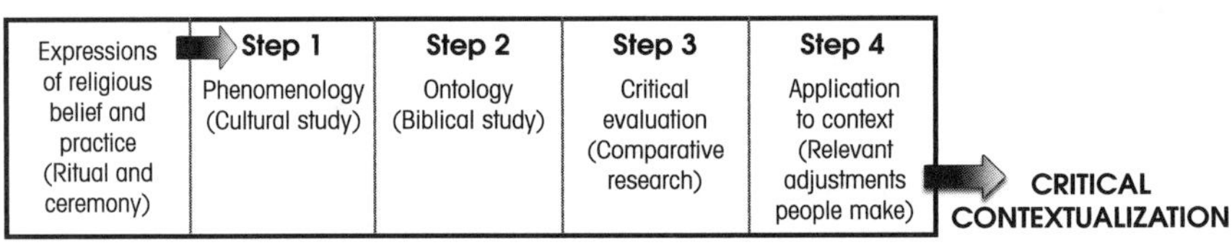

(Adapted from Hiebert, Shaw, and Tiénou 1999, 21–28)

Hiebert used this progression to encourage thorough investigation of all the socioreligious aspects of the behavior in focus (step 1). Once understood, that information can be used to appropriate God's perspective on the particular experience under review (step 2). Once the cultural and the biblical aspects of a particular expression are understood, Hiebert encouraged a critical evaluation that compares and contrasts the key elements of each in light of an appreciation of God's intent (step 3). Hence, the critique comes from direct engagement with Scripture, not from another culture's history and context-limited *interpretation* of Scripture. Finally, all this is applied to establishing new religious expressions that Christians and non-Christians within a society will recognize as reasonable adaptations of their cultural expressions (step 4), as Mantae Kim proposes for the Korean death rite.

When Hiebert designed this evaluative progression, his objective was to provide message bearers with a tool to help people appreciate the contrast between what they experience and what God intends (Hiebert 1987). Such an understanding, he reasoned, would enable people to make crucial decisions about the kinds of adjustments necessary to bring their religious experience in line with God's Word. Today, cross-cultural communicators must allow local pastors and church leaders the dignity of working out the transformation in ways that make sense within their churches. The process we have been speaking of puts Western influences into perspective and encourages people to worship God in meaningful ways. In sum, we are dealing here with a *process* that appropriates a need for *discernment* and listens to the Holy Spirit through Scripture.

Contextualization, then, in its deepest sense serves as a self-critique on religious experience in a specific time and place. In that critique, God's view of reality as found in Scripture is accounted for and wrestled with. Doing so enables people to make changes they understand to be necessary for them as they interact with God and with each other. Doing so empowers people to answer for the rationale behind the adapted behaviors that reflect their ancient rites and direct them toward God's intended purpose. In effect, through the critical contextualization process, they are developing a biblical theology that connects their phenomenological experience of all three zones of reality to God's ontological intent. When people understand what God is saying to them and, out of that perception, recognize that their reality needs adjustment, the result brings a gradual transformation that conforms to God's invitation to be one in Christ in the power and presence of the Holy Spirit (Rom 8:29–30). This in turn (because they have been the decision makers and affirm their own rationale for the adjustments) should radically reduce nominal complacency and replace syncretism with what Bill Burrows calls "hybridity" in chapter 2. What has frequently been considered syncretism is actually distinctive elements creating a new experience that enhances both and results in what scientists call "hybrid vigor" or "heterosis." Through it all, God, rather than culture, is in focus, but always from the understanding of a particular context.

Throughout the Bible we see God seeking a right relationship with people, trying to lure them into a pattern of life in harmony with God's intentions for creation. The title of a book by a great Jewish theologian, Abraham Joshua Heschel (1976), catches that dynamic perfectly: *God in Search of Man*. From an anthropological perspective, the entire expanse of myths, dance, music, and all manner of religious rites demonstrates at one level a focus on survival in a hostile world. Viewed from a biblical perspective, the God who seeks to bless humanity has implanted an implicit desire to worship the creator, even if people do not realize it. The human propensity for independence, however (as manifested in the biblical story of Adam and Eve), shifted the trajectory over time. The result is that people can miss God and find themselves in a self-perpetuating cycle of middle-zone religious experience that John Strelan called a "search for salvation" (1977). Such a proliferation of religious expression boggles the Western mind and forms the basis of the anthropologists' instrumental view of religion.

TRANSFORMING TRADITIONAL RITES TO REFLECT GOD'S INTENT

Redirecting people's rituals and ceremonies for the purpose of worshiping God is crucial for Christians in any context. The host of beliefs, values, and experiences generating rituals and ceremonies reflects human relationships with superhuman beings. My contention is that when people become aware that God has an intended purpose for the rites they depend on, they adjust their traditional assumptions and redirect their religious experience toward the creator's intention. This emphasis on a vertical relationship with God is then reflected in horizontal relationships with all human beings. Why? Because behind the diversity of human socioreligious experience is a collective human commonality that binds people together more than may initially be apparent when only examining their phenomenology. Lawson and McCauley make this point when they note, "the cognitive apparatus for the representation of religious ritual form is the same system deployed for the representation of action in general" (1990, 61). Moreover, the intent that undergirds human action is shared beyond the contrasts of specific behaviors (see Pike 1967, chapter 2). True worship of God, in all its cultural glory, will be the result if careful discernment is practiced. As an example, I roll the calendar forward fifteen years from the opening scene in my introduction to this chapter. Samo Christians clearly demonstrated a conscious adaptation of shaman-centered ancestor singing to the context of prayer during a church service. Again, I turn to my journal record of a Sunday morning service.

> During the course of the meeting, my co-initiate, Toyo, indicated it was time to pray and asked people what they wanted to pray about. Then, to my surprise, everyone began to pray in unison, something I had not experienced in a Samo church service in the past. As prayer continued, I began to hear sounds that were definitely not Samo speech, and as I looked around and listened carefully, it became clear that various ones were speaking in tongues. My first reaction was to wonder when a Pentecostal missionary had visited here. As the crescendo lessened and it became quiet, I expected to hear Toyo bring the prayer time to a close, but instead an older man who had been speaking in tongues began to sing in Samo. People paid close attention and then repeated his words. The man sang another phrase and the congregation picked it up and repeated it, and soon the meeting house was filled with an antiphonal song that reminded me of *kogwa fonio* (ancestral singing) years before.
>
> Maybe I was wrong to question what God was doing here; this may have nothing to do with Pentecostal missionaries. As if to reinforce my thought process, a younger woman who had also been speaking in tongues began to sing, and again people listened and

> repeated the phrase and the whole congregation received a message from the Lord. These folks were not engaged in a Pentecostal experience, but were reflecting on their cultural understanding of 1 Cor 12–14, and Paul's injunction to "interpret so the church may be edified" (14:5). (Personal journal, August 1987)

Toyo was acting as pastor in 1987. In 1973 he was one of the group with whom I was initiated. He and several in that group were subsequently instrumental in leading a popular movement that swept through the society in the mid-1980s. The Samo combined their use of shamanic glossolalia I was familiar with in the 1970s with their scriptural understanding of prayer in a Sunday morning service in the late 1980s. The objective in both expressions was seeking guidance from a superhuman agent. When the Samo heard glossolalia, it was evident to them that there should be an interpretation (an understanding that Scripture reinforces in Ac 2:14–37). For Toyo, this was a direct connection with God's presence among them, following cultural expectations and then following scriptural injunctions to clarify words people could not understand.

Without having read Hiebert, the Samo followed his critical contextualization process, harmonizing their own intentionality with God's purpose for them. If their rituals and ceremonies could be transformed to honor human relationships with God through Jesus Christ in the power of the Holy Spirit, then people would begin to realize God's intention for them and engage in culturally appropriate Christian expressions of their faith. In so doing, the experience will be intentional and meaningful and will reduce syncretism. Complacency will no longer be a factor. This outcome coincides with McCauley and Lawson's model, the attraction shifting from the tedium effect to emotional, sensory pageantry (2002, 51).

RELEVANT CULTURAL ADJUSTMENT

In order to anticipate the direction of needed transformation to ritual and ceremony, we can apply a cognitive adjustment model developed by Harriet Hill (2006). As a Bible translation consultant, Hill needed to appreciate how people perceived a particular text so that relevant adjustments could be made. What she discovered was the hermeneutical role of human expectations that reflect cultural experience: What do people think they share with the people of the source text, and what needs to be adjusted in order to move them to understanding what I call "God's truth" as reflected in the translated text? The contrast of what people thought they knew and what was biblically true enabled her to develop a matrix of possibilities I present in Figure 1-5.

Quadrant 1 recognizes people who actually share information and know what was intended in the text. This combination creates a conceptual match of understanding the intended textual message: God's truth and local understanding closely match. Quadrant 2 characterizes those who actually share awareness but do not realize it. Quadrant 3 is an expression of those who do not have an understanding of the intended meaning, but think they do. Finally, Quadrant 4 reflects those who do not share information and agree that, in reality, they do not know what is going on.

Figure 1-5: A Cognitive Adjustment Model Showing Mutual Cognitive Environment Possibilities

	Think it is shared	Do not think it is shared
Actually shared	1 KNOWN, RECOGNIZED ASSUMPTIONS (God's truth) The intended message is understood	2 UNRECOGNIZED ASSUMPTIONS (hocus pocus) Know the truth but do not recognize it
Not actually shared	3 UNINTENDED ASSUMPTIONS (hocus pocus) Do not know the truth but do not recognize inadequacy	4 UNKNOWN, MISSING ASSUMPTIONS (hocus pocus) Do not know the truth and recognize inadequacy

(Adapted from Hill 2006, 29)

Each quadrant, then, represents a different degree of understanding (what I call "hocus pocus," drawing on my 2003 hermeneutical discussion [Shaw and Van Engen 2003]) with its concomitant need to adjust for a faithful connection of a contemporary context to God's intention as reflected in Quadrant 1. Quadrant 2 indicates that people know much more of the truth than they realize and can apply their knowledge to appreciate the text. Quadrant 3 focuses on those who are not aware of their misunderstanding and therefore misrepresent God's truth. Quadrant 4 emphasizes people's honesty in not understanding the truth and transforming their lack of experience to an appreciation of God's perspective. Appreciating the socioreligious environment subsumed by the text as it is juxtaposed to a present-day context will go a long way to reducing misunderstanding. This model can be applied to any information reflective of what people need to know in order to understand a particular Scripture passage (Hill 2006). Hill also notes that Bible translation should only be part of a missiological strategy. Message bearers must also foster right contexts in which receptors can understand the Bible and the God behind it (Hill 2003, 180ff.). This focus on knowledge and how people relate what they know to what they need to know in order to appreciate what is being communicated is reflective of the application of cognitive studies to Christian mission (Sperber and Wilson 1986, 38ff.).

Appreciating local expressions of religiosity in light of this model should, over time, diminish syncretism with its focus on the temporal and enhance the eternal with its ontological emphasis from above. The transformation from religious expressions intended to influence superhuman agents to God-honoring rituals and ceremonies is a conscious part of the critical contextualization process. The protection and care human beings so intensely desire will come as they redirect the focus of spiritual presence from local spirituality to a recognition of God among them. I depict this progression in Figure 1-6.

Figure 1-6: Culturally Appropriate Styles Impact How People Worship God and Counteract Spiritual Forces

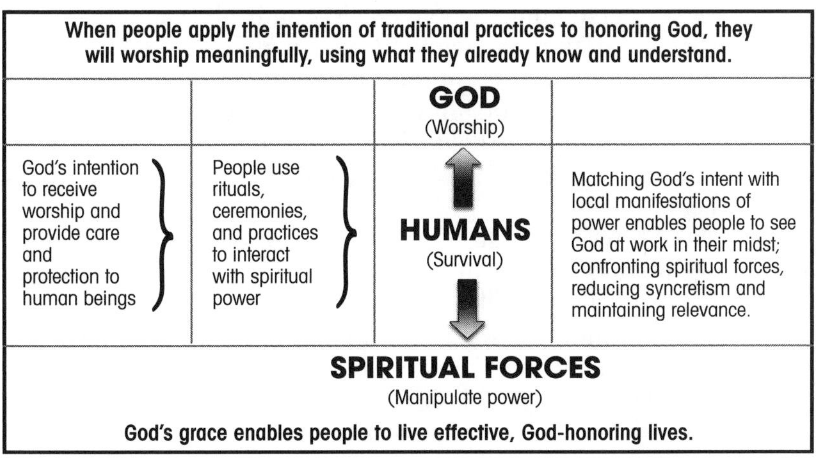

As people come to realize God's plan for them, they are able to take possession of their beliefs and practices and reorient these toward Christ, who was sacrificed on their behalf, redeeming them and reinstating God's intention for them. This action requires that people receive Scripture, analyze both the Scripture and their cultural understanding in light of their new awareness of and relationship with God, and adjust their practices in ways that bring honor to God. Doing so will enable people to appropriately worship God, who, by grace, will ward off evil, provide loving care, and accept the worship that God alone is worthy to receive (Ps 148; Rev 4:11).

Anthropologists have long realized people traditionally use a wide assortment of religious expressions to influence superhuman power. If people can recognize God's intent and redeem their rituals and ceremonies (as well as all the other spiritual expressions) in such a way that these become reflective of their relationship with God, they will increase their appreciation of both the expressions and of God; this result is hybridity. And the more they understand their own objectives in light of God's expectations, the more they will desire to bring honor to God and thus reduce the split-level Christianity so pervasive in today's world. The objective is to redeem ritual and ceremony for the glory of God and the realization of the purpose of the church within a society.

CONCLUSION

How do people take culturally familiar, pre-Christian structures and bring them into the church in order to conform to God's expectation for them? What processes can people use to ensure their rites are adjusted to meet God's objective of relationship with human beings who can then bring glory to God? I believe the answers lie in reviewing Hiebert's models and applying them to contemporary cultural expressions of Christian truth within specific human expressions of reality—what anthropologists call "culture." Understanding people's beliefs and values and the practices that are associated with them, while recognizing God's intentions, affects how people manifest goodness in their place. By acknowledging the role of spiritual expressions of worship we may be able to encourage people to recognize their assumptions in light of God's purposes—that is, release them from assumptions of unrecognized truth, and move them closer to God's intent for them.

God, through Jesus Christ, incarnated in a human environment. And Jesus, in turn, used the power of the Holy Spirit to accomplish everything the Father intended (Jn 17). All who seek to enable God's message to incarnate in societies around the world must do the same. By building on the understanding of fundamental contrasts between Western and non-Western perspectives while developing relationships and experiencing life with other human beings, cultural outsiders and insiders alike can encourage the transformation of traditional, non-Jewish and Christian rituals and ceremonies for the purpose of worshiping the one true God. From an appreciation of these models and the principles behind them, I encourage readers to consider how all this might affect Christian worship in their varied ministry contexts. The following questions may serve as triggers to precipitate adjustments to culturally appropriate behavior—encouraging a conscious processing in order to realize God's intentions and bring people closer to acting out God's truth in their socioreligious environment:

- What do people know about their beliefs and the practices based on those beliefs? What is their intent in utilizing those practices?
- How are ritual and ceremony used: to manipulate superhuman agents for human benefit, or to recognize superhuman beings?
- How can what people know and what they do be transformed to worship God in relevant, culturally appropriate ways?

These questions assume a careful study of a people's socioreligious experience. However, as members of their own Indigenous cultural communities, the contributing authors to this book demonstrate that they are able to find answers to such questions and thus help previously marginalized voices express their own religious reality. Many of their beliefs and practices can be appropriated to bring honor to God. In turn, these newly adjusted behavior patterns can counteract evil in all its cosmic, social, and structural manifestations. God wants the very best for creation. God wants people to conform to their recognition of what is relevant within the expectations of their community. As Hill has made clear, new information changes the cognitive environment; the actors are not left the same. Message bearers and local people both make adjustments to their understanding based on mutual interaction with God's intent and the circumstances under which the message takes root. Gospel communicators and local recipients benefit and are changed (Shaw 2010, 211); hybridity happens.

It remains, then, to listen to others, to hear how they respond to these ideas, and to answer these questions. In the chapters that follow, authors explore the transformation of contemporary ritual and ceremony to reflect God's presence in each context and how people respond to that presence and worship God in ways that make sense to them. Their responses demonstrate how to utilize supernatural power to survive spiritual hostility. They present their interpretation of socioreligious experience in light of what they perceive God saying to them through Scripture.

As human beings we interact with superhuman agents every day, whether we realize it or not. Using that interaction for human benefit has been the pattern since Adam and Eve. God provided the means to cope with spiritual realities and survive accordingly. At issue is how the resulting rites are used—as traditional rituals with a focus on survival as an end in itself, or for Christian worship of God, who extends grace to all who give him honor. The authors of this book demonstrate how traditional rites can be transformed to their God-intended purpose.

2

Theological Ideals, Cross-Cultural Realities

Syncretism and Hybridity in Christian Culture Crossings

William R. Burrows

As it examines the question of using ritual elements from other religious and cultural traditions in Christian worship and prayer, this book pivots on the problem of achieving true mutuality and understanding between peoples reared in vastly different cultures. More particularly, this volume involves the issue of people from diverse cultures trying (1) to understand one another and the Christian message while (2) determining what constitutes genuine worship of the God revealed archetypically in Jesus and mediated down through the ages by the Holy Spirit. While this book puts rituals in the foreground, worship is actually the broader category—that is, rituals by which Christians recognize who God is and what God has done for humanity through Jesus the Christ.

Often forgotten is that, from its earliest days, Christian worship was the result of a hybridization process that borrowed elements from the religion and culture of those who became followers of Jesus and used to worship the Triune God manifested and incarnated in Jesus. I will not argue this point, but I do refer readers to the work of the Benedictine scholar Odo Casel, especially his *The Mystery of Christian Worship and Other Writings* (1962). The monumental *Oxford History of Christian Worship* (Wainwright and Tucker 2005) is the standard work in the field, and the work of Paul Bradshaw (2002; 2004) on the origins of the Eucharist and Christian worship will quickly abuse anyone open to evidence that early Christian worship has been faithfully retrieved by post-1517 attempts to return to pure worship.

The development of Christian worship has from the earliest intertestamental times been a hybridization process. With a prayer that this paragraph has not alienated readers from "nonliturgical" churches, let us proceed to develop what I consider a responsible and sound biblical and theological foundation on which to enter the conversation on the principles that should guide the process of discernment on what constitutes authentic Christian ritual and worship.

A BIBLICAL-THEOLOGICAL PREMISE

To be clear, God does not need our rituals. We do. As the great penitential Psalm 51 says so eloquently,

> For you are not pleased with sacrifices;
> should I offer a holocaust you would not accept it.
> My sacrifice, O God, is a contrite spirit;
> a heart contrite and humbled, O God, you will not spurn.
> (vv. 18–19)

If worship is based on an inward recognition of who God is in regard to us (i.e., our creator, redeemer, and savior), the biblical-theological premise for everything that follows lies in Genesis 12:1–3, the story of Abraham and God's election of Israel. God called Abraham and his descendants to become a revelation of both God's blessing and judgment to all nations:

> Now the LORD said to Abram, "Go from your country and your kindred and your father's house to the land that I will show you. I will make of you a great nation, and I will bless you, and make your name great, so that you will be a blessing. I will bless those who bless you, and the one who curses you I will curse; and in you all the families of the earth shall be blessed."

The thrust of the text is threefold: (1) God's election of Israel was an invitation to a covenantal relationship between Abraham's descendants and God; (2) this election was for Israel to become a source of blessing to the nations as Israel said yes to the requirements of the covenant, on the one hand, and a cause for judgment, on the other hand, both for Israel (if it violated its terms) and to those who wished Israel ill; and (3) as would become clearer as the history of Israel unfolded, a teaching that God's people have a key role in making God known to all peoples. Nor should it be forgotten that the covenant with Abraham is foreshadowed by God's covenant with Noah (Gen 9:1–7), wherein God promised not to destroy humanity again and entered symbolically into a saving relationship with all humankind.

Ideally, worship and the ritual that expresses the human acknowledgment of God's presence and purifying action stem from an acknowledgment of who God is and what God promises to those who are faithful. As different as are the cultures of Abraham's descendants, so the expressions of worshiping God may vary as God's peoples show gratitude (i.e., our *eu-kharistia*), as prefigured in Ezekiel's vision of stony hearts being transformed by God's spirit (Ezek 36:24–30). For Jesus-followers, the Christ is the one whose life, death, and resurrection are re-membered, brought to life in worship by the Holy Spirit. Jesus is, as the ancient Latin adage has it, the *norma normans non normata* (the [living] norm [for Christian life], which is not [himself] normed). The metaphor rests in the Greek word for a carpenter's square, *gnômôn*, figuratively a *standard* or *pattern*. The Spirit brings the Christ-event to us in time and is made present in the living Christ, the effects of whose work we celebrate *now* even as we await their revelation fullness in a *not yet*, eschatological dimension.

TWO BASIC HERMENEUTICS OF "PAGAN" RITUALS AND BELIEFS

What follows are examples that typify the approaches historically taken by the two largest bodies of Western Christianity to approach other religious traditions in their attempts to bring Christianity to the followers of those religious ways. Having said this, I am fully aware that numerous exceptions exist to what I present as "typical." For every gifted Matteo Ricci (1552–1610) of the Catholic Society of Jesus and Timothy Richard (1845–1919) of the British Baptist Missionary Society, many thousands of more routine-minded men and women followed the typical patterns emanating from a Western-dominated colonial hegemony.

The Classic Roman Catholic Orientation

Catholics have had a more ambiguous relationship to pagan rituals than Protestants, as is well illustrated in a letter from Pope Gregory the Great (540–604) to St. Augustine of Canterbury (d. ca. 604–9), who was sent to be the "re-founder" of the church in Britain. Gregory had a dual task: (1) reaching an agreement with the ancient Celtic Church on discipline and practice, and (2) finding a way to accommodate Christianity to the traditional (i.e., pagan) religion. In brief, Augustine represented a process in which the Celts would lose in the face of Romanization at the Synod of Whitby in 664. In the *Ecclesiastical History of Britain* by the Venerable Bede (ca. 673–735), Gregory entrusted a message to Augustine in which the monk Mellitus was commissioned to tell Augustine,

> What I have long been considering in my own mind concerning the matter of the English people; to wit, that the temples of the idols in that nation ought not to be destroyed; but let the idols that are in them be destroyed; let water be consecrated and sprinkled in

> the said temples, let altars be erected, and relics placed there. For if those temples are well built, it is requisite that they be converted from the worship of devils to the service of the true God; that the nation, seeing that their temples are not destroyed, may remove error from their hearts, and knowing and adoring the true God, may they more freely resort to the places to which they have been accustomed. (Bede 1907, 67)

I would be oversimplifying to say that Gregory's instructions were carried out as written. What is certainly true is that the inculturation of Catholicism in Europe led to what James Russell calls the "Germanization of Roman Catholicism" (Russell 1994), which is to say a Catholicism marked by a complex mixture of Christian meanings placed on pagan rituals and beliefs. Precisely this accretion of "nonscriptural" elements led to the Reformation. Nevertheless, as recently as the Second Vatican Council, while in essence admitting these accretions had occluded the Christomorphic nature of Christianity, the Council still advises patient dialogue in the process of inculturation (Vatican Council II 1965a, § 22).

What are the dangers of the Catholic approach? At least the following:

- Praying to saints in ways that eclipse the centrality of the Triune God, who is nearer to us than we are to ourselves.
- Creating the impression that the church and its priests have God's power to use as their own, thus elevating reception of the sacrament of order over the primacy of baptism and thereby obscuring the equality of all Christians, and the vocation of all who become Christ-bearers.
- Emphasizing rites, catechisms, and doctrinal formulations arrived at in one culture's history over patient dialogue to discover, mutually, what God is about in any given context.

Against such tendencies the sixteenth-century Reformation occurred. Alas, instead of reforming the church as a whole, the unity of the church was weakened and a splintering process begun.

The Classic Protestant Orientation

Nowhere is the groundwork behind the classic Protestant judgment on the possibility of salvaging anything from other religious traditions clearer than in Calvin's great sixteenth-century synthesis of Christian theology and wisdom, *The Institutes of the Christian Religion* (especially book 1, *The Knowledge of God the Creator*). My contention is that even in churches and denominations that do not stem from the Reformed tradition, Calvin's thought underlies the hermeneutic they employ. I also believe that any fair-minded reader of book 1 of the *Institutes* has to be impressed by the cogency of the arguments for relying on *sola scriptura* (nothing but Scripture) to guide us. Calvin brought that concern to bear, as Brian Gerrish has shown, in his writing on the Reformation heritage, primarily to introduce the Bible

> as a supplementary aid, in addition to God's disclosure of himself in mankind's innate awareness of him (chap. 3 [of *The Institutes,* book 1]) and in the works of creation and providence (chap. 5). The Scriptures are like a pair of spectacles that clarify weak and defective vision. So grave is mankind's myopia that, without the Word, there would be no sound perception of God in the world at all. (Gerrish 1982, 51)

Calvin's strategy in book 1 was to show the sufficiency of Scripture and the danger of relying on human traditions. In book 1, chapter 3, indeed, his view of the *sensus divinitatis* (natural knowledge of God) "serves, in practice, to render man inexcusable, since he deliberately smothers it," that knowledge being "nullified by man's perverseness" (Gerrish 1982, 58–59). Above all, Calvin was trying to bring his hearers and readers to understand how the clarity of Scripture under the guidance of the Spirit (*Institutes* 1.7.1) surpasses all natural wisdom.

What are the dangers of Protestant approaches? As I did above in speaking of Catholic weaknesses, I will not argue the case here, but boldly give the following caveats:

- Creating a movement that relies so heavily on particular elements of Scripture (i.e., creating a veritable "canon within the canon") that the dynamic of the revelation as a whole gets lost in arguments and causes divisions.
- Converting to Christ can become so emphasized that dialogue about "other" spiritual entities or insights (for example, the wisdom of Confucius) tends to end up in condemnations of these entities and insights as demonic.
- Words begin to dominate worship, with the effect that elements from traditional rituals are suppressed.

TRANSCENDING THE CLASSIC HERMENEUTIC

I have a great deal of empathy for the Reformers' vision and goals, but what we are dealing with throughout this chapter and the larger project of this book is the following question: given the polemical hermeneutic of the Reformers—who were attempting to overcome Catholic abuses—can their *sola scriptura / solus Christus* hermeneutic be used today in the far different situation of peoples who come from cultures formed by primal or local religious beliefs and values and the practices that emerge from these cosmologies?

Without downplaying the dangers, I suggest a hermeneutic that may be more useful. It takes shape in God's election of Israel in the age of Abraham. That covenant has roots in pre-Abrahamic covenants, of course, but the election and vocation of Israel started—literarily, at least—with Abraham and Sarah, moved into the stories of Isaac and Jacob, and followed through the Joseph and Moses cycles (telling the history of Israel's migration, captivity in Egypt, liberation, wandering in the desert, and conquering the promised land). It is a story full of colorful men and women who acted faithfully as well as shamefully, and it continued through the judges and kings to the destruction of the First Temple by the Babylonians in about 587 BC and of the Second Temple by the Romans in AD 70.

Although many consider it dated and others overly "Christian," the work of Gerhard von Rad remains persuasive to me, both as he dwells on the possibilities of messianic expectations being fulfilled and the difficulty of making Old Testament prophecies into straightforward predictions of Jesus that Christians hail as their realization (see von Rad 1965, 2:169–72, 336–87). Deuteronomic history became the most important, postexilic interpretation of Israel's historical traditions. The interpretive theme of Deuteronomy taught what God wanted from Israel: much more than faithfulness to rules regarding public worship and obedience to the Law—the love of a people who appreciated their creator and redeemer. What God had done and who God was were critical realities (see Deut 6:1–8). The gospel of Deuteronomy was news of God's faithfulness to the promises made to Abraham and Moses, and a clarification of the need to love God in response. In our context, the Law is celebrated as God's great gift, and idolatry is an abandonment of the Law. This perspective underpins the way in which Moses counseled the Israelites before they entered the promised land (Deut 4:25–41); Moses emphasized the great commandment, words that Jesus borrowed centuries later.

The story of Jesus and the interpretation of his person, life, teaching, and work in the twenty-seven books that Christians call the New Testament are so rich that isolating any single element as central is dangerous. That said, creating a "canon within the canon" was inevitable when Christian cross-cultural agents and their Indigenous helpers selected elements from both the Old and New Testaments that were considered to be particularly relevant in a given situation. Making such selections is intrinsic to the "translation process," which is revealed as central to appropriating the Christian message in the work of Professors Walls (1996, 26–42), Sanneh (1989), and Bediako (1992), to whom we owe a debt of gratitude for bringing its dynamics to the fore.

With much caution I want to emphasize that the deepest teaching of the New Testament about Jesus is embedded in the multifaceted, paradoxical manner by which he taught both by word and deed. His entire person and story reveal Godself and God's promise to save. Like Jesus before them, evangelizers must employ analogies that their conversation partners can grasp. Inevitably, though, analogies lead to a short version of Christianity that emphasizes morality and makes Christianity a new set of laws taught by Jesus. This result occurs in spite of the paradoxes of Jesus's parables and the great reversal of his death, which made it clear who God is and what God is about in Jesus. Christ's salvific act cannot be understood in a straightforward fashion. Much more is going on in the life, death, and resurrection of Jesus than ethical ideals, logic, and the analogies necessary for translations to teach. Indeed, in cross-cultural evangelization the greatest difficulty is that we are dealing with paradoxes and reversals of logic. God and God's manner of self-revelation and ruling are a mystery, and a whole new mental apparatus needs to replace the worldly eyes of the non-Christ-follower:

> You must no longer live as the Gentiles live, in the futility of their minds. They are darkened in their understanding, alienated from the life of God because of their ignorance and hardness of heart. . . . You were taught to put away your former way of life, your old self, corrupt and deluded by its lusts, and to be renewed in the spirit of your minds, and to clothe yourselves with the new self, created according to the likeness of God in true righteousness and holiness. (Gal 4:17–18, 22–24)

Indeed, the summit of the revelation of God and God's relationship to all of humanity lies in Jesus's ignominious death and logic-defying resurrection. The one executed at Calvary is portrayed as God's unique son. His resurrection is testimony that the promises made to Israel and the followers of Jesus will be honored. The good news, in short, is a promise that if we follow Jesus and allow his Spirit to live in us, our sins will not be counted against us and we shall rise with Jesus as all of creation is redeemed.

The temptation is to ignore or downplay the complex process of intercultural dialogue that should be at the heart of evangelization. For all its ambiguity, misunderstanding, and mutual incomprehension, it is also a fact that we are only beginning to acknowledge the way in which the culture of evangelizers and the culture of hearers of the Word interact with one another, as Dean Gilliland pointed out in his definition of contextualization: "the way in which the Word, as Scripture, and the Word as revealed in the truths of culture interact in determining Christian truth for a given people and place" (1989, 10). This sounds very much like what we are calling "hybridity," and is the focus of where I take my argument as it emerges from my discussion of classic Catholic and Protestant hermeneutics.

DOES HYBRIDIZATION NAME THE PROCESS OF INCULTURATION?

I wish to suggest that "hybridity" is a good word to name the intercultural dialogue process that comprises evangelization and inculturation. I do so with an analogy to horticulture. The result of crossing genetically diverse plants to form a new plant is called a "hybrid." I am, in essence, asking readers to call into question the adequacy of the long tradition of calling the result of the cross-cultural process a "synthesis" of gospel and culture. In my view, religious hybrids inevitably result when a religion is carried across a cultural boundary and is adopted and adapted by people in that milieu in light of their biblical understanding. I would also point out that this process is not a fact only in Christianity as it crosses into new cultures.

Concretely, in regard to Christianity, Robert Schreiter suggests that it is important to look at this process from the perspective of the receptor culture rather than from that of the missionaries of the incoming church.

> By taking the perspective of the receiving culture rather than that of the incoming church, we can get a better sense of which options are most likely to be engaged within the culture, given the range of incorporate possibilities. If the encounter between church and culture is often an incomplete one, the reason for that could well be that the church does not adequately understand the culture. Starting from the culture's perspective is a firmer base from which to envision the whole dynamic. (1985, 152)

If we apply Schreiter's insight to the classic understanding of how faith develops, the total act of faith is always a combination of transcendent grace and the immanent, all-inclusive cultural reality of the persons who say yes to the message.

Missionaries have long preferred to speak of the goal of evangelization as a "synthesis," wherein the transcendent and universal message of the communicator interacts with a local culture to produce a new expression that retains all the essential elements and understandings of the messengers' home church. This, in reality, is what my good friend, the late Father Joseph Donders, called one day in conversation "inculturating the Western interpretation of the gospel." It is easy to accept that a church is inculturating itself when hymns are translated into, say, Banjara in Andhra Pradesh, or Kuman in Papua New Guinea. Going further with that idea, it is possible to imagine slightly different structures of ordained ministry or lay governance when the texts of the Roman Missal are translated into Simbu, or Chalcedon Christology is explained to Jamaican Maroons.

The main point of this chapter is that not only is syncretism inevitable—from an anthropological perspective—but that the metaphor of hybridity better describes the results of the syncretic process that occurs when Christian faith begins to mature among a people. In terms of what we are about in this project, in the place of the ideal being "synthesis," I offer the concept of hybridity. It is an analogical use of the term, rooted in the biological process of blending traits as two related but diverse entities come together to create something new. Applied to evangelization, hybridization is the process whereby peoples who accept the gospel of Jesus Christ express and understand their faith in light of Scripture and local cultural symbols. Saying this is the case, of course, is not the same thing as proving it. Nevertheless, I believe that the anthropological and linguistic sources Dan Shaw cites in chapter 1 represent a discerning distillation of what social science has demonstrated over the past century and a half. In addition, if one reads Arbuckle's magisterial work (2010), one finds in his explication of insights from mission history confirmation that syncretism is the all too frequent outcome. Mention of syncretism, Arbuckle observes, strikes fear in the hearts of those who hold power in institutional churches. Nevertheless, he goes on to say,

> At no point in time is there ever a pure Christianity. It has never existed and never will. The fact is that both the faith of Israel and the faith of the first Christian generations developed processes of inculturation involving syncretism in assimilating influences of other cultures. (2010, 183–84)

In the first part of this chapter, my biblical-theological proposal involves the idea that the cross-cultural transmission of Christian faith initiates a complex intercultural dialogue, not merely the translation of a message—although it is *also* accompanied by translation. This has been the case since the beginnings of Christianity: it occurred when apostles like Thomas founded Syriac churches in Mesopotamia and India, when an Ethiopian eunuch returned home, when Mark went to Egypt and other parts of North Africa, when James went to Spain, when Peter and Paul went to Rome, when Patrick went to Ireland, and when Winfrid (St. Boniface) went to Frisia and later to peoples along the Rhine.

The same process occurred when Martin Luther and John Calvin cashed in on the "new knowledge" of the Renaissance and began the attempt to reform Latin Christianity by a radical return to the Scriptures as the sole source of revelation. Calvin produced one of the great syntheses of Western Christian doctrine, and Luther's retrieval of the gospel as "promise" is enormously important. However, before the Reformers produced their theological artifacts, they had a vision of something new that could be created if the church were purged of a thousand years of cultural accretions. Yet, for all their good intentions, in the end the Reformers produced a hybrid that resembled more the Catholicism they sought to reform than the primitive church they wanted to reinstate.

Saying that a cross-cultural passage of Christianity to parts of the world that followed local or primal religious traditions forms a hybrid is not to say that God is absent from the process or that Jesus is falsely understood. Rather, it is an admission that the words of Jesus still ring true:

> "What is born of the flesh is flesh, and what is born of the Spirit is spirit. Do not be astonished that I said to you, 'You must be

> born from above.' The wind blows where it chooses, and you hear the sound of it, but you do not know where it comes from or where it goes. So it is with everyone who is born of the Spirit." (Jn 3:6–9)

The typical Protestant suspicion of syncretism assumes that we can return to the Bible to find pure teaching, unencumbered with later accretions that crept into Catholic Christo-paganism. The remedy was to condemn syncretism and instill pure biblical Christianity.

The typical Roman Catholic form of denying the legitimacy of syncretism and keeping it at bay is to maintain that popes, Vatican congregations, and bishops have the authority to intervene in any local church to maintain traditions of interpretation or practice or to condemn what does not comport with that tradition and practice, often to the extent that it exemplifies Bernard Lonergan's dictum that members of hierarchies "possess authority in inverse ratio to their familiarity with the concrete situations in which the new ideas emerge" (1957, 234–35). Practically speaking, the Catholic question boils down to how many elements of church practice and doctrine need to be maintained if churches in places with far different cultural histories are to remain *Roman* Catholic? (See Burrows 2007 for a longer development of these ideas.) On the other hand, confronted by the splintering tendencies and the rush to adopt new ideas, it is important to remember what Lamin Sanneh says well:

> Catholicism's doctrinal core is arguably more stable than that of many other variants of Christianity. Even if its directives are contested, the church's magisterium is recognized for what it is. The catechism and the instrument of papal encyclicals together have defined Catholic faith just as that faith is enshrined in the church's liturgical life, with Jesus Christ at its core. Against the cultural fragmentation of modern life, that is a considerable advantage. While in the mood, Catholics may crack wise at this heritage and from the flanks even nibble away at it, but it's hard to dismiss it as of no value. (2012, 259)

Alas, despite oceans of ink sprayed onto mountains of paper in scholarly articles and books and synthesized into ever more impressive encyclopedias, no one has succeeded in re-creating purely biblical Christianity in a way that convinces everyone that his or her canon within the canon is uniquely valid. Indeed, Homi Bhabha expressly cites the British use of the Bible in India as a form of hegemony that illustrates colonial authority (1985). Sadly, he missed the need of the British to account for the Indian expressions that concomitantly reflect the hybridity that resulted, and that he later extols.

HYBRIDITY IN RELIGIOUS DEVELOPMENT

As I hope is apparent by now, I am recommending we expand our recognition that Texans, Swedes, Italians, Peruvians, and Xhosa are all hybrid Christians. And, just as individuals can be absolutely sincere in saying yes to Christ and still have to deal with the incompleteness of their individual conversion right up to the hour of death, churches in a given culture must go through a similar process of development. My view on the incompleteness and process nature of Christian conversion is part and parcel of a Roman Catholic orientation to these issues; I ask Protestants to suspend judgment until I have made my case.

Concretely, in this book we are dealing with what happens when Westerners exclude other cultures' understanding of human beings within reality as a whole. For many such peoples there is a cosmological middle ground between heaven and God, on the one hand, and Earth and humanity, on the other hand. That middle ground must be taken into account as individuals and peoples negotiate their way along the Christian path. I speak especially about the reality of a people's experience with ancestral spirits (or "presences") in the surrounding world that may be a source of power, blessing, or danger. These realities, when disregarded by missionaries and the churches they found, create bifurcated Christian identity in the new context.

In essence, I am suggesting that hybridity is not only possible but inevitable in the process of an individual's or a people's achieving mature Christian identity in a cultural setting such as Korea, Papua New Guinea, Costa Rica, the United States, Jamaica, or India. At another level, I suspect that judgments on the part of Westerners who relegated ancestral and other spirits to the realm of syncretism, superstition, sorcery, idol worship, and other evils to be shunned were misguided and premature. Such an approach resulted from insufficient dialogue with cultures found in most of the world outside the West.

For Melanesians, dealing with such spirits is part of the drama of continual conversion, self-transcendence, and trusting oneself to God. It is equally true of the Igbo of Nigeria. This phenomenon is structurally similar to the belief of many US citizens who maintain that divine approval has been given to everything authentically American. At a corporate level, dealing with spirits and traditions is an integral part of the theological and cultural analysis required of believing communities. People particularize the gospel in ways that enable individuals and societies to see the way of Christ as a way that offers a path to liberation and salvation in their cultural and historical context.

For me, this was driven home when I felt the spontaneous energy and interest on the part of my students in a course on eschatology that I regularly taught at Holy Spirit Seminary in Bomana, near Port Moresby, in the mid-1970s. Eschatology, in the days before the Second Vatican Council, was the first half of a semester course devoted to official teaching on the fate of the soul after death, and the second half was devoted to Mariology (doctrines concerning Mary, the mother of God). I, of course, was much too up to date to follow that pattern. In part my approach stemmed from the fact that in 1965 (the year the Vatican Council ended) Jürgen Moltmann published his groundbreaking bestseller, which was translated into English and published in 1967 as *Theology of Hope*. It made a great impression on me. Between Moltmann and Oscar Cullmann, many Catholics, including myself, were plunged into the world of the Bible. We also discovered Bultmann and took on the task of demythologizing both the Bible and doctrine. As we delved into biblical and early patristic writings, medieval traditions that Catholic manuals of doctrine taught on topics like heaven, hell, and purgatory began to look hopelessly mythological and quite outdated.

Throwing away my notes from my own eschatology course under Candido Pozo, SJ, at the Gregorian University, I decided to teach Vatican II's *Gaudium et Spes* (*Pastoral Constitution on the Church in the Modern World*; 1965b) as an introduction to "realized" eschatology and the Christian's vocation in a world that was a sign of a "real but not yet fully realized" inbreaking of the kingdom. I supplemented that with Moltmann's and Cullmann's ideas about hope and the centrality of the kingdom of God. Eschatology, I taught, was our attempt to understand what we could about the advent of God's reign on a cosmic scale; salvation of individual souls, I taught, was a much later preoccupation. My focus was on the obligation that the *now* of the kingdom imposed on us to make this world realize "kingdom values."

I won't say that the students at Bomana were uninterested in the way I explicated *Gaudium et Spes*, following Cullmann's rendition of the New Testament teaching about the kingdom being with us *already now* but *not yet* in its fullness. The same was true for their reaction to Moltmann's showing that eschatological hope had a present-day political-liberation dimension. But the fact is that the real energy was kindled when we talked about what I thought then was the outmoded Catholic tradition's three potential fates of souls after death. Upon reflection, I realized that the older schematic opened an avenue to address two typically Melanesian concerns: the salvation of their ancestors born before Christianity arrived and the role of both ancestral spirits and other spirits or "presences" in nature and in daily life. My students began resonating with the idea that those who had gone to be with God were also still within the village community as a source of blessing and wisdom. Others who had died were experienced as corresponding to souls in purgatory, needing purification and enlightenment and the good example of the community of the living to embrace *trupela rot bilong Jisas* (the true way of Jesus). The third class of souls were evil ones whose hearts were set against God, perhaps jealous of human beings who were able to enjoy *gutpela sindaun* (the good life) that came to the living who were following the Christian way. These souls could make mischief and even cause serious suffering to those who had not put themselves under the protection of Christ; his mother, Mary; and the rest of the saints.

I finally began to understand what my students were trying to tell me, and I added a section titled "A Phenomenology of Spirits." When the students went home at term's end for pastoral assignments, I asked them to interview village elders to see how the typology of spirits we were arriving at corresponded with the way their traditions pictured the role of ancestral and other spirits. I would be teaching them ecclesiology and Christology the next term, and we would continue to explore these issues.

How had we tentatively classified the spirits? First, some spirits were experienced as being a blessing to the people; this fit with the doctrine of the communion of saints, since some of these were felt to have a special ability to guide a clan or family to make good decisions, such as choices about marriage partners, whether to begin laying out a new garden in this place or that, or warding off a sorcerer's spell. Members of a second group were felt to hover around the village or a particular family. These were perceived to be in a sort of confused state, perhaps calling attention to themselves by knocking a jug off a shelf or making an arrow shot at a bird miss an easy target. Members of a third class of spirits were experienced as malevolent. They could cause illness; make people go crazy; stir up disputes over land; engender fear, mistrust, and war between clans; cause spells to be cast by witches; and in some places (with the assistance of *sanguma*—see Zocca 2009 for research on this vexed topic), they could cause death.

I remember spending time in class discussions with texts such as Galatians 5:16–26 on spiritually appropriate behavior. The following came out of one discussion:

- If spirits are not leading people to wisdom, patience, kindness, love, and understanding, then they are not of God and should be shunned.
- If spirits produce the fruits of the Spirit, we needed to deepen our theological reflections on the relationship of the earthly and heavenly communion of saints.
- We needed to ask, could purgatory be a place from which ancestors who had not known Christ in life—but had lived basically sincere, good lives according to the customs of their people—might be admitted to heaven, having been shown the way by their descendants' living in Christian community?

To make such a jump, remember that, for Melanesians, the dead are still an integral part of the community, as Daimoi makes clear in chapter 13. Moreover, the physically "living" members of the community have obligations to these souls, who in turn have obligations to the community. Also remember that Catholicism has long taught that the souls of saints in heaven (and even those called "the poor souls in purgatory") could intercede for us with God. It didn't seem too big a step to consider whether the spirits of the dead might directly provide benefits to us, and we to them.

This sort of thing, of course, is foreign to those who populate Western Protestant churches—and rejected by many "modern" Western Catholics. By the time of the Reformation, devotion to the saints and abuses in areas like indulgences had crowded out Christ to become the center of many people's faith life. I recognize the merits of the Protestant disapproval. But I also emphasize that, in the international culture of Catholicism in which our students had been nurtured, the idea that some of their ancestors might be the source of blessings and be saved is not a long leap. The phrase "in a way known" to God is taken from *Gaudium et Spes* (Second Vatican Council 1965b, § 22). This section of *Gaudium et Spes* deals with the universal effects of Christ as the "New Man" on the salvation of the world and its peoples. The relevant portion reads,

> The Christian is certainly bound both by need and by duty to struggle with evil through many afflictions and to suffer death; but, as one who has been made a partner in the paschal mystery [of the death and resurrection of Jesus], and as one who has been configured to the death of Christ, he will go forward, strengthened by hope, to the resurrection.

Article 22 goes on to say,

> All this holds true not for Christians only but also for all men of good will in whose hearts grace is active invisibly. For since Christ died for all, and since all men are in fact called to one and the same destiny, which is divine, we must hold that the Holy Spirit offers to all the possibility of being made partners, *in a way known to God*, in the paschal mystery. [emphasis added]

My threefold phenomenology of spirits and other presences, I will be the first to admit, is amateur anthropology. It would be laughed out of a serious doctoral seminar. Indeed, I need to apologize in advance to my good friend and colleague from our days together at Bomana, Jerry Arbuckle, whose recent book (2010) criticizing the misuse of anthropology by theologians is obligatory reading for anyone musing on these questions. But in my defense, participants in my classes came from vastly different language and culture groups. Marriage customs, gender identity, social structures, religious rituals, narratives told to make sense of the universe—and so much more—all differed, sometimes radically. Yet this taxonomy of spirits and presences came out of dialogue with these Melanesian men at Holy Spirit Seminary. Alas I became seriously ill during the school holidays, and in February 1977 my doctor packed me off to Australia suffering from a serious case of hepatitis. I returned to the United States several months later and began doctoral studies, thus missing the chance to discuss these things under the rubric of a Christology and ecclesiology class. My plans to return to Papua New Guinea and devote my life to exploring these issues never materialized.

DRAWING THREADS TOGETHER

The theological warrant behind my speculation regarding spiritual presence rests in the conviction that people who enter into the evangelization process will, in God's good time, come to recognize, at ever deeper levels of interiority, God's sovereignty over themselves and over ancestral and place spirits. This process of growing discernment is rooted in the insight that the most important communication in religious matters is nonverbal, as summed up in the saying, *cor ad cor loquitur* (heart speaks to heart), the motto adopted by Cardinal Newman (1801–1890), who got it from St. Francis de Sales (1567–1622), who in turn used the phrase as he sought to transcend the theological bickering of a troubled age. De Sales, like Newman and today's Pope Francis, knew that in order to lead the poor to Christ, authentic love of the poor is required.

In this regard, the church needs to take seriously the excluded cosmological middle ground that Hiebert depicted and Westerners have shoved aside in our rush to instrumentalize nature. It also suggests that David Tracy is correct when he notes that Westerners have today "become conscious of those other traditions whose power we sense, but whose meaning for us we do not yet begin to know how to interpret" (1987, 8). To cite one random example, the use of dreams to impart important information is testified to throughout the Pentateuch and elsewhere. In Genesis 28:11, an angel spoke to Jacob in a dream. In Genesis 31:24, God comes to Laban the Aramean in a dream, and several chapters later (Gen 37) Joseph has a dream that sends his entire family into a state of high anxiety. In the New Testament, Matthew 1:20 has angels appearing to impart important information to Joseph. In Matthew 2:12 Mary and Joseph are warned in a dream to avoid falling into Herod's clutches.

Modern exegesis, rooted in reductive literary theory, sees dreams as a way to get information to a biblical figure so that the drama can move toward its conclusion—in much the same way that ancient Greek drama would introduce a god to move the story ahead. While it is impossible to get behind the biblical story to prove that God sent a dream in which Yahweh spoke or sent an angel to deliver a message, the point I wish to make is simple. In ancient times, people were sophisticated enough to know that some literary devices are constructed to move a plot ahead. But the literary devices worked because the cultural environment was saturated with experiences of real messages being imparted in them. My Melanesian students made the distinction between *lukim driman nating* (having a mere dream) and *lukim driman* (having a [message-laden] dream). No doubt the dramatis personae of biblical stories and their editors made the distinction as well.

At another level entirely is the question of discernment of good and evil. Biblical images of spiritual warfare and its condemnation of traditional rituals remind us that Jewish and Christian Scriptures are replete with examples of false gods and evil spirits leading people astray. The reality of spiritual tempters is not questioned, and discernment between them and messengers from God (such as angels) is required. The ultimate New Testament criteria of genuineness in Christian growth are (1) the teaching of Galatians 5 on the fruits of the Spirit, and (2) experience that spiritual maturity leads the follower of Christ into both hope and belief that God is directing all toward eschatological completion. This completion, not the salvation of individuals, is God's intention; individuals and the human race as a whole will be saved as the whole reaches fulfillment for each person.

Such biblical principles help us formulate the primary goals of mission: helping people everywhere understand the full dimension of what they are saying yes to and becoming a witness of when they accept the invitation to become disciples of Jesus. Stating this sort of thing or quoting and paraphrasing Scripture is one thing. It is quite another for individuals, communities, and societies to grasp what it means in their inmost being and then to give witness to it in the concreteness of their lives. It is precisely here where wise evangelizers make their own the prayer of Paul: "I pray . . . that the eyes of your heart may be enlightened in order that you may know the hope to which God has called you" (Eph 1:18).

In the context of such discussions, the relevant issue is that Christian evangelism is not complete when the Scriptures are understood intellectually and candidates behave ethically at a level sufficient for baptism. Nor is it as simple as confessing, "Jesus is Lord," even when that act of faith is done under the inspiration of the Holy Spirit (see Rom 10, especially v. 9). Put in a slightly different manner, what I am asking readers to consider is this: Can individuals not genuinely be moved by the Spirit to believe in the *gospel of promise* even though they may fall short of a *total* act of trusting faith? Why? Because Christian life *is* dialectical at the individual level, where we struggle both with the dark side of our nature and with resistance to trust fully in the promises of Christ. Furthermore, at a cultural level, we struggle to discern which are the false gods and practices that keep communities from understanding the Lordship of Christ in their context.

CONCLUSION

Finally, let me return to the issue of this book as a whole, the question of traditional or other, "non-Christian" rituals in Christian worship. God's purpose in leading us to become disciples of Jesus is to encourage a deeper level of awareness of where we fit in creation. The two principal rituals of Christianity are baptism and Eucharist. The first, a ritual of transformation, externalizes the act of trust involved in saying yes to God's promises. Believers go down into the water and come up again, cleansed of sin, open to the transforming power of the Holy Spirit. The Eucharist is a ritual of remembrance, forgiveness, communion with Christ in his death, and resurrection, as well as in his anticipated return. No one exhausts the depths of these two sacraments. Instead, as we grow, we *participate* in them as they re-present the life, death, and resurrection of Christ and teach us how to bring him into the everyday world of family, work, play, and public life.

A community committed to the symbolic expression of the Christ-life must seek to incorporate that expression in the reality of their worship. Such faith communities rejoice in being part of a greater communion of saints who have gone before us. These sacramental rituals lead us more deeply into life's mystery and are central to the life of the church. The ultimate norm is whether worship utilizing such rituals is in accord with the fundamental rule of faith: Christ as the *norma normans non normata*. That is to say, Christ is the one who establishes the standard of Christian ritual and worship, while not himself being subject to human standards. Christ, sitting at the right hand of the Father, is celebrated in the recognition that all peoples express in all the richness of their creativity.

Part One
Traditional Rituals

Rituals provide a means for humans to worship God and for God to bring human experience in line with God's intent for them. Rituals reflect what people consider important and serve as a vital way to connect people to God, who desires people to live fulfilled lives (Jn 10:10). The chapters in part one all reflect on use of traditional (i.e., pre- or non-Christian) rituals in Christian worship. They demonstrate how pre-Christian socioreligious traditions can be adapted to enable people to focus their praise and thanksgiving to God. Despite some overlap, these chapters divide into an emphasis on the rituals themselves or a focus on the context in which those rituals make sense.

WITH FOCUS ON RITUAL

In chapters 3 through 5, the authors emphasize the nature of ritual itself: the behavior associated with ritual and ceremony and what it means for those who practice them. Osias Segura-Guzman discovers the myth behind the festival of El Baile de la Yegüita and applies it to reconciliation between Catholics and Protestants. Gabriel Kuman in turn makes a connection between Old Testament Passover rituals, New Testament Eucharist rituals, and the Shimbu pig-kill. Like the peoples who populate the Bible, the Shimbu draw on Dema myths to provide a rationale for their ritual behavior. In chapter 5, Emmanuel Obasare shows how present-day Maroons still evade outside contact while seeking to relinquish their "rights" of association with the Kromante spirit in order to develop a dependence on the Holy Spirit.

WITH FOCUS ON CONTEXT

The authors of chapters 6 through 8 put ritual in contexts that, though highly specific, highlight general principles for human worship. In chapter 6 Paul Mantae Kim locates Korean death rituals within the context of the family to demonstrate the importance of family worship for identity. Bradford Haami then elucidates the need for applying Māori rituals common in mid-nineteenth-century New Zealand to the contemporary reconciliation movement so that all inhabitants of Aotearoa may be restored. In chapter 8, Petros Malakyan and his protégé, Dan Hopkins, close this section of the book by demonstrating how pagan third- and fourth-century rites contributed to the sensory experience that is present-day Armenian Orthodoxy.

All these rituals and the contributory elements of each context demonstrate that relevance is reflective of context, which in turn provides purpose, structure, and sensory impact of traditional rituals giving shape to contemporary worship.

With Focus on Ritual

3

A Folk–Costa Rican Festival of Reconciliation

El Baile de La Yegüita

Osias Segura-Guzman

Understanding and appreciating rituals and their supporting symbols and myths are important tasks for missionaries and pastors. These religious categories provide opportunities for dialogue and for understanding that God is at work in every culture, even outside of Christianity. The best way to appreciate a ritual is to understand the story that lies behind it: the myth. If pastors and missionaries would read the Scriptures narratively, a better appreciation of sacred stories would open a desire for greater dialogue. For those who participate in ceremonies, such experiences impact their spirituality and can only be appreciated and understood on their own terms as expressions that are sometimes difficult to put into words.

For decades, anthropologists have been broadcasting the importance of appreciating symbols, rituals, and myths to understand the faith of the people they study. Missionaries, in contrast, have feared idolatry and resisted the belief that God could be at work in cultures outside Christianity. Today, in the second decade of the twenty-first century, this lack of appreciation and understanding of symbols, rituals, and myths still remains common among some Christian missionaries and pastors. Why is this understanding important? Traditional rituals are being supported in many parts of Latin America today by governments and universities as a way to allow communities to rediscover their cultural origins and to bring tourism to the local communities. That is, rituals are in a revival mode in many societies around the world, and pastors and missionaries may be missing opportunities to missiologically engage local cultures.

In what follows, I present an ethnographic case study from my experience in Latin America. Then I present a missiological discussion centered on a creative tension of insights from theological studies and the social sciences. To accomplish this interdisciplinary task, I draw upon symbolic anthropology (e.g., Paul Hiebert), which seeks to study the fundamental questions about human life by studying the arrangement of symbols and their meanings in rituals. Enriching Hiebert's approach, I also use the discipline of religious studies (e.g., William Paden), which helps us understand cross-cultural patterns of religious behavior. I conclude the chapter with a missiological proposal of recommendations for how pastors and missionaries can approach rituals missiologically; a few insights from biblical theologians and missiologists help us do that.

THE FESTIVAL OF EL BAILE DE LA YEGÜITA

One need only travel a few hours from the capital city of any Latin American country to find cultures that have not been assimilated completely into the Western paradigm. They still remain largely premodern, though influenced by Christian elements initiated by a Catholic history largely from Spain and reflected in the Protestant movement of eighteenth- and nineteenth-century missionaries from Europe and North America. These historical religious excursions are further maintained by the contemporary evangelical expressions reflecting the impact of North American missionaries during the twentieth century. The old and the new coexist to reflect "split-level Christianity." I discovered this convoluted mixture in one of the rural areas of Costa Rica in a local Methodist church.

The local Methodist church in the town of Nicoya, in the province of Guanacaste in Costa Rica, was founded around 1988, and its sanctuary and parsonage were built in 1993. The church has a membership of about two hundred people, and it is one of the well-known Evangelical churches in the area. I met the pastor, Gerardo, during the last weeks of June 1999 when I took two short-term mission teams to serve there for a period of three weeks. A few years later Gerardo was in my class at a local seminary in San José. One day I said, "We can be 100 percent Costa Rican and 100 percent Christian." After class, Gerardo came to me saying, "Osías, I understand what you have said about being 100 percent Costa Rican and 100 percent Christian, but in my town of Nicoya, I have to say that we cannot be 100 percent Nicoyans and 100 percent Christians."

"Why?" I asked.

He responded, "Well, figure this out: in Nicoya, as you know, they celebrate the festival of El Baile de la Yegüita" (the dance of the young mule).

Trying to be a good listener, I said to him, "Tell me about it." He explained,

> This festival celebrates the time a young mule appeared to some Indigenous people who were fighting with each other. The mule came from nowhere and separated them from fighting. It is a big festival and, thus, a big deal for the people of Nicoya to participate in. They re-create the ritual dance, and the young mule dancing behind the Virgin Mary in a parade. Even people from my church like to go there and participate in this festival. I have interpreted this as being like eating food dedicated to the idols and giving money to the Roman Catholic Church. As well, this story about a young mule sounds kind of diabolic. You know, this is Indigenous stuff mixed with Catholicism. That is idolatry! Now, tell me what do you think about it? As a pastor, would you participate in this festival?

While I knew about this cultural tradition, being from the capital city, my cultural background is very different from that section of the country. Being in Nicoya was a cross-cultural experience for me. So, in order to respond to Gerardo's question, I needed to ask this question: "What is this story of *la Yegüita* all about?" What follows is my journey in discovering El Baile de la Yegüita as ritual and myth. It became more than a case study; it became an experience that impacted my missiological understanding of contextualization.

The Festival of El Baile de la Yegüita

For over four hundred years, every year between November 12 and December 12, los Nicoyanos (the natives of the town of Nicoya), have been celebrating El Baile de la Yegüita with fireworks and a gala dance to the Virgin Mary who once granted them a miracle. The people explain that during the colonial times, while returning from work, two Indigenous men from the ethnic group of the Matambugueños began discussing their love for the same woman. They pulled out their machetes and were ready to kill each other. Their companions were afraid, and loudly requested to the Virgin to grant them a miracle by separating them. She granted it! The Virgin sent a *yegüita* (a young mule), who came down from a hill to dance between the two men, separating them and putting an end to the fight. Today this myth is part of a deep spiritual devotion to the Virgin Mary for the Nicoyanos; a traditional dance, the *yegüita*, is still danced with flute and drum in honor of the Virgin.

These sacred days begin in the month of November with the day of the *contadera* (day of counting) when the days are counted with kernels of corn until the arrival of the official celebration. One month before the big festival begins, oxcarts come loaded with firewood that is taken to the Cofradía (the place of fellowship) for the event. The logs will be the fuel used to prepare the food and drinks, made of corn, which will be distributed freely during the festival. The official rituals begin at dawn on December 11 with the first prayer made to the Virgin. Then the Nicoyan image of the Virgin (a local version of the patroness of Costa Rica) is carried from the main Catholic church "dirty," as the Nicoyans say, to be given new clothes for the party. Once the image is well dressed, the procession begins in the streets and, later, in the church. On this day the image visits the Cofradía amid shouts of "Long live the Virgin!" with loud bursts of firecrackers. Then the image is taken to the church around 6 p.m. to preside over the first Mass. Around 10 p.m., the Virgin receives a serenade by a professional choir. The party continues the next day at 11 a.m. with a major Mass. Once the Mass has ended, the Virgin is with the town people for the last time and dances with the yegüita, which has accompanied her during the whole festival.

Traditionally, the dancing of the yegüita in the streets was a sign of reconciliation. Those with issues or differences in the community would tell each other, "See you at the yegüita dance." Then, at the reenactment of the ritual, they would jump into the street and fight each other, and the yegüita would seek to separate them. At that moment they would hug each other and forgive the past. About one hundred years ago, however, the Roman Catholic Church considered that fighting an act of savagery, and the central expression of reconciliation was removed from the ritual. To make things worse, the first Protestant pastors and missionaries taught that conversion to Christ implied abandoning anything Roman Catholic. Thus, participating in such communal events was considered idolatry and therefore syncretism.

Understanding the cultural background of this celebration, I came to realize why Gerardo asked his question and doubted the main hypothesis of my class. Knowing his fundamentalist-Pentecostal background, I could somewhat understand his theological perspective. Churches like his have a legalistic interpretation of "avoiding idolatry." They believe that God expects them to be holy, and to do so they must keep pure from other forms of spiritual practice, including Roman Catholic rituals. Their conclusion is that the world is sinful and corrupt, and their local church is a holy place and a safe haven. Therefore, everything that does not fit into the parameters of what they consider "holy" is unholy and sinful.

Understanding El Baile de la Yegüita

In my class, I had challenged Gerardo's approach and proposed that nothing is wrong with evangelicals contextualizing this ritual for themselves. The point of contextualization is to allow a hybridity to continue bringing God back into the equation (see Burrows, chapter 2). The problem does not lie in the ritual itself but in those who cannot see God at work. Understanding and embracing God in the culture as an expression of incarnation is often a problem for evangelical leaders like Gerardo.

A ritual such as El Baile de la Yegüita is the reenactment of the myth, a sacred story about the Virgin allowing a young mule to bring reconciliation. Every such story reveals values, explains the divine, and reflects how people in this society organize time and space. A "ritual," as I am using it here, is a re-creation of the story that reminds the people of a time when God interrupted reality with a divine presence. "Although myth has a similar function across religions, its content and style is different in each" (Paden 1988, 92).

In all cultures, humans interact with superhuman agents or gods through spiritual practices that occur in sacred places and times (e.g., festivals).

> Gods, whatever they may or may not be ultimately, present themselves to human experience as "other" and as primordially given. Even from the point of view of invention, gods and their worlds would surely be among the astonishing creations and creative acts of our human species, and unavoidable subject matter for any student of how humans choose to live. (Paden 1988, 140)

William Paden defines rituals as a "sacred action and time deliberately created" (1988, 95). A ritual is human activity that structures action and time with the purpose of focusing on the sacred. In rituals, humans dramatize or re-create the myth that "expresses the world foundation in terms of words and image; ritual dramatizes world foundations in terms of performance" (Paden 1988, 93).

Therefore, for those who engage it, a "ritual is authoritative . . . and is instrumental in creating new forms of life and relationships" (Paden 1988, 100). Through ritual, the stories of the community are re-created and celebrated as an enactment of the myth. Thus, a ritual like El Baile de la Yegüita is authoritative because it is the dramatization of the sacred story, the communal myth of an entire ethnic group. Rituals often express the ideal relationship between superhuman agents, human beings, and the rest of creation. With this cultural understanding and an awareness of the festival of El Baile de la Yegüita, I can now work with Gerardo to deconstruct this festival in light of his evangelical position in the community of Nicoya.

CONTEXTUALIZING THE EL BAILE DE LA YEGÜITA FESTIVAL

What we have here is a Methodist pastor in a majority Roman Catholic town struggling with folk-Catholic rituals. It is a good example of what William Burrows describes in chapter 2 as hybridization.

There are layers upon layers of meaning in a ritual. In chapter 1, Dan Shaw develops Paul Hiebert's model of critical contextualization, which lays out a process of enabling evangelical leaders like Gerardo to appreciate their own culturally appropriate expressions in light of a biblical view for the purpose of making relevant adjustments that both celebrate their culture and recognize God's presence with them (see Figure 1-4). This process, initiated by a phenomenological study of the ritual itself, would help the evangelical and Roman Catholic churches describe and analyze, without premature judgments, the spiritual practices and experiences of folk-Catholics.

After understanding folk-Catholic practices and experiences come the second and third steps, which help evangelicals and Roman Catholics do a biblical study of ritual in the Old and New Testaments. God loved a party, as reflected in his elaborate instructions for the Passover and the many other festivals in the books of Leviticus and Deuteronomy. How those festivals were focused on honoring God was important to how people worshiped God in the context of their celebration.

Once people appreciate the cultural expressions and have reflected on the biblical expressions, there can be a critical evaluation as the Scripture and the local culture are brought into dialogue. This process helps Roman Catholics and evangelicals alike evaluate and respond to their own existing beliefs and practices in light of their new scriptural understanding as it relates to folk-Catholic rituals. The process, then, becomes an exegesis of the theological theme behind the myth of El Baile de la Yegüita and its enactment. Allow me to clarify that I do not intend for the Catholic Church to change folk-Catholic rituals, but I hope the Catholic Church can enrich them with biblical understanding. Engaging in this contextualization process not only helps evangelicals and Roman Catholics respond to folk-Catholic needs but also may help in prompting them to know each other as well as themselves even better.

The final step provides the people's own missional response by creating transformative ministries in order to guide folk-Catholics from where they are to where God may intend for them to be. Thus, the key is for leaders like Gerardo to be willing to mobilize their churches and empower their congregations to discern what ministerial actions should take place in the context of such a festival. Each religious community brings a different understanding, but together with God's view, as expressed in Scripture, they may evaluate and bring their religious perspectives together in order to develop a new contextualized enactment of the myth.

I must, however, be clear about Hiebert's objective for developing this critical contextualization model within a missiological framework. First, Hiebert never meant for his model to appear linear. Rather it is an ongoing process in which every hermeneutical community needs to engage as part of their spiritual development—knowing God. Second, Hiebert never meant for outsiders to execute his model. The missionaries' task is not to serve as spiritual sheriffs, naming what is good and bad and how things are supposed to be done. As Hiebert put it, "Contextualization is ultimately the task not of individuals or leaders, but of the church" (Hiebert 1991, 40). Third, although we are interested in a biblical theology in context, this should not be separated from the global church. The Catholic Church in Costa Rica should not ignore that our brothers and sisters in Africa, Asia, Europe, and other parts of Latin America may be going through similar challenges. Why not seek to listen to and learn from all of them? Again, quoting Hiebert,

> Critical contextualization does not equate the gospel with any culture. Nor does it allow theologies developed in different contexts to become islands to themselves. Rather, it calls individuals and churches to listen collectively to what God is saying to them and to the church. (1991, 40)

Fourth, in order to understand this model of critical contextualization, we need to appreciate it within the framework of Hiebert's concern about syncretism in his model of the excluded middle. As Hiebert notes, in such an approach, "We first study both the Scriptures and our cultural and historical settings, and then let the text transform us and our context" (1991, 40).

Extending the Critical Contextualization Model

With all this in mind, I present in Figure 3-1 an adjusted model that will clarify for people I know and love how to apply Hiebert's model in their context. My intention is not to alter the model but rather to clarify Hiebert's intention in order to avoid syncretism. Thus, I like to see Hiebert's model in the form of a church—a community of believers recognizing the supremacy of God, who reconciles the whole of creation through the incarnation, death, and resurrection of Jesus Christ, all through the power of the Holy Spirit.

Figure 3-1: A Community of Believers in Dialogue with Global Theologies

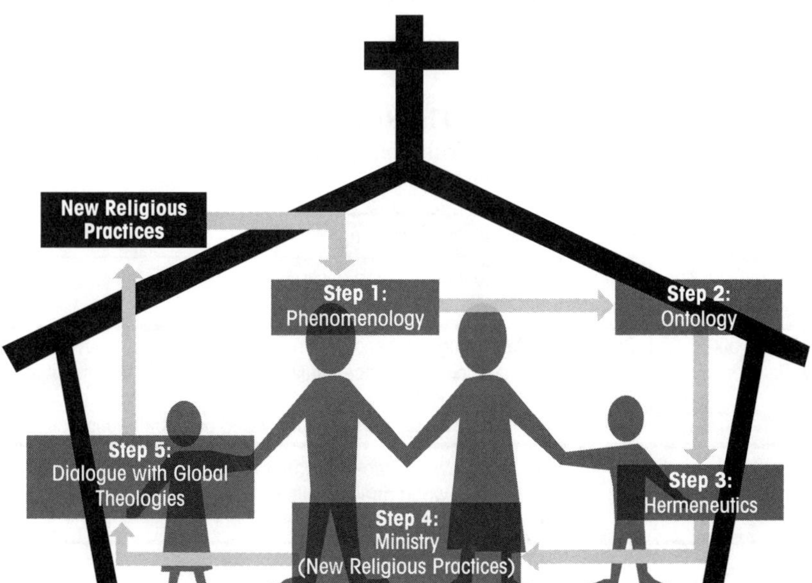

In the model as depicted, the church serves as a hermeneutical community and is the context in which the circular process of critical contextualization takes place. The steps are basically the same as Hiebert encouraged, beginning with an evaluation of religious practices in light of cultural and biblical understanding within a particular socioreligious context. Developing new practices that are critiqued by Scripture rather than outside cultural expressions is important for the well-being of the community of believers. The new step I am adding is Step 5 on global dialogue, which means listening to the global church. Then an arrow goes back to begin the process all over again. What does this mean? The key point here is for the church, after a few weeks, years, or the next generation of Christians, to reevaluate the new religious practice in terms of the old religious experience and go through the process of critical contextualization all over again. Doing so regularly will avoid any uncritical acceptance of old beliefs and practices. The process is never complete.

The practice of contextualization must be an ongoing process because culture and the people in it are always changing. Practices developed in one time and place may not be appropriate in the emerging environment of global change. This circular process will help believers avoid syncretism, which reconnects this model to Hiebert's intention for developing the model in the first place.

For leaders like Gerardo, syncretism means idolatry, which is a huge sin. Hiebert's best model to explain this concern is in his work on the "flaw of the excluded middle" (1987), as reflected in Figure 1-3 in Shaw's introductory chapter. Hiebert's love for mathematics, anthropology, and the Church made possible this brilliant expression of culture clash. I represent the three categories for his model in Figure 3-2.

Figure 3-2: The Relationship of High Religion, Folk Religion, and Science

Level	Focus	• Questions Concerning ...?
High/Orthodox Religion	Truth	• Ultimate origins and destiny • Meaning and purpose in life
Low/Folk–Religion	Power	• Well being diseases, famine, drought • Guidance: Fear, uncertainty of the future • Success: Failure • Peace: dealing with the Spirit world and spirit possessions
Science	Control	• Control over nature by technology • A hostile world and difficulties • Social harmony: Social conflict, wars, rivalries, feuds

(Adapted from Bradshaw (1993, 13) following Hiebert)

For Hiebert, high religion responds to the ultimate questions of the origin and destiny of life—the meaning and purpose of human existence. On the other hand, a middle level of religion responds to those life questions related to fear, suffering, and other "unexplained" issues. Hiebert helps us understand that religion must also respond to the everyday life issues that humans confront. As Shaw stated in chapter 1, "Missionaries unwittingly ensured that Christianity would be considered irrelevant." Therefore, a church that is not able to help people deal with their middle-zone questions is a church that has removed God from where God was meant to be all along.

For Hiebert, syncretism takes place when we allow the cultural context to be the final authority for determining the boundaries of Christian experience. Rather, following Hiebert, we must seek the following principles in every process of contextualization. First, "Christian beliefs and practices must be biblically based" (Hiebert 1991, 39). Second, it is the Spirit who instructs us and guides us in all truth. Third, the church should act as a community of interpretation, avoiding any hermeneutical privatization. Fourth, we need a biblically based theology in order to avoid any religious pluralism when it comes to the person of Christ. Shaw calls this a "biblical theology in context" (2010, 211–12).

Critical contextualization is a very good model for not falling into the problem of syncretism when working with rituals. These principles can help a leader like Gerardo understand that it is not about accepting the ritual as it is, but allowing the Spirit through Scripture in the context of the church as a hermeneutical community to engage the ritual for missiological purposes.

MISSIOLOGICAL IMPLICATIONS OF A CONTEXTUALIZED EL BAILE DE LA YEGÜITA RITUAL

Now, allow me to provide further implications for missionaries that emerge from engaging with the festival of El Baile de la Yegüita. Western theological schools have trained pastors and missionaries to mainly handle written texts. We need a different hermeneutical approach to other religions and religious practices—something more than a focus on literacy, as Dyrness notes: "The exposure of most people to religions other than their own is more likely to be via aesthetic or ritual objects and practices" (2013, 1). Thus, written accounts are not the best way to appreciate most religious practices in the world. Religious experiences are sometimes not easy to explain in concrete words. We need to pay attention to what rituals "*do* for people, how people feel and respond to them and what the consequences of this might be for their lives" (Dyrness 2013, 8). That is, it is not about *what* but *how* people believe. This approach has been a hermeneutical handicap for Western missionaries and protégés like Gerardo. If missionaries and pastors could be trained to apply oral and narrative approaches instead of written and propositional reasoning, they may learn to "read" culture as a text and Scripture as a tool for religious dialogue. Comparing and contrasting sacred stories can open a desire for dialogue between sacred expressions.

Appreciating Local Narrative

Reading the culture as a text is all about narratives. Behind every ritual there is a myth or sacred story, and behind any godly worship event there is a biblical narrative. When facing culturally established rituals, Christian workers need to approach the Scriptures from a narratival perspective. This is also a good way to hermeneutically learn to read cultures as texts. Every community has a basic history, which is their story, and the key is to relate that story to God's narrative in the Bible. Scriptures are not fragmented doctrinal propositions.

In the Scriptures, we find one overarching storyline (with multiple topics) that goes from Genesis to Revelation. The narrative revolves around God's reconciling work in creation together with restoring what was lost in the Garden of Eden. This story provides human beings with a script for living in their socioreligious context with an eye toward God's intentions for them. Looking at the Scriptures from this perspective helps people connect the story behind the myth with the holy, biblical story. That intersection is a redemptive task that demonstrates how Christ complements every culture. Christian workers in a context like Nicoya should, then, express the relevance of the myth behind the ritual of El Baile de la Yegüita and thereby gain the right to demonstrate how the myth may ultimately have its origin in Scripture and thus complement their cultural desire for reconciliation with what the Scriptures say about God's reconciliation through Jesus Christ. The intentions of the biblical narrative and the cultural myth are the same. "In order to understand our world, to make sense of our lives, and to make our most important decisions about how we ought to be living, we depend upon some story. . . . Which story a person lives out of makes a huge difference in how one interprets events in life" (Bartholomew and Goheen 2004, 18, 19).

Nicoyans are seeking miracles of reconciliation, and it turns out that the Bible is full of them. "To be human means to embrace some such basic story through which we understand our world and chart our course through it" (Bartholomew and Goheen 2004, 19). This is a great hermeneutical tool for leaders like Gerardo. In the same way that Gerardo is able to find himself in the biblical story, ritualists also find themselves in the myth, reflected in their understanding of the cosmos and their place in it. Once Gerardo reads the Scripture from a narratival perspective and appreciates the folk-Catholic myth, I would pray for the possibility of a vulnerable dialogue between evangelicals and folk–Roman Catholics who share sacred stories and experience the wonder of recognizing the same root metaphor.

Ensuring a Narrative-Based Dialogue

The contextualization process is about dialogue. One way to exchange sacred stories is through vulnerable dialoguing about one's faith. The imperialistic arrogance of outsiders showing off their apologetic prowess as the only "true Christianity" is no longer an option. The idea of an *elenctic* dialogue without an apologetic intent was proposed by J. H. Bavinck over a generation ago. The term "elenctic" is based on an attitude of vulnerability in which dialogue allows others to share their faith as well. This interaction creates an environment where the Holy Spirit is the one who will convince others what is right. Mathias Zahniser, however, developed this term further, suggesting the addition of the element of dialogue to take "the convictions of others worthy of serious consideration and make an earnest effort to understand and to appreciate them" (1997, 1). This is the next step Gerardo needs to take.

Furthermore, Zahniser mentions three crucial dimensions of Christian witness through dialogue: the importance of intimacy, the work of the Holy Spirit, and the need for vulnerability in order to be convincing. These three dimensions bring together a dialogic approach he calls "close encounters of the vulnerable kind" (Zahniser 1994b, 72). In this model, one must be willing to be just as vulnerable as the other person in the conversation. Are we willing to perhaps have our mind changed as a result of the dialogue? If not, then it is not truly elenctic dialogue. If we desire that the other person be open enough to be convinced by the Holy Spirit to change their position, then we must be willing to be as open as we are asking them to be. This is where we learn from each other and allow the Holy Spirit to apply that learning to the point of the discussion.

The importance of intimate dialogue and the recognition of God's grace cannot happen with just preaching because "proclamation without dialogue will miss the rich fruit born of discerning the work that God is already doing in the life of those to whom evangelistic witness is directed" (Zahniser 1994b, 75). In dialogue, two kinds of vulnerability are encountered. "We experience both (1) the threat of being impacted by the faith and life of our partners in dialogue, and (2) the pain of having to put them in a position of anxiety and suffering" (1994, 76). This type of vulnerability enables Christian workers to be open to the point of being convinced by the other person. When a person is in that state of vulnerability, the Holy Spirit, not the logic of argumentation, does the work. This vulnerability in dialogue implies a phenomenological understanding by evangelicals of the other's religious background, where the other person's faith is appreciated as real and valuable because God has already been working in that culture.

Developing a Biblical Theology in Context

This vulnerable approach is about finding a theological substance for dialoguing narratives. In El Baile de la Yegüita we can see how the Holy

Spirit has been present and at work (i.e., prevenient grace) before pastors and missionaries preached the name of Christ for salvation. If the grace of God is not limited to the proclaiming work of the church, then evangelicals may more easily appreciate the work of the Holy Spirit in Nicoya as evidenced in God's intervention in El Baile de la Yegüita. God's presence was evident in the way the Virgin provided the mule as an instrument of peace. While Mary was viewed as a superhuman agent, God's presence was the reality behind the myth. Clark Pinnock's insights are helpful here:

> People are saved by faith, not by the content of their theology. . . . People are judged on the basis of the light they have received and how they have responded to that light. . . . People cannot respond to the light that did not reach them. They can only respond to revelation that did. . . . God cares about the direction of the heart, not the content of theology. (1992, 157–58)

Considering that the festival of El Baile de la Yegüita is about reconciliation, the narrative that Christian workers should seek to present in elenctic dialogue is the theological theme of reconciliation by way of the cross. This is a clue for leaders like Gerardo. The myth explains that the first miracle the Virgin granted them was sending a young mule to bring about reconciliation between the two men who were trying to kill each other. Thus, reconciliation can become the main principle behind this myth and the theological clue to engage the Scriptures accordingly.

Now, in order to find a symbol to represent this theological theme, evangelicals can ask themselves, *What symbol is mentioned in the Scriptures to express God's reconciliation with humanity? What about the cross of our Savior?* What an opportunity for the evangelical church to proclaim in word and deed the evangelical meaning of reconciliation during this festival, held every year during the advent season as Christians everywhere prepare for Christmas!

> A theology of reconciliation can be discerned on three levels: a Christological level, in which Christ is the mediator through whom God reconciles the world to God's self; an ecclesiological level, in which Christ reconciles Jew and Gentile; and a cosmic level in which Christ reconciles all the powers in heaven and on earth. (Schreiter 1998, 42)

Judging whether this myth is historical or not is irrelevant. I propose that the supplication of the Indigenous Nicoyans asking for help so that their two siblings could be reconciled was genuine. To this request, through prevenient grace, God responded in cultural terms they could understand. This festival of El Baile de la Yegüita is a tradition of how Nicoyans articulate their relationship with the spiritual realm. Rejecting or labeling this tradition as idolatry or in some way evil would only make it more difficult for the gospel to penetrate in Nicoya, because culturally this is such an important part of their existence. Pastors and missionaries during this festival can proclaim that reconciliation is reflected in relational terms as the work of God through Jesus's death on the cross. Reconciliation first comes from God and is then expressed in rituals such as El Baile de la Yegüita. Therefore, rituals may be transformed to express the work that God has already done through Christ on the cross and through the resurrection.

Presenting a Relevant Gospel Message

On an ecclesiological level, church workers must consider the historical facts that may help them appreciate the "spiritual phenomena" of the festival of El Baile de la Yegüita. The first non–Roman Catholic church came to Costa Rica during the second half of the nineteenth century, around three hundred years after this miracle happened in Nicoya. How can we expect Indigenous peoples under the Spanish Crown's control, and "evangelized" by the Catholic Church, to have a further Christological knowledge of the gospel (as evangelical pastors and missionaries may expect) when even the Latin Bible was only read by the clergy? According to what the native Nicoyans were taught about Christianity, they prayed to Mary, whom they understood to be the Christian deity who performs miracles.

> There are many Virgins throughout the world, especially in Latin America, that share these iconographic and semantic characteristics: she appears to Indians, mestizos, and mulatos; she is related to pre-Columbian cultures by some means; and she represents the defense of the people. (Mullenax 1992, 9)

Mary was the light of revelation that the Catholic Church preached to these natives. Can God choose to answer a call that is not to him? What about those who, spiritually speaking, prayed to Mary for salvation and miracles but did not have adequate knowledge of the work of Christ on the cross?

Finally—and I recognize I am presenting a linear logic that borders on an apologetic, but in light of Nicoyan experience I do it narratively—evangelicals like Gerardo must remember that all things have been reconciled in Christ. Therefore in Christ, people—evangelicals and Catholics alike—can find peace through the blood of the cross. As Colossians 1:19–20 reads, "For in him all the fullness of God was pleased to dwell, and through him God was pleased to reconcile to himself all things, whether on earth or in heaven, by making peace through the blood of his cross." In this passage Christian workers may see how Paul mentions the cross as a symbol for reconciliation. The concept of reconciliation has its own symbol—the cross—and its signs can be applied in many ways: peaceful living, healing, and forgiveness of sins, not to mention peace between brothers.

Thus, the cross can be the symbol for pastors like Gerardo, who seek reconciliation and forgiveness among Roman Catholics. The cross was an instrument on which Jesus bore human sins in his body. As such, the cross may serve as a symbol of unity for Costa Ricans, evangelicals and Roman Catholics alike. This culturally sensitive gospel can guide folk-Catholics from their focus on the festival of El Baile de la Yegüita to an awareness of the reconciliation of human beings to God through Jesus's death on the cross and the power of the Holy Spirit in raising Jesus from the dead. A humble attitude of dialogue to exchange stories is key for this theological topic to be communicated successfully.

CONCLUSION

Religious practices, like the ritual of El Baile de la Yegüita, are a response to deep, meaningful needs in human life. Through rituals, people make sense of life. Today we need missionaries with cultural intelligence to capably and critically engage folk beliefs. Rituals allow the creation of an ideal picture of how the world should be for the people who use the ritual; this action brings hope and strengthens people's faith. Symbols and rituals should not be rejected as part of an evolutionary spiritual agenda. Christian workers such as Gerardo need to be creative in order to contextualize the gospel of the kingdom on earth. A way to help pastors like Gerardo capture that Christian understanding and emerge from an appreciation of people's spiritual experiences is through their rituals and ceremonies, which are replete with cultural symbols that hold great meaning for the people who experience them.

Therefore, we need to enable people to read culture as a text, because a text is all about narratives. Behind every worship event there is a story, just like myth often informs ritual. Stories can be brought into dialogue and allow a hermeneutic approach to understand deep human needs as people seek the divine presence. Furthermore it is necessary to connect the biblical story with the story of people's sacred narratives, the origins of which may be the same. The importance of exchanging sacred stories by dialoguing one's faith in a vulnerable way teaches us to listen and fight our impulsive evangelical arrogance. A dialogical attitude creates a sacred environment for the convincing work of the Spirit to take place. In so doing, we can begin to comprehend that, behind every ritual, there is a sacred story—a mythical narrative.

El Baile de la Yegüita is about reconciliation, a topic that opens a space to dialogue the Scriptures from Genesis through the cross, all the way to Revelation. This is an example of how we can locate theological themes in every Christian or non-Christian ritual. Every culture thus becomes an open book that needs to be read. Understanding the narrative behind the myth forces a hermeneutical exercise of realizing that God has been at work in the context long before outsiders arrived. Indeed, as I maintained in that humble classroom at the seminary in San José, by God's grace, "We can be 100 percent Costa Rican and 100 percent Christian." Without a doubt, Christ can appear in our humble dialogical approach, and we, through the power of the Spirit, can be a living witness of God's reconciliation.

Gerardo came to appreciate this revitalized understanding of the festival of El Baile de la Yegüita. Both he and I, as well as his congregation, came to recognize God's reconciling work in the town of Nicoya as well as in their community of believers. Together they came to value the festival, not for its mythic value, but as an appreciation of a folk-Catholic expression of God's work on the cross of Christ and the power of the Holy Spirit to enlighten their entire community of God's presence in their place. May God be glorified!

4

The Simbu Pig-Kill Festival and the Eucharist

A Paradigm for Building Christian Community in the Highlands of Papua New Guinea

Gabriel Kuman

> When the Simbu people experience the pig-kill, they celebrate the life given to them through the violent death of their ancient ancestors, the dema.
>
> The memorial feast of the exodus took on a new meaning when Jesus had the thanksgiving meal with his disciples on the night he was betrayed (Lk 22:19–20).
>
> Taken together these images express God's self-revelation, and abundant life flows continuously.

The Simbu (pronounced "Chimbu") Pig-Kill Festival is a traditional religious feast that is celebrated in the highlands of Papua New Guinea (PNG) to make present the life-giving event of the death of *dema* (mythical ancestors). According to Ennio Mantovani, who has spent many years investigating both the pig-kill rite and the function of dema in Melanesian cultural history, the lives they gave up provide new life in fullness—an enhanced life both for humans and the natural world (Mantovani 2009; 2014). When the dema die, blood flows. Similarly, when pigs are killed, blood flows; the people see pigs' blood as a sign of new life. In other words, blood symbolizes the flow of new life, strength, blessing, peace, and harmony. It is a cosmic symbol that keeps the whole creation in order.

During this period of a pig-kill festival, all the neighboring tribal friends and distant relatives of a given line (a better word than clan or tribe) are invited to help, participate, and share in the festival together. As a communal, *memorial* celebration, the pig-kill has elements that remind us of the Jewish Passover and the Christian Eucharist. In this chapter I discuss some of the similarities found in these three celebrations.

It may seem awkward to compare the pig-kill festival, the Passover, and the Eucharist. Indeed, one may disagree with drawing an analogy between a Melanesian festival and ancient Jewish and biblical rituals. However, I believe it is fruitful to take a closer look at the three celebrations in their proper cultural and religious contexts in order to appreciate and deepen our understanding of the shared role of death and regeneration in all three and the implications for the Simbu today.

The contemporary view of the traditional pig-kill festival of the Simbu people may presage and aid in understanding the salvific action of God. Maintaining that the Simbu rite has similarities with the Jewish Passover and the Christian Eucharist stems from the interpretive work of pioneer missionaries. For the Simbu people, elements of the traditional religious feast can greatly influence and give new Christian meaning. The guiding principle of this chapter is that it is life-giving for a people to understand their culture and its traditional religious feasts, in order to grasp better the meanings of Christian celebration such as the Eucharist.

My desire for this discussion is to (1) help Simbu Christians see how God prepared our ancestors to appreciate and accept the gospel long before the arrival of the missionaries, (2) help Simbu reflect on their cultural practice of the pig-kill festival and see how it connects to the Christian feast of the Eucharist, and (3) help other Christians see the significance of ancient and contemporary meals that transform families and communities by bringing them into communion with one another and the natural world. Doing so can enable those who participate to remain open to the future with Christian hope.

THE HISTORICAL BACKGROUND OF THE PIG-KILL FESTIVAL

The pig-kill festival is one of the most significant cultural events for the people of Simbu Province; the pig is one of the most prestigious animals. They were valued by our ancestors and continue to be valued today. As such, the pig was and is commonly used to celebrate life in this culture. Since the pig is highly valued as far back as memories go, it is fair to assume it had significance in the history and origin of these people who depend upon and value their pigs. One can raise technical questions: Where do pigs originate? Why is the pig important to the people of Simbu? Such questions have their place, but in asking them it is easy to miss the point of their local meaning in the past and for today. Of course, with the help of modern archaeological and anthropological methods we may come to know these details, but we also need to realize that before contact with Europeans, before scientific documentation, the people had no knowledge whatsoever about how, where, and when the pigs came to them. All that is important to us, who engage in these practices, is to understand how our ancestors responded to the arrival of the pigs and the resulting traditions they have passed down to us.

According to James Knight (1979), pigs arrived among the Simbu more than five thousand years ago, probably through trade with the coastal people. In the past, the people lived a seminomadic lifestyle of hunting and gathering, but this changed completely when the pigs arrived and the Simbu moved into a more sedentary lifestyle. *Kaukau* (sweet potato) arrived in the PNG highlands about five hundred years ago, much later than the introduction of pigs. The nutritious value of the sweet potato, for humans and pigs alike, required that people learn to cultivate them. People began to build homes, make gardens, and live in small family settlements, which later developed into clans and tribes, or family lines, as I prefer to call them. The arrival of the pig marks a significant event in the history of the Simbu people and the establishment of their communities. Hence they need to account for this great changing event (Rynkiewich 2004). Since written records of such events have not been part of our tradition, people kept memory of the event alive from generation to generation by maintaining an oral history of myths and stories.

What follows is an English translation of one mythic version of the pig-kill and the genesis of the dema:

> Long, long ago in Simbu Province there lived two brothers. The elder brother was Mondo and the younger was Gande. One day Mondo invented the *arigl* [a wig made of birds' feathers and the hair of their grandparents worn during the pig-kill festival] and usually he wore this headdress and went to the bush and stayed there till night. Then he came home and slept. One day the younger brother decided to follow him to the bush and see what he was doing every day. When Mondo dressed and left the next day, Gande followed him secretly. As soon as Mondo arrived at the usual place, he removed the *arigl* from his head and placed it on a branch of a tree. Then he grew pig's teeth and started digging the soil just as pigs normally do. He kept on digging until dusk. Gande saw him from behind the bushes with tears running down his cheeks.
>
> Late at dusk Mondo took his *arigl* and put it on but it kept slipping off his head. Then he asked, "Did Gande come and see me that you act like this?" After saying this he placed it on and it stood perfectly on his head. When he arrived at home, he asked Gande. "Did you follow me to the bush and see me?" With tears flowing, Gande replied, "Yes." Then Mondo continued, "You must take me to the place where you saw me digging and kill me and bury me at the place where I hung my *arigl* and put a strong wooden fence around it. A few days later *kumgi* grass [a weed that was the first to

grow in cleared gardens or new burial sites] will grow on the burial place, and when this happens you must go and look."

So Gande took Mondo to the place where he dug the soil and killed him and buried him there and put a wooden fence around the grave just as Mondo had prescribed. Three weeks later when *kumgi* grass began to grow on the grave, Gande came to see the place and, to his surprise, within the fence he saw several pigs of varied colors—black, white, red, and some with black spots, and many others with stripes. He went home and returned with his clansmen and put ropes round the legs of the pigs and took them home. Since then they have bred pigs and eaten them, and they have made *arigl* and also many other decorations of their ancestor Mondo, who had given them life and prosperity through the gift of the pig.

This history of the pig-kill festival was preserved, interpreted into new circumstances, and handed down for many generations. T. W. Guzie aptly notes, "Myth can give genuine meaning to an event or person. It can move us outside the world of history and finite experience into a world of pure meaning" (Guzie 1974, 18). This cultural meaning is far more important to us than the technical details investigated by outsiders.

CHRISTIAN INTERPRETATION OF THE PIG-KILL FESTIVAL

We note that in the Simbu myth the elder brother freely offered himself to be killed by his younger brother so that an abundance of life and prosperity might flow to the people. The story does not say how Mondo was killed but emphasizes what emerged from the grave: pigs of varied colors. So the question arises, what does the pig really mean for the Simbu people?

Anthropologists including Ennio Mantovani and Mary MacDonald provide the answer: "The pig is what keeps Simbu society together. It stands for good and stable relationship" (1982, 13). Through the gift of the pig, peace and harmony have prevailed in Simbu societies. Furthermore, the gift strengthens the existing relationships and restores those that are broken. The pig also symbolizes wealth and prestige, the social status of a community, the power of community leaders, and many other things.

We do not know exactly why Mondo was killed by his brother. One would assume that, between Gande seeing him growing pig's teeth and digging the soil and the role of the *arigl*, there was rich cultural and religious significance associated with these symbols as well as the death. As in many Melanesian societies, the myth portrays a community that was lacking in something essential. In other words it was as if the society lived in want, chaos, or darkness and required somebody to bring forth light to illuminate their condition. This situation required a very courageous person to give up his life freely to remedy the state of deprivation (Mantovani and MacDonald 1982, 13).

In the myth we notice how a remedy is made available to the whole unstable community. The person who sacrificed his life to perfect an incomplete creation is thus a heroic person whose work must be remembered down through the ages; that is the role of myth. Whenever there is a lack of abundant "life," the only way to restore it is to reenact the death of the dema, by carrying out the prescribed "rituals, which make present the life-giving death in order to increase life" (Mantovani and MacDonald 1982, 14). Some of these rituals of life are birth and death celebrations, marriage, and planting and harvesting ceremonies. According to Mantovani and MacDonald (1982), the various occasions for the rituals may differ, but the meaning and purpose remains the same: rendering in the present the primordial event that brought forth true and abundant life.

The story of Mondo and Gande resembles the biblical account of Christ's salvific action. Jesus's celebration of the Jewish Passover and his own passion, death, and resurrection are encapsulated in the Eucharist. In the Bible these events are presented as history, but in their shape one cannot but admit similarities to Melanesian and other mythology. In this sense at least, Mondo can be seen as a cultural representation that foreshadows the pattern of Jesus, who came, suffered, and died that an abundance of life might flow continuously to the entire needy human race. What I want to emphasize is that the myth of Mondo and Gande is only a Simbu representation of what Christ has gone through and its significance for all human beings. Taking the images further—through God's self-revelation in the incarnation, teaching, life, and death of Jesus—abundant life flows continuously, not just to one people, but to all people everywhere. People make sense of the story in their own cultural context and according to their own thought and linguistic patterns. As Guzie states the case in regard to the Christian tradition in the Mediterranean, "All the Church Fathers' imagery regarding Christ's victory over Satan is very much in line with Ancient mythology" (1974, 12).

In this sense, therefore, Mondo can be understood as a prefigurement of Christ who becomes the mediator between God and the Simbu people at this point in time in their cultural experience. Put another way, it is natural for the Simbu to understand Christ's significance against the background of their dema stories. Unlike the historical Jesus, the incarnation of the Logos in John's Gospel has the potential to take human form in every culture and use events and symbols of any society to reveal and identify himself to the people and thereby become part of their history. Considering the Simbu myth, we can say that Jesus reveals and identifies himself with the Simbu people through the gift of pigs. Similarly, through the crucifixion and resurrection, Christ reenacted this memorial schema in the bread and wine of the Eucharist.

Salvation, according to Scripture (Heb 7:27), came only once and for all and at a specific point in time and history. But the redeeming and saving action of God must be intimately experienced by all people everywhere, as it first dawned on the people of Israel more than thirty-five hundred years ago.

The dema myth is presented in a holistic manner that expresses the genuine purpose of religious ritual and celebration, the significance of which is fully manifested in the events recorded in Scripture. Is this radical and new in terms of Catholic teaching? Not if one follows the line propounded by Capuchin Father Ronald Lawler and his associates, who maintain that "among God's chosen people who were favoured by the guidance of his special revelation, there were sacrifices that foreshadowed the one sacrifice which truly merits salvation for all nations and all ages" (Lawler, Wuerl, and Lawler 1976, 421–22). Pioneer missionaries were fully aware that there are unacceptable (from an outsider's point of view) elements of magic and superstition involved in the pig-kill celebrations, but this did not mean that the whole process was evil and sinful (Schaefer 1981). These missionaries were aware that elements closely tied to traditional religion had to be transformed into new Christian practices. But other elements revealed the footprints of God as reflected in the incarnation of Jesus. The pattern is similar to that recorded when Israel came in contact with the religions of Canaan. According to Guzie, "The Ancient Hebrews inherited pastoral rituals from the tribes surrounding them," but he also maintains, "After they escaped from Egypt, the old rituals acquired a new significance," and were ultimately fulfilled and illuminated by Jesus, who became the real embodiment of both the old and the new traditions (1974, 55).

Today's attempts by Simbu Catholics to incorporate elements from the pig-kill is premised on the belief that God was in Melanesia before the arrival of the first missionaries. If we say that God abandoned Melanesia and did not reveal himself to our people until the pioneer Christian missionaries arrived, then Christianity will be misunderstood and treated as an alien religion. Instead, we can say that the pioneer missionaries brought us a second salvation. Let me state that God's covenant choice and partnership with Israel should be understood not exclusively but inclusively, for it encompasses the entire human race. As summed up well by Franco Zocca, "God has chosen an obscure people . . . (Deut 7:7) only to show that his love embraced all people, even the lowliest, especially the lowliest. In the concrete case of the one people, all people were chosen" (1997, 15). The divine covenant covers all of humanity and is based on unconditional love and mutual relationship that transcends all realities of life.

Writing about the pig-kill rituals in Simbu, veteran missionary Alfons Schaefer notes, "When I witnessed them I said to myself that we cannot simply abolish them even though they are associated with aspects of the old pagan religion and with magic, since they effect much that is good" (Schaefer 1981, 214). While some may argue with this point, our Simbu Christian faith rests on the fact that, when God created the world, Melanesia was part and parcel of his immense creation. Therefore, to say that God had been absent from Melanesia until the missionaries arrived is unrealistic. What can be said, however, is that the full meaning of these rites was hidden until the first missionaries came. Those who embraced Christianity felt that it had better explanations and could purify the people's previous practices and beliefs. Burrows is making this point when he discusses hybridity in chapter 2.

Old Testament Background of the New Testament Eucharist

Since the grandparents of my generation became Christians, we have grown familiar with the celebration of the Eucharist as a memorial and re-presentation of the paschal mystery. We need to become more familiar with its historical background in the history of Israel, for this will deepen our understanding both of our own dema myth and of the depths of the Eucharist we now celebrate.

As Stuart Dauermann notes in his chapter in this volume, the celebration of the Passover is the prime antecedent of the Eucharist. When Jews celebrated it in the promised land, it was a memorial of their having passed over from slavery, death, and danger to a life of freedom and peace. The later ritual of Passover recalled the midnight meal the Israelites celebrated the night before they left Egypt under the leadership of Moses. The question can be asked, did Moses invent this Passover celebration? Probably not. Instead he reenacted and transformed with new meanings the celebration that his ancestor Abraham and his family celebrated when they were living a seminomadic life (Kwesi 1970, 47). If this is true, the question arises, what could have been the sort of events that motivated Abraham and his people to have this celebration?

A plausible explanation is that in the seminomadic culture of Abraham, people killed an unblemished male animal, roasted it, and ate it with bitter herbs. They poured blood on the tent post to ward off evil powers. This ancient nomadic pastoral feast, celebrated before moving to new pastures, was intended to ensure that the herds were safe while traveling in the wilderness and to seek divine protection and fertility. In other words, God would protect them and their animals and drive away any evil forces that might come to destroy them.

In commemorating the Passover and Exodus, the meaning of the older festival practices of the seminomadic people was transformed into a new experience reflecting their relationship with God. According to Old Testament scholar Lawrence Boadt, "The Israelites took over these traditional feasts and transformed them into a great celebration of the Exodus events so that further religious experience adds new meanings to existing rites" (1984, 266). This does not mean that all the original meanings were suppressed, but they were subordinated to the celebration of Israel's intimate relationship with God. God promised to be with them and to protect them. For us it illustrates the dynamics of appropriating the pig-kill into Christian worship, for "the basic ritual symbols have not changed, but their meanings have been newly defined" (Guzie 1974, 56). In the words of Scripture, "And when your children say to you 'What do you mean by this service?' You shall say, 'It is the sacrifice of Yahweh's Passover, for he passed over the houses of the people of Israel in Egypt, when he slew the Egyptians but spared our houses'" (Exod 12:26–27). Let us now examine further this ancient ritual, which Jesus transformed into the celebration of the Eucharist.

The Eucharist as a Passover Remembrance

The writers of the New Testament saw Jesus as a new Adam and a new Moses, the high priest who came not to save Israel alone but to deliver all humanity from the bondage of sin. The Gospel of John says, "Here is the Lamb of God who takes away the sin of the world" (1:29), showing that Jesus was regarded as the new paschal lamb slain for our salvation. This interpretation of Jesus as the paschal lamb of the new covenant radically transformed the ancient Passover feast, giving new meaning to the old tradition by the one who said he came not to condemn and destroy the old laws and the traditions but to fulfill them (Mt 5:17–20).

According to Robert Grant, in the Synoptic Gospels, the Last Supper was a Passover meal celebrated on the night before Jesus's death. During the Passover meal, Jesus identified himself, however, "not with the lamb, but with the bread and the first of the four cups, characteristic of the meal" (Grant 1963, 354). The bread became his body and this cup became his blood, which was the seal of the New Covenant, "a Covenant between God and the disciples" (Grant 1963, 355), who symbolically represent the whole of humanity.

Grant, however, shows that the Last Supper in John's Gospel should not be considered a paschal meal. According to him it was a "fellowship meal" (Grant 1963, 357) that took place before the actual Passover began, because the next day the priests were still waiting to celebrate the Passover (Jn 18:28). This may seem to run counter to the account of the Synoptics, but the important aspect for John, Grant says, was the sacrificial death of Jesus on the cross, which completely transformed and renewed human intimacy with God. According to John's Gospel, Jesus died as "the Lamb of God" (Grant 1963, 356). And after giving his body and blood, he called upon the disciples to reenact the Passover meal in memory of him (Lk 21:19; Mt 26:20–30; Mk 14:17–26). To this effect, I now turn to the Simbu pig-kill as a reenactment of God's intention for the redemption of my people.

THE PIG-KILL AS A FESTIVAL OF REMEMBRANCE

It takes seven to ten years for one community to prepare for and host a successful pig-killing festival. In preparation for this festival, the people make large gardens and raise many pigs. When the gardens are ready and the pigs have matured, the people send word around that they are ready to host the festival. When that happens, the men of the host community gather together in *yagl ingu* (a specially built men's house) to discuss and plan for the forthcoming celebration. After this, they go to the festival ground to erect *bugla tekand ingu* (long pig houses) on the periphery of the main festival ground. These houses are built to accommodate visitors and store both raw and cooked food for the festival.

In the central part of the ceremonial ground, a very special round house called *bugla-bogln* is erected. Louis Luzbetak called this "the House of the *Bolim* Spirit" (1954, 65). Even though the people build the Bolim Spirit's house, little is known about this "super-human being" who lives somewhere in the clouds. Even less is spoken about him, because "his name was greatly feared." According to Luzbetak, the Simbu people became very frightened when they heard Bolim's name pronounced (1954, 104).

A special post called Ende-Mondo (a sacred tree that people cut during the pig-kill festival) is erected in the center of the Bolim Spirit's round house. The name Mondo is given to this tree as a reminder of the mythical ancestor who dug the ground and placed his *arigl* on this tree.

When the houses are completed, the village elders call for the *kua ombuno* (bird call initiation), which is a rite of passage for young boys between the ages of seven and fourteen. During this initiation a select group of initiated men blow the *kua kumba* (spirit flutes) usually in pairs during the night. One represents the female partner and the other a male; Luzbetak reported, "In the evenings and late into the night the monotonous hooting of the Spirit-flutes filled the valley" (1954, 63). The men blowing the sacred flutes show them to the initiated boys for the very first time. This signifies their passage from boyhood to adulthood. At around the same time, the children of the host community put on their traditional dress and begin to dance. During this period of several weeks, the entire community is in the process of cutting firewood, collecting bush ferns, and gathering other necessary items in preparation for the feast. Thus, the blowing of the Spirit-flutes and the dancing of the children signal to neighboring peoples the imminence of the pig-kill festival.

At the conclusion of the period of blowing the Spirit-flutes and the dancing of the host children, every family of the host community kills a medium-sized pig near the place where the pigs' huts are located, or sometimes in their respective *gigl-pene* (an ancestral burial place), which Luzbetak described as the "place of the Spirits" (1954, 61). This is done primarily to appease the bush spirits as well as Simbu ancestors and to ensure that the piglets roaming in the forest will grow quickly to replace the pigs that are about to be slaughtered. The single slain pig is then shared and eaten among the family members, and especially the dancers, as a foreshadowing of a successful festival to come.

Immediately after the medium-sized pig is killed and eaten, the men of the host community prepare for the *sing-sing* (song and dance), dressed in traditional dancing regalia. The dancing always accompanies wonderful traditional songs that go hand in hand with the beating of the *kundu* (handheld wooden drum). The dancing has many significant meanings, especially as an opportunity for young people to come together to begin their courtship. The dancing continues for about three to four weeks as it takes time for people to come from distant places with gifts to participate in the event. When the sing-sing is nearing its end and before the actual pig killing begins, the entire society gathers together to perform a special ceremony called *buga kurak* (purification rite) (Luzbetak 1954, 106). Normally it occurs at the center of the ceremonial ground where the Bolim house was erected.

In 1998 I interviewed Joseph Kenna, an elderly Simbu, who explained the impact of the purification process. According to Joseph, the traditional ritual experts speak to their Yaglavano Ande (the Great-Grand-Spirit) so that he may give them blessing and prosperity. When the family kills its pig, it serves as a memorial of an event that occurred in the primordial past and that brought to the entire society new and abundant life, strength, growth, peace, and harmony. In effect it is a "ritual cleansing," since it involves sprinkling pig's blood and water on food, crops, and humans alike. New sweet potato vines are blessed so that they may produce an abundant harvest in the new gardens. Women and children are also included in the ritual to cleanse them from the contamination of menstrual blood, which for the Simbu (as in many PNG societies, especially in the Highlands) is considered impure and contaminated (Kyakas and Wiessner 1992). This purification rite is performed before the actual pig-kill begins so that the contamination cannot affect the rest of the event. Joseph explained the symbolism of sprinkling the blood of the slaughtered pigs:

> On the floor there are sweet potato leaves, sugar cane suckers, taro and banana suckers, which are ready to be planted. Besides these there are also digging sticks, axes, ropes for tying pigs, etc. Furthermore, there are also women with their babies standing to be initiated. Then a special traditional ritual expert takes some of the pig's blood and sprinkles it onto the various things that are laid on the floor, including the women and their infants. Then he rubs some of the blood on the Mondo post which is planted in the center of the Bolim Spirit's house, with the recitation of some incomprehensible words. (Personal interview with author)

With this ritual cleansing complete, the pig-kill proper begins, culminating in the grand celebration. Normally it takes two to three days to slaughter all the pigs because each man must butcher five or six pigs and cook them in a *mumu* (earth oven). It is a tedious job that requires many strong men.

When the slaughtered pigs are cooked, every adult man of each family takes the best parts of the pig, especially the heart, and climbs up to the roof of the Bolim house using a bush-thatched ladder. The erection of the

Mondo post in the center of the Bolim house symbolizes the presence of the dema and the Yaglavano Ande. Each man stands on the side of the roof and cuts the pig's heart into pieces and throws them to the awaiting crowd below; whoever catches a piece eats it. This display of plenty shows that the community bred enough pigs and would like to share the best parts with their friends and relatives as well as the watching spirits. A ritualistic chant is recited by one of the elders as a token of appreciation for the ancestral dema and to invite the spirits to partake in the meal: "Good spirits, we have all worked together in raising the pigs and now we bring this heart to share and eat together. Come and eat with us and continue to help us raise more pigs in the future."

Sometimes the uncooked belly fat is hung in the *gerua* house where men gather to make *gerua* boards (special panels are made from the Mondo tree and painted in colorful diamond-shaped patterns that symbolize female sex organs and represent fertility, life, and growth). Men customarily wore these boards during the days of the pig-kill festival in recognition of women's contribution in rearing the pigs for the festival (Luzbetak 1954, 66). After distributing the cut-up pig's heart, other cuts of meat are shared within family groups and with invited friends who partake in the festival.

There are many reasons for killing so many pigs. First, the ritualistic chanting at the ancestral sacred Bolim house signifies people's obligation to renew their relationship and connectedness with the whole cosmos, including the spirits. This ultimately culminates in the final sharing and eating of the pork together. Second, for many years, people have worked hard to breed pigs, and now they want to eat pork and relax. People lost weight by doing all the hard work of raising the pigs and preparing for the festival, so now they want to eat pork and grow strong and healthy again. Their hard work has paid off and now they have lots of pigs, so they can call their friends to share with them and enjoy the fruits of their labor together. When the friends depart, they take with them the blessed sweet potato runners; taro, banana, and sugarcane suckers; and beans that they use to make new gardens and breed new pigs for the next festival. And so the flow of life continues into the next generation.

CHRISTIAN INCULTURATION OF THE PIG-KILL FESTIVAL

The whole process of the pig-kill festival I have described might seem complex and focused on the activity of spiritual beings. However, as we have seen with Moses and the Exodus and Passover traditions, many customary elements assumed meanings within the new (and still developing) Yahwistic faith in Israel. Similarly, elements of the pig-kill have been changed and adapted, and new Christian meanings have been given to the old symbols since the missionaries arrived. For example, when missionaries saw the erection of the round Bolim house in the center of the sacred festival ground, they sought to abolish it. But it was difficult to persuade the Simbu people to abolish a symbol with such deep cultural significance. The Bolim house signifies the presence of the ancestral dema, who brought forth true and abundant life for them as well as the presence of the grand spirit Yaglavano Ande. The future achievement of the community rested on the success of this magnificent celebration. Observing all this, the missionaries realized that the whole celebration would collapse if they abolished this house in the center of the festival ground. The result would make the people enemies of Christianity, and they would regard the church as alien. Instead the missionaries allowed the cultural practice, but infused it with Christian meanings and values similar to Hiebert's critical contextualization process (1987).

The missionaries used their understanding of the festival to encourage the people not to plant the Mondo post but to make a cross from the Mondo tree and erect it in the center of the Bolim house (Knight 1979). From then on, when the pig-kill festival was about to begin, the Simbu would no longer call the traditional ritual expert to initiate the ceremony, but instead called a priest (or the ritual expert turned catechist) to inaugurate the festival using Christian rites. Moreover, instead of chanting the sophisticated ritualistic words of the traditional ritual expert, a priest was invited to say a prayer over the preparations. The priest now typically sprinkles holy water on those garden plants and tools to help foster growth and the flow of life. This holy water replaces the traditional rite of sprinkling pig's blood. At other times the people build a small altar inside the Bolim house, and a priest celebrates the Mass there before the large pig-kill. The women and infants no longer received the blessing from pig's blood; instead the sacrament of baptism was given to them, making them members of Christ's family.

THE EUCHARIST AS A RITUAL OF REMEMBRANCE

The term "Eucharist" derives from the Greek word *eucharistia* (thanksgiving). It is rooted in the celebration of a Second Temple–era Jewish thanksgiving meal that was not invented by Jesus but transformed by him and derived from the ancient Jewish feast of Passover or Pasch.

This ancient Jewish feast of Passover became significant after the exodus when the Israelites fled Egypt and traveled to freedom in the promised land. As stated in the book of Exodus, "This day shall be a memorial feast for you which all your generations shall celebrate with pilgrimage to the Lord, as a perpetual institution" (Exod 12:14). The memorial feast of the exodus took on a new meaning when Jesus had the thanksgiving meal with his disciples on the night he was betrayed (Lk 22:19–20). The words of Luke imply that Jesus became the new paschal lamb and that, whenever the disciples have the same celebration later, they commemorate the saving events of Jesus's passion, death, and resurrection. This call for remembrance means not only to remember Jesus but also involves Christians calling on the Holy Spirit to be present with them. In the Catholic faith, it entails belief that every time we receive his body and blood in the form of consecrated bread and wine, we proclaim Christ's actions until he returns with his Father's glory.

> The Eucharist is "the source and summit of the Christian life." The other sacraments, and indeed all ecclesiastical ministries and works of the apostolate, are bound up with the Eucharist and are oriented towards it. For in the blessed Eucharist is contained the whole spiritual good of the Church, namely Christ himself, our Pasch. (*The Catechism of the Catholic Church*, § 1324)

Today's Eucharistic celebration existed long before the birth of Christianity; these ancient rites were transformed when celebrated in remembrance of Jesus. As the Acts of the Apostles states, Christians "spent their time in learning from the apostles, taking part in the fellowship, and sharing in the fellowship meals and the prayer" (2:42). And in 1 Corinthians 12:26, St. Paul reassures the early Christians that "every time you eat this bread and drink from this cup you proclaim the Lord's death until he comes." Even today the Eucharist remains the central and most essential part of the church's celebration of Christ's passion, and it will continue until the eschatological kingdom of God comes, when Christ shares this meal with the whole of humanity again.

Significance of the Eucharistic Meal for Building Christian Community

Lawler maintains (as integral to Catholic teaching) the idea that even before the incarnation of the Word, people all over the world were led by God to seek him and to find mercy. Accordingly Christ reveals himself in each culture and teaches people to offer sacrifices and to remain open to God's future action, even if God is but dimly known. Nevertheless, in following their spiritual expressions they are implicitly acknowledging God's Lordship and bind themselves together as his people (Lawler, Wuerl, and Lawler 1976). This perspective may seem suspect to Christians who root themselves only in the *sola scriptura* (explicit words of Scripture), but it follows the line of reasoning one finds clearly stated in Vatican Council II's *Dogmatic Constitution on the Church*:

> Those who have not yet received the Gospel are related to the People of God in various ways. . . . Those who, through no fault of their own, do not know the Gospel of Christ or his Church, but who nevertheless seek God with a sincere heart, and, moved by grace, try in their actions to do his will as they may know it

> through the dictates of their conscience . . . Whatever good or truth is found amongst them is considered by the Church to be a preparation for the Gospel and given by him who enlightens all men that they may at length have life. (1965c, § 16)

Is the Church blind to the ways in which humans deceive themselves? No, for this section goes on to say,

> But very often, deceived by the Evil One . . . [people] have exchanged the truth of God for a lie and served the world rather than the Creator. . . . Hence to procure the glory of God and the salvation of all these, the Church, mindful of the Lord's command, "preach the Gospel to every creature" (Mark 16:16) takes zealous care to foster its missions. (Vatican Council II 1965c, § 16)

In the Old Testament, we notice how Abraham and his people sought God and offered sacrifices to him. In the Mosaic period we also notice how the feast of Passover derived its significance and became a memorial of the exodus for the people of Israel from Egypt. Ultimately, the Passover reached its fulfillment when Jesus celebrated his final meal with his disciples the night before his death. All that had been done by Abraham and Moses prefigured what Jesus fulfilled in the Pasch and resurrection, which Christians commemorate as they eat his sacramental body and drink his blood, in a way prefigured when the Israelites consumed the Passover lamb.

Today many Papua New Guineans, including the Simbu, receive the Eucharist without knowing and understanding its significance. Many doubt the personal presence of Christ in the consecrated bread and wine. The case I am developing, drawing upon the structural similarity of the pig-kill festival and the Eucharist, could shed light on the significance of the Eucharist for the Simbu. Both the Eucharist and the pig-kill celebrate the presence of someone offering up his life to give the people an abundant life. I say "both" because in the Eucharist we celebrate the personal presence and sacrificial death of Christ, while in the pig-kill festival, the sacred Bolim house symbolizes the presence of Yaglavano Ande, as well as the ancestral dema that sacrificed his life for the abundance of everything people need to live well. Therefore, in correlating the Eucharist and the pig-kill, we can identify important similarities that bring transformation of the people involved.

The main reasons behind the pig-kill celebrations for the Simbu are threefold:

- While celebrating a historical rite, they are able again to experience past events, which opens them to future hopes.
- Since it is a communal celebration, many friends and neighbors are invited to participate throughout the entire event.

- The joys and happiness they experience together encourage them to uphold the spirit of solidarity both at that time and for years to come. This, in turn, helps them make connections to the economic, social, political, and religious dimensions of their lives.

The important social elements involved in a prosperous life are the spirit of making contributions to the community by participation and sharing. In Simbu culture these elements are important factors in achieving a successful pig-kill festival. In this culture, action means participation, and participation means the action of contribution and sharing.

In the same way, the idea of acting, contributing, and sharing can be experienced in the Eucharistic liturgy. The Eucharist is an action Jesus asks us to enter into, the paschal action, saying, "Do this in memory of me" (Lk 21:19; Mt 26:20–30; Mk 14:17–26). Everyone is invited to become active participants, which means that all Christians should become active participants who are intimately immersed in the celebration through singing, reading Scripture, and taking part in the Holy Mass.

For the Simbu people a meal is a meaningful expression of keeping members of an entire community, in all its manifestations, intact: family, clan, line, and the cosmos. Food shared restores broken relationships and brings peace and harmony. The traditional pig-kill festival was the culmination of everyone's hard work and preparation over seven to ten years in order to achieve *gutpela sindaun* (life in its fullness). It gives them vivid connections to events in a mythic past and enables them to make sense of the present and to remain open to future hopes.

Due to modernization, the tradition of the pig-kill festival has been gradually dying out, but its lessons and meaning remain unchanged as it is adapted into modern meals (see Knight 1979). Mantovani (1984) once said that the leaves have changed but the roots remain unchanged. In contrast to the missionaries's initial response, they sought ways to keep the cultural significance of the Bolim house alive by encouraging people to build a small house around the Tabernacle in which the Eucharist is kept between celebrations of the Mass. This helps maintain the people's faith in the living presence of their ancestral Spirit, the Yaglavano Ande, which now is understood to be the God of the Bible. This missionary approach was complemented by the Second Vatican Council's *Pastoral Constitution on the Church in the Modern World*, which says, "God spoke according to the culture proper to each age. The Good News of Christ continually renews the life and culture of fallen men; it combats and removes the error and evil" (Vatican Council II 1965b, § 58).

CONCLUSION

The contemporary practice of families and communities gathering together to celebrate and have a common meal together signifies mutual solidarity, oneness, connectedness, and interdependence. All celebrations of cultural significance (such as birthdays, marriages, graduations, peace ceremonies, and burials, as well as the opening of new churches or other significant events) assume sharing food, which symbolizes the solidarity of communities, families, and lines. While the Simbu Pig-Kill Festival is no longer what it used to be, its key elements remain abiding principles that drive the society and frame relationships. Celebrating life events together renews the people's sense of obligation to be responsible and serve their families and communities well.

The Eucharist, in turn, while not a Simbu ritual in and of itself, provides many of the pig-kill elements Simbu people recognize as relevant to them. These elements, then, represent both fundamental Simbu and Christian values that must be upheld, encouraged, and proclaimed in all activities of the communities, churches, and more broadly throughout PNG as a nation. For Catholic Christians, the feast of Passover during Holy Week, Christmas, Easter, and other holidays can be used as venues for remembering mythic expressions of Simbu cultural significance, which now contribute to a meaningful remembrance of Christ's "Last Supper" with his disciples. That event, in turn, is steeped in the paschal memory of Israel's exodus from Egypt that Jesus deeply embedded into the disciples' psyche, initiating expressions of remembrance as long as they eat bread together and drink from the cup. When the Simbu celebrate the Eucharist, families should be encouraged to bring food to share after Mass. The sacramental encounter with Jesus at Communion time should not end in the church building. Rather, it must be a daily living encounter experienced by every Christian in their everyday life and work.

Actively connecting the Eucharist with the dema myth binds the collective Simbu memory of their past to Christ and the reality of his presence with us. Every time a family comes together and recites the Lord's Prayer and shares a meal together, it makes present the Eucharistic significance as well as their cultural identity. As Daimoi notes in chapter 13, time typically collapses in PNG; history becomes the present and anticipates the future. Together the family, as in days remembered, share food together and celebrate their memories until they receive the body and blood of Christ in the next Holy Eucharist.

5

Jamaican Maroons Seeking to Confront the Kromante Spirit

Manni, A 'Elp Wi Need

Emmanuel Obaro Obasare

A MAROON CRY FOR HELP

Sometime in 2004, four Jamaican Maroon *opunges* (mediums) came to me for help in dealing with their ancestral traditions.* These four men had been introducing me to their traditions, and I was greatly honored that they sought guidance from me, a non-Maroon from Nigeria. Kwadwo, their leader, was a science man (that is, a diviner); Gordon, a dancer; and the other two, *ɔkyerema masa* (drummers) of *mpintin* (an ancestral drum).

This chapter is about developing a hybrid model of Jamaican Maroon ancestral experience. The mediums desire to shift from the "shadow" power of the traditional Kromante spirit to the true power of the Holy Spirit on ancestral activities for the purpose of honoring Yenkipon, also called Onya–me (the Almighty God), in the Twi language of Ghana. Developing the model revolves around my attempts to respond to the mediums' call for help. Somehow, they recognized in me, a Nigerian, a similarity in things spiritual, cultural, and psychological that could connect with their deepest concerns (see "My Cry for Help" at the end of this chapter).

Kwadwo opened the discussion by reminding me that Maroons have a strong desire to satisfy and enjoy Yenkipon but have not been able to achieve this since 1655, when their ancestors arrived on the island of Jamaica. They had come to believe that I could help by guiding them and wanted to know if I would do so. Tears rolled down my face as I absorbed the reality of the respect and trust they displayed. I acutely felt the responsibility involved if I said yes. Embedded in the cry for help was almost four centuries of fear to come out from under the power and influence of the

* A glossary of Jamaican terms appears at the end of this chapter.

Kromante spirit. Despite the hold this spirit has on the Maroons, they are determined to shift from the Kromante spirit to the Holy Spirit dominating their activities.

I saw this call for help as a desire to satisfy and enjoy God in a context where traditional, pre-Christian ancestral ceremony was a way of life. On the positive side, these traditions have had a role in fulfilling the Maroon desire to know God. Negatively, the power and influence of Kromante (an African spirit originating from Kromante village in Ghana that dominates ancestral traditions in Jamaica and Suriname), whose manifestations are often destructive, cannot be ignored by Christians. Kwadwo, his head down and close to tears, spoke of mediums who feel helpless and frustrated with the dilemma of wanting to achieve their desire to experience God as relevant to their lives while participating in activities dominated by Kromante. After listening to Kwadwo and the other mediums who came to me, I thought it was essential for me to provide them help. The cry for help was, in effect, a prayer that said, "Manni [the name by which I am known among the Maroons], help lift us up from our fear to resist and flee from the Kromante spirit." It is a cry buried in pain and frustration that hitherto has been held in their hearts. This chapter reflects my journey with these Maroon spiritual specialists to arrive at a relationship with Yenkipon that dispels the power of Kromante. It is my attempt to accept their call and work with them as we learned together how to adapt their understanding of the rituals they know so well and restore them to God's intended purpose as Shaw calls for in chapter 1.

MAROON IDENTITY

Contemporary Jamaican Maroons are descendants of enslaved Africans who were forced out of their homes in Ghana and brought to Jamaica during the era of the Atlantic slave trade. Rebelling against enslavement, the ancestors left the plantations of their slave masters and fled into mountain and cave hideouts across the island of Jamaica to live as free and independent people. Nana (widely known as "Nanny of the Maroons") is considered the mother and principal ancestor of all Maroons in Jamaica. She was crowned as one of Jamaica's national heroes. Others who led the resistance to enslavement included Kojo, Accompong, Jonny, Mesante, Mesanpong, Sekesu, and Kwaku. Together these enslaved Africans sought to overcome slavery and the plantation system that dislocated the lives of people who were taken against their will from Africa to the Caribbean. Along with their tradition of refusing to be part of an immoral system, these Maroon ancestors left behind the legacy of ancestral traditions that tells today's Maroons who they are as a people. These stories and traditions preserve their history, culture, and religion. They are passed down from generation to generation. The Maroons "simply removed themselves from the influence of the Europeans, to re-create their own life style in other places. As such, they were at first considered to be 'Maroons,' a term which was connected to the Jewish system of Marronage, which was to practice their traditions (mainly religious ones) in secret" (Carey 1997, 1).

Richard Price speaks of Maroons as people who see themselves as Africans in the diaspora. Their ancestors "stood together as the heroic, living proof of the existence of a slave consciousness that refused to be limited by the master's conception or manipulation of it" (1996, xi).

The cry of the mediums has been a silent plea for help continuing for over 360 years, following the uprooting of the ancestors from Africa. Their cry for help is reflected in their eyes when they play drums, dance to ancestral songs, blow the *abeng* (cow's horn), speak in the Kromante language, pour out libations (by blowing rum in the air and pouring some on the ground to appease spirits), and use *nsa* (alcoholic drink) at any of the ancestral ceremonies. The principal ceremony is the annual celebration held in each of the four main Maroon communities. The psychological dimension of the cry for help is also present when community heads and mediums speak of the ancestral traditions.

I recall Kwabena, a drummer who had become a Christian and now played drums for the church. At one church service, Kwabena drummed in a Kromante style and an ancestral spirit manifested itself. The congregation ran out, afraid that the African spirit could accost them. The pastor quickly went for divination substances at her home to dispel the spirit. Despite Kwabena's participation in ancestral ceremonies, his real desire was to satisfy and enjoy Yenkipon but he knew he needed help to be free from the power and influence of the Kromante spirit.

To advance our understanding of what is involved, in this chapter I present some ancestral experiences illustrating the fear and helplessness of mediums and show how essential it is that I help guide them in their quest to shift from the Kromante spirit to the Holy Spirit dominating the ancestral activities for the purpose of worshiping Yenkipon.

MAROON FEAR OF RELINQUISHING KROMANTE SPIRIT POWER

The stories that follow present the intentional design of the Kromante spirit to dominate the Maroon ancestral tradition for its own benefit. The behavior of the spirit is painful to the Maroons and causes them to show an air of sadness despite being a people who, at one point in their history, were celebrated for their role in dismantling slavery in Jamaica and the wider Caribbean.

Fear to Resist Kromante-Inflicted Deaths

Some years ago a woman named Marcia was gravely ill, and her condition could not be medically diagnosed. Her community leaders decided to treat her condition using the ancestral tradition, and they organized a

Kromante healing session. The community believed that evil spirits had attacked Marcia. In this case, a number of mediums, including Afua, tried to heal her using the ancestral method but were unsuccessful. Afua was unhappy about the situation because she thought she had the experience to access ancestors at the level required for Marcia to be healed.

Kwaku, Marcia's father, recognizing the delicate nature of the situation, decided to take control by allowing more powerful ancestral spirits to "mount" him (a term reflecting the spirit jumping on the person's back and controlling their behavior). As the healing session continued, a more powerful ancestral spirit took possession of Kwaku and gave him instructions for the treatment of Marcia. Kwaku followed the instructions and Marcia was healed. Marcia still lives in her Maroon community, but sadly, Kwaku died after Marcia was healed. Normally, when an ancestral spirit has completed the purpose for taking possession of a medium, it exits the body after performance of certain rituals. Without this procedure the medium will die. In this case, the Kromante spirit gave instructions in spirit language, but Afua (the only person who understood it) refused to execute the instructions because she was jealous of Kwaku possessing more divinatory power. The other mediums present were helpless, and persons in the audience who could pray for Kwaku's deliverance were afraid to do so; Kwaku died. Much like a drug overdose, Kwaku's body could not contain all that power.

Fear to Exercise a Choice to Be a Medium

To become a medium usually requires an individual making a choice whether to accept the offer from ancestral spirits. There are, however, exceptions, as was the case for Labi. He became a medium at age eight when he innocently crossed a trap set for Ado, who had hurt a number of people in his community; one of the victims, Yeboa, was so angry that he decided to retaliate by sending an evil spirit to a particular location to accost Ado. He hoped that Ado would cross the location but he did not; instead, Labi came by. The evil spirit acted on Labi, who immediately, despite his young age, became a medium. When Ado realized what had happened, he was too afraid to make any attempt to deliver Labi of the spirit. Labi continued to be possessed by the spirit because he was afraid to resist it. Later, even when Labi heard the voice of Yenkipon calling him, he was afraid to resist the spirit that possessed him. Now, at over forty years of age, after getting help from me, Labi finally accepted Yenkipon's call.

Fear to Be without Jege

Whenever mediums leave their homes, they carry their *jege* (divinatory device; also known as a *pocket*) with them. This charm or amulet is given to mediums by the spirits attached to them. These powerful devices cannot be stolen or lost, because the spirit can see them and show its medium where they are. In some cases, if a jege is stolen, the Kromante spirit may instruct mediums to kill the thief; mediums are obliged to carry out the instructions or the spirit will kill them. Mediums will sometimes carry their jege for assurance of spirit protection. Such power is addicting, and mediums fear that if they shift from Kromante-dominated to Holy Spirit-dominated activities they may be unable to exercise their powerful role as diviners, dancers, singers, drummers, and *abeng* blowers. If possessed by God's Spirit, they fear the Kromante spirit will no longer attach to them and they will not be able to participate in traditional ancestral ceremonies. These activities become an essential aspect of their identity and life, and they are afraid to give up their jege and accept true power from Yenkipon.

Fear of Reprisals from the Kromante Spirit

Community leaders known as *colonels* (a term dating back to the period of war between the Maroons and Great Britain) fear reprisals on them and their family members if they refuse to participate in annual ancestral ceremonies. Ancestral spirits expect the colonels to permit and take a lead in the performance of the ancestral ceremonies. Daniel, a church leader and also a colonel, decided at the planning meeting of an ancestral ceremony that he was not going to lead the commencement. As a result, the ancestors struck Daniel's father, Okonjo, with a fatal illness. Okonjo was taken to the doctors for medical attention, but the cause of his illness could not be diagnosed. Okonjo's condition worsened. Members of the community were concerned and thought divination was necessary to identify the cause of illness and treat it. A Kromante healing session was organized, and ancestral spirits revealed that Okonjo's illness was caused by Daniel's refusal to carry out his role as colonel. They said if Daniel did not perform his role, his father would die. Daniel, wracked with the pain of frustration and manipulated by ancestral spirits and cultural expectations, decided he had to enact his role, notwithstanding his Christian convictions. He was afraid of reprisals from the ancestral spirit if he exercised his faith in Yenkipon.

I also recognized fear of reprisal in Kwesi, a blind medium. Kwesi treated me as his eldest son. He taught me the deep aspects of the ancestral tradition, including areas he would not teach his own family members. While reciting his life story, Kwesi would ask me, "Manni, a wen yuh a go bring de light fi mi?" (Manni, when will you bring the light to me?). I did not realize at the time that although Kwesi was teaching me, his ultimate goal was for me to help relieve him of his pain; he wanted to cease being a medium but feared reprisal from the Kromante spirit.

One day, I approached Kwesi and said, "Papa, time cum. Time cum fi satisfy an' enjoy Yenkipon" (Kwesi, the time has come for you to satisfy your desire to enjoy God). I asked Kwesi to give me his jege. He handed them over to me and said that was all. Anna, Kwesi's wife, who was there, said, "Manni, papa don' give yuh everything yet yuh kno' because him 'fraid, but me a get de res' o' tings fi yuh." Anna was telling me that her husband, whom everyone in the family called "Papa," had not given me everything. Kwesi had something hidden in the room and was afraid of reprisal from the ancestors if he handed it over to me. Mama went into the room and came back with what was left of the divination substances. I took it, prayed, and destroyed it. Later, Anna told me that she had long prayed for this and gave thanks to God.

Fear to Resist Kromante's Call

Wayne was a pastor who was a medium in his earlier years of ancestral experience. Prior to his death a few years ago, Wayne had an experience that has remained in the memories of community members. Wayne was in church one day, and Kromante drumming was being performed nearby. Notwithstanding the fact that Wayne had answered the call to be a pastor, an ancestral spirit mounted him, compelling him to dance right there in church. The senior pastor of the church prayed, and the ancestral spirit was dispelled.

Because Wayne had taken his jege to church with him, the Kromante spirit was able to connect with him and compel him to dance to the Kromante drumming. As long as a medium has the jege, the owning spirit has authority to do whatever it pleases with the medium.

Kwadwo, the lead member of the mediums who approached me for help, often reminds me that he is an evangelist at his church. When I visited Kwadwo at his local church, I watched him play the harp, sing, and dance. Then Kwadwo said to me, "Manni, a nuh Kromante alone mi hear an' speak yuh kno). Mi do it too with de Holy Ghost" (Manni, I can speak the Kromante language of spirituality but I can also speak in tongues). Kwadwo wanted to be released from the agony of this dual life but was afraid of giving up the Kromante spirit.

Fear to Reject Kromante's Deceptions

Mediums, who have knowledge of truth, are afraid to reveal two distinct areas of deception. The deceptions pertain to the Maroon understanding of Yenkipon as the source of all power and authority. Yet, according to their tradition, Yenkipon has delegated his power to air spirits like Kromante for access by human beings who, in turn, must use the "proper" divination methods. The deception relates to spiritual delegation of power emanating from Yenkipon through Kromante tradition and the mediums to control spiritual power and the use of libation, which in turn appeases Yenkipon—a deceitful cycle that forces obedience to Kromante rather than to Yenkipon, the source of all spiritual power both in heaven and on earth. I now present the principal misconceptions precipitated by the power of Kromante spirit.

YENKIPON ESTABLISHED THE KROMANTE TRADITION

For about 360 years, mediums have led the Maroons to believe that Yenkipon legitimized initial establishment of the Kromante tradition in Nana's Maroon community in Portland, Jamaica. This belief is centered around the historical origin of the Kromante tradition.

Oral tradition says the Kromante tradition in Jamaica is traceable to the period when the ancestors worked on plantations under extremely harsh conditions. At a certain point, the ancestors complained bitterly to the *bacra masa* (plantation owners, slave masters) through the slave drivers, the overseers, and asked for negotiation. The slave masters gave no room for dialogue. Conditions of enslavement worsened, dialogue was not forthcoming, and the ancestors resorted to singing ritual Kromante songs.

Robert Fisher (1988, 42) has written that ritual songs have coded messages about life and realities of the world. I illustrate with the lyrics of a song the ancestors sang:

time cum oh, nankaka deh,
time cum oh, nankaka deh,
time cum fi wi fi gu way nankaka deh,
time cum fi wi fi gu way nankaka deh. . . .

Loosely translated: "The time has come for the simple yet strong Maroons to leave the plantations."

Faced with no alternative, the ancestors were forced to leave the plantations and flee to the mountains and caves to live under rain and sunshine. The slave masters realized that the Maroons had escaped and searched for them. This started the "slave wars." But the Maroon ancestors had no physical weapons and were on the losing end. At a critical point, when the ancestors were losing the battle, they heard a voice, and Nana tested it to determine whose it was. She used her jege and confirmed it to be Yenkipon, encouraging his people. The oral tradition speaks of Yenkipon promising to fight for the ancestors. The Maroons began to fight with renewed vigor, and their primary focus was to assault the British (Brathwaite 1977, 9). After more than eight decades (1655–1739) of intense war, Britain was compelled to sign treaties with the Maroons, recognizing them as free and independent people living on the island of Jamaica.

The Kromante tradition has thus been taught as a historical reality legitimized by Yenkipon because there was victory in the voice discerned to be Yenkipon's, using Nana's jege. The ancestral experience shows that a number of mediums who once thought Yenkipon established the ancestral tradition now realize it was the Kromante spirit all along and that this spirit has been deceiving mediums during all of this time. It was the Kromante spirit they heard, impersonating Yenkipon.

Mediums such as Kwabena, Kwadwo, Wayne, and Kwesi know that Yenkipon forbids the use of divination to determine his voice. Kwabena, Kwadwo, Kwesi, and some other mediums who have come to know the truth would prefer the Holy Spirit dominating their ancestral activities rather than Kromante. They are, however, afraid to make the shift.

Mediums believe that permission must first be obtained from Yenkipon and Asase for a successful Kromante activity. They further believe that the way to obtain this permission is to appease Yenkipon using libations. Kwadwo and a number of mediums know that Yenkipon is not to be appeased through the use of rum, as though he is a mere ancestor spirit.

Mediums are aware that the Kromante spirit is the one that manifests during any ancestral activity, not the Holy Spirit. Despite this knowledge, they have continued to pour libation using rum because they are afraid to discontinue the practice. The mediums know the real and psychological power of Kromante manifestations do not reflect the true attributes of Yenkipon. I now turn to developing a model that goes beyond the deception of the Kromante spirit and reflects the true power of Yenkipon.

DEVELOPING A HYBRID MODEL OF ANCESTRAL POWER

I have been working with these mediums for over ten years to develop a sustainable hybrid model. The model needs to be robust as there are issues of life, patience, African identity, and ancestor remembrance that must all be taken into account. After all, this is the first time in the history of the Maroon ancestral tradition that mediums exhibited the courage to ask for help despite the realities of reprisals from the Kromante spirit. My duty is to follow up with them to ensure the success of their inquiry.

Developing this model is reminiscent of Hiebert's critical contextualization model (1987), mentioned by Shaw and several other authors in this book. In developing this hybrid model with Maroon mediums, we have been aware of the need for biblical understanding applied to the practices and their impact upon how the mediums express spiritual power and how the Maroons respond to it. The result, which I present here, is a work in progress, as my description makes clear. But what is very important is that people in the churches are a dynamic part of encouraging the adjustments and making the shift from a Kromante spirit focus to a Holy Spirit of God focus. The mediums and I are doing the hard thinking, the people are praying, and together with the impact of the Holy Spirit, God's presence is being manifest among the Maroons.

The model has five key elements, as shown in Figure 5-1. In my description of the model, I explain how some of the specifics of the ritual and ceremony—such as drumming, dancing, singing, the use of prayer, and anointed olive oil (instead of rum)—can fuse into the five elements.

FIGURE 5-1: Key Elements for Mediums Shifting from Kromante-Dominated to Holy Spirit-Dominated Activity

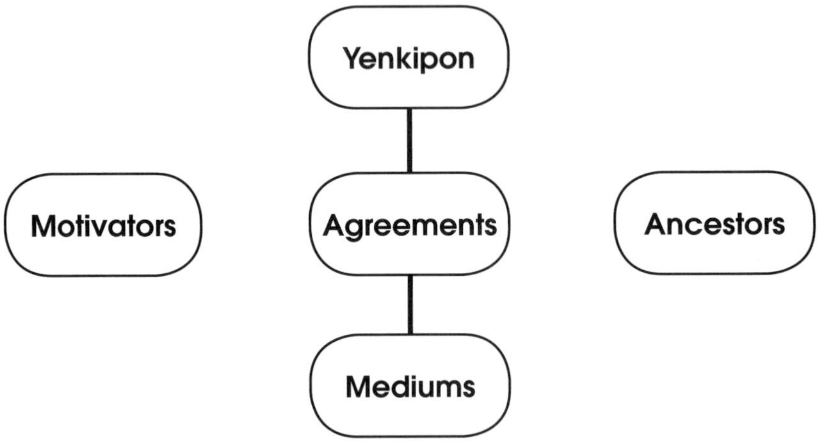

Mediums, Yenkipon, and Agreements

These three elements, put together, are the engine of the model. The mediums do not want to lose this combination of elements and the connection between them. These representatives of spiritual power treasure the gift of *sabi* (knowledge), which includes the presence of wisdom and discernment.

Yenkipon, Onya–me, and Sovereignty

In the new model, sabi comes about by anointing from the Holy Spirit, the carrier of all wisdom, knowledge, and understanding that resides in Onya–me (the Twi identity for God), which can be translated "find me and be satisfied." Onya–me (of whom the Maroon ancestral tradition speaks) has always said that if they seek and find him, he will give them satisfaction. They can seek him for an anointed understanding, and he will freely give spiritual gifts.

In a different context, mediums celebrate Yenkipon lavishly and receive healing of pains they have shouldered for almost four centuries. In celebrating Yenkipon with African songs from the Redemption Song Book, drumming, dancing, and speaking in tongues, the Holy Spirit will manifest and join in the ceremonies to produce a harmony of unspeakable, pure enjoyment for which the mediums have always yearned. As the model emerges, mediums emphasize the importance of singing African songs they believe to be especially powerful and spirit filled.

Mediums

The mediums already know how to receive power from the spirit world. However, rather than seek corrupted power from the Kromante spirit, many mediums desire to cleanse themselves and receive power from the Holy Spirit. They will no longer use rum but the word of Yenkipon (the Bible) and prayer as their source of power. In fact, for those mediums who are serious about this shift, Yenkipon himself may cleanse them and appear in a dream as he did for his vessel of honor, the prophet Ezekiel.

Rum, abeng, and drums are key in ancestral ceremonies. Rum is used for libation, the abeng mediums invoke the Kromante spirit, and drums create the atmosphere. Following the tradition, the mediums can replace the use of rum with olive oil and prayer. This will place the attention fully on the Holy Spirit rather than the Kromante spirit. The abeng can be anointed with olive oil and used as a trumpet in church, and drums (with a different rhythm) can enhance worship. What a joy for the mediums to reempower cultural symbols everyone knows and anoint them with new power from above.

Transformation of the ancestral experience to a Holy Spirit experience will spill over to the church, where a new form of passion for Yenkipon will manifest as never before. Mediums will be happy to know they are contributing in a significant way to the mutual satisfaction and enjoyment of Yenkipon. Churches in the Maroon communities will be revived, new churches will emerge, and the way church is done will change as this hybrid model takes its full effect. The people in Maroon churches will learn new ways of doing church, while mediums continue their open-air worship. As churches follow the mediums' example, they will find an open door for ministry, both individually (as those who have found Onya–me) and collectively (as a community of believers in Yenkipon).

Agreements

Mediums know what it is to adhere to agreements with the Kromante spirit. Agreements that were hitherto held with the Kromante spirit will shift to the Holy Spirit, and relationship with Yenkipon will be restored. Church members will also learn this and prepare to be anointed to become better vessels of honor for Yenkipon. Kwadwo reminded me of the tremendous power in the Psalms, especially Psalms 121 and 122. All Maroons look to the hills, the interior of Jamaica, and recognize their help has come from Lord Yenkipon. He is their protector and keeps them from stumbling, as they personalize the words of Psalm 121:

> We look to the hills. Where does our help come from?
> It comes from the Lord, the creator of the heavens and the earth.
> Lord Yenkipon is our protector!

> He does not sleep. He protected Israel and he will protect us.
> The Lord watches over us. He stands at our
> right side to give shade from the sun.
> We will not be harmed by the sun during the
> day or by the moon at night.
> The Lord will keep us safe from all dangers. Yenkipon
> will keep us safe wherever we go.

Mediums like Kwadwo will read the Psalms and the whole Bible in their new experience as part of a commitment to the agreements with Yenkipon. As they do, Yenkipon will enable them to prosper for sticking to the terms of the agreement they have with him—a covenant much like between Yahweh and the people of Israel. A people who at one time were timid to hear the voice of Yenkipon or were inhibited by fear of reprisal will be empowered by the Holy Spirit. They will be able to think through issues with him directly rather than through the Kromante spirit professing to have powers he does not truly possess.

Ancestors

The ancestor element has an ancestor-faith-remembrance theme. The purpose of this element is to help mediums continue to hold annual thanksgiving ceremonies in appreciation of their ancestors who fought for the freedom and independence of Jamaican Maroons during the slavery period. The freedom-fighting spirit of the ancestors resulted in the signing of the 1739 treaties that now allow Maroons and their descendants to live on land occupied by them without any form of control by the Jamaican government.

Werner Zips noted the view of one Maroon: what the ancestors did in destroying the bondage of slavery meant more to him than life itself (1999, vi). One colonel said to me that there is a significant reservoir of life in the glory of the ancestors that we simply cannot allow to die. Malidoma Patrice Somé has also expressed that in most non-Western societies, ancestral traditions are inseparable from life (1994, 9).

Ancestral ceremonies can be held in the open, reflective of how the ancestors held their meetings. There could be displays of cultural items and songs but nothing to do with the Kromante spirit. A Maroon national thanksgiving Sunday can be declared a thanksgiving day for all churches in Maroon communities to set aside time to thank Yenkipon for using the ancestors to fight for freedom.

Motivators

This emerging hybrid model suggests that the continuing role of motivators, or helpers, is essential and not to be ignored. The Kromante spirit will not sit by and watch mediums shift allegiance to the Holy Spirit for the purpose of giving honor to Yenkipon and worshiping him. The African spirit will fight. The experiences of Wayne, Kwesi, Daniel, and Kwabena support the inclusion of this element. Let me narrate an extended experience with Labi and the story of Frimpong, another medium.

Labi was under the significant and powerful influence of the Kromante spirit for over thirty years. So powerful was the influence and connection with the spirit that sometimes, sitting over a hundred yards away from locations where an *mpintin* (ritualized drum) was being played, Labi would be pulled to the location to dance, fully possessed by the spirit. I subsequently invited Labi to an African church away from his community. He did not hesitate to attend and did so more frequently as the years passed.

Occasionally, Labi would telephone me to say his head was feeling funny or his bed was shaking. Since I wanted to learn more as a helper, and he also needed to learn new behavior that would help him overcome his challenge, I asked many questions. I wanted to know what he meant by saying his head was hurting him and the bed was shaking and what his suggestion was to stop both. His response was, "Manni, yuh nuh kno'? A de big people dem. Yu cou'd a pray fi mi an' sing de African song weh she, 'Jehovah is your name,' right now and gi' mi a Bible later?" Labi was telling me he was troubled by the Kromante spirit and needed help. He defined the help he needed to be singing African songs, giving him a Bible, and praying with him. I would pray and sing the song every time he made the request. I also eventually gave him a Bible with my name on it.

I encouraged him to read small portions of the Bible and to use the Psalms and the name of Jesus Christ when under attack by the spirit. Whenever we both practiced what we agreed, the Kromante spirit found it difficult to possess him.

I was encouraged by Labi's progress. However, despite his best intentions, on one occasion, Labi was at a traditional ceremony possessed by the Kromante spirit. The spirit used Labi to lift up a heavy man and drop him down in the presence of onlookers at the function. In my devastation, I asked Labi to explain what had happened and why he was at the function. All he could say was, "Manni, dem tell you? Mi nuh kno wha' 'appen. A wha' you a go lef' mi *now*?" Still shaken but recognizing my lifetime commitment to be used by Yenkipon to bring Labi to a point of fulfilling his real desire to satisfy and enjoy God, I assured him that I was not going to leave and that no matter how difficult, one day he would experience the fulfillment of his desire. I was conscious of the power of ritual and ceremony Shaw presents in chapter 1. Developing hybrid expressions takes time and patience and a continued focus on the ultimate desire of God to reconcile unbelievers to himself.

Labi continued to practice his new learned behavior and attended the African church while I continued my role as a local motivator. The members of his church prayed for him as well. Gradually Labi was able to shift allegiance from Kromante to the Holy Spirit. Labi now lives abroad but keeps in close touch with his community. Occasionally he will call me and say, "Manni, yuh is mi fren' fi life, yuh cou'd a sing de song fi mi again?" I will sing the song, and he'll be there crying as he reflects on Yenkipon's goodness.

An important point that the emerging model highlighted regarding motivators is the need to engage the youth of the community quite early and use African Christian worship styles in the Maroon communities. Help from African Christian leaders will be considered authentic, and the mediums will more readily identify with such helpers. These motivators are better placed to offer much-needed help to the Maroons who are crying out for assistance.

Four years ago Frimpong invited me to his community on a Sunday. I went and was told by community members that he was at the church. I found him at the *ae poco* (revivalist) church Jamaican Christians normally have nothing to do with. On entering the church, I observed some elements not usually part of church worship: burning candles, a basin filled with water, drawings on the walls depicting African spirits, and the use of incense. The Mother, serving as pastor, asked me to greet the congregation. I did but then also decided to teach an African song. When I finished, I sang a Jamaica chorus they were familiar with but did it in the way African worship leaders would. I was later asked to bring the sermon. I did but not before explaining my appreciation of the visible African setting around the church. I also explained that some of the African retentions no longer existed in African churches in Nigeria where I was born, and encouraged them to use these African religious symbols to bring honor to Yenkipon.

As I interacted with the church members that day, I was conscious of the long-term dimension of what mediums expect of motivators and the fact that these helpers must respect mediums and be truthful. At the end of the sermon, with tears in his eyes, Frimpong told me I was the brother he never had. He reached into his pocket and gave me a jege and asked that I go do whatever I was led by the Holy Spirit to do with it. I received the jege, cried out to Yenkipon, and destroyed it in his presence. Frimpong could not resist carrying the jege with him to church, even though he knew he should not be dealing with it. However, he was afraid the Kromante spirit would kill him if he didn't. Well, Frimpong is still alive even though his jege was destroyed. The Kromante spirit could not kill me either. Frimpong needed to be empowered by a Spirit-filled motivator.

As I bring this section to a close, I must emphasize that motivators use the Word of God as they engage the mediums. The mediums recognize the power of God's word and make reference to it as appropriate. Preaching and teaching the Word of God are of vital importance to reducing the power of Kromante spirit and energizing the Maroon church with the power of the Holy Spirit.

CONCLUSION

My objective in this chapter has been to describe Jamaican Maroon understanding of ancestral experience in their quest to satisfy and enjoy God. I presented the description from the Maroon perspective they consider more relevant, but pegged it to the discussion framework established in chapters 1 and 2 by Shaw and Burrows.

Essentially, the Maroon ancestral experience shows that persons who are under the power and influence of ancestors have a strong desire to satisfy and enjoy God and that the ancestral experiences have a significant role in the fulfillment of that desire. I presented background information on contemporary Jamaican Maroons in order to appreciate the cry of the mediums for help. I demonstrated that embedded in that cry is the fear of helplessness to shift from Kromante spirit-dominated to Holy Spirit-dominated activities. I also explained how essential it is for me to help the mediums achieve their desire to implement this shift.

After characterizing the rationale of fear behind the cry of the mediums, I presented a hybrid model that has emerged as I have learned from them. My prayer is that this model will enable the mediums to achieve their hoped-for shift from a Kromante-dominated experience from below to Holy Spirit–empowered activity from above, for the purpose of honoring and worshiping Yenkipon. In the model, I presented five key elements—the role of the ancestors, mediums, Yenkipon, agreements between mediums and Yenkipon, and the role of motivators like me.

I hope readers appreciate the Maroon ancestral experience as an expression of critical contextualization (Hiebert 1987). As the Maroon mediums express increasing spiritual maturity within their believing communities, they will honor God, worship him, and encourage church growth. My message here is that motivators who apply anthropological and historical methods in understanding the power and presence of ancestors, as well as those under their influence, will have a strong potential to communicate the gospel message. They will understand the deep psychological dimensions of the ceremonies and be better equipped for mission work. Motivators and Maroons who respond to the gospel will benefit and develop a new appreciation of the power of the Holy Spirit who fulfills the longing of human hearts to experience the fullness of relationship with Yenkipon. This, in turn, will enable fulfilling worship experiences that will be most pleasing to God.

MY CRY FOR HELP

I began this chapter with the story of mediums who came to me for help, and I explained how this informed the chapter. I, too, have a story.

A few years ago, I was flying from Los Angeles to Kingston, Jamaica. I began to watch a movie when we were airborne, and five minutes later I began to cry. I was crying because the movie caused me to reflect on my own pains in relation to my grandmother (a medium in Nigeria), two daughters of the Ga spirit of a shrine I often visit in the Asante region of Ghana to do research on ancestors, and the pains embedded in the cries of the Maroon mediums with whom I am working. The cries of Frimpong, Kwadwo, Wayne, Kwesi, Labi, members of Kwaku's family, and the Maroon communities at large were taking a toll on me. We had truly become family.

My grandmother (who died in 2015) was a medium for more years than I can remember. It is painful to know she was used by African spirits to cause the deaths of some of her children and grandchildren. She also tried to attack me but failed because Oghene (the Urhobo name for God) would not permit her. I held an unforgiving spirit against her. The pain of being in that state affected me for over thirty years until I cried to the Holy Spirit for help and asked God to release my pain. God did, and I was freed of my pain of having lost the will to forgive my grandmother.

The cries of the Maroon mediums are also mine. Our collective cries are of people experiencing common pains resulting from African spirits dominating ancestral activities. These spirits do not reside in Africa alone; they hold sway wherever Africans were taken during the curse that was the African slave trade. The good news is that the ancestral expressions we encounter have a missional effect that can help shift the focus from African spirit-dominated to Holy Spirit-dominated activity in honor of Yenkipon, so that the whole earth might worship and enjoy God forever.

GLOSSARY OF JAMAICAN MAROON TERMS

The following Jamaican Maroon terms have varied meanings and must to be understood in the context in which I have used them.

abeng. An instrument made from a cow's horn.
colonel. A community head among the Jamaican Maroons. Sometimes also called *teacha*.
jege. A divinatory device used for more critical situations; often called *pakit* (pronounced pocket).
mpintin. A special drum used in the ancestral tradition. *Mpintinkam* is the Akan Twi word for a drummer of the ancestral tradition.
nsa. Any alcoholic drink.
nsuo. Water.
Okyerema masa. A drummer of the ancestral tradition. The Akan Twi people call this person mpintinkam.
Onya–me. Lit., "find him/her and get satisfied." In this context, God is seen as Agya, Father, and Ɔbaatampa, good Mother. The Akan of Ghana use this term in relation to the Almighty God, whom they also call Ɔnyankopon.
opunge. A spirit medium, sometimes also called a horse.
science man. A diviner.
Yenkipon. The Almighty God; also called Ɔnyakopon or Ɔnya–mƐ.

With Focus on Context

6

The Korean Ancestral Rite

Cultural Significance and Implications for Christian Faith

Paul Mantae Kim

In this chapter I explore the Korean ancestral rite for the purpose of suggesting a relevant evangelical, Korean engagement with that rite. The Christian controversy over this traditional rite has continued for more than two hundred years in Korea. This rite persists today and still holds an important place among the Korean people. I begin with an introduction of the issue followed by the nature and motifs of the ancestral rite. In the rest of the chapter I address a relevant Christian engagement with the rite. My intent is to encourage discussion over the issue rather than give a definitive solution.

Before proceeding further, let me give a brief historical overview of the issue in Korean Christian history. Christianity first encountered the Korean ancestral rite when Catholics came to Korea in the late eighteenth century. At the outset, the Catholic mission rejected the ancestral rite and then had to face strong opposition from the Korean people (Y. S. Kim 2005, 317). For this reason, many Catholic missionaries and their Korean converts were martyred. At that time, the Catholic mission considered the ancestral rite to be idolatry. Protestant missions began in Korea in 1884. They also disapproved of the ancestral practice (Ok 2005, 219–27). Radically changing its initial position, the Roman authorities revisited the so-called Chinese rites controversy and allowed Catholics to observe many traditional Confucian ancestor rites. The Korean Catholic Church followed suit. Today, many

Korean Catholics conduct either the traditional ancestral rite or an alternative practice that incorporates traditional elements and Catholic faith. The majority of Korean Protestant churches continue to disapprove of the ancestral rite while providing a Christian form of memorial service.

SIGNIFICANCE OF THE STUDY

Why do we need to conduct a serious study of the Korean ancestral death rite? How does this study relate to evangelical Christian life in Korea? I see at least three reasons why this discussion is both necessary and important:

- Korean Christians frequently clash with their unbelieving family members about the observance of the ancestral rite.
- Korean Protestants recognize a need to go beyond current Christian memorial services and generate a better alternative.
- A resolution of the issue is essential to improve the public image of Protestantism in Korean society.

I expand on each of these points in this chapter.

My family was sincerely observing the ancestral rites when I became a Christian at age twenty-two. At that time, I had a combative attitude toward my parents and determined that I would not betray God by attending the rite. My parents were unhappy about my absence, but they were tolerant of me. Later when my parents became Christian, my father decided to replace the traditional ancestral rite with a Christian memorial service. When they did so, regrettably my uncle and his family never showed up for our new Christian ancestral practice. They were gradually disconnecting from my family since we adopted Christian practices for ancestral veneration. In the example from my own family, we note that many Koreans are reluctant to become Christian because they do not want to abandon the traditional ancestral rites.

Marriages between Christians and non-Christians produce a serious conflict over observance of ancestral rites. According to a news report, a Christian Korean woman who refused to attend the ancestral rite was divorced by her husband (Kang 2001). When someone becomes a Protestant Christian, the key question focuses on how that person should deal with the ancestral rite. Korean Christians need to discover a proper resolution for the problems relating to the traditional ancestral rite in their relationship with unbelieving family members. In relation to this issue, Charles Lowe did an in-depth study of how churches should respond to Chinese popular ancestral practices. He recommends that churches should not ignore people's social and cultural traditions and that Christian converts should be able to celebrate family occasions and traditional festivals without either offending their relatives or compromising their Christian faith (Lowe 2001, 271).

Korean Protestants increasingly recognize a need to reexamine traditional ancestral rites and to go beyond current Christian memorial services to generate a better alternative. In this chapter I endeavor to carry that discussion forward. Statistical data show that many Protestant Christians feel their current memorial services are spiritually insufficient. In this regard, 24.8 percent of Protestant respondents agreed, 27.9 percent disagreed, and 47.3 percent were undecided when asked if they think their Christian memorial services are spiritually satisfying (Hansin University Theological Institute 2005, 229). Furthermore, 36.7 percent agreed, 33.2 percent disagreed, and 30.1 percent were undecided when asked if Korean Christianity needs to positively incorporate traditional funeral or ancestor rituals without damaging the essence of Christian faith (Hansin University Theological Institute 2005, 228).

Bongho Son, a Protestant Christian ethicist, has stated that Protestant churches urgently need a new memorial service that does not ignore the traditional rite but still retains biblical teachings (Y. Kim 2011). Korean sociologist Sungyoon Cho has shown that Protestant forms of memorial services clash with traditional forms of the ancestral rite. He claims a need to harmonize these two forms and points out that Protestant churches are reluctant to address this issue for fear that they will be condemned as heretical (Y. Kim 2011). Inwoong Son, a Korean pastor with a solid reputation, argues that we should not reject the ancestral rite simply as idolatry, but give attention to *hyo* (the essence of filial piety). He suggests that Protestant churches have sincere conversations over the issue and search out an appropriate method that avoids a clash with Korean traditional culture while at the same time evangelizing the society (Ko 2013).

Furthermore, I hope this chapter leads to an improved public image of Protestantism in Korean society. According to national survey results, Korean Protestantism experienced a modest decrease in 2005 after the previous few decades of explosive numeric growth. Concretely, the number of Korean Protestants decreased by 1.4 percent from 1995 to 2005, according to the results of the Korean national survey; in contrast, Catholics were reported to have increased by 74.4 percent during the same period (Cho 2012). The Protestant decrease may be attributed, in some measure, to the decline of its public reputation in Korean society; one of the major reasons is that many Koreans think Protestantism has an exclusivist stance regarding Korean traditional culture, according to the Korean Ministerial Sociology Institute (2006). Subsequently, society at large regards Protestantism as culturally extraneous and prefers Catholicism, which is more accepting of traditional culture.

Statistical research on Koreans' perception of culture shows that the ancestral rite still occupies an important place in Koreans' lives. When asked if they agreed with the practice of the traditional ancestral rite, 66.5 percent of the respondents replied positively, 22.1 percent disapproved, and 11.4 percent were undecided. On the other hand, 50.9 percent of Protestant Christians disapproved of the ancestral rite and 32.7 percent approved of it. By contrast, the majority of other groups approved of the rite: Catholics at 71.4 percent, Buddhists 83.3 percent, persons without religion 73.4 percent, and others 66.7 percent. Clearly the majority of Koreans attach importance to the traditional ancestral rite (Hansin University Theological Institute 2005, 229).

Other data indicate that respondents without religion regarded the disapproval of the ancestral rite as the second greatest mistake of Korean Catholics in the past (Kim, Park, and Park 2004, 54). Ancestral rites are a most eminent Korean traditional cultural practice. Their observance predicts if a person acknowledges Korean cultural tradition. Korean Protestantism cannot disregard the issue of the ancestral rite. If Christians want to be accepted by non-Christian Koreans, who comprise about 80 percent of the population, they must deal with this important cultural expression.

DESCRIPTION AND MOTIFS OF THE KOREAN ANCESTRAL RITE

Ancestral rites typically account for up to four generations of ancestors. Today, it is not rare to commemorate only two or three generations of ancestors (Kim 2001, 94). There are some other changes in the ancestral practice we can see today:

- Not a few families perform the rite in the evening instead of midnight for their convenience (Kim 2007, 279).
- Some families offer food that ancestors preferred during their lifetime (Yoon 2005, 331).
- Ancestral couples can be jointly venerated (Kim 2007, 284).
- More and more women are allowed to participate in the ritual (see http://www.korea4expats.com/article-ancestral-memorial-rites-g.html).

Two kinds of ancestral rites are performed at home: One is *charye* (holiday rites), and the other is *kijesa* (death-day rites) (Janelli and Im 1982, 86). Two holiday rites are performed annually on Goojung (lunar New Year's day) and Choosok (Korean Thanksgiving day). Holiday rites are offered to multiple ancestors up to four generations collectively (Kim 2001, 94), whereas death-day rites are offered for an individual ancestor near midnight of the day before the person died (Janelli and Im 1982, 93). Thus, a typical family conducts ten ancestral rites a year (two holiday rites and eight death-day rites) if they memorialize four generations of ancestors. In this chapter I explore only the death-day rites, which are currently performed more frequently than holiday rites among Korean people. Hereafter, when I speak of the "ancestral rite," I am referring to the death-day ritual memorializing the death of a particular person.

The ancestral rite is usually performed at home, although it may be held at a shrine. The most prominent object at this ritual is the table that holds various objects. All the objects must be put in places designated by ritual codes. Various kinds of food are offered, as shown in Figure 6-1. In the traditional Korean belief system, the spirit of the honored ancestor is believed to come and eat this food. An ancestral tablet is usually attached to a folding screen just behind the ritual table. This tablet is believed to be the place where the ancestor stays during the rite. *Shinju wipae* (wooden tablets) were originally used, although paper tablets are more common today. The tablet contains the ancestor's name, title, and place of origin written in black ink. Candles and incense are lit, being assumed to invite and welcome the ancestor's spirit.

Figure 6-1: A Typical Ancestral Rite Table with Objects

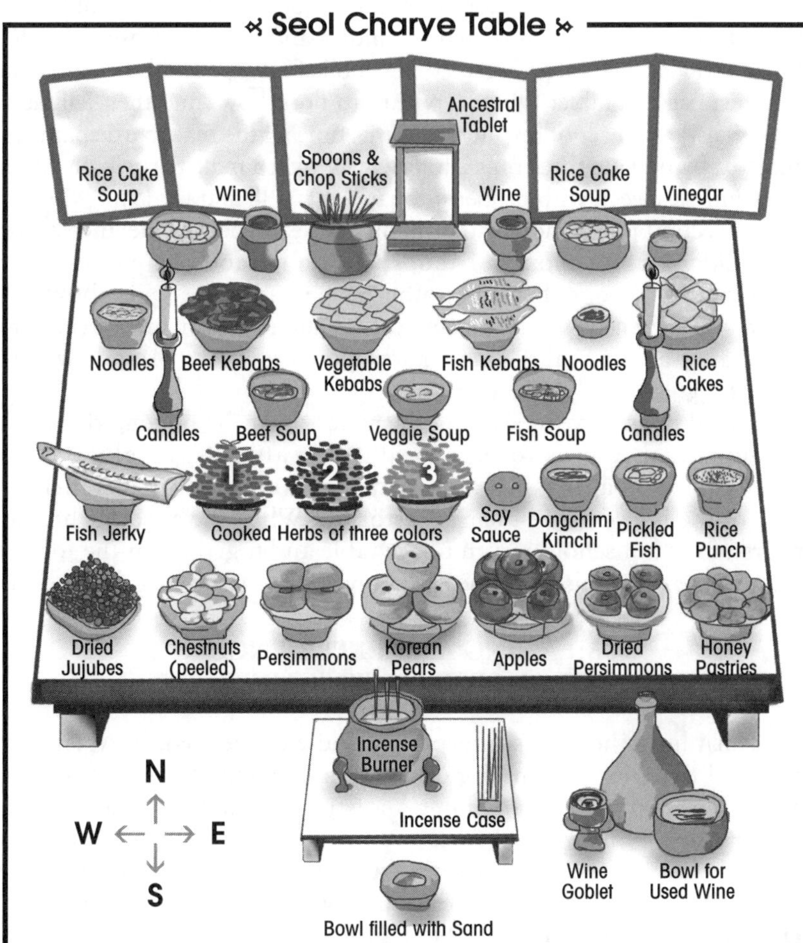

(Adapted from http://k.daum.net/view.html)

The eldest son of the household presides over the ancestral rite, and only males participate in the ritual procedures as such, although women prepare food for the ritual table. Male participants follow the direction of the ritual presider, and the ritual itself is usually performed in an *anbang* (master bedroom). The Korean ancestral rite comprises four major phases: inviting and welcoming the ancestor who is being honored, serving food to the ancestor, seeing the ancestor off, and participating with fellow descendants by eating the food that has been provided.

The rite begins with the eldest son inviting and welcoming the ancestor. As presider he goes to the gate of the house and opens it so that the honored ancestor may enter. He welcomes the personage by bowing his head to the ancestor who is believed to return (as a spiritual being) to visit its descendants on the death anniversary (Bae 2002, 292). Members of the household arrange the ritual table, and the presider lights candles and burns incense (Kim 2001, 101). The presider then offers a glass of alcoholic beverage and bows three times toward the ancestral tablet (two deep head-to-floor bows and then a light bow from the waist) as an act of invitation. At this time all the male participants greet the ancestor by bowing three times, following which a male participant chants a written Chinese speech with proper intonation (Janelli and Im 1982, 87).

In the second phase, household members serve food to the ancestor. The ritual presider lays a spoon and chopsticks on the food he wishes to offer them, moving from one dish to another as he and other males bow to the ancestor. They then leave the room so that the ancestor may freely enjoy the meal; after an interval the male participants return to provide water for their special guest.

The third phase involves seeing the ancestor off by bowing three times, as the individual returns to the world of the afterlife. Finally the ritual presider burns the paper tablet and written address. Participants then go to the gate of the house to see their ancestor off. When the ancestor has gone, members of the household return to the table and together eat the food that has been presented. This is a time of fellowship for the living descendants.

MEANING AND EXPERIENCE OF ANCESTRAL PRACTICES

To learn how the rite is interpreted and experienced, in April 2013 I interviewed two Koreans in Los Angeles and Orange County, California. Both interviewees had been attending ancestral rites and showed enthusiasm for the practice. I interviewed each one for about an hour—one in person and the other by phone, using a semistructured interview with three major questions: (1) What motivates you to carry out these ancestral practices? (2) What do you experience during these ancestral practices? (3) How do you think ancestral practices influence your family?

Respondent Jun Kim (all names are pseudonyms) was fifty-one years old with a wife and three children. He emigrated from South Korea and has been living in the United States for about ten years. His mother and three sisters also live in the United States. He grew up in a Buddhist family and has participated in traditional ancestral rites since childhood. He still practices the rites in the United States, although he became a Catholic at the age of thirty. He said that he had somewhat simplified the ritual for convenience.

1. *Motivations for doing ancestral practices.* The respondent has been doing ancestral rites because he used to do it for so many years from his childhood. Although Catholic churches provide their own forms of ancestral practice, he opted to follow the Korean traditions with which he was familiar.

2. *Feelings and experiences.* When the respondent was young, he did not understand his father's strictness and ways of performing the ritual. However, having raised his own children, he can now understand his late father's heart and mind. He said, "When I was young and my father was alive, I was very afraid of him. However, I see myself becoming the same as my father. I now realize that my father was a good person. I respect him."

3. *The influence of the practice on the family.* When the respondent bows down toward his late father during the rite, he says, "Enjoy these foods. Please look after and prosper this family," so that his children may hear it. In this regard, the respondent wished blessings upon his family and reminded his children of their relationship with their grandfather. He emphasized that the ancestral rite offers a chance for his siblings and their children to gather together and observed that without the rite they would seldom get together. He sees the ancestral rite functioning to enhance family gathering and fellowship.

Respondent Hyun Lee was forty-five years old. He emigrated from South Korea to the United States about five years before the interview. He is married with two children. His father lives in South Korea, and his mother passed away many years ago. Although his family converted from Buddhism to Catholicism, they continue to perform the traditional Korean ancestral rite for his late grandmother. Since coming to the United States, his family, together with his three sisters' families, gather together to practice the Catholic form of ancestral practices, which combines Catholic and traditional Korean practices.

1. *Motivations for doing ancestral practices.* The respondent says that he performed the ancestral rite to observe Korean tradition, to memorialize his mother, and to assist her soul in moving from purgatory to heaven.

2. *Feelings and experiences.* The respondent said that he believes his mother visits the ancestral practice as they perform it. He remembers his late mother during the practice. He feels grateful and remorseful to his mother. He and his sisters share a memory of his mother. He comes to understand his parents' heart as he himself lives as a parent.

3. *The influence of the practice to the family.* The respondent believes that ancestral practices positively influence his children, who are reminded of their grandmother, and this enhances family relationships and deepens

their sense of belonging. It offers a chance for his children to meet their cousins. The ancestral rite brings his siblings together and sustains their relationship even though they once had conflicts with one another. The late mother functions as a relational link between her offspring. These practices help them establish their identity as family.

MY FAMILY'S TRANSITION FROM THE TRADITIONAL RITE TO A CHRISTIAN MEMORIAL SERVICE

My family was Buddhist, and I participated sincerely in observance of the ancestral rites until I became a Christian at the age of twenty-two. My family practiced these rites no fewer than eight times a year. Upon becoming a Christian, however, I stopped attending these rituals because I thought that if I continued to join in them I would compromise my Christian faith. My father continued to preside over the rites and was not happy with my absence, although he never scolded me about it and was outwardly tolerant. When he became a Christian, he chose to celebrate a Christian memorial service instead of the traditional ritual, and I was happy about his decision. I realized over time, however, that something vital was missing from our observance of the Christian ceremony in comparison to the feelings that accompanied the traditional ritual. This led me to reflect on the deeper significance of the ancestral rite and to come to several conclusions about my family's experience.

My first observation has to do with my father's loss of position as the ritual leader. In the past, as the eldest in the family, my father presided over our traditional ritual, while my brothers and I followed his direction. When my father became a Christian, he did not know anything about conducting a Christian memorial service. As a result, he asked me to lead the service, since I was a seminary student. I felt guilty that as the youngest of the three sons, I robbed my father as well as my older brothers of their noble position.

Second, I came to reflect on the exclusion of ritual symbols in our Christian memorial service: the emphasis was on words rather than the richness of visual elements. In contrast, our previous ancestral rite was full of symbolic artifacts and actions and few spoken words. Verbal expressions replaced the cultural symbols in our new memorial service.

Third, I became aware of what might be termed the "insufficiency" of the Christian memorial in honoring ancestors. Our Christian memorial service was meaningful in worshiping God and being attentive to God's will for us, although it did not seem to recognize or honor ancestors enough during the service. We were not remembering and honoring their contributions to the family, nor were we paying tribute to them as the focus of the expression.

Fourth, there was what I call a "shortage of dedication." My mother used to prepare special food and other ritual objects from morning until night for the ritual table. My father and his sons showed great respect to our ancestors by bowing toward their photos. My family's attitudes toward our ancestors, as expressed in the rite, were expressions of sincerity, politeness, earnestness, and dedication. I felt these emotions diminishing in our Christian memorial services and considered it a great loss. Robert McCauley and Thomas Lawson predict this loss when the focus shifts from sensory pageantry with a strong agent to more routinized expressions that emphasize a patient (2002, 43–44).

UNDERLYING MOTIFS OF THE ANCESTRAL RITE

I noted above the two main aspects of the Korean ancestral rite (Choi 1983, 89–91): (1) the rites are *religious* and regarded as a "worship" of ancestral spirits; (2) the rites are social by nature. This second aspect of the rite points to *hyo* (filial piety) in the rite, as ancestors are honored, respected, and venerated by descendants. Some Koreans emphasize the social character of the rite and thereby rule out an interpretation of the rite as true ancestor worship. To these two dominant socioreligious aspects, I suggest adding a third aspect to the ritual motif: (3) the *psychological dimension*. In so doing, I am noting the deep psychological and emotional attachment that descendants develop and which deepen as a result of performing the rites. In summary, I believe that the Korean ancestral rite embodies three major motifs—religious motifs, social motifs, and psychological motifs—and that each of these three main motifs have further submotifs.

The traditional Korean ancestral rite is *religious* in that it presupposes that the spirits of ancestors are still alive and present. Descendants venerate ancestors as living beings through the rite and reflect belief that the ancestors may assist or harm their lives on earth. Thus, they seek blessings and protection from their ancestors by offering food and showing honor to them. Accordingly, the religious motifs of the Korean ancestral rite include belief in ancestors as living spirits, veneration of ancestors, and anticipation of the ancestors bestowing blessings upon descendants. Miyoung Kim notes that rituals are used to affirm social orders in the Confucian view of how society should be structured, reflecting the fact that Korea has been greatly influenced by Confucianism over the centuries (2007, 57). Kwanguk Kim draws attention to the fact that the rite recognizes and affirms the special status of the eldest son (1986, 126). And it must be noted that women do not participate in this ceremony, although they prepare food that makes the ritual possible.

The rite ends in family fellowship and a meal that promotes family cohesion and solidarity. One can legitimately demonstrate how the social motifs go beyond just honoring the ancestors and affirming relationship between ancestors and descendants. They also enhance family solidarity and enforce social position in the family. Wi Jo Kang articulates the significant social meanings of the ancestral rite in Korean life:

> Thus, ancestor worship [the ancestral rite] became a powerful institution in Korean life and culture. It was a sacred symbol in which all Koreans found meaning and purpose for their lives and the enhancement of their sense of belonging. Without both ancestor worship and family, Koreans lost the sense of meaning of their existence; but through the observance of these rites Koreans maintained the values of filial piety and loyalty which in turn strengthened family life and solidified the fabric of Korean society. (1988, 74)

Finally, the ancestral rite is the channel through which Korean people express their psychological and emotional attachment to the dead. Through the rite they mourn and acknowledge the individual's absence, which makes them sad. In the context of the rite, I have seen my mother missing my father, who passed away in 2000. She has a feeling of sorrow and remorse for my father. On the other hand, my mother usually expresses her gratitude for my late father, commending his commitment to our family. When Koreans remember and long for their late spouses, parents, and grandparents, the ancestral rite is what allows the psychological elements of longing, gratitude, remorse, mourning, and remembrance to manifest in relation to the dead.

ARTICULATING CHRISTIAN ENGAGEMENT WITH THE RITE

In the preceding sections, I addressed the elements, procedure, and motifs of the Korean ancestral rite. In this section, I seek to identify a relevant Christian engagement with that rite.

Multiple Facets of Ritual

Note the multidimensionality of the Korean ancestral rite; it exemplifies the social, cultural, personal, and cosmic dimensions of rituals (see Hiebert, Shaw, and Tiénou 1999, 283–84). If we see it only from a religious perspective, we will inevitably condemn the rite and exclude it from Christian life. But to come to terms with positive elements in the rite, Korean Protestants must also face the fact that we have traditionally been unable to accept the belief that ancestors are present in the form of spirits in this world.

Nevertheless, the Korean ancestral rite embodies other significant meanings that enrich Korean people's lives and social relationships. If we abandon these traditional practices, we lose the opportunities through which Koreans may enjoy social and psychological constituents through which God's word may speak to non-Christian family members. At a minimum, the ritual should be condemned only after careful study and discernment, for while traditional religious beliefs permeate human cultural practices, a way may be found to maintain other sociocultural values that are compatible with biblical teachings.

As a matter of principle, we need to view these practices in their entirety and should not denounce a cultural practice as totally unacceptable simply because it contains nonbiblical religious elements. If we do so, we lose sight of significant sociocultural values of which the Bible may approve. I have portrayed the motifs of the Korean ancestral rite as displaying religious, social, and psychological aspects. A Christian analysis of this rite requires us to denounce antibiblical elements and to maintain its biblically affirmed elements in our practice regarding ancestors. If we determine this to be the case in the areas we are considering, we as Koreans who are Christian may continue to enjoy our cultural heritage without fear we are compromising our faithfulness to God.

In summary, the Korean ancestral rite entails religious motifs, social motifs, and psychological motifs. The question we must ask is: Which of these motifs are compatible with biblical teaching? In the next section I analyze the Korean ancestral rite in light of biblical teachings.

A Critical Assessment for Evangelical Christian Practice

If I am correct, evangelical Christians reject the traditional Korean ancestral rite on the basis that it entails "worship" of ancestors and the use of symbolic objects and actions such as food, incense, candles, and prostration to carry out the ritual. As I noted earlier, in principle we should exclude elements incompatible with biblical teachings, while carefully discerning whether it is possible to maintain or transform elements that the Bible can affirm. Paul Hiebert calls this approach "critical contextualization" (1985, 186), an orientation that examines traditional cultural practices in light of the Bible and creates new Christian practices that take culture into account. To achieve this sort of critical contextualization, we need to deal with the components as well as the manners of expressing requisite evangelical beliefs and practices in regard to ancestors.

Proposing Components for Evangelical Christian Practice

Evangelical Christian faith centers on the uniqueness of Jesus as Savior and the Bible as the ultimate norm for Christian faith and life. On this basis, evangelical Christians cannot accept believing in and worshiping ancestors as living spirits, as practiced in the traditional Korean ancestral rite. The Korean rite presupposes ancestral sprits moving between the afterlife world and this world. They are believed to affect their descendants' earthly lives. In contrast, evangelical Protestant faith holds that people go to eternity after their death and are not further involved in the earthly world. This is exemplified in Luke 16:19–31, the story of Lazarus and a rich man that portrays the state of the dead as either at Abraham's side (in heaven) or in hell, with a gulf fixed between. In addition, the Bible nowhere teaches us to contact or seek help from the dead. Instead, the Bible guides believers to seek help from God alone (see, for example, Ps 115:9–11; 121:1–8). Therefore, in my opinion, evangelical practice needs to renounce the elements of the rite that amount to the worship of ancestors. Accordingly, in my view, evangelical practice should not offer food to ancestors, because this action presumes the presence of ancestral spirits. In regard to a traditional Korean belief in ancestors conferring blessings on descendants, evangelical Christians may instead ask for God's blessing. Thus we see that the religious aspects of the death rite need some adjustment to bring them in line with biblical truth.

The social and psychological motifs of the rite, however, do not contradict biblical norms. The Bible emphasizes the importance of honoring parents and elderly people (Exod 20:12; Lev 19:32; Mt 15:4). Israelites in the Bible remembered and reflected on the lives of their ancestors (Exod 4:5; Mk 12:26; Heb 11:1–40). Therefore, it does not contradict biblical teaching to remember and honor ancestors. With regard to the social dimension of the Korean ancestral rite, evangelical Christians may express their respect, honor, and gratitude to their ancestors without believing in or worshiping them as living spirits. Descendants may recall and reflect their ancestors' care and dedication during their earthly lives. They may recognize the importance of learning from their ancestors' life experiences and living harmoniously. Some Protestant Christians use photos of their ancestors to better recognize them. Furthermore, they can prepare food to eat together, thereby enhancing their fellowship and sense of mutual belonging.

In regard to the psychological elements of the Korean ancestral rite, participants may express their respect and gratitude for ancestors, for each generation receives much from its predecessors. This is a very positive element; in addition, participants in the rite can be relieved from remorse and regret that they did not serve their ancestors as well as they should have during their lifetimes.

In this vein, as Shaw makes clear in chapter 1, a reformulated evangelical alternative to the traditional rite should focus on God, and the eventual goal of the practice should be to worship and thank God for what he did and continues to do within the family. In addition, Christian participants need to be reminded of their commitment to God and his call. At the same time, unbelieving relatives participating in the Christian ancestral rite are given witness to God. As evangelicals commemorate ancestors, we need to properly incorporate elements of Korean belief and practice in order to create a culturally meaningful Christian expression.

Proposing Ways to Express Evangelical Faith

Religious faith is always communicated by particular ways of expression. Each church tradition carries its unique forms of Christian expression. For instance, some churches conduct baptism by immersion while others sprinkle. Catholics use a variety of symbols, art, and images while Protestants seldom do. Instead, Protestants use verbal and written languages to express their faith—namely speaking, singing, and writing words. They use auditory music rather than visual media. The four major methods of communicating Christian faith among evangelicals are praising, praying, preaching, and teaching. In contrast, the traditional Korean ancestral rite contains numerous symbols with few words. With this in mind, we need to devise culturally appropriate ways to express and communicate the components of evangelical Christian practice as I have proposed in this chapter.

When non-Christians become Christian, they may feel that the Christian memorial service without symbols is insufficient; they were accustomed to honor their ancestors by prostration, but the Protestant practice does not allow them to do so. This is presented as a contradiction to the second of the Ten Commandments, which prohibits bowing down to or worshiping idols (Exod 20:4–5). Rather than seeing prostration as worshiping the ancestors, however, would it be possible to conceive of prostration as a deeper expression of honor more than merely spoken words? In this regard, might prostration be interpreted as a way of fulfilling what is demanded in the fifth of the Ten Commandments, that is to say, "to honor your father and your mother" (Exod 20:12), in culturally appropriate ways? On New Year's Day, many Korean Christians honor their *living* parents by bowing to them. Could they honor their deceased ancestors in the same way? In addition, could we accept prostration as an expression of respect rather than worship? After all, bowing is portrayed in the Old and New Testament as paying respect, honor, and reverence to God, angels, and certain persons. In the Old Testament, people bow down to God (Gen 24:52–53; 1 Chr 29:20); to angels (Gen 19:1; Josh 5:14); to other gods (Num 25:2; Deut 17:3); to idols (Exod 20:5); as well as to kings (2 Sam 9:6; 1 Kgs 1:23); to parents and elderly people (Gen 33:6; 48:12; Exod 18:7; Ruth 2:10); and to ranking people (Gen 42:6; Esth 3:2). The New Testament includes many occasions when people bow down to Jesus (Mt 8:2; 9:18; 14:33; 15:25; 20:22; Mk 5:6; Jn 9:38). Cornelius, in turn, bowed before Peter (Ac 10:24). The Bible forbids bowing down to other gods or idols, but honoring certain persons and worshiping the one true God by bowing down is encouraged.

Can candles be used for the evangelical practice regarding ancestors as they are in Christian weddings? We might also consider using the photos of ancestors to help recall them and preparing flowers to commemorate them, remembering that Jung Young Lee distinguishes images and idols, pointing out that an image itself is not an idol and that an image becomes an idol only when it is an object of worship (1988, 83). Some Protestant churches allow these elements. Most Protestant churches are unfamiliar with the use of symbols and tend to think such practices are wrong or unbiblical. Nevertheless, the Presbyterian Kyoungdong Church allows the photo of the deceased, candles, incense, flowers, and bowing in their practice regarding ancestors (Kyoungdong Church Home Ceremony Research 1995, 33–42). Given these precedents, Korean evangelicals need to define their biblical and theological perspective of symbols in general, as well as Korean traditional symbols in particular.

Current Protestant memorial services take the form of four basic elements: prayer, reading Scriptures, delivering a message, and singing praise songs. I have suggested the components for the Protestant evangelical practice for the ancestral rite in terms of four directions: toward God, toward Korean culture, toward believing participants, and toward unbelieving participants. As a result, the components employ verbal prayers for God's blessings, reflecting on and learning from ancestors' lives, exhorting commitment to the family, articulating longing and gratitude, reaffirming commitment to God and his call, and witnessing about God. For family cohesion and solidarity, evangelical Christians can prepare food and eat together, as in the traditional Korean ancestral rite.

RETHINKING EVANGELICAL ATTITUDES TOWARD TRADITIONAL CULTURE

As we have seen, the ancestral rite remains significant for Koreans in terms of religious expression, social relationship, and psychological well-being. I have urged a point of view that maintains it is important not to totally condemn the rite because some aspects appear incompatible with the Bible. Instead, I suggest, we should follow Shaw's recommendation in chapter 1 to take stock of the rite's social and psychological importance and then develop evangelical practices that are both faithful to God's word and respectful of Korean culture.

Following Burrows's suggestion in chapter 2, an appropriate death ritual for Korean Christians must incorporate elements of both biblical and Korean belief and practice. Only then will it be viewed as both Korean and Christian and become acceptable to both. In this vein, I have suggested components and ways of expression for an evangelical alternative for the Korean ancestral rite. The components are designed to worship God, affirm Korean culture, strengthen believing participants, and impact unbelieving participants. They include the Protestant tradition of oral prayer, praise, and spoken words, as well as the possible use of symbols familiar to Korean people in general. Korean Protestantism, I argue, needs to redefine its view of symbols in its ecclesial practice.

In the absence of such proper alternatives, many non-Christian Koreans accuse Protestants of distancing themselves from Korean culture and are reluctant to accept Christ if they have to turn their backs on their cultural heritage. Our commitment to God does not require abandoning our cultural identity. Indeed, as Shaw points out, such rejection of traditional culture leads many Koreans to regard Christianity as unrelated to their own cultural ethos and roots, thereby rejecting Christianity as alien and irrelevant to their lives (Mantae Kim 2010, 424–25).

While we must reject cultural elements that contradict biblical truth, we can also maintain cultural traditions compatible with the Bible. We honor and worship God, and we anticipate eternal life, but we also live in social relationship with others within history. As Protestants we need to value our relationship with other people as well as with God, and provide proper Christian mechanisms that fulfill our social relationships. In this regard, Eunjung Cha points out that Korean Protestant worship services are insufficient to fulfill the role of rituals that connect individuals with a community and strengthen communal ties in their life situations. Conversion to Christian faith should not mean abandoning social relationships with non-Christian Koreans (Cha 1999, 122). On the contrary, we can maintain such relationship in biblically transforming ways. We can honor our ancestors and solidify social relationships in the family through an appropriate Christian alternative for ancestral practices, ultimately focusing on worshiping and glorifying God while honoring the ancestor.

In this study, I have articulated that the Korean ancestral death rite can be transformed in ways that simultaneously offer glory to God and value Korean cultural heritage. When Korean evangelical Christians properly respond to traditional culture in biblical faithfulness and cultural relevance, they will enjoy both God's grace and cultural heritage and make Christianity more meaningful and relevant to non-Christians in Korea.

7

Sacred Feet—Waewae Tapu

Pathway to Cultural Reconciliation in New Zealand

Bradford Haami

Tauihu e, arahia te waka—Sacred prow guide this canoe,
Tauihu e, whakatere hūhunu—Illustrious prow, hasten the
double-hulled vessel,
Ki runga i te mata o te moana—On the face of the ocean.
Kawea atu au ki waho—Carry me out to sea,
Kawea atu au ki uta—Carry me to land,
Kawea atu te korero—Carry my address
Ki te taunga tapu—To the sacred anchorage,
Hei turanga waewae—Where my feet are firmly placed,
Hei taumata kōrero e.—A platform to speak.*

My name is Bradford Haami. I am an Indigenous Māori from *Aotearoa*, "Land of the Long White Cloud" (the Māori identification of what is now New Zealand), with a mixture of bloodlines running through my veins: Māori, Scottish, and British. I was raised in the coastal town of Whakatāne, situated within the Ngāti Awa (family of Awa) tribal region. I identify most with my Ngāti Awa tribal roots because I was raised in this territory of my grandmother's people. Her lineage also included the Waikato tribes of the Māori King movement. Both Ngāti Awa and Waikato had British war and confiscation thrust upon them, the effects of which my people still feel. Our founding ancestors voyaged across the Pacific south to Aotearoa, approximately one thousand years ago. They were the last humans to inhabit an unknown land and the first to colonize Aotearoa.

* A glossary of Māori terms and English equivalents appears at the end of this chapter.

We are described as a people of protocol, strongly driven by maintaining our *whakapapa* (tribal genealogical links, language, and culture). As a young journalist I was exposed to the deep historical grievances of our people as the tribes sought justice, self-determination, and freedom from an ever pervasive Westminster cultural and legal worldview that now dominates the Māori landscape. I dwelt in a world focused on past racial conflicts where political solutions seemed the only answer to our people's socioeconomic woes. While the government recognized its obligation to settle historical grievances with the tribes through the Waitangi Tribunal process, I grew increasingly aware that political apologies and minimal compensations would not heal the hearts of a hurting people. Something else had to come.

I became a firm believer in Jesus, which mellowed my heart and shifted my mindset to a more reconciliatory approach to relations between Māori and non-Māori New Zealanders. This chapter focuses on a particular reconciliation-repentance journey that was ushered through the country between 2012 and 2015 using Māori protocols and ceremonies of engagement, as a process for restoring Māori-British relationships. In 2012, when UK peacemakers sought to bring British repentance to New Zealand, this journey was placed partly in my hands. I questioned God: Who am I to accept this? Where do I take these people? How was this journey to move forward? Amid the questions and uncertainties, I felt led by the Holy Spirit to step onto the land and assist the British among our people—to break up the hard ground of bitterness in our nation. We needed this.

In this chapter I highlight the context for this particular British repentance journey but emphasize more the cultural expedition through the Māori world of protocol and ritual. It was my privilege to help the team walk as *waewae tapu* (restricted feet; newcomers to the land). They needed Māori assistance if they were to receive a platform from which the Māori people could hear them. This journey through the Indigenous doorway sets precedence as an approach to local protocol on which other prayer and reconciliation journeys in other nations may build.

As a Māori leader from Aotearoa in this British-Māori repentance journey, I wanted to share academically as well as personally. For any reconciliatory embrace to occur, it was imperative that tribal protocols of engagement from the victimized be recognized and adopted. The British organizers were adamant that their team would not come to Aotearoa unless specifically invited by Māori. In the past their British kin imposed imperial rule over the Māori world, but on this journey it was their desire to enter the land, without agenda or motive, in humble submission to Māori expectations.

Consequently, the visiting British team of intercessors made a commitment "in faith" to walk through any customary process required in order to confess, repent, and pray for the people and their lands. As a result, the hybridity of Māori cultural custom and British expression of a biblical call to bring reconciliation to this land were essential to the outworking of this journey. No particular theological or academic model was followed. Rather, by agreement, we simply followed the leading of the Holy Spirit and walked the land, meeting with people, following our cultural instincts, and moving among the tribes in a manner reflecting biblical principles of reconciliation. Our combined objective was to place repentance before the people with the hope it would be accepted, forgiveness given, and a closer relationship between *tangata whenua* (Māori people of the land) and Pākehā (non-Māori New Zealanders) might occur. More importantly, the British team was determined to follow in obedience to God's will while behaving in accordance with Māori protocol.

In this chapter I offer insight by hindsight into moments of this journey with accompanying comments to contextualize the narrative. I briefly outline the current Aotearoa situation with regard to historical events and reconciliation and then explain the lead-up to the British intercessors' arrival in Aotearoa. Then I explain the tribal customs of engagement involved in this process and highlight the expression of Christian repentance offered on two occasions by the British team and the Māori response. These two occasions serve as case studies of how rituals of engagement were expressed dynamically in two completely different situations and became integral to a Christian repentance process.

In conclusion, I comment on the validity of experiencing a mutual level of embrace while walking in this way and how this enabled *hohou-rongo* (binding peace) between former protagonists. Furthermore, both groups desired to create an environment for a greater movement of God in tribal territories and the manifested healing of the land as espoused in 2 Chronicles 7:14.

THE AOTEAROA CONTEXT

In recent days, the commemoration of the New Zealand land wars of the 1860s—particularly in the Waikato, Taranaki, and Bay of Plenty districts—has highlighted the lack of public knowledge of these pivotal historical events that shaped New Zealand as a nation. These commemorations created momentum to have the truth of these battles, their origins, and their ramifications exposed and remembered. We want to pull aside the blanket of shame.

The Crown Tramples on Māori Tradition

Many of those Māori leaders who stood against the British, to defend their territories against colonial onslaught and land sales, were missionary-educated chiefs who held a prophetic office, but who were eventually silenced by war, incarcerated, or otherwise disempowered. Colonization and war greatly marginalized not only the Māori voice but the Indigenous prophetic voice in New Zealand. For Robert Consedine, coauthor of the book *Healing Our History*, Aotearoa's colonial history was a shocking revelation:

> The Colonial History of New Zealand since the signing of the treaty of Waitangi in 1840 was a history of dishonoured promises, fraud, theft and violence against *Māori* by the government through a process of systematic colonisation. At every level of the political and economical system *Māori* had been marginalised. In that process *Māori* have continually been divided which undoubtedly has compounded the problem. (Consedine and Consedine 2001, 20)

This history and its aftermath have been a source of tension between Māori, the Crown and Pākehā for generations. In recent times a formal commission of inquiry known as the Waitangi Tribunal, formed under the 1975 Treaty of Waitangi Act, has had the power to hear claims against the Crown pertaining to breaches of the Treaty of Waitangi as submitted by tribal groups. The Treaty of Waitangi is a binding agreement signed by some five hundred chiefs and representatives of the British Crown in 1840. The objective was to allow the British to settle and govern Aotearoa with full rights of citizenship given to Māori as British subjects, with Māori retaining control over their valued possessions, including land and natural resources (State Services Commission 2004, 20).

The official Waitangi Tribunal website, www.waitangitribunal.govt.nz, gives its own history, showing how the tribunal was awarded power to make findings of fact and make recommendations only to the Crown that would lead to settlement of claims. Many of the claims investigated the breaches of the treaty in light of Crown actions, inactions, laws, and policies and that Māori suffered harmful prejudice as a result (Waitangi Tribunal Official Website n.d., The Claims Introduction). This has meant looking into the ramifications of the Aotearoa land wars, confiscation of lands, the establishment of the Māori Land Courts, the numerous laws that contributed to the loss of Māori lands and other treasures. More than two thousand claims have been lodged with the tribunal since 1975 (Treaty FAQs 2014). For the valid claims that have been heard, the tribunal has produced a report for the Crown with recommendations to negotiate for settlement. Many of these claims have been settled with a formal apology from the Crown. Māori, however, often feel the settlements are only a small percentage of the full value of the original loss, with others suggesting the Crown's apologies do not have full public sympathy (O'Sullivan 2005, 208).

The Church Forgets the Past

More recently, the church in Aotearoa is having to reevaluate its own historical involvement regarding its position and redress of these issues. This reevaluation has further been compounded with the bicentennial commemorations celebrating the first sermon preached to *Māoriat* Ōihi by Rev. Samuel Marsden on Christmas Day 1814. The arrival of the gospel and the pioneering role of the missionaries are foundational to the story of modern New Zealand. Many believe the church should be integral to the healing of the nation's historical past, as well as the shaping of its present and future. In this shaping process, I must acknowledge many strong Christian communities like the TeKohinga Reconciliation Network in Tauranga City and crucial individuals in the faith who have been diligently committed to uplifting the Māori cause for the building up of the church and the nation.

However, some believe the church has suffered from historical amnesia over the stories of this land, with many Christians believing that the story of the Māori-Pākehā-Crown conflict has little to do with the church. Interestingly, Keith Newman, a Christian "prophetic" teacher, proclaimed in 2013, "The time for endless forgiving is over. For Māori: Get over it, we are now one people, one nation" (2014, 9). Newman based this statement on an overly simplistic, clichéd version of history—"that was then, this is now"—which he uses to brand Māori who seek compensation for past grievances as moaners and complainers (2014, 9–10).

While many years of work and a great deal of effort have occurred in the arena of reconciliation, the word itself has lost much of its value for Māori. Too often, the term represents a generalized Christian reconciliation with little recognizable behavior change toward Māori, and no real restitution offered. The Consedines believe that apologies "without changed behavior lack credibility and become another political tool, which risks devaluing their meaning." Such apologies are "most believable when they are accompanied by reparations, and reparations are least offensive when they really are about apology" (Consedine and Consedine 2001, 208).

Therefore, the Aotearoa team supporting the British peacemakers had to be clear what answer they would give if asked about tangible restitution or reparation associated with this British attempt at reconciliation. In a political environment where settlements are being signed off and tangible restitution offered to *iwi* (tribes), how would we as Christians answer this question? To this end the team worked on preparing an answer. Suffice to say that for those of us, as Christians, we must appreciate what God means when he claims to be a God of justice and restoration. Furthermore, what role do believers in Christ have in bringing about meaningful reconciliation in all of its fullness? Māori communities often hold deep offenses against the work of past colonizers whom they perceive were ushered into the country by Christian missionaries. Thus, the case studies I present here show how both Māori and British intercessors honor God by being obedient to the Scriptures as the Holy Spirit informs each team on how to behave and gives specific actions to do or words to say at each place. The Holy Spirit was the one spelling out how the British team was to move under the authority of Māori protocol.

THE BRITISH MANDATE

David Tidy had been concerned about the plight of the Māori for over twenty years. He had been working alongside other UK prayer organizations to bring repentance and reconciliation to countries once colonized by England. While in the Philippines in 1998, he met Joan Edmondson (a New Zealand intercessor of non-Māori origin with a heart for reconciliation), who invited him to come to Aotearoa. When I joined the team early in 2012, I challenged the British to come, initially just to meet Māori people *kanohikitekanohi* (face-to-face) before any preparations to negotiate could begin. This provided the encouragement necessary for David Tidy and Martin Smith of Prayer Warriors International to visit Aotearoa and to meet with Māori representatives in order to find a way to fulfill a call for the British to repent for their historical sins. During their visit in July 2012, David and Martin were able to share their vision of reconciliation with many Māori people. Their wish was to proceed with this movement only after receiving an invitation from the Māori people. Moreover, this invitation needed to be clearly seen as guidance from the Holy Spirit.

Setting Feet on the Land

During their initial visit, Māori from the Northland, Auckland, Waikato, and Bay of Plenty regions all extended personal invitations for them to come to Aotearoa. Based on those invitations, these British peacemakers agreed to return with a team. In preparation for his and his team's return in October 2012, David invited me to witness their nation's repentance before God for the sins associated with the colonization of Aotearoa at Westminster Chapel in London. Along with myself, a small contingent of Māori and Pākehā Christians attended this significant ceremony at Westminster on September 14, 2012. It was here that David Tidy and his team were commissioned to go and literally walk on Māori land in Aotearoa. They were tasked to repent of the sins of their forefathers and to deal with historical grievances created between the British and the Māori. It must be clear that this journey was only one of a multitude of reconciliation movements to have visited Aotearoa as a nation over many years. However, this particular *hikoi* (journey) had a particular focus on repentance and the essential element of spiritual warfare under the authority of Māori protocol guided by the Holy Spirit.

God Will Heal the Land

The key Scripture for this journey was 2 Chronicles 7:14. God appeared to King Solomon and said,

> If my people, which are called by my name, shall humble themselves, and pray, and seek my face, and turn from their wicked

> ways; then will I hear from heaven, and will forgive their sin, and will heal their land. . . . But if you turn away, and forsake my commandments, which I have set before you, and shall go and serve other gods, and worship them; then I will pluck you out of the land I gave you.

This passage reiterates the notion of a restored relationship with God; the central components of that restoration are humility, prayer, searching for God, repentance, and turning away from sin. In return God said he would hear the people's plea, forgive them, and heal the land. Applied to the Aotearoa repentance journey, this Scripture verse demonstrates how humanity must come humbly before God and bow to the ways of Indigenous people with whom they need to be reconciled—and this is not only for the sake of people but also for the healing of the land.

Another key Scripture was Ephesians 2:14–16:

> For He himself is our peace, who made both groups into one and broke down the barrier of the dividing wall, by abolishing in His flesh the enmity, which is the law of commandments contained in ordinances, so that in Himself He might make the two into one new man, thus establishing peace, and might reconcile them both in one body to God through the cross, by it having put to death the enmity.

Here Christ is the perfect image of reconciliation—sacrificing his own body so that people might be one with God, abolishing enmity between warring factions. We ourselves must break down the dividing walls between us so that we might walk as new persons before God and each other. While Christ has already achieved this, we ourselves must deal with our deep-seated hatred and prejudices by accepting what Christ has already accomplished (Haami 2013, 2–3). For my purpose here, I see our task of reconciliation as a journey of "spiritual warfare."

British team leader David Tidy's view of the importance of British repentance and spiritual warfare was based on the notion that, without repentance on their part, there could be no remission of sin. By his estimation, the remission of sin also included the removal of the power and iniquity of that sin that continually impinges on and rules over land and people. One of this team's particular mandates was to remove the spirit powers underpinning Freemasonry, which greatly influenced the colonization process and still has a stranglehold over many Pākehā communities. This work was a duty that the British peacemakers believed they had to deal with—to root out the source of colonial iniquity and oppression.

In my view the notion of reconciliation as a goal of restoring relationship is a concept that incorporates a number of essential components reflected in the scripture passages I have mentioned. Each element brings with it a microcultural world of its own, replete with appropriate ritual and ceremony, as I discuss shortly. Gathered together, these protocols comprise a series of engagement ceremonies. Using these acts of worship brings true liberty and freedom to my people. I have labeled this journey a "British repentance journey." The core tenets of this journey were humility, repentance, confession, and spiritual warfare, with forgiveness as a reciprocal expectation. With invitations offered and travel preparations made, the British team was ready to bring their brand of repentance and prayer to Aotearoa.

WALKING THROUGH MĀORI PROTOCOLS

Entering Māori tribal territories, especially with first-time visitors, is best achieved by adhering to cultural protocols of engagement. When people gather, a *pōwhiri* (welcome ceremony) takes place on the tribal *marae* (sacred tribal space). Visitors are welcomed to this sacred ground that lies in front of the *whare-tipuna* (ancestral house), a separate *whare-kai* (dining hall), and other communal buildings. Once welcomed in an appropriate way, visitors are shown hospitality commensurate with the size of the group, the rationale behind the gathering, and the nature of the ancestral connections between the joining groups (Mead 2003, 96–97, 117).

Called onto the Marae

The protocols of appropriate engagement include correct procedures for introducing the right people, often in the form of a *karanga* (public call) performed by women, singing as they move from a private home onto the *marae* (grounds). Speeches may include the recital of genealogies to ascertain relationships, formal requests, the singing of *waiata* (traditional songs), and the laying down of *koha* (gifts) to honor hosts. Orations in the Reo (Māori language) are essential. After orators banter and formal greetings are completed, visitors and hosts ceremonially perform the *hongi* (traditional greeting) by pressing noses to finish the welcoming ritual. This act is followed by eating together to bind each other in relationship. This pōwhiri process is a metaphorical enactment of two enemy armies meeting, the home guard and the visitors each trying to ascertain each other's hidden intentions. Only after this welcome is complete can people be unified through the embrace of the hongi and eating together as one people ready to sit in peace, settle disputes and create relationship. Once this extension of welcome is made, a pathway opens to discuss the issue that precipitated the gathering. Variations of this process reflect tribal differences, which the British peacemakers needed to account for as they approached each group.

The marae and the pōwhiri customs center around formal engagement. They are traditionally designed to create and strengthen relationship with the objective of securing an appropriate peace. Traditionally, the marae courtyard was considered to be the *marae-o-Tū* (the realm of war), while the inside of the elaborately carved and painted meeting house represented the *marae-o-Rongo* (the realm of peace and resolution) (Tate 2010, 200–201). Tū is the Māori god of war, while Rongo is the Māori god of peace and the pōwhiri process seeks to move the people from the realm of Tū to the realm of resolution with Rongo—moving from outside, where confrontation is the focus, to the inside where people sit in peace and work out their differences. In my mind, the marae becomes the perfect location for bringing an old issue to a reconciliatory resolution.

Hirini Moko Mead sees the pōwhiri as the gradual reduction of *tapu* (that which is forbidden), culminating in the sharing of food, which ends the ceremony and brings about *noa* (a state of freedom) (2003, 118). "Tapu" is a concept of sacred or ritual restriction, implying the presence of supernatural power that demands respect. There is a sense of danger or fear involved but also of safety reflected in tribal lore but formalized through enabling noa, which is defined as a "freedom from *tapu* or any other restrictions" (Metge 2004, 60). These complementary spiritual states are symbolized by the enactment of the pōwhiri process, thereby removing all restrictions and returning people to normalcy (Williams 1957, 222–23).

Inviting the British to Aotearoa

Initially the Aotearoa team had to identify the locations where major historical conflicts, incidents, and battles occurred between British and Māori in the years from 1800 to the 1870s. This required searching out the local tribes and the leading families involved in these old conflicts with the British and seeking the appropriate location for an audience. As emissaries or message bearers, we made contact with people who could usher us to the family and tribal heads for *kanohikitekanohi* (face-to-face) meeting.

On meeting the assembled folk in the different regions, we engaged in a pōwhiri during which I tactfully recited my own ancestral genealogy to establish tribal links to their families. After the correct salutations to everyone gathered, I then laid down the *take* (issue for discussion): the British desire to come and make amends for the past sins of their kin. I then made a case for why this would be important for these people to receive. The *wero* (challenge) I laid down before these families was couched as a political apology by the Crown with the return of limited land and a monetary settlement. Though it may bring some relief for past historical grievances, it will not heal the wounded heart of the tribe.

In most cases my overtures were welcomed, but some people were suspicious. In many cases, elders understood that there was a foreign spiritual control over their lands, but they were unable to discern or remove it by traditional means. Removing this unseen power created an open door for the British team. I also conveyed to the families that they were not obligated to accept or even forgive the British, and the decision how to answer this *tono* (request) was entirely in their hands.

While there was intense wrangling to obtain clear invitations, almost all the curious tribal groups and families agreed to receive the visiting British team. What follows are two of the many scenarios where the British repentance team met face-to-face with Māori. I offer a local historical context for each visit and share the ritual processes the team walked through to bring about repentance and a context of worship that honored each side.

MANOEKA—SCENARIO 1

On April 26, 2014, David Tidy and his British Intercessory team were scheduled to meet with the wider family of the ancestors of the Prophet Hakaraia TeHēpara (Zechariah the Shepherd) at the Waitaha tribal marae at Manoekaon on the Bay of Plenty. The story that connects these people and the British began in 1818 with Hakaraia of the Waitaha tribe being taken prisoner at Mauao (Mount Maunganui, Tauranga) by the NgāPuhi warlord HongiHika. He was enslaved for a number of years in the Northland, but while there he heard the gospel preached and was converted to Christianity in 1834. He was subsequently baptized by Rev. William Williams at Waimate North and given the name Zechariah (Hakaraia).

The Waitaha Land Grab

In 1845, after returning to the Bay of Plenty, Hakaraia led his own Waitaha people and the closely aligned Tapuika tribe back to their traditional lands at Te Puke, where he established Christian villages in the region. At the time of the war at Gate Pā in May 1864, Hakaraia was living in the Tauranga mission station as a senior Christian teacher and prophet. He stood to support his people at TeRanga where he escaped British guns by running into the Kaimai ranges. The Crown regarded those Māori who fought at Gate Pā as rebels, and in May 1865 the British confiscated 214,000 acres of land and labeled Hakaraia a "fugitive" and a "cunning old man." For the next two years he led a guerrilla campaign against land surveyors preparing confiscated lands in the Bay of Plenty for military settlement. He was likened to a kind of Robin Hood character with people calling him Hakaraia TeHēpara (Hakaraia the shepherd), the head of a disparate landless community of tribal people.

British troops pursued Hakaraia, destroying settlements, gardens, and livestock owned by the Waitaha tribe. It was an unnecessarily brutal campaign against the people, their land, and their crops. Hakaraia was further named in the press as "the son of Satan" but was actually a fervent student of Scripture, trying to live by the tenets of the Bible. In 1870 he and the prophet leader TeKooti were pursued as far as Waioeka near Ōpōtiki, where Hakaraia along with seventeen others were shot in cold blood. Hakaraia was decapitated and his body left lying on Mokoia Island at Rotorua. In the aftermath of the land confiscations Hakaraia's people were left landless, with only 2.5 percent of their former territory in their hands in 1900. Furthermore, their links to the God that Hakaraia believed in were all but severed.

While Hakaraia the prophet's story has been largely forgotten, his family and the local tribes still remember well his life and the way he was belligerently treated by the British. In 2011 the Crown recognized the wrongs done to the Waitaha people and agreed to compensate the tribe, including a pardon for Hakaraia. The settlement documents end with a Waitaha proverb, dating from the 1845 peacemaking ceremony Hakaraia had made possible: *Kua tau te rangimarie ki te whare o Hakaraia ake, ake, ake* (The peace has been settled in the house of Hakaraia now and forever more) (McCulloch 2014).

The British Step into the Waitaha House

In 2014, 144 years after Hakaraia's death, the visiting British team assembled at the front of the house of Hakaraia to bring a message. At the behest of the *karanga,* by the senior woman of the tribe, the British team, flanked by Māori and Pākehā support, were ushered onto the marae and into the carved meeting house to present themselves before the Waitaha tribal elders. Inside the house, the seating was arranged with the hosts gathered at the back of the house while the visitors were designated seats along the left-hand wall.

After an initial prayer, the first host orator stood to greet the visitors. Reference was made to the British visitors as *waewae-tapu* (sacred or restricted feet). This acknowledgment indicated their inability to move among the tribal people until the "reduction of tapu" freed their feet to interact without restriction. In this symbolic condition, the British could do nothing without the formal agreement of the elders until the pōwhiri ceremony was completed. The orator intoned the names of the tribes and families gathered and explained the protocols of the house (all formal speeches had to be spoken only in the Māori language until the traditional orators completed their speeches). In reply I stood to greet the elders and announce who was gathered in the visiting group, quoting genealogies to solidify connections between my own Ngāti Pukeko tribal group and the Waitaha people. I then explained the reason the British team had come: to repent for past sins of the British and bring prayer to Waitaha lands. After my speech I laid down a *koha* (monetary gift) before the hosts to honor them and to indicate there would be no more formal Māori language speakers on our visiting side.

The senior orator of the marae, Tame McCausland, then stood and welcomed the British, inviting them now to speak in English. He reiterated how the descendants of Hakaraia and the other Christian chiefs killed at the battle of Te Ranga were in their midst and were keen, along with their progeny, to hear the words of the British team. Carved effigies of dead ancestors lined the walls of the tribal house while their living descendants listened to every word and connected the past and present to future generations who would benefit from what was about to take place.

The British team immediately knelt inside the carved house, wishing to be below the eye line of the Māori people and at their feet. On his knees David Tidy, the team leader, confessed out loud before the people the deplorable sins of their ancestors. Each of the team members then confessed the specific sins of the past, including the persecution of Hakaraia, his horrendous death, and silencing his prophetic voice to his people. The British team then bowed their heads to the ground before Hakaraia's family and waited for a reply. The descendants of Hakaraia had never seen such deference and the emotion of the moment brought silence and tears. After all was said the Kaumatua (elder) Tame stood to answer their confession and spoke out the history of Hakaraia, who never wavered from his scriptural teaching and died standing up for justice. The Kaumatua then publicly received their apology with gratitude.

Lifting the Tapu from Restricted Feet

When the local families regained their composure, they lifted the British from the floor and embraced. I stood to further explain how the confiscation lines created by the Crown had spirit power to keep the people in bondage. Everyone in the house agreed that this was true, but the Māori had not known how to destroy the power. David Tidy was given permission to share about the power of Freemasonry in the colonial process to bring war and especially in the shifting of ancient boundaries. The lines they drew on the maps are aligned to the *ley lines* (spirit lines). These lines form a net of control and oppression over entire regions of people. The Waitaha people were then asked if the British could pray to cut off the power of these confiscation lines, and they were in total agreement. The visitors spoke of how the British historically placed these confiscation lines across the land, and their duty as British representatives was to remove the spiritual powers of these lines in the contemporary context.

Waitaha lost thousands of acres of land to the Crown and were allocated to live on reserves. The local people pointed out how the confiscation line traveled straight through the marae grounds, splitting the house and continuing up through the middle of the mountain called TeUpoko o Taranui (The head of the ancestor Taranui). With all in agreement, David led the British team to stand at one end of the carved house and to walk to the other side of the house, crossing over that line while declaring prayers to cut the spiritual presence. In the end all the Māori people gathered with the British to declare a unified "amen." In faith everyone in the gathering knew the line had been severed in the spirit realm.

All the visitors were then led in a line to greet the host elders with a hongi ritual to complete the formal part of the pōwhiri ceremony. A beautiful feast was laid out by the Waitaha people in honor of the occasion, with shared food removing the state of tapu (restriction) and restoring noa (freedom). This allowed everyone to move among each other, free from formalities and restrictions. After a resounding farewell from the marae, the local people took the British to another area where the confiscation line crossed over the Te Puke state highway. They wanted this line spiritually severed. As Māori, British, and Pākehā prayed together, the unified team marched in close rank over a section of the invisible line on the land in loud voices, asking God to cut the power of the line and pull down the nets of oppression. In that moment of agreement, the British team openly prayed for the Māori men of the tribe who had ushered the team to this location. Because the tribe had honored God and allowed repentance to be spoken and forgiveness had been offered, the British declared that God would come in a special way to bless their lands, their lives, their families, and their futures. These prayers were received with open hearts and completed by blowing shofars (**adapted by some Māori as spiritual symbols**) three times into the heavenlies as an amen.

This state of restored freedom allowed the British to move and share without encumbrance with the local Māori. It enabled a form of *hohourongo* (binding peace) that ensured restored relationships and acceptance. Later the British team was told how the people of Waitaha reflected for hours on what had occurred that day, and the news mushroomed out to the whole community of Manoeka and the Te Puke region. The full fruit of that day is yet to be seen.

RUAPEKAPEKA—SCENARIO 2

This second scenario differs in location but follows a similar ceremonial process of lifting tapu to bring about noa. Māori families who had invited the British team into Northland desired to usher them to the battle site of Ruapekapeka (the bats nest), fourteen kilometers south of the town of Kawakawa. This stockade was constructed with thick timber palisades, dugouts, and underground caves designed to withstand cannon fire. The massive fort took six hundred men and women nearly two months to build (Moon 2001, 143).

The British Military Destroyed Ruapekapeka

In December 1845 the chiefs Hone Heke and Kawiti were dissatisfied with the 1840 Treaty of Waitangi and the continuous demand for land. Governor Fitzroy tried to resolve the land dispute, which had become a major obstacle for race relations (Belich 1998, 54–57). Old Kawiti said to Fitzroy, "You shall not have my land—no, never! Sir, if you are very desirous to get my land, I shall be equally desirous to retain it for myself" (Cowan 1955, 73). As long as Kawiti would not give up one single acre of land, Hone Heke was resolute not to desert him, since Heke believed the governor was trying to deprive them of their lands (Moon 2001, 143). Without peace, Governor Fitzroy was dismissed and replaced by Governor George Grey who organized a large British expedition, a combined naval and military force to quell Māori defiance in the Northland. According to historian James Belich,

> The British had to crawl 18 miles of hill, bush, river and ravine, hauling thirty tons of artillery along with them and cutting their road as they went. It took them three weeks to get the whole column up but by Christmas the whole echelon (700 men) and a couple of guns were before Ruapekapeka. (1998, 59)

Figure 7-1: Location of Scenarios 1 and 2

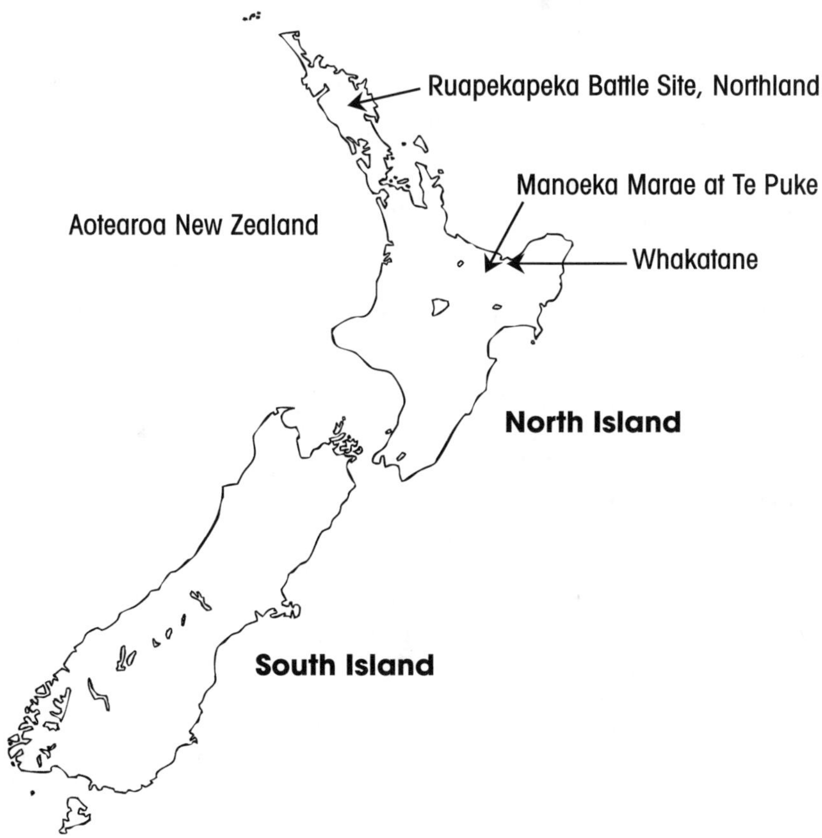

The result was an overwhelming British bombardment of the fort. Finally, Kawiti and his surviving warriors were overwhelmed and abandoned the valueless fort. Some say the British won a huge victory while others believe Kawiti scored a greater strategic success (Belich 1998, 64). Later Kawiti found himself in a divine struggle with Te Atua o te pō, the unseen God, after which he relayed to his people the following words:

> My beloved people. I have stood before the God of the unseen realm, and I was not destroyed. Therefore, from this day, trample hatred under your feet. Do not dishonour your ancestors' peace memorials in greenstone that lie on many seas. Observe the white objects of the ocean. You shall be Pakeha boys. Be firm to retain religion, turning only when the sand fly bites upon the page of the book. Also, whosoever weaves a net let him set it himself, and let him draw it in himself. (*TeAoHou: The New World* 1956, 45)

Since that time, many repentance ceremonies have taken place on this battle site, but the local family regarded it important to gather here again with the British team. On arriving at the open site it was decided that a battle reenactment would be appropriate to reverse the impact of the original war.

The British Peacemakers Restore Ruapekapeka

At the base of the entrance to the battle site, the British and supporting New Zealanders gathered at the gate and waited to be called on to the site, as is traditional for the pōwhiri process to unfold. Pastor Paul Wihongi then appeared as a traditional Māori warrior sent out to wield a *taiaha* (long fighting staff) before David Tidy and his team to test their intentions. After a warlike performance he laid down a token of peace on the ground while grimacing warlike at the British team. David Tidy was informed to pick up the token and hold it up in front of the warrior to indicate peaceful intentions. The warrior then led the team up the walkway to the top of the battle site where the descendants of past warriors waited in a line to face their new foes. The British were ushered before the local Māori, and two lines of people faced off; it was like a scene on a killing field where two armies were about to seal the rules of combat.

Despite formal protocols of engagement having been decided the day before, there was still a protocol of meeting required on this site where blood had been spilled so long ago. Laurie Anderson, one of the Māori elders, stepped forward and prayed. He then spoke of the battle waged on the site and introduced the local people. Once the formal introductions had been made, he encouraged the British to reply in their own way. David Tidy and his team immediately bowed to their knees, and each began to confess aloud the sins of the British who arrogantly bombarded this land with British firepower in a bid to subdue the so-called rebellious Māori.

When their confession and repentance were completed there was a long silence before a reply. Stunned, Paul Wihongi picked up his taiaha, which was inscribed with the Scripture Zechariah 4:6—"Not by power nor by might but by my spirit"—and dragged the blade along the earth. He then performed a warrior's dance in the gap separating the two parties. Symbolically, this broke the dividing spiritual wall between the two peoples. After that definitive, prophetic action the Māori people acted in the opposite way to the original battle and walked across the separating line of engagement to hongi with the British team and their supporters.

Discerning that the spirit of anger and hatred had ruled over the mountainous tribal landscape for nearly 170 years, those gathered decided to reenact what the chief Kawiti had stated to his warriors: *takahia te kino ki raro i ou koutou waewae* (trample hatred under your feet). In unity, Māori, British, and Pākehā linked arms as believers in Christ. Assuming the traditional Māori stance, we stamped our feet across the whole of the *pā*, chanting in *reokē* (glossolalia), as experienced in Acts 2, enacting Luke 10:18–19 by trampling on the enemies' power that had prevailed on that hill. At the edge of the site we all declared hatred and anger to be removed off that mountain and replaced with heavenly glory and joy. At the conclusion of this event, the new family in Christ traveled back to Moerewa, where a *kai-hakari* (feast) was served and eaten together, sealing the unity between everyone involved.

In journeying with the British peacemakers to this battle site, the social Māori protocols of engagement quite easily complemented the desire for a past enemy to meet the Māori people on Māori terms to broker the beginnings of restoration. The local Māori people who met the British team on the site were all Christians who chose to express the peacemaking proceedings in a traditional Māori fashion. There we saw the *wero* (challenge) and *takahi* (trample customs) applied. The trampling of the land was a prophetic action designed to enact what the old chief Kawiti had proclaimed his people must perform.

CONCLUSION

The Hebrew custom of offering a bowl of water to guests to wash their feet upon entering a home was the first duty of a host. To omit this was a sign of disrespect and unfriendliness, as Jesus reminded Simon the Pharisee (Lk 7:44). Such a ritual constituted a customary form of crossing the threshold of engagement directly applicable to the pōwhiri process. Throughout Scripture we see that God has set a pattern by which each nation has its boundary-crossing protocols—ways to properly cross over a threshold, to rightly enter and leave a formal occasion, a house, or a territory through the public front door of honor. Mechanisms for finding resolution and reconciliation have established protocols in Māori culture. I have utilized these recognized rituals and ceremonies to examine this repentance journey of the British peacemakers.

In retrospect, the visitors awaiting invitations and submitting to Māori protocol became a public sign of their humility and willingness to take tribal custom seriously. This resulted in an overwhelming acceptance by their Māori hosts. Due to this show of humility, Māori engagement in the formalities became integral to the acting out of 2 Chronicles 7:14 in a meaningful way.

In prayer and supplication, the visiting British team, their UK intercessors, and the Aotearoa supporters sought the face of God for almost a year. They sought God regarding how to move and what to do on this journey. Answers were discerned through Scripture under the guidance of the Holy Spirit. What emerged was that the British should walk in submission to the Māori way. Through continued humility and submission to local protocol, old enemies openly entered on to the land of past victims where confession and repentance reflected a turning from wicked ways. The combination of traditional ceremonies, enacted scripturally through faith in Christ, created a welcoming atmosphere in these territories. This hybrid expression brought liberty to the regions where local people, hearing the gospel again, might have the freedom of will to choose Jesus as a restorer of hope rather than one who took their land. In some areas the name of Jesus has been openly desired and entered back into the conversation of local marae.

Wherever forgiveness, repentance, and embrace were extended to the British, people are enjoying a new freedom in Christ. We believe these heartfelt words and actions were not simply between men but were witnessed by God, who will accomplish his desire for our land and its people. The British team in Aotearoa had a twofold purpose: seeking release from the workings of British iniquity over Māori people and their lands and obtaining merciful healing of their own lands in the United Kingdom.

By repenting on Aotearoa soil and pulling down ungodly networks over the land, the British team have not only fulfilled a call by God but have left an example from which we can learn to walk out 2 Chronicles 7:14. I suggest that when reconciliation teams are called to represent their dominant cultures with repentance, they should walk in a humble way on the Indigenous lands of their victims. Good tribal negotiatiors are needed to usher them through the appropriate protocols of peacemaking in that territory. This process sets a precedent for the way the British walked in through Māori land. By crossing our threshold through invitation and appropriate Indigenous protocols relating to restoration of the land, everyone participating was redeemed for the purpose to which God has called them.

Those of us Māori who supported and ushered the British team over the killing fields and on to our tribal marae were forced to consider our own past hurts, offenses, and prejudices toward other tribal enemies as well as the Pākehā. Despite the past sins of their British forebearers, together we can now look to renew the land on which we both depend, celebrating God's plans for us all. We have honored God through our ancient rituals and protocols and applied them to reconciliation.

By welcoming the British peacemakers, we experienced a demonstration of how to apply the tenets of Scripture to our own walk of faith. This, in itself, is a form of worship. We have laid down the *koha* (gift) of peace before each other. This suggests that we all accept God's koha, none other than Christ's sacrifice on the cross, as atonement for our past sins but also for the sake of our future. It also suggests our ongoing interaction between ourselves, as well as with the Pākehā.

This point brings me to one final Māori ritual, a song composed and sung for a particular occasion. On the occasion of this chapter in this book, I take a section from Psalm 85 as an appropriate closing chant. This psalm is often sung in Māori by the Ringa tu people of the Prophet Te Kooti.

Kua tutaki te mahi tohu rāua ko te pono—
Mercy and truth have knit together
Kua kihi ki a rāua te tika me te rongomau—
Righteousness and peace have kissed
Ka tupu ake te pono i te whenua—
Truth shall spring out of the earth
Ā, ka titiro iho te tika i te rangi—
Righteousness shall look down from heaven
Āe, ka homai e Ihowā te pai—
Yes the Lord will give what is good
Ā ka tukua mai ōna *hua e tō tātou whenua—*
And our land will yield its increase
Ka haere te tika i mua i a ia—
Righteousness will go before him
Hei whakatū i a tātou ki te ara o ōna *hikoinga—*
And shall make his footsteps our pathway.

GLOSSARY OF MĀORI WORDS

Aotearoa. Land of the Long White Cloud, New Zealand.
Atua. God.
hohou–rongo. Binding peace.
hongi. Greetings by pressing noses.
hui. Gathering.
iwi. Bone(s), tribe.
kai-hakari. Feast to eat.
kanohi ki te kanohi. Face-to-face.
karakia. Prayer, incantation.
karanga. Woman's call.
kaumatua. Elder.

kaupapa. Matter for discussion.
koha. Gift.
māhaki. Humility.
mana. Authority, spiritual power.
Māori. Indigenous person/people of New Zealand.
marae. Meeting place, open courtyard.
noa. State of freedom.
pā. Fortification.
Pākehā. Non-Māori.
pō. Darkness, unseen realm.
pono. Faith, genuine.
pōwhiri. Traditional welcome.
reo kē. Glossolalia, speaking in the spirit, speaking in tongues.
Rongo. God of kumara, peace.
taiaha. Long fighting staff.
takahi. Trample.
takahi-whare. Trample death out of the house.
take. Issue.
tangata whenua. People of the land.
tapu. Restriction, sacred.
tikanga. Correct procedures.
tipuna. Ancestor.
tono. Request.
Tū. God of War, war.
waewae. Feet.
waewae-tapu. Sacred or restricted feet.
waiata. Song.
wero. Challenge.
whaikōrero. Speech.
whare-kai. Dining room.
whare-tipuna. Carved house.

8

Pagan Rituals and Orthodox Beliefs

Hybridity, Prayer, and Worship in the Armenian Orthodox Church

Petros G. Malakyan

From 1921 to 1991 the Christian Church in Armenia was oppressed and persecuted. As a result, Christian faith and Christian worship were reduced to mere rituals and ceremonies, with little relevancy to a search for truth and meaning in life, social responsibilities, or experiencing God. As a result of the Soviet takeover, Christian worship was gradually nominalized. For the first time in the history of the first Christian nation, Armenians embraced atheistic ideology and were forced to abandoned their Christian identity and faith. Despite the Soviet attempt to uproot Christianity, which had been around since apostolic times and as a national religion since AD 301, their plan failed and the atheist ideology vanished with the fall of the Soviet Union in December 1991.

Ironically, what St. Gregory the Illuminator (who was the pioneer and initiator of Armenian conversion from paganism to Christianity) did to pagan rituals and festivals at the beginning of the fourth century, the Soviets attempted by eliminating Christian feasts and rituals and substituting them with Soviet festivals and celebrations. Despite the seventy years of the Soviet experiment in Armenia, the seventeen-hundred-year-old Christian traditions prevailed, yet the Soviets succeeded in alienating people from the church and the Bible by prohibiting public access to the Bible and Christian literature. People were misinformed about God and the church, resulting in a decline of faith in God and knowledge of the Bible and Christian worship. The Soviets were able to kill the missional spirit of the church by prohibiting Christian charity, preaching, teaching, and discipleship.

During the twenty-five years since state-regulated atheism was abandoned, contemporary Armenian society has quickly replaced socialism with free-market capitalism and atheism with theism. The Armenian Church has gained her previous leading position and power in the society as the state church. The Christian feasts and rituals have been restored. However, post-Soviet Christianity in Armenia has become a combination of secular materialism and highly ritualistic and superficial Christianity. The hybridity of Christianity and secularism has produced economic inequality, corruption in political leadership, and an unprecedented gap between poor and rich. On one hand, the society is submissive to the spiritual authority of the church and her leadership; people seem to crave spiritual revitalization. On the other hand, the society continues to become increasingly secular and materialistic. Armenians put high moral expectations on orthodoxy, but also on the orthopraxy of their spiritual leaders. My real question in this chapter, then, is as follows: what are the role and the responsibility of the Armenian Church for (1) restoring God-human relationships through worship and the administration of sacraments and (2) actively participating in the reconstruction of a just society that honors God and God's creation? Before we address this question, let me give a brief historical overview on the Armenian Christian past.

HISTORICAL BACKGROUND OF THE ARMENIAN APOSTOLIC CHURCH

Before the fourth century, Armenians were pagans. The first Christian communities in Armenia date back to the time of Jesus. Bartholomew (one of the Twelve) and Thaddeus (one of the Seventy) came to Armenia with their evangelistic message, established apostolic communities, and were martyred by pagan Armenians in the second half of the first century. Armenians embraced Christianity only after St. Gregory the Illuminator (AD 232–325) established the Armenian Apostolic (Orthodox) Church in the late third and early fourth centuries. Considered "apostolic" because of Jesus's disciples, it was the enduring message and long-suffering faith of Gregory (who later became the first bishop—see Thomson's translation and commentary on *The Teaching of Saint Gregory*, 2001) that Armenians embraced Christianity (Cowe 1991, 19). Today, the Armenian Church celebrates *Lusavorchi ton* (feast of the Illuminator) every June (Thomson 2001).

The invention of the Armenian alphabet by Mesrop Mashtots (AD 361–440) at the opening of the fifth century marked the beginning of the golden age of Armenian scholasticism and Christian education. St. Mesrop translated the Bible into Armenian with his six disciples. Later, more than one hundred translators, following Mesrop's steps, laid the foundation of patristic literature in Armenian.

After the last Armenian kingdom of Cilicia fell in the late fourteenth century, Armenians, who had been living around the slopes of Mount Ararat since the days of Noah, lost their independence. For the next five to six centuries, the Armenian Church served a dual political and religious role in the life of the Armenian nation. In the early twentieth century, the national independent state of Armenia lasted only two years (1918–1920) before a militant atheism was imposed on Armenians by Russian and Armenian Bolsheviks from 1921 until 1991.

My story fits into this general context and serves as a case study of how cultural understanding and spiritual discipleship fit together to change people's lives within an Orthodox community.

BEYOND RATIONALIZED FAITH: MY EXPERIENCE WITH GOD

After the completion of my doctoral studies in 1999 I took my family back to Armenia to implement my research and establish a new ministry among my own people. Coming from the Armenian Evangelical Baptist community, I knew very little about the rituals and ceremonies of the Armenian Apostolic Orthodox Church. As a long-term goal and as an act of obedience to God's Spirit, I had a desire to find ways in which I could immerse myself in the life of the Armenian Church, one of the oldest Christian traditions in the world. Somewhat by coincidence, I became acquainted with Archbishop Shahe Ajamian, the founding dean of the faculty of theology at Yerevan State University (YSU). In 2000 he invited me to teach courses at the university on Christian education, Christian doctrines, and eschatology.

Archbishop Ajamian also invited me to lead Bible studies for the university students and organize pilgrimage-retreats to ancient monasteries throughout Armenia. During this time I began experiencing God in new ways. I found myself participating in Christian rituals and ceremonies dictated by the Armenian Church calendar with its daily scriptural readings and prayers. These rituals and ceremonies served as the foundation for me to teach the Bible to young adults and help them develop an I-Thou relationship with God through daily prayers and weekly worship services (Buber 2000). Moreover, the celebrations and feasts within the church calendar provided a structure to take university students on regular pilgrimage-retreats. Those two- or three-day travels and sharing life together were transformational not only for my students but also for me and my family. As a result, I have been able to disciple a select group of twelve to fifteen young adults out of eighty to one hundred attendees. God opened doors for me to implement a lay leadership program among young adults within the Armenian Apostolic Church in Armenia by establishing the National Leadership Institute (NLI).

Upon reflection, I realize that I became more open to the importance of rituals and ceremonies in my own Christian traditional roots. Following the lead of Shaw and Burrows in the first two chapters of this volume, I show in this chapter how their main points relate to enabling young Armenian adults within the context of NLI and the structures of Armenian Orthodoxy to enthusiastically use Orthodox rituals and ceremonies to engage in meaningful worship and grow in faith.

THE NEED FOR CHRISTIAN RELEVANCE: THE PEOPLE EXPERIENCE GOD

Since national independence in 1991, Armenians recognize the need for revitalization and rediscovery of their spiritual past and Christian heritage. The society is in the process of transformation, shifting from atheism back to its traditional Christian roots. A new challenge that the Armenian Church is facing today is to overcome the spiritual losses of the past and the contemporary materialism of the present generation. The Christian message and the centuries-old Armenian Divine Liturgy or Surb Patarag—a Mass where believers are united with the Holy Trinity, angels, and saints in worship—is considered largely irrelevant by the younger generation. There is a lack of biblical and theological understanding of what it means to be a people of God or a follower of Christ. On an individual level, most Armenians are still in search of deep meaning—connections to their ethnic and spiritual heritage. Some blame Christianity for physical and territorial losses since the fourteenth century and are turning to ancient neopaganism as a replacement for Armenian orthodoxy.

Nonetheless, the Christian rituals and ceremonies continue to provide spiritual, ethnic, and cultural significance for the Armenian people. The Divine Liturgy, particularly, has been designed for holistic worship and experience of God through all five human senses: sight, smell, touch, taste, and sound. It seems that the relevancy and restoration of religious rites reflect the hybridity of biblical orthodoxy, which enlightens contemporary Armenian Christian spirituality, culture, and ethnic identity.

Worship and Spirituality: Individual and Communal

Armenian Christian worship focuses on daily prayer hours, the weekly Divine Liturgy, and annual feasts. Together these establish a calendar of spiritual engagement originally designed to promote individual and communal spirituality. The Armenian Orthodox Liturgy encompasses collective and individual responses to God in worship through all five senses and thus is considered holistic worship. This approach includes

- *Liturgical hearing* through prayers and responsive singing of *sharagans* (hymns) as people are invited to participate in the liturgy.
- *Liturgical seeing*, which engages a plethora of visual expressions of icons, lit candles (heralding Christ as the light of the world), and even the church buildings that envision theological insights.
- *Liturgical touches*, where parishioners greet one another with a holy kiss of peace and are touched by the Holy Spirit through the *muron* (holy oil).

- *Liturgical smelling*, whereby the specific odor of the incense creates a subconscious prayer and worship mood or mental posture to honor God.
- *Liturgical tasting*, as the faithful participate in the Eucharist and taste the goodness of the Lord (Ps 34:8).

Put together, congregants experience through the Divine Liturgy the totality of holistic worship expressed through celebrating the Eucharist, which they can see, feel, smell, and taste while hearing the priest intone, "Sa e marmin yev aryun Kristosi" (The body and blood of Christ) (Anjewac'i 1991). By breaking the bread of *nshkhark* (love feast), believers experience together the love of God through Christian fellowship (Ac 2:42).

During the expression of this holistic worship, people are encouraged to engage with God's entirety in a community context. On one hand, the liturgy draws people to an intimate relationship and union with God through the Eucharist; on the other, the faithful share solemn peace and union with other members of the sacerdotal community: together they form the mystical body of Christ (Jn 15:5–8; Eph 4:4–13). Furthermore, the liturgy also unites the congregation with all the saints, including deceased loved ones, who by faith take part in the Divine Liturgy as members of the invisible church (Nersoyan 1970). Thus, unlike other religious traditions, where physical and metaphysical worlds are distinct and strictly separated, Armenian Orthodox Christianity unites rational and mystical faith in balance with the past, the present, and the future, thereby blending life and death, humanity and divinity in an eternally timeless and spaceless experience of spirituality embodied in the Eucharist. This holistic worship guarantees spiritual and psychological well-being for individuals as well as the community that is the congregation. The ongoing worship thus remains as the main mission of the church until Christ returns: celebrating Christ's real presence in the Eucharist, fellowshiping with others faithfully through communal worship, and union with God and the glorified church by engaging the Holy Spirit through the Divine Liturgy.

Cultural Identification

Through the ages, liturgical rituals, feasts, and ceremonies have been incorporating Armenians into the life of the church. Thus, the Christian tradition has become a part of Armenian culture. The Armenian culture has long been identified with Orthodox Christianity, extending almost unobstructed to the time of St. Gregory. In chapter 2 Burrows's use of the hybridity concept has been practiced by Armenian Christians since the fourth century. Through Christian feasts dedicated to Jesus Christ, the Virgin Mary, the cross, and the saints, the Armenian church fathers were able to intermingle "remnants of pagan feasts and popular customs" (Manookian 1986, 14). For instance, the celebration of Christ's birth in the winter season began in the second half of the fourth century, symbolically connecting the Virgin Mary's nine-month pregnancy with elements of the pagan festival of Saturnalia—a farmer's festival to mark the end of the autumn planting season in honor of Saturn. Moreover, as in other Orthodox Churches, the Armenian Church celebrates Christmas on January 6, along with Christ's baptism and the first miracle.

Furthermore, the use of water has become a significant element for spiritual commemorations. Water has always been a highly symbolic element in Armenian worship, combining the use of water in pre-Christian pagan celebrations with Christian traditions. During the feast of Epiphany, water is blessed and distributed among the faithful, as a reminder of Jesus's baptism in the Jordan. Water is also used at the feast of the Transfiguration, which is celebrated with the pagan feast Vardavar, as people pour water on each other as a symbol of purification and kindness. Pouring water is also a reminder of the flood and the salvation of Noah's family. This reminder in turn highlights the pagan symbolism of water with the worship of the goddess Astghik, the daughter of Noah. The fire-worshiping rituals of our pagan ancestors were also merged with the Christian feast of *tyarnendaraj* (presentation of Jesus in the Temple), and the pagan festival of fortune telling for personal luck with the Christian celebration of the ascension of Jesus Christ to heaven. It seems evident that the Armenian Church attempted to substitute pagan festivals with Christian celebrations by giving biblical meanings to adapted pagan rites.

The feast of the Assumption is a great feast exalting Mary in the month of August. It is also one of the five *daghavar* (feasts) of the Armenian Church (along with Theophany, Easter, Transfiguration, and the Exaltation of the Holy Cross). According to church tradition, Christ himself took Mary's body into heaven. Sometime between the ninth and twelfth centuries, the church endorsed this belief, observing this feast for nine days, during which priests bless the grape as the noblest of first fruits and the essence of joy tracing the narrative back to the Genesis account of Noah (Boyajian 2011, 153–54). It is evident, then, that the Armenian church fathers intentionally made Christianity very Armenian by connecting pre-Christian feasts with Christian worship as well as to the land. Pagan rituals and ceremonies have shaped Armenian culture as well as how people perceive God. They establish habitual attachments, memories, and a sense of cultural belongingness in the minds of Armenians through the ages while serving as a means to appropriately worship God in fullness of mind, heart, and soul. Readers interested in further information on the nature of Armenian culture and the role of the Orthodox Church should see Arzounmanian (2014), Devrishian (2013), Karmeian (2010), and Ormanian (1955). NationMaster.com also has a wealth of information for interested readers.

Ethnic Sustainability

The Armenian Orthodox rituals and ceremonies also provide ethnic sustainability. Armenians, anywhere in the world, build sustainable communities by establishing churches and schools and following the traditions of their ancestors. William Saroyan, an Armenian American author, wrote what has become a famous quote on Armenian ethnic cohesion:

> I should like to see any power of the world destroy this race, this small tribe of unimportant people, whose history is ended, whose wars have all been fought and lost, whose structures have crumbled, whose literature is unread, whose music is unheard, whose prayers are no longer uttered. Go ahead, destroy this race. . . . Burn their houses and their churches. See if they will not live again. See if they will not laugh again. See if the race will not live again when two of them meet. . . .
>
> (Saroyan 1936, 437–38)

Food and habits of eating familiar food together, much like in the Divine Liturgy, sustain Armenian families. Moreover, marriages foster ethnic sustainability within the ethnic group both at home and in the diaspora.

The general public possesses basic knowledge about feasts and ceremonies. However, the number of people who actually know the meaning of the rituals and their theological significance is limited to the clergy. For instance, most attendees of the Divine Liturgy in the Armenian Church lack biblical and theological knowledge to understand the stages of the liturgy. Moreover, since the liturgy is in Grabar (classical Armenian), most Armenians do not possess the necessary language skills to understand and interpret the words of the liturgy.

Much like any ethnic religion, a significant number of Armenians are nominal Christians who seek healing and protection by appropriating the blessed elements but do not understand the intent behind them. Less than 10 percent of Armenian Christians practice their faith weekly or monthly. For any given worship event, less than 1 percent of Armenian Christians actually participate. While nearly 95 percent of the 2.8 million Armenians consider themselves Orthodox Christians, most do not actively engage in regular worship (NationMaster.com n.d.). Yet it is not uncommon to see holy water, salt, amulets such as crosses, evil-eye handkerchiefs, and other physical objects regularly sold in marketplaces, monasteries, or other holy places throughout Armenia. People find peace and comfort in the church building even if they understand little of what the priest is chanting. People seem to faithfully follow what has been passed through generations in their search for God's protection from evil. Intellectual knowledge is only a small part of their experience in knowing God.

Since the collapse of the Soviet Union and renewed spiritual freedom and authority of the Armenian Apostolic Church, people tend to know more about God through the Bible and church traditions. Over the last twenty years the Bible has become increasingly visible and taught from all the altars of the Armenian Church. Moreover, Sunday schools and educational centers called "Hyordats Toon" have been organized to provide the necessary education and knowledge about God and his intent for all humanity. To appreciate this relevance of God throughout the Orthodox community, I turn to Harriet Hill's helpful expression to move people into God's intention for them.

APPRECIATING GOD'S PRESENCE: THE PEOPLE WORSHIP GOD

The Armenian Church experience brings a number of challenges to Hill's cognitive adjustment model (see Shaw, chapter 1). First, knowledge about God's truth and God's intentions for Armenian Christians comes from the Bible and church tradition, as well as the experience of God, which is perceived to be intimate, sacred, and mystical—knowledge that is not easily expressed or shared. Even the weekly Divine Liturgy must be studied outside of the worship it defines. In other words, an average Armenian may not cognitively understand the liturgy but is still welcomed to experience God with one's human senses.

Determining God's Intent

It is important to respond to Hill's model from the Armenian Church perspective, despite the fact that less than 1 percent participate at any given time. In Quadrant 1 would be people who actually share information and know God's truth; they are the minority within the Armenian Church. Seminarians, seminary graduates, clergymen, and lay leaders who serve in the church have been exposed to God's truth. They not only understand and recognize the importance of the rituals and ceremonies within the calendar but also share it with other Armenians as a call of duty. Making others aware of God's intention for people's lives is important to this group of religious specialists.

Quadrant 2 comprises those who actually share awareness but do not realize they know God's truth; this group represents the majority of Armenian Church attendees. While they participate in most, if not all, church rituals and ceremonies, they lack adequate biblical and theological knowledge to relate to or recognize God's truth in relation to their own spiritual experience. While they seem aware of God, they do not know God despite their participation in the Armenian Church celebrations.

Quadrant 3 includes those who do not share understanding but think they do. These people are the remaining population of Armenians who claim they are Apostolic Christians but who, in fact, do not understand what the religious expression is all about and, as a result, do not truly worship God. Despite being baptized and being Armenian, they do not realize that their ethnic, social, and cultural identities bring them into association with Christian identity. Thus, for them, being Armenian is the same as being Christian.

In Quadrant 4 are those who do not share information and agree that they don't. These Armenians used to advocate for the atheistic ideology of the former Soviet regime. The former intelligentsia, for instance, may fall in this quadrant, as well as those nominal Christians who know enough about Christianity to claim that their baptismal identity is insufficient to know the truth about God.

Worshiping God

The main worship practice that takes place in all Armenian Churches worldwide is the Divine Liturgy. This regular liturgy contains many elements of biblical worship patterns, scriptural citations, intercessory prayers, confessions, thanksgiving, and praise. Yet it is mystical as well, allowing parishioners to experience God through the Holy Spirit as they worship the Triune God, and also experience angels, saints, and deceased loved ones. For Armenians, it remains the most powerful worship practice for blessings and protection in the entire Orthodox encounter.

The Divine Liturgy of the Armenian Church commemorates and venerates saints not only from the Armenian Church tradition but also from the New Testament (St. Mary, the mother of Jesus; John the Baptist; Stephen the first martyr) as well as the universal church (e.g., St. Sarkis, Voskiank, Sukiasiank). These saints are perceived as rested souls, but not dead. They take part in the communal worship of the Divine Liturgy and thus can be communicated with through intercessory prayers. Moreover, although they are considered the glorified church, while those who are still in their physical body are part of the struggling church, an eternal unity in the body of Christ transcends time and space. Thus, according to the teaching of the Armenian Church, there should be no separation between the visible and the invisible church. When the Church of Jesus Christ is worshiping its Lord, everyone participates and is present, including the Holy Trinity, angels, and other heavenly beings. The cosmos collapses and coexists with those who worship.

Thanks to Mesrop Mashtots, the Holy Scriptures have been available to Armenians from the beginning of the fifth century. Unfortunately, the Bible has not been systematically taught to the public in Armenian churches for nearly one hundred years. Today, the Armenian Church leadership is well aware of this need and is making numerous efforts to reintroduce the truth of the gospel to their own people. The clergy—the main mediators between nominal Christian Armenians and the mysteries of God in the Armenian Church—are called not only to administer the seven sacraments of the church and officiate rituals and ceremonies but also to educate the general public with the richness of the Scriptures and church traditions. This is an enormous task. Thus, parachurch organizations such as the National Leadership Institute are engaged in practical ministries and lay leadership development (see www.clinternational.org and www.nli.am for additional information). Such movements appear to be the answer to moving Armenian Christians from Hill's Quadrants 2, 3, and 4 to Quadrant 1.

Human and divine intimacy in prayer is another characteristic of Armenian Christianity. St. Gregory of Narek reached a deep intimacy with God through his prayers that surpassed the common experiences of the Middle Ages. As a monk himself, Gregory took courage to speak to God without any other human mediator. He was able to transcend time and space and pray to God with those who went before him. Moreover, through his conversations with God, Gregory was also able to somehow reach out to those who would come after him to join in prayer that transcended his own time:

> If a pure hand lifts incense to you, may my voice join with the
> sound and sighs of prayers and reach you. (Prayer 3C, 49)
>
> If my offering of the words of my soul is pleasing,
> may they be offered to you with those who
> have gone before. (Prayer 3C, 51)
>
> If a confused heart is wounded by doubt, may these words
> make it whole through your sweetness. (Prayer 3D, 51)
>
> May you perfect what I have started and may your spirit be
> mixed with it. May the breath of your great might infuse
> these verses with grace so that you may brace the wilting
> heart and accept praise from us all. (Prayer 3E, 53)

HYBRID WORSHIP

Grigor Narekats'i was a monk who lived during the Armenian Renaissance in the tenth century. His work serves as both a prayer omnibus and a powerful worship guide. Portions of his writings are read every day within the Armenian Church as part of the Divine Liturgy. These words need to penetrate the average, nominalized Armenians and revitalize their worship as well as the way they live their lives. The church structures and Orthodox experiences holistically enable believers to experience God through all five senses, acquire knowledge of the good news of the gospel, and exercise orthopraxy through Christlike living and actions. The Eastern understanding of mystery, humility, repentance, and obedience needs to become the four cornerposts that hold the spiritual house together for every Armenian. The dynamic process of give and take with St. Gregory needs to impact every area of life: spouse, parent, worker, and friend cojourneying through human existence on earth.

Parishioners who desire to know God need to move from a notion of faith and worship to a deeper appreciation of timeless rituals and worship—a return to their Christian roots as well as a profound awareness of the implications of their faith to life. They need to reflect on Scripture and apply biblical truth to worshiping and following Christ individually and corporately. These insights will result in increased supernatural awareness to face spiritual hostility in daily life with joy and creativity. Much like Narekats'i, Armenians must find courage to speak with God daily through prayers by using their own words. Praying through the Lord's Prayer was not enough for Narekats'i. Nor should it be for any Orthodox Armenian.

French neuroscientist Michael C. Clanet proposed a theory of interculturation that requires three intrapersonal and interpersonal processes: (1) "acculturation" of values other than one's own; (2) "differentiation" through the recognition of one's own uniqueness; and (3) "synthesis," which assumes creation of a new and encompassing reality (Sam and Berry 2006, 360). Interculturation refers to the integration of a plurality of cultural references (acculturation or adaptation), which differentiates a variety of individual experiences into a synthesis of collective experience—unique specificities blended into a synthesis of common experience held together by the Eucharist. It is defined as "the set of processes by which individuals and groups interact when they identify themselves as culturally distinct" (Clanet 1990).

Interculturation, then, seems to do justice to Shaw's quest for going "beyond contextualization," while also embracing Burrows's hybridity concept by creating a new reality of worshiping and honoring God. The average parishioner's experience should be clearly affirmed on the basis of Scripture. Because their encounter with God connects biblical understanding with their life experience, it moves them toward Hill's Quadrant 1. Through their life and testimony, they bring ever greater honor to God. Thus, every sincere experience or expression of God appears to result in a God-intended worship that brings honor and glory to God (see Appendix to this chapter for Dan Hopkins's discovery of the relevance of orthodox praxis to the reality of contemporary life).

CONCLUSION

The teaching and the practice of the daily prayer in the Armenian Church were developed over hundreds of years and addressed a wide variety of individual and social needs. Although most prayers have been canonized and recited ritualistically during the daily prayer hours, they continue to provide meaning and comfort to those who participate. As priests and deacons administer daily intercessory prayers for peace in the world, the prosperity of the land, and the protection of the nation, people experience God's presence and worship God in spirit and in truth (Jn 4:23–24).

The Armenian Church tradition has gone beyond the New Testament practices of worship and developed unique approaches to what it means to honor God in its own tradition. It has integrated the Scripture with the Armenian experience but did not limit itself to first-century Christian practice. Rather, it developed further and made Christian worship relevant to the once "pagan" culture and social identity. These integrative approaches have found expression in the daily, weekly, and annual Christian rituals and ceremonies that have emerged from centuries of engagement with Armenian identity and Christian experience with God.

To some extent, Hill's cognitive adjustment model seems to be a one-sided approach to human-God interaction (see Shaw, chapter 1). This model appears to reduce worship to mere human initiatives. In the Orthodox context, however, mystery of God is taken into account in worship. Worship is perceived as both a divine and human endeavor. Without external (divine) intervention (divine revelation and God showing up), worship cannot occur. Thus, the Armenian shift from unrecognized pagan assumptions to recognition of God's intended message may not be realized through a solely human cognitive exercise. God's sovereign role in worship cannot be minimized. Worship is not only human, but it recognizes Christ's presence in the church with God's people—incarnation. This is what makes worship a reality. The average Armenian Orthodox Christian showing up in church comes with anticipation for mystical fellowship with God, knowing that it cannot be preplanned and that worship is the result of the Holy Spirit's controlled presence.

Armenian liturgical worship is built upon the historical accounts of Christ's followers through the centuries—the ancestors, if you will. Without their participation there can be no experience of Divine Liturgy. Understanding of participation should thus go both ways (Shaw): human as well as divine participation. The faithful are called to worship God in the presence of ancestors (as opposed to ancestral worship), intercede for one another, and in so doing, be united with the Triune God and with one another through the Holy Spirit, which is honorable to God.

Many pagan rituals and ceremonies were brought into the Armenian Church calendar by integrating biblical and theological meaning and interpretation to feasts already celebrated by Armenians before their Christian conversion. Moreover, despite all the efforts of the church, ordinary people continue celebrating pagan feasts and practicing pagan rituals. Even today, sacrificing a lamb or dove as an act of covenant is not uncommon in Armenia. Armenian priests bless the salt as a part of the ritual before slaughtering the animal. However, they constantly remind people that this ritual should not be associated with remission of one's sins and that the sacrifice of the Lamb of God is the only way for sins to be forgiven. As

Jesus reoriented the Jews from their religious rituals to true worship of God, contemporary Armenians need to give new meaning when worshiping in truth and spirit. Armenians must recognize that folk practices of sacrificial ceremonies are still part of a hybrid Christianity in Armenia. They have survived along with Armenian Orthodoxy since the fourth century. Thus, a hybrid approach should not assume a complete assimilation or integration. Both may coexist side by side indefinitely.

Finally, the diaspora Armenians, the survivors of the 1915 Armenian genocide who have not been affected by the militant regime of atheism in Armenia, are the new hope for contemporary Armenia. They seem to be more exposed to the Armenian orthodoxy and orthopraxy than to neopaganism in Armenia. This new generation of Armenians, who have become citizens of the world, bring new spirituality to their fellow Armenians who seek and hope for spiritual meaning and renewal in post-Soviet Armenia.

Appendix

A Modern Friendship in Ancient Armenian Orthodoxy

East by Midwest

Dan Hopkins

"Please pray one prayer a day on your knees until you finish this prayer book."

I took the little book from his hand as I looked into his smiling face. He was a slim, well-dressed man of Armenian descent, with a trim salt-and-pepper beard and dark eyes that twinkled as he spoke. He continued,

> This book that I am giving you is incredibly powerful. It was written over one thousand years ago by a great mystic who dedicated his life to intimate communion with God. His prayers were so powerful that for many generations Armenian warriors rode into battle with them under their armor and in amulets around their necks. His prayers have great healing power as well, and many have been healed through their use. His name is Saint Grigor Narakatsi (also known as Gregory of Narek) and he was a celibate monk who lived his entire life in a monastery near the city of Narek on the shore of Lake Van. He and his prayer book are so inseparable that both are known as The Narak. So, you must realize ahead of time that to pray these prayers is to open your very soul to the transformative power of the Holy Spirit. You must count the cost before you start praying these prayers. Are you willing to be profoundly changed? You will have to pay a price; it will cost you a great deal.

I had never in my life read someone else's prayers. I had only read a written prayer of my own a couple of times, and it did not sit well with me. It seemed too contrived and formal. I had a certain learned disdain for "high church people" who read prayers with their eyes open. I was definitely approaching the edge of my life experience map, but I was willing to do anything that this man told me to do. I had reached a point where I told God that I was taking just about everything I believed, all I'd been nurtured in and taught, off the table, and he would have to tell me what he wanted me to put back on. In turn, God told me to trust this man with the little book.

MISSIONARY BACKGROUND

I am a Western missionary-pastor whose eyes were opened to the socio-religious limitations of my ministry and relationship to God by embracing the rituals and ceremonies of the Armenian Orthodox Church. My life as a child of God, husband, father, teacher, pastor, and servant-leader is different now because of spiritual direction and friendship within ancient Eastern Christianity. During this transformative journey I have had two constant companions: an Armenian monk who is a revered mystic and theologian, and Dr. Petros Malakyan, who became my spiritual guide. Both of these men are my friends and teachers. From them I have learned about humility, confession, obedience, faith, and mystery, all from an Armenian Orthodox perspective. This has changed how I now pastor and disciple young people. I am not the same man I was, but I never expected that the most profound changes in my spiritual life would happen because of Orthodox Christianity.

In juxtaposition to the context that Dan Shaw has focused on, the context that Petros and I shared was reversed. Petros, an Armenian majority-world scholar, introduced Armenian Orthodox rituals and ceremonies to me, a Baptist pastor living in Indiana. I had a thoroughly Western understanding of the Christian faith. Petros, on the other hand, had an Eastern understanding of God and faith. In many ways our beliefs about God were about as far apart as the countries of our birth. After the Holy Spirit brought us together, Petros invited me to enter into his Orthodox world. He helped me reframe my understanding of God in light of my Western misunderstandings, or at least blind spots. He helped me gain new appreciation for union with God and what that actually looks like in real life.

Coincidently, Petros and I approached our mutual understanding from diametrically opposed life experiences. He was a majority-world believer who interacted with Western missionaries in Armenia. He was the son of a highly respected evangelical pastor who defied the Communists in Armenia. Following the fall of the Iron Curtain, they experienced first-hand the ministries of both good and bad Western missionaries. Petros saw the condescension of missionaries who made it clear they were there to instruct and lead, rather than to learn from others. I, in turn, was a Western missionary serving in Brazil. My wife, Cindi, and I became disillusioned with the restrictive presence and ministry of American missionaries who, as Shaw notes, imposed Western thinking that almost always reacted with rejection and replacement. In fairness, Petros and I also have lifelong friendships with Western missionaries who inspire us with their devotion to God and others.

I was born in the upcountry of South Carolina and raised in a cotton mill culture that revolved around the Baptist church. We were independent, militantly fundamentalist, sword-of-the-Lord Baptists of the strongly dissenting variety. We proclaimed, "No creed but Christ, no book but the Bible (as long as it was an Old Scofield / King James Version), and no law but love!" At best we were two for three on most days, with love falling low and away. Our understanding of church history went back about as far as the day our Beacon Baptist Church was planted in Lancaster, South Carolina. Growing up I was taught that from the cross to the present there have been Baptists, or at least "Baptistic" Christians, who spread the good news, taught dispensationalism, and kept the faith. We were neither Protestants nor Catholics and saw little difference between the two. At heart, we were dissenters who delighted in boycotting and protesting everything from Crest toothpaste to Oreo cookies. Spirituality could be measured, quantified, and graphed based upon a myriad of factors such as daily Bible reading, church attendance, souls saved, and the length of one's hair and hem of a skirt. Over the years a lot has been pruned away and grafted in by the Lord. It has taken a great deal of patience on his part (and pain on mine) to uproot legalism and cultivate grace and love.

My exodus out of legalism began when I met my wife, Cindi. During college, we were still members of a Baptist church and later, at the urging of our pastors, attended Grand Rapids Baptist Seminary. It was during the three years of seminary that there was a subtle, internal, ego-defying shift toward the acquisition of knowledge about God, the Bible, and theology. I think the quest for knowledge came from a sincere desire to know God and help others, but over time, it devolved into the necessity of having all the right answers to all the questions that might ever be asked by anyone, ever. This was great for Bible trivia, but eroded an intimate love relationship with God.

Following seminary, we became missionaries with a Baptist mission agency, and our family spent the next ten years in northeastern Brazil. My primary responsibility was teaching as a member of a church planting team. I was dismayed by the entitled attitude that many veteran missionaries exercised toward Brazilians. Instead of partners in ministry, the "nationals" were often treated as a resource to be used to the project's best advantage. In my limited experience, the worst offenders were often missionary kids who manipulated their status as insiders who had grown up in the culture speaking the language but yet outsiders who benefited from education in American Bible colleges and seminaries. So much of Western culture is performance-driven toward the holy grail of "success." Where we ministered, success in the "missionary environment" was defined by hard numbers: churches, converts, students, members, church plants, and so on. At the end of two terms, we returned home disillusioned with life and ministry.

I joined the staff of a large Baptist church in Cindi's hometown in central Indiana. We would be there for five years, and the first three years were the happiest of all my years in ministry. Historically, the church was similar to the church I grew up in, but the senior pastor was intent upon changing the "church culture." That process did not go well. In a story as old as the Israelites in the wilderness, a segment of the membership resisted all change. As our time there drew to a close, there were secret meetings, petitions, false accusations, hate mail in the offering plate, and hijacked business meetings. The senior pastor had a nervous breakdown and our entire staff resigned, along with the deacon board. The injustice of it all gnawed at me, and I was stuck for a while in a vicious cycle of bitterness and anger. However, through this process the Lord led us to a Christian and Missionary Alliance church plant in a nearby town. There we found a home to heal, regroup, and relearn. I entered into a new kind of relationship with God—one in which I listened to God more than I spoke. Prayer became more of an interactive conversation.

And as I listened, God spoke. The first thing God asked me to do was give away my library. It had taken me years to put my library together, so this was a hard ask. However, I sensed that God was telling me to come know him in a new way. I could quote chapter and verse about him, but God wanted me to know him with my heart, not just my intellect. He wanted an intimate, love relationship with me. Over time, I came to want that, too. God began to lovingly show me the areas of my life he wanted to change—things like pride, unforgiveness, and bitterness. It was both awful and wonderful. I began to cooperate and entered into the painful, but necessary, process of being dead to Dan Hopkins and alive to Christ (Gal 2:20).

ENTERING SPIRITUAL DIRECTION

One of the podcasts I had started listening to was by Frederica Matthews-Greene, a Greek Orthodox author and speaker. This new world made me a little nervous because it seemed so different from everything I had known. At the same time, my best friend, who had been the administrative pastor at the church we all left, was now going to another church in the area. He and his wife were in a small group, and he kept telling me about this guy who was Orthodox. One of my coworkers at Indiana Wesleyan University was taking a class at the same time, and she kept telling me about her professor and how much she admired and respected him. She said that he was from the Orthodox Church, and I realized that it was the same guy my friend mentioned. At this point I had been praying and listening more, and then trying to do whatever God told me. He kept bringing up this guy's name in our talks. I asked God what he was trying to tell me. This went on for some time, until one day God told me that he wanted me to go to see this professor and ask him if he would be my spiritual guide. I asked God several times to retransmit. It sounded crazy.

I was ready to have a conversation, but spiritual direction? I understood enough to know that this was serious, and I was pretty sure that I was supposed to be invited by the director, not me seeking him out. I wrestled with this for a while, until I submitted and told God I would obey. The next day my feet dragged as I approached Dr. Malakyan's office. I thought, This guy is going to think I'm crazy. What in the world is he going to think when he opens the door and there's this big guy with wild hair and a beard saying that he has a message from the Lord? My mouth was bone dry as I hesitatingly knocked on his door. He opened the door, and at first I just stood there speechless. He smiled and with a quizzical expression asked if he could help me. All in one breath I said, "Hi! My name is Dan Hopkins and you don't know me but I believe that God told me to come here and ask you if you'd be willing to be my spiritual director." His smile broadened, and without saying a word he opened his arms, stepped forward, and embraced me. He said that he would be honored to serve God in this way. We talked for a few minutes, then set up a time to meet the following week. During that meeting Petros offered me the Narak with the warning that it would change my life.

Yes indeed, spiritual direction with Petros changed my life, even as reading St. Grigor Narakatsi's prayer book on a daily basis gave me a new perspective on things spiritual. I learned that Petros never seeks out or chooses disciples. He waits for the Lord to send them to him, then he knows with certainty that God is leading him to invest in someone. That is why my sudden appearance and word from the Lord did not surprise him in the least. He opened up whole new worlds to me: servant leadership, spiritual direction, ancient Christianity, Armenian history, listening prayer, meditation, and the necessity of humility and a teachable spirit. I submitted myself to him in all things.

THE "PRAYERS" OF THE "SAINTS"

Reading a book is a singular act of faith and hope. I began with the expectation that something would resonate and that transformation in heart and mind, or at the very least worthwhile reading, would be the result. A few books (few in relation to the millions that have been written since pictographs were scratched on the wall of a cave) have the power to inspire and move the reader to tears. The Narek is such a book. It unites the triumvirate of faith, hope, and love. In the last one thousand years, millions of people have taken up this little book by faith, hoping that it would bring healing, encouragement, strength, and direction. In that process, love, the greatest of the three graces, reassured them that their faith and hope were well placed. Readers received assurance that whatever dreadful circumstances befall them, from losing a child to national genocide, they would never face suffering alone. The Narek, though small, is a book of great import and power; it is spiritually "heavy." Petros was right; one cannot pray these prayers and remain unchanged. St. Grigor is a guide on the road to spiritual transformation, and his prayer book is like a map drawn with tears, blood, and the sighs of many hearts.

One of the fundamental issues in learning about and adapting to another culture is dealing with the fear of change that border crossings entail. Worship, because it is so highly relational, is especially fertile ground for fear and resistance to change. As Shaw points out, people worship God through the rituals and ceremonies that reflect what they already know and understand from their own cultural as well as spiritual experience. Efforts to change those rituals and ceremonies most often create fear and resistance. Words like "syncretism" and "pluralism" become labels, then battle cries, for the faithful to control their membership. Clearly, fear cannot stand in the presence of the Holy Spirit and should be equally denied a place in the life of believers. Rituals and ceremonies are like an engraved invitation from the Trinity for deeper intimacy. If you really want to nurture a deep, abiding friendship with someone, you need to spend time together talking, sharing, laughing, and crying. It's the difference between talking with someone on the telephone or sitting down in their kitchen face-to-face. For me, fearing the possible changes that would occur, the Narek became a kitchen conversation between the Trinity, Grigor, and me, enhanced by my interaction with Petros. Without question, change was the result.

In most mainline denominations within the Western church, an impenetrable wall exists along the border between the natural and the supernatural. Paul Hiebert calls it the "excluded middle"—maintaining a separation between them. It is common to hear, "One day I'll sit down with the apostle Paul for a thousand years. . . ." Other than the direct line to God, the rest of heaven apparently remains in a permanent blackout. Eastern Christianity, on the other hand, understands the veil of separation between the natural and the supernatural to be gossamer thin. Time, in the ancient Near East, is always in the present. Grigor and the saints who have gone before suffer no time constraints. He is contemporary with me; he is modern. The glorified church in heaven continues to learn and be creative as it worships and talks with God. We are as connected to people in heaven as we are to one another and to God. To think that the only intercessory resources available are contemporary is spiritual naivety, which is doubly ironic considering our Western penchant for maximizing resources in every situation. So while I do not worship the saints in heaven, I do venerate them as followers of the Way, those who fought the good fight and made it to my future home. Our brothers and sisters in heaven are our "great cloud of witnesses" (Heb 12:1) to whom we have access. Asking Grigor to pray for me is no different than asking my friend Grant to pray for me. In fact, from his vantage point, Grigor is in a much better position to intercede on my behalf. I'm not asking him to mediate with God for me; rather I believe that Grigor's prayers for me are special because he is reigning with Christ and is even more devoted to God's cause now than when he was praying for the saints past, present, and future in the monastery at Narek in AD 980. I want, I need, praying for me a person who understands prayer, breathes prayer, and is prayer.

I am a hybrid. I now have a Western foundation with an Eastern framework. Like Shaw and Burrows, I am driven by the question, what honors God? If it honors God, it is good, period. Allowing rituals and ceremonies to be redeemed and religious experience to be restored requires humility and a teachable spirit. The missionary must embrace the role of follower as readily as the role of leader. Like Peter on the Mount of Transfiguration, we must stop talking and listen, stop making judgments, stop imposing, and stop controlling. Humility, like the honeybee, is an effective pollinating agent that enables missionaries to recognize God's intent and to embrace anything that deepens their relationship with God. I have learned that not everything that is missing is lost. I was given rituals and ceremonies that were missing in my faith tradition but were never lost in Christendom.

I am a learner. I am learning . . .

- How to worship God through rituals and ceremonies that my Orthodox brothers and sisters share with me.
- About the beauty of mystery in prayer and worship, the power of the Divine Liturgy, and the sacraments.
- Who the Holy Spirit is through words of knowledge, dreams, healing, and prophecy in the history and tradition of the Armenian Orthodox Church.
- To live a God-saturated life in union with Jesus Christ. The sacramentalism of historic Christianity is extremely Christocentric, enabling me to make sure that Jesus is the focus and that he is in focus.
- How to talk with God face-to-face.

We are all trying to find what the Greek philosopher Archimedes called "a lever and a place to stand," so that we can move our world just a bit closer to God. Grigor's little prayer book became my lever. Grigor reached across one thousand years of human history to communicate in a language he never spoke, to help a man he never met, who lived in a country that did not exist when he wrote his prayer book. Initially the prayers were his; then they became his prayers for me. Then, through daily use, they became my prayers. Now these prayers have become, more and more, our prayers, mine and Grigor's—representations of faith, hope, and love (1 Cor 13).

"Please pray one prayer a day on your knees until you finish this prayer book."

I followed Petros's instructions; I did it and have been immeasurably blessed. Blending ancient orthodoxy with the reality of twenty-first-century living has changed my life. May God be praised.

Part Two
Christian Worship

All the authors in part two note how Christianity is more than an artificial, imposed religion. Rather they portray the Christian life as expressions of recognizing God's presence among them. Their people, in turn, give honor to God in meaningful Christian worship that incorporates elements from traditional rituals. As in part one, these chapters loosely divide into a strong emphasis on relevant worship per se, or on the context in which worship demonstrates relevance.

WITH FOCUS ON WORSHIP

In chapters 9 through 11, the authors focus on the nature of worship that draws from pre-Christian spirituality. In chapter 9, Chinaka DomNwachukwu shows how, despite long missionary influence, the authenticity of Igbo worship builds on Igbo cosmology to bring a renewed appreciation of spiritual and social authority. Billy Nishioka's Japanese case study of the "bone-ash" church in chapter 10 demonstrates the need for empathy with the living in order to establish a memory of the deceased that demonstrates Christian relevance in a context where less than 1 percent of the population is Christian. In chapter 11 Stuart Dauermann closes this section of the book with a focus on Jewish family worship. By highlighting the need for rabbinic-style praise and honor of Yahweh, he draws attention to Yeshua as the Messiah.

WITH FOCUS ON CONTEXT

In chapters 12 through 14 context shapes the nature of worship and gives meaning to its manifestations. Thus, in chapter 12 Cheryl Bear demonstrates how, regardless of the many expressions of the smudge ceremony, cleansing is the focus among Indigenous North Americans who seek to develop expressions of their faith that will, in the words of Richard Twiss, "rescue the gospel from the cowboys" (2015). In chapter 13 Joshua Daimoi's exegesis of the Epistle to the Hebrews demonstrates the importance of understanding the richness of Hebrew as well as Sentani cultural metaphors. Both societies value the role of ancestors and provide a history to appreciate Jesus as the Great Ancestor. Finally, in chapter 14 the late John Sanjeevakumar Gupta shows how Indian and Hebrew traditions can be traced to similar contextual roots. Connecting those traditions to contemporary village religiosity draws attention to the role of deity meeting ordinary people.

Christian worship, then, draws its strength from the rituals and ceremonies that anticipate worship forms that honor God in all God's glory. It reflects local expressions while recognizing the larger picture of God's infinity, majesty, and grace. Indigenous expressions provide the sense-making enablement humans need to exercise faith in the one who entered our realm so that we might reengage with God's intent for all human beings, avoid syncretism, and celebrate hybridity.

With Focus on Worship

9

Indigenous Igbo Worship in Nigerian Churches

Reconfiguration of Worship and Spiritual Encounters

Chinaka S. DomNwachukwu

In the theological literature of the West, worship patterns that have differed from the traditionally known Western experiences found in the liturgical Catholic and Episcopal churches, or the free worship found within the evangelical traditions, are regarded as alternative worship. Thomas Schattauer (2011) distinguished between traditional or what he called "conventional" worship and "alternative" worship. These designations assume that worship experiences found within the traditional European and American churches should be regarded as "conventional," while those worship practices and experiences of Christian bodies outside of these traditions would fit into the "alternative."

Schattauer sees alternative worship as standing in opposition to conventional worship and "ultimately to conventional ways of being Christian" (2011). In 1972 Juan Mateos argued that the practice of Christian worship should not be seen exclusively as a set of historical and institutional conventions, but rather must be seen in relation to the communication of God's life to the world in Christ. Mateos saw the need for a "constructive reimagining of the Christian assembly and its purpose in present circumstances" (Schattauer 2011, 144).

Traditional worship among my people in the Igbo society of southeastern Nigeria was a dynamic interaction between humans and the Supreme Being. Humans responded to God's revelation of himself through prayers, songs of worship, and the totality of their earthly being. In this chapter I focus on worship among the Indigenous Igbo churches of Nigeria. I begin with a look at the worship and rituals of the African traditional religions that predated the inroads of Western Christianity to this part of Nigeria. I further examine the forms of worship and rituals that came with the inroads of Christianity, the history and development of the Indigenous Igbo churches, and the worship experiences that have emerged from them. I conclude with a review of how worship in the Western evangelical churches of the Igbos has been influenced by new worship experiences that have emerged from among our Indigenous Igbo churches, and the prospect it holds for authentic Christianity among the Igbos.

In this chapter I make the argument that worship in Indigenous Igbo churches should not be seen as alternative worship; rather it must be seen as truly conventional from the perspective of my people. We Igbos should be allowed to experience God in our own ways and through our own cultural forms and practices.

IGBO RELIGIOUS EXPERIENCE AND THE WORSHIP OF CHUKWU

The Igbo cosmology is dominated by the supremacy of Chukwu (God the Creator). We know God as a personal being, the source of all forms of existence. Whereas the Western mindset questions the existence of God and scrambles to explain the origin of the universe, the Igbo mind does not dwell on those exigencies. The person of the Supreme God and his creative abilities in bringing the universe into being are givens for us, hence the common name among our people, Chukwukere (God created). My name, Chinaka, which can also be rendered Chukwunaka, is a declarative. In naming a son "Chinaka," my parents were making a declaration that Chukwu (or Chineke) is the one who shapes or determines their destiny. Simply put, they were yielding to God's will for their lives.

Igbo Cosmology

The Igbo cosmology comprises complex interactions between the forces of nature, human personalities, and the spiritual forces of good and evil that together affect human quality of life and life after death. Vincent Mulago outlined four essential elements of the African religious worldview as follows: belief in two worlds, visible and invisible; belief that both worlds involve community and hierarchy; belief in the intersection of the two worlds (the transcendence of the invisible world in no way contradicts its immanence); and belief in a Supreme Being, Creator, and Father of all that exists (1991, 119).

All these elements are reflective of our Igbo view of the world; the visible and the invisible intersect in a seamless precision. The transcendence and the immanence do not cancel out each other; rather they exist in a symbiotic unison. The visible and the invisible coexist in a constant cycle of harmonization made possible through prayers, sacrifices, and appeasements.

As depicted in Figure 9-1, the complex interactions between humans and the Almighty Chukwu reflect a vertical, hierarchical relationship. Humans are unable to influence or manipulate Chukwu to the degree they are able to influence ancestors, the divinities, and the spirit forces. Worship, then, is at the heart of our Igbo interaction with Chukwu, while veneration is at the heart of our interactions with ancestors and other spirit beings. This approach is apparent in rituals and sacrifices that show respect, reliance upon beings for favors, appeasement, and cordial relationship in order to continue a cycle of interaction between the living and the living dead.

Figure 9-1: Igbo Cosmology

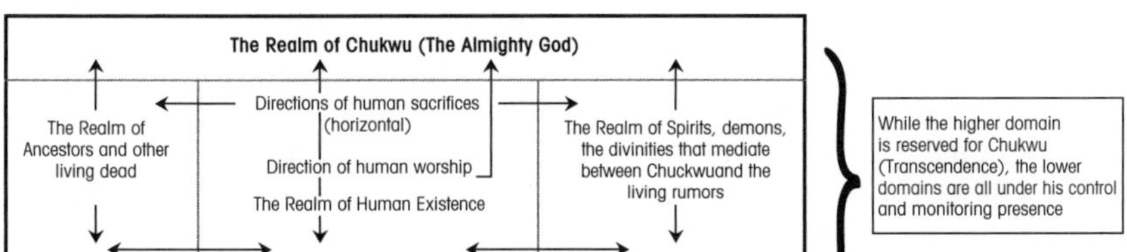

According to John Mbiti (1975a), worship in the African experience is a means by which living humans link the spiritual and the physical worlds, creating a bridge between the two. In our Igbo cosmology, through the bridge with the spirits and divinities, we have a complex relationship that includes but is not limited to fear, appeasement, manipulation for personal and/or communal good (through sacrifices), and resentment. Among my people, it is common to resent certain deities and avoid interaction with them unless forced to do so by illness or other life-threatening circumstances. I must, therefore, make clear that while the Igbo cosmology is replete with a web of interactions between the worlds of human existence, the ancestors, and the spirits, our interaction with Chukwu is an exclusively worshipful interaction, which may take the form of petition, prayer, supplication, or an oral invocation of God's name into life's situations.

Worship and Rituals of Traditional Igbo Religion

Multiple channels of interaction exist between Chukwu and humans, and each one of those channels is a means for worship and spiritual engagement with God and his messengers, the divinities. Worship takes various forms among the Igbos.

Worship

"Worship" can be defined as human beings responding to God's revelation of himself. Worship could happen as a result of observance of regular rituals or celebrations of rites of passage: birth, initiation, death, burial, and other life situations such as acquisition of new titles. Each life experience prompts an occasion for worship (Hillary 1995, 290). My people regard obedience to the moral and legal codes of the community as one of the primary vehicles for showing reverence to Chukwu and the divinities (Ilogu 1974, 39). A person who violates social norms and legal codes is seen as irreverent to God, the land, the divinities, and the community. So worship is not necessarily what we say to Chukwu as much as what we do in response to God's self-revelation. The way we live our lives in society is the outermost display of our worship of God. We Igbos take special notice of a man or woman who fears God, saying, "*Onye a n'atu egwu Chukwu*" (This person fears God). That's the best of compliments anyone can receive from an Igbo.

While traditional Igbo societies were replete with public and private shrines, collective worship was not a common Igbo experience. There were very few occasions for public communal worship. However, in response to disasters or misfortune, the community would gather to make collective sacrifices. Occasions for communal worship would arise from a positive spiritual encounter, when the elders of the land would gather to make a collective sacrifice. Families often congregate at the family shrine when sacrifices are made for the birth of a new child, appeasement of the deity, initiation into manhood, new yam celebration, or any other occasion that calls for it (Ilogu 1974, 49–50). These forms of worship would fit into Robert McCauley and Thomas Lawson's Type 2 rituals, which they called "sensory pageantry" (2002, 51). All in all, the daily act of worship was more personal than communal in Igbo society.

Sacrifice

Sacrifice is another pronounced form of worship to God among my people. While in the traditional societies we did not make sacrifices directly to Chukwu, the sacrifices made to the deities were believed to ascend ultimately to God, for those deities were simply God's messengers here on earth. In Igbo cosmology most of the deities of Igbo traditional religion are regarded as God's messengers. While some were prone to evil and mayhem, they and those who bless and prosper us are both seen as emissaries of Chukwu, charged with different roles. This perspective does not provide much accommodation for dualism, since even Ekwensu (Satan) was seen as Chukwu's messenger.

Our Igbo traditional religion was essentially shrouded in a variety of sacrifices almost the same as seen in the Old Testament Levitical sacrificial system. There were sacrifices of expiation (to regain favor from the higher divinities), petition (to obtain favors from the divinities), thanksgiving (to express gratitude for favors received), and sacrifices to ward off evil (Arinze 1970, 34–44).

Reconciliation

For the Igbo the concept of reconciliation is known as Oriko. Damien Onwuegbuchulam (2008) introduces a very powerful traditional Igbo practice, which he competently links to the Christian practice of Holy Communion. In Oriko, we believe that reconciliation and reinstatement take place. People who were otherwise in enmity are brought back into fellowship with one another. Oriko normally takes place between humans and does not involve animal sacrifice. Rather, a simple use of *nzu* (clay chalk) and *odo* (medicinal gold dust), sometimes mixed with other medicinal herbs, serves to bring people together and resembles the Christian concept of forgiveness and restoration. Onwegbuchulam suggests that this practice can precede participation in Holy Communion—reconciling relationships with God and other people as recommended in Scripture.

Prayer and the Role of the Ofo Staff

T. Adeyemo states that prayer is "the commonest act of worship" in African traditional religion (1979, 35). Laurenti Magesa describes prayer in Africa as "comprehensive, requesting the removal of all that is bad and antilife in society, and demanding restoration of all that is good . . . African prayer acknowledges the mutual interdependence of the visible and invisible worlds" (1997, 195–96). According to Magesa, prayer emphasizes the dependence of the living on Chukwu and the ancestors; it assigns the source of order and harmony in life to a power or powers greater than human beings (1997, 196). The forms taken by these daily acts of worship vary, but one uniform and consistent form is the daily morning prayer, which men and women both do.

In a typical Igbo family, the holder of the *ofo* staff (which is usually the family head) would lead the family in morning prayer. While he does not call the members of the family together, every family member—male and female, young and old—sits up in their huts to listen as he loudly leads the morning round of prayers. He would typically start with washing hands, face, and mouth, for you do not speak to men or the gods with a dirty mouth; neither should you shake hands with anyone in the morning without first washing them. Following the cleansing, he picks up the ofo staff and sits at the entrance of his *obi* (parlor), speaking at the top of his voice. He may choose to break a piece of kola nut and throw it out to the deities (Arinze 1970, 24–26).

Holding a cup of palm wine, the household head calls on God the creator, then greets the ancestors, the family deities, and the gods of the land. The hierarchy is acknowledged in the fact that Chukwu is always the first to be called. He offers thanks for life and the wherewithal for life. He gives thanks for the health and well-being of family members. He confesses to his sense of justice in relation to others, making defense against all who would wish him and his family ill. He hurls curses on his enemies, pleading the power of the spoken word in protecting himself and family and taking offense on any enemy. Then he makes petitions for his family for the day and the future. He concludes his prayer by pouring a libation of wine and hitting the ofo staff on the ground. Chinua Achebe presents a detailed prayer by a chief priest, Ezeulu:

> Ezeulu took the Ofo staff from the others and sat in front of the shrine. . . . He held one end of the shorter staff in his right hand and with the other end hit the earth to punctuate his prayer: Ulu [local deity], I thank you for making me see another new moon. May I see it again and again. This household may it be healthy and prosperous. As this is the moon of planting may the six–villages plant for profit. May we escape danger in the farm, the bite of a snake or the sting of the scorpion, the mighty one of the scrubland. May we not cut our shinbone with the machete or the hoe. And let our wives bear male children. May we increase in numbers at the next counting of the villages so that we shall sacrifice you a cow, not a chicken as we did after the last New Yam feast. May children put their fathers into the earth and not fathers their children. May good meet the face of every man and every woman. Let it come to the land of the riverain folks and to the land of the forest peoples. (1964, 6)

Throughout this lengthy process, he is likely hitting the ofo staff on the ground at intervals to affirm his prayer. His family members sitting in their huts would at intervals affirm his words with loud “Amens.”

In our Igbo traditional worship, sacred objects played a prominent role. The primary object is the ofo staff, held by the family/clan head. The ofo staff is the family or clan insignia, handed down from generation to generation. The ofo can be carved into any form the family or clan chooses to make it. It could be an animal, a human, or a neutral form. It is usually small and easily held, like a cane.

Ofo staffs are never carved in any specific form with any particular markings; rather they are carved however the user chooses to fashion them. They are made to be stuck into a man’s carrying bag, to be pulled out when needed in a village gathering for collective worship or oath-taking. These staffs must be made from the ofo plant (called *abusi* in some areas). Once carved, it stays in the family, passed from generation to generation.

While we can claim that we do not worship any inanimate or animate object apart from Chukwu, our traditional cosmology encouraged reverence of sacred trees, clay objects, wood and stone carvings, and sacred animals dedicated to the deities. We Igbos strongly believe that the spirit of the deities resides in these objects. Our veneration, then, is meant for the spirits inhabiting those objects. Other objects that feature prominently in Igbo worship include small petri dishes used for presenting food to the spirits, sacred water, the kola nut used as a fellowship meal with the gods, salt, nzu (clay chalk), odo (medicinal gold powder), egg, and day-old chicks.

IMPORTED CHRISTIAN WORSHIP PATTERNS

Probably the best way to explain the worship patterns of the Western churches that came to Igboland is to examine the theological views of those who came. Roman Catholic and Protestant theologies have had significant impact in shaping the nature of Christianity among the Igbo. The early missionary gospel, although confrontational in its encounter with our Igbo understanding of spirituality and cultural patterns, often did very little to address the deep spiritual and social crises of my people, consequently proving incapable of transforming many lives. As Dan Shaw points out in chapter 1, the Christian gospel confronted Igbos with a demand to an uncompromising separation from the past in order to connect with the future. My fellow Igboman, Chinua Achebe, noted this when he cited the story of Okonkwo's son, Nwoye, who made the fateful decision to leave family and join the church. He wrote, "Mr. Kiaga's joy was very great. Blessed is he who forsakes his father and his mother for my sake. Those that hear my words are my father and mother" (Achebe 1959, 108).

Many of my people embraced the call of the gospel, not necessarily because they fully appreciated the new spirituality, but because it was their passport to a better economic and social future. Salvation in this context meant disconnecting with the past to embrace the new and the future. This disconnect with the past called for a worship pattern that significantly departed from the authentic Igbo experience. Within the two major branches of Christianity that dominated Igboland, worship took a new form, though not entirely detached from the Igbo cultural experience.

The church promoted corporate and private worship. Whereas the church building provided the context for corporate worship, private family worship was encouraged among the Protestant groups in the form of morning family prayers with songs and Scripture reading, and personal prayer of the rosary by Roman Catholic adherents. Sadly, no connection was made between Christian manners of prayer and the older traditional prayers. In addition, African drums, flutes, and other musical instruments were replaced with organs. The Roman Catholic Church, more than the Protestants, replaced the ancestors and local divinities with devotion to saints, who were depicted as intermediaries between God and human beings. Worship took the formal structure of European practices without much understanding of its meaning. While Onwuegbuchulam (2008) has attempted to relate the sacrament of Holy Communion in the Catholic Church to Oriko, the Igbo covenant of reconciliation, such connections are far removed from the Igbo understanding of the sacrament, especially given the Roman Catholic belief in transubstantiation. The result was that the average Igbo Christian observed rituals and went through worship experiences that meant little to them. Instead, given the fact that the church was the primary vehicle for upward mobility in the new Igbo world of colonialism, mission schools and hospitals offered my people incentives to convert to Christianity and enjoy the benefits it offered.

Richard Niebuhr captured the crises of Western mission in Africa. He outlined five streams of thought on the relationship between Christ and culture. His first position (and the only one I focus on here) presents Christ as opposed to culture, which very well captured the Igbo Christian dilemma. This position sees culture as evil and something from which Christians must separate themselves (Niebuhr 1951, 40). This approach to conversion of people and their culture is the thrust of the missionary gospel that came to Igboland. The host culture was seen as evil and irredeemable, so the focus was not just a transformation of individual lives, but a cultural transformation. This emphasis on transformation missed the opportunity to learn the ways of my people and present to them a Christianity that could become incarnate among them. In chapter 1, Shaw laments the fact that a contrast of worldviews led Western missionaries to consider the many practices people used to interact with and manipulate spiritual power as incompatible with Christianity. In so doing they banned many meaningful religious practices that the people could use to connect with the God of the Bible. They were left with an impotent faith that fails to address everyday challenges in a meaningful way.

A significant inference, therefore, is that Western missionaries, who came with a "conversionist" version of gospel interpretation, stepped into non-Western cultures of Africa bearing the conviction that a close affinity existed between Christianity and the West. They preached a mixture of the Christian gospel and superior Western culture and thought they had a mandate to transform "heathens" into "civilized Christians." A fundamental flaw of this approach is that the very missionaries who could not separate their Western cultures from the gospel saw no need to allow the gospel to merge with African cultures. Indeed, they made deliberate attempts to keep the two separate, thereby creating a major spiritual disconnect between Africans and Christianity. African Christians have struggled ever since to bridge this gap for our many African brothers and sisters who have not believed.

EMERGENCE OF AFRICAN INDIGENOUS CHRISTIANITY

Unwittingly, Western missionaries were setting up a situation in which the only way Africans could truly enjoy worship was to seek to worship

Chukwu as seen through their own cultural lenses. In retrospect, as Burrows points out in chapter 2, the cross-cultural translation and transmission of Christian faith produces a hybrid. According to him, hybridity is fundamental to the process whereby peoples who accept the gospel of Jesus Christ express and understand their faith in a new way. The faith of the first-century Jewish and Gentile Christians cannot be the same as the faith of the twenty-first-century Igbos of southeastern Nigeria. Each society must accept biblical faith and interpret it to suit their spiritual awareness within specific African cultural contexts. This is what Burrows, in my perspective, refers to as "hybridity," the very thing the missionary gospel prevented Igbo Christianity from attaining. Similar to what was happening in many other parts of Africa, the result of this refusal to allow for cultural fusion with the Christian gospel was, for my people, to break away from the missionary churches and establish Igbo Christian churches that would suit our own cultural need: hence the emergence of Indigenous Igbo churches.

Benetta Jules-Rosette (1991) outlines certain factors that led to the emergence of Indigenous churches in Africa:

- The disappointment of local converts with the premises and outcomes of Christianity.
- The translation of the Bible into local African vernaculars, which stimulated a reinterpretation of Scriptures from African perspectives.
- The divisions in denominational Christianity and its failure to meet local needs.
- The impotence of Western spirituality in the face of personal problems, psychological disorders, epidemics, and natural disasters.
- The failure of mission Christianity to break down social and cultural barriers and generate a sense of community.

While the major Indigenous churches of western Nigeria, such as the Christ Apostolic Church, Cherubim and Seraphim, Church of the Lord Aladura, Celestial Church of Christ, Evangelical Church of Yahweh, and many others arose in the 1920s and 1930s (Adogame 2004), their inroads into Igboland were not significant until the 1950s and 1960s. The end of the Nigerian civil war in 1970 saw a new wave of revival that swept through Nigeria, especially southeastern Nigeria, through the combined forces of the Scripture Union and the Pentecostal revival. These movements gave rise to more authentic Indigenous Igbo churches. These charismatic Indigenous churches are increasingly significant among the Igbos today, and their worship patterns reflect a true incarnation of the gospel among my people. On the other hand, many people remained loyal to Western Christian forms and practices.

Worship in Indigenous Igbo Churches

Worship in Indigenous Igbo churches could be described as a protest against Western impositions. They served as a claim to freedom from the chains of the spiritual impotency that resulted from patterns imposed by outsiders. It is also a celebration of personal and cultural affirmation in the presence of the Supreme Chukwu, the source of all life. African drums found their way into the Christian church. Igbo music took on Christian lyrics, and such instruments as *ogwe* (Igbo drums), *udu* (clay pot), *ekwe* (wooden gong), *ogele* (metal gong), and many others became credible instruments used in worship. Igbo music found its way into the church. In Indigenous Igbo churches, Igbo worship objects met Western styles of worship, and a new hybridity emerged, one that departs significantly from Western worship patterns.

Physical Objects in the Concretization of Worship

The emotional and expressive forms are likely among the strongest features of contemporary Indigenous Igbo worship patterns. The use of physical objects—candles, crosses, anointing oil, holy water, hand bells, and the like—are still prominent in the Indigenous Igbo churches, with roots in the Yoruba Aladura movement. C. G. Oosthuizen wrote about the significance of symbols and icons in what he called Afro-Christian religions. Accordingly, "Iconography of the Afro-Christian religions was not born in the context of the growth of African art, but in the context of African traditional and Christian religious expression" (Oosthuizen 1979, 4). Whereas Oosthuizen saw these symbols as indebted to motifs common to Christianity, E. Bolaji Idowu (1973), a Nigerian scholar, wrote about traditional symbols and liturgy in African traditional religions that predate Christianity. Their significance and efficacy underlie the many "Christian" symbols and liturgies found in African Indigenous churches today. Oosthuizen's study focused on the Zionist movements that span East, Central, and Southern territories of Africa, yet the symbols he addressed have parallels to those used in the Indigenous Igbo churches as well, where the symbols and liturgies are vast and varied. I discuss only a limited number of these to illustrate my point.

Candles

In services of deliverance in the Indigenous Igbo churches, candles serve as salvific instruments of light to illuminate the worship environment and symbolize the illuminating presence of the Holy Spirit coming into a life that is held in bondage by demonic powers. Candlelight creates an air of divine presence. This symbol is most prevalent among the Indigenous Igbo churches with Aladura roots. Indigenous Igbo churches believe that light is able to expel the demonic forces and reduce them to submission. The use of candles in Indigenous Igbo churches has biblical parallels in Exodus 25:31–35 and Matthew 5:15. Darkness represents the works of the enemy; light dispels darkness and brings agents of darkness under submission (Oosthuizen 1979, 18).

The Cross

A second significant physical object is the cross, an important object of healing and deliverance. The cross of Jesus is the object that stands for our redemption and physical healing. The cross is a point of meeting with the redemptive power of Jesus Christ. In the Indigenous Igbo churches it is believed that physical contact with a cross is able to effect healing. Many Igbo also believe that in the process of deliverance, the cross, as a symbol of the victory of Christ over Satan and all demonic forces, repels evil spirits and clears the way to a successful deliverance. The cross, therefore, is a salvific instrument even today. Unlike the Protestant theology that sees the cross as symbolic, Igbo church members see the physical cross as efficacious, almost as in the traditions of Roman Catholicism (Oosthuizen 1979, 16). Crosses are often planted at the entrance of Igbo homes and hung on walls inside homes.

Water

Another significant object in the deliverance programs of many Indigenous Igbo churches is water. Natural water is believed to be a powerful instrument for cleansing and is often used to symbolically cleanse the sinner and restore the fallen, bringing them back in relationship with Chukwu and his people. Research on the use of water in Indigenous Igbo churches reveals that different sources of water are used. Tap water, believed to be contaminated with chemicals, is rarely used. According to Oosthuizen, seawater is considered to be extra powerful, so powerful that leaders and members often travel hundreds of kilometers to fetch it for its "potential holiness" and perceived curative power (1979, 10).

Water from various sources may be combined to formulate special "holy water." Adding salt into water, then praying over it to purify and make it holy, is also a common practice. Holy water is consequently used for healing and seen as a life-giving source. Water has a very important place in the whole of the salvation program, which is initiated at the cross, and has been made a continuous expression of the church in the ongoing events of deliverance and restoration. Pentecostal Indigenous Igbo churches emphasize water baptism by immersion, in keeping with their interpretation of New Testament teachings. Today's use of candles, holy water, and the cross as worship objects connects very well with the Roman Catholic symbolisms that were the first expression of Christian faith to enter Igboland.

Oil

Yet another important object in the life of the saved community is oil. In the Old Testament, oil was used for anointing and consecration, so the Indigenous Igbo churches consider it an essential ingredient of healing and protection. Oil is used in spiritual as well as physical healings. The anointing of the sick with holy oil effects healing. It also has the power to break satanic bondage in a person's life, thus opening the door for spiritual salvation and physical deliverance (see Jas 5:14–16).

Just as the traditional Igbo worshiper would manifest a sense of justice in regard to others while praying and defend against all who would wish the family ill—hurling curses on enemies and pleading the power of the spoken word to protect the entire family—the contemporary Indigenous Igbo churches have Christianized this practice. Christians commonly use the power of the spoken word to assault those who would do them harm.

WORSHIP AND AFRICAN CULTURAL HERMENEUTICS

Many Indigenous Igbo churches refer to the Bible to warrant their theological positions. This tendency, while in sync with biblical theology and traditional standards for Christian orthodoxy, is also rooted in Western missionary theological discourse that did not see our culture as compatible with the gospel. Igbo worshipers, however, relate to these theological interpretations because we see direct connections between the biblical world and our own. This makes the ostensibly Western hermeneutic palatable and more pragmatic for us. Despite the sad truth that the gospel came to us through a missionary cultural straitjacket, Igbo Christians are now bringing worship into our own place, time, dress, artifacts, and music to convey our passion for the supremacy of Chukwu.

The Supreme Being, as recognized in Chukwu, is no stranger to our land; nor did missionaries bring God to us. To suppose that they did is to invalidate what Paul wrote in Romans 1:20: "For since the creation of the world God's invisible qualities—his eternal power and divine nature—have been clearly seen, being understood from what has been made, so that men are without excuse." This biblical passage underlies Joseph Enuwosa's claim that "the God-king, redeemer, Savior-creator of the New Testament Christology . . . existed in Africa long before the coming of Jesus" (2005, 86). The concept of God as supreme creator of the universe is central in Igbo cosmology; Chukwu is lord over the universe, and the universe is God's creation. About these cardinal principles we entertain no doubts. That said, contemporary Igbo Christianity has yet to recapture certain essential aspects of Igbo traditional style that could enrich our worship today. Some of these elements include:

- Access to the supernatural or the mystical dimension of life.
- The idea of sacrifice as an essential aspect of human interactions with supernatural presence.
- The ofo staff as a typology of family, spiritual seal, insignia, or even the Bible.

I briefly explore how these expressions can become effective avenues for Igbo Christians to see God, overcome Satan and his attacks, and engage in more enriching spiritual encounters with God and his Son Jesus, through the power of the Holy Spirit.

Access to the Supernatural and the Mystical

The argument can be made that our Igbo world is at a crossroads, at the intersection of natural and supernatural, secular and sacred, human and spiritual—in a state of hybridity. Igbo cosmology is a sphere of endless interaction between the spirit world, the ancestral world, and the world of living humans. Given such a perspective, traditional Igbos depended on access to supernatural and mystical powers to hold their ground amid the realm of nonhuman influences. Traditionally for the Igbo, the spiritual world was as real as one's arm, which remains true today. The Igbo know without a doubt that survival in the world of the living depends on meaningful access to the resources of the supernatural world. They have no excluded middle, as Hiebert's model makes clear for my people. By means of prayers to God, sacrifices, and offerings to ancestors, spirits, and divinities, human beings reached for supernatural strength to overcome illness, spiritual and physical enemy attacks, and the negative influence of demons and wandering spirits (Magesa 1997, 195). Spiritual encounters were not limited to certain initiates and titled men. Rather they were common phenomenon of the Igbo world, which Western Christianity hopes has been dispelled by the power of the Western gospel. On the contrary, these encounters have and will continue to persist.

In *Arrow of God*, Chinua Achebe painted a picture of such a supernatural encounter between Obika, a young son of Ezeulu, and the divinity Eru, described by Ezeulu as "the magnificent, the one that gives wealth to those who find favour with him" (1964, 9). In this encounter, Obika saw an apparition of a human figure who was, "Taller than any man I know . . . His skin was very light . . . like . . . like . . . He was dressed like a wealthy man. He had an eagle's feather on his red cap. . . . He carried a big tusk across his shoulder" (Achebe 1964, 8). Judging from the description, Ezeulu knew immediately it was the divinity Eru, as it was common for people to see his likeness at the same spot Obika had seen it. Ezeulu reassured his son that the encounter was a good omen, not a bad one, as Eru did not mean him any harm. According to Dominique Zahan (2000), the value of the African experience of spirituality and mystical encounters reflects the nature of the relationship between the believer and the "invisible," as the encounter is different for each person.

While one would expect that the entrenchment of Western Christianity in Igboland would have eroded such stories and possible occurrences from the people's experience, it is not so. Achebe's book was telling a story that must have taken place between fifty and one hundred years or so before his writing, but stories like this did not die with the passing of time. Even in the twenty-first century, stories of supernatural encounters continue to occur, and the church's inability to deal with the supernatural drives many Christians back to traditional shamans.

In 1983, while I was serving as a pastor in a small village church in Ugirike, in Imo State, a member of my congregation came home from the farm and ran straight to my house asking me to pray for him. He had just had an encounter with some spirit beings. While riding on his motorcycle on a path by a stream, he encountered three women who were light-skinned, expensively dressed, and very beautiful. They stood by a crossroad in the middle of the jungle, with no homes around. The sight overwhelmed him, and he fell off his motorcycle. By the time he got up, unhurt, and looked around, they were nowhere to be seen. I did not know what to do but obliged him in his request and prayed, not sure I believed his story. I am certain he went home unsatisfied by my inability to deal more meaningfully with his situation. Unlike Ezeulu, who readily told his young son the name and mission of the visiting spirit, I had no idea whom this elder had encountered; rather, my Igbo mindset, biased by Western Christian schooling, assigned the apparition to the category of a manifestation of demonic spirits. Clearly, the Igbo church desperately needs a dynamic response to the world of spirits and the supernatural encounters in the name and power of the risen Christ.

Sacrifice as an Essential Aspect of Interaction with Supernatural Presence

A fundamental challenge that confronts the Igbo concept of sacrifice within the context of Western Christianity is the very fact that New Testament Christianity does not provide for a continued engagement of the sacrificial practices of the Levitical priesthood. The writer of the Epistle to the Hebrews stated unequivocally that the blood of goats and bulls proved unable to cleanse and sanctify us from sin, so the blood of Christ, "who through the eternal Spirit offered himself unblemished to God," cleansed our conscience from acts that lead to death (Heb 9:13–14). Any attempt to resurrect the sacrificial practices that existed among the Igbos would undoubtedly compromise the New Testament gospel and render the fidelity of our faith questionable to the world of Western and New Testament Christianity. One must ask, however, is there a way sacrifice can be adopted and made an integral part of the Igbo Christian experience, without necessarily returning to the slaughtering of goats and bulls?

Igbo Christians, within the Indigenous churches as well as Pentecostal circles, have responded very positively to certain practices of televangelists of the West, such as giving a large sum of money to the church as an act of "sacrifice" to God in response to favors received or anticipation of favors yet to be received (sometimes referred to as a "seed of faith"). These practices are clearly anchored in so-called prosperity theology, which has become part of the African religious experience in many Indigenous churches (Nkwoka 2006, 122).

A reinterpretation and application of the idea of sacrifice in contemporary Igbo Christianity could significantly reshape Christian theology in Igbo churches for the better. Through sacrifices, the Igbo actively participated in the process of improving a situation such as illness or misfortune, or even responding to good fortune. Sacrifice has been the point at which the Igbo engaged in a dynamic spiritual intercourse with the supernatural through the exchange of gifts for favors. While fully accepting that Christ, once for all, paid the price for sin on the cross of Calvary, Igbos still desire to actively participate in the process of making that salvation a daily reality through active spiritual engagement. A reinterpretation of sacrifice as gifts may provide this platform.

A classic reinterpretation of God's grace bestowed on sincere worshipers is epitomized in the story of a lady whose faith and commitment to Christ persuaded her that serving God must involve a substantive sacrifice. In response to the call to help share the gospel with unreached peoples, she pledged to give the totality of her family's annual income to advance the gospel. Such a pledge surprised the husband, who nevertheless stood by her. By year's end they not only paid out what they pledged, they earned much more than they had ever made in their business, and in so doing attained a new height in their recognition of God's provision and his dealing with human beings. This made their faith more personal than ever.

The Ofo Staff

I have discussed the ofo staff as the central symbol of Igbo spirituality. It is a sacred staff of authority and an emblem symbolizing the links between Chukwu Okike (the Creator of all) and humanity—the dead and the living, the living and the unborn. Ofo symbolizes justice, righteousness, and truth, and it played an important role in the social, political, and spiritual lives of our people in the olden days. No serious rite of ceremony could be performed without ofo.

The Igbo ofo staff, like many other Igbo symbols, has strong biblical parallels. In Numbers 17:1–7, God instructs Moses to select twelve staffs to represent the ancestral heads of each tribe of Israel. The names of the ancestral heads of each tribe were to be inscribed on the staff, and the staffs were to be placed in the Tent of Meeting, where God met with Moses. Similarly, the ofo staff represents family and ancestral lines. Ofo staffs were sacerdotal objects that connected the living with the divine and the world of ancestors. In Igboland, the ofo staff was not taken from just any tree, but specifically from an ofo tree. The sacerdotal nature of this tree warranted the fact that people were forbidden from putting a knife on a living ofo tree to cut it down or cut off its branches, as it was believed that, "the Supreme Being created the ofo tree purposefully to be sacred and for its branches to fall off unbroken" (DomNwachukwu 2000, 26). Ofo staffs were made from the fallen branches, bespeaking the sacred nature of this object.

Without necessarily advocating a resurgence of the Igbo ofo staff, the Igbo Christian experience could undoubtedly be enriched with a renewed appreciation of an ancestral staff. This step could allow for the communication of a common Christian faith across generations. In the West, noble families devised coats of arms as insignia to represent their family. The coats of arms are passed down from generation to generation, and as the family expands and disperses, these insignia become an identifying mark for connecting family members. Some families pass on a family Bible from generation to generation. Finding some symbol or ritual to give a sign of handing the faith over to the next generation has been taken away from Igbo Christians. A Christian representation of the ofo staff (possibly taking the shape of a family Bible) is somewhat analogous to the biblical consecration of Aaron's staff in Numbers 17. It could provide a theological basis for a new tradition of handing the faith from one generation to the next (DomNwachukwu 2000). Our culture is replete with many objects that have Old Testament symbolisms and similarities, and I believe we can collectively identify objects and symbols that can effectively carry that role while upholding the purity of our Christian faith in sound biblical truth.

CONCLUSION

We Igbos knew God long before the first European set foot in Africa. God was Chukwu, the supreme, the one above all other spiritual and physical beings. We interacted with Chukwu and continue to do so. We appreciate the new and more complete revelation of God that has come through a biblical presentation of Jesus Christ. According to Joseph Enuwosa, "In the plan of salvation, God seems to have considered that his only begotten Son should be trained and nurtured within African culture just as Israel was nurtured in Egypt. . . . Africa is the channel of divine salvation" (2005, 90). The role that the West has played in reconnecting Africa with the new and final revelation of God in Jesus will continue to be appreciated. However, the time has come when the West must allow Africans to represent our experiences of God and his revelation within our own history and culture. This is important because God is in Africa; he speaks our languages, attends our village councils, and participates in our daily rituals. We are his people, and he is our God.

The idea of an Igbo cultural hermeneutic is a call for the West to allow us to explain ourselves to them. Africa, as a whole, has undergone decades of political, economic, and religious rape and is currently undergoing what Simon Kofi Appiah (2003) has called a "crisis of identity." Long before Europeans came, we were connected with each other as a community of people, with Chukwu as sovereign Lord of the Igbo. Europeans brought with them a new story, which supplanted the African narratives, and we were compelled to allow Europe to assign identity to us, tell our stories for us, and practically assign us a place in the world. Appiah describes the stage we are at today as the age of radical hermeneutics. Within the limits of this radicalization, we must define ourselves and tell the world about our experience with Chukwu and his ongoing revelation to us. In short, we must be allowed to be ourselves, even when it does not make sense to the West.

10

A Creative Death Ritual

Receptor-Oriented Sense-Making in Japan

Yoshiyuki Billy Nishioka

The Christian mission in Japan has stagnated for decades. One of the reasons is that the church and her message have not been contextualized into the Japanese culture. Overseas missionaries who have served in Japan should not be blamed. Given the nearly four-hundred-year history of Christian mission in Japan, the Japanese church leaders should have contextualized the gospel in a way that significantly expanded God's kingdom and made an impact on the Japanese people. However, the gospel, which was contextualized into the Western culture, faces difficulty as it is being made relevant in Japanese culture.

ISSUES OF MISSION IN JAPAN

At least four issues relate to how Japanese Christian leaders have historically not contextualized the gospel message and practice. First, the Japanese highly respect long-standing tradition, and Japanese Christian leaders are therefore reluctant to contextualize the historical precedence seen in Western-style Christianity. The value for historical continuity is harmonized with the Japanese worldview, cultivated through ancestor reverence, which stresses the continuation of the ancestral line. Thus, it is natural for Japanese Christians to accept Westernized Christianity as the ancestor of their faith.

Second, Western Christianity tends to be absolutized as a sacred entity. It arrived intact in Japan during the sixteenth century. The Japanese took it at face value without change—a foreign religion in their context. In keeping with Japanese culture, the attitude toward religious traditions can be compared to the Japanese people's attitude toward their ancestors. For Japanese Christians, Western Christianity is seen as their Christian ancestor—it must be revered and unaltered. This attitude toward Western Christianity suppresses the possibility of contextualization.

Third, the forging of a Christian identity, in the midst of a pluralistic and globalizing Japanese society, strongly suggests a socioreligious model. In the Meiji era (1868–1912), Western technology and civilization led to an inferiority complex among the Japanese and motivated some to become Christian. For early Japanese Christians, accepting Christ was closely connected to accepting Western forms and meanings; some Japanese equated Westernization with accepting the religion of the West. Similarly, many Japanese viewed Westernization as a way to advance Japanese society and escape their technological and civil poverty. As a result, the last 150 years of Christianity in Japan has been predominately Western in form.

Fourth, this tendency gradually blurred the difference between identification with Christ and identity as a Western Christian. Ironically, this blurred boundary has to do with the Cartesian boundary between the gospel and culture. The Cartesian way of understanding and presenting the gospel has deeply influenced the attitude of the Japanese people toward Christianity in their context. The transmission of a Westernized gospel in Japan created a dilemma not only in the process of contextualization but also in the content of the gospel itself. The missionary transmission of the gospel made it nonparticipatory for the Japanese, because the content of the gospel had already been decided. In such an approach, receptors of the gospel did not participate in constructing gospel meaning; they simply accepted it as presented. However, transmitting the gospel through ritual encourages participants to create meaning relevant to the experience at hand. Therefore, to negate the hard boundaries and connect culture with the message of the Bible rather than with another culture requires paying attention to a participatory approach for transmitting the gospel, as Lesslie Newbigin pointed out:

> The idea that one can or could at any time separate out by some process of distillation a pure gospel unadulterated by any cultural accretions is an illusion. It is, in fact, an abandonment of the gospel, for the gospel is about the word made flesh. Every statement of the gospel in words is conditioned by the culture of which those words are a part, and every style of life that claims to embody the truth of the gospel is a culturally conditioned style of life. There can never be a culture-free gospel. (Newbigin 1984, 4)

Newbigin's insights, grounded in Western cultural assumptions which were formed by the Enlightenment, suggest this question: "To what degree does Enlightenment-influenced Western understanding of the gospel challenge Western culture with the gospel presented in Scripture?" Here I want to reinforce Newbigin's point regarding the concept of a "culture-free" gospel. Once we are mistakenly convinced that we have reached a gospel that is free of culture, then meaningful construction of the gospel is no longer an issue. The task of mission, then, is applying the gospel into a specific culture, such as Japanese, Filipino, and so on. If the gospel is culture-free, recipients need not be active in theologizing. They are active only in the process of applying a Westernized gospel to a non-Western context. This results in a gospel that is irrelevant to a particular context and only transmits the issues assumed by the "presenting" messengers.

To summarize, the concept of communicating the gospel in a context other than that of the presenters' must start with the Bible, not with culture, as Dan Shaw makes clear. When the gospel arrived in Japan clothed in Western forms, God's intentions, as reflected in biblical content, were not communicated. Therefore, the Japanese naturally associated Christianity with the religious experience introduced to them. To make changes to those expressions would have changed the religion and violated, in their thinking, the continuity of Christian traditions. Furthermore, the Japanese desire for technological advancement resulted in their equating the Western religion with the advancement that came with it. Taken together, these conditions resulted in acceptance of Christianity as a foreign religion that did not match up with Japanese lives and hearts. Consequently, the religion was not accepted, while the technological advancement proceeded to secularize Japanese society. In short, culture provided the critique of behavior but was never aligned with biblical principles that could have impacted Japanese spirituality.

Without biblical content, or more important, an understanding of God's intent for all human beings, the Japanese people could not develop a biblical theology in their context, as Paul Hiebert called for (1994, 96–97). The problem, now as then, is threefold: (1) the sense-making process regarding the gospel has been done by Western missionaries rather than Japanese communicators, (2) the content of the gospel was culturally laden rather than biblically focused, and (3) the Japanese recipients misunderstood the culturally conditioned gospel. It is difficult to transfer a contextualized gospel to the heart of recipients in a culturally different milieu. Instead, we need a culturally contextual model for the Japanese who are invited to construct the meaning of the gospel through participating in meaningful rituals that reflect biblical intent.

A CASE STUDY OF "ASH CHURCH"

Let me illustrate with an example from Tsuchiura Megumi Christ Church in the Ibaraki Prefecture, where traditional Japanese culture and practices are still prevalent. The senior pastor, Katsuhiko Seino, who studied missiology at Fuller Seminary's School of World Mission, decided to build a beautiful ossuary called Pisgah, the place from which Moses saw the promised land (Deut 34:1–3). One of Seino's major reasons was to contextualize the gospel for the people living around the church facilities. These people are predominantly conservative and have ancestor veneration as a foundation for their family and social life. According to Rev. Seino, the value of bone ash for the local people should be reconsidered for evangelism, since bone ash is deeply associated with family ties. Bone ash is not just the remains of a corpse; it also represents a physical continuity between a deceased person and his or her living family members. As a result, funeral and memorial rituals are crucial for commemorating the deceased person and addressing the psychological needs of the bereaved family. They are also important for reinforcing family and social ties as well as connecting invisible spiritual ties between the ancestors and their living descendants. The local people shame and ostracize those who deviate from the communal and traditional attitudes toward bone ash. If Christians do not pay appropriate attention to the multifaceted issues surrounding its use, application, and spiritual meaning, they will be considered irrelevant by the local people. Rev. Seino pointed out that the church in Japan has often disregarded Japanese cultural forms, leaving the church irrelevant to the concerns of the Japanese people.

The Structure of the Ossuary

The shape and structure of the Pisgah ossuary is significant for the participants of the rites. As diagrammed in Figure 10-1, the ossuary has three parts: an entrance (C), a chapel (B), and a space for bone ash (A). When people come into the entrance of the ossuary, its dome shape with its high vaulted ceiling signifies a holy space. The chapel is an ornate sanctuary that can accommodate about seventy people. Though used primarily for funerals, it is also appropriate for weddings and other events—a practical multifunction building that serves as a channel for holy and ultimate spirituality in which non-Christian Japanese may feel a sense of awe. In other words, the ossuary is designed to be a place for worshiping God. Finally, space for the bone ashes of at least two hundred people is located behind the altar (A).

Figure 10-1: Diagram of Pisgah Ossuary

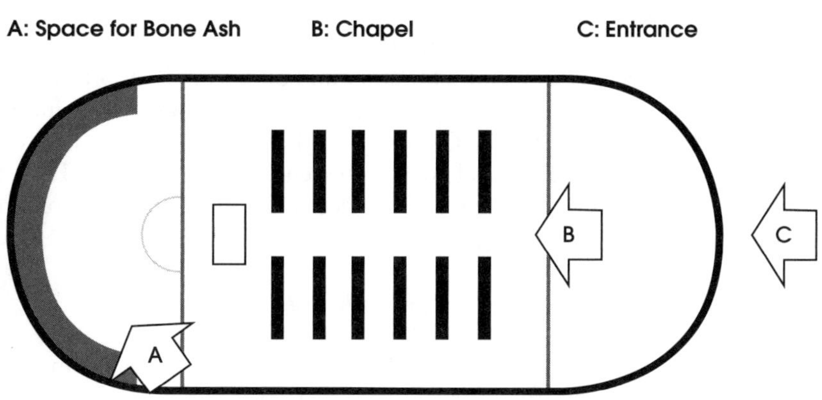

Visitors come to the space to remember a deceased person and to strengthen their family ties. The bone ash remains in the designated storage space of the ossuary for up to thirty-three years. After this period, the ash will be thrown into the special space of mud located in the center of the inner ossuary. This practice of mixing the ash with soil signifies the verse from Genesis 3:19: "You were made from soil, and you will become soil again." The way the church handles the ash is in accord with local traditional Japanese culture; thirty-three years is considered a responsible period for decedents to honor their loved one in order to avoid a curse from the deceased's spirit. In this way, the local Japanese people may feel "at home" in the ossuary when grieving the loss of their family members.

Conducting Funerals at Pisgah

There are at least two important aspects for all funerals held at Pisgah. Rev. Seino uses these as metaphors for constructing Christian meaning from people's participation in the ritual that accompanies a responsible handling of the bone ashes as recognized by the Japanese people.

Flower Arrangements

The way of arranging funeral flowers is significant. The altar flowers on the left side are arranged to reflect the person's life. If the deceased person comes from a mountainous village, the flowers may be arranged as a beautiful mountain. Flowers arranged in a checkered pattern signify an urban landscape. If the person was a shipbuilder, the flowers are arranged in the shape of a ship or with a decorative painting of a ship. In this way the flowers communicate something about the deceased person's life in a way that all the funeral participants recognize. The right side of the altar has flowers arranged as a road up to heaven. If the person is a church member and expressed clear faith in Christ, a cross sits in the center of the stage.

All these details signify the deceased person's life story and are arranged with the cooperation of Rev. Seino and the bereaved family. By doing so, Rev. Seino can hear the deceased person's life story and understand important events in the person's life. If he learns of any favorite poetry or songs, Rev. Seino may use them in the funeral message. The image and arrangement of the flowers, poems, and songs encourage participants in the sense-making process. Thus, the participants can not only commemorate the deceased person but also construct the spiritual significance of the person's life.

A Person's Life Story Must Be Carefully Told

Rev. Seino invites the funeral audience to construct gospel meaning from the way he presents the person's life story. He shares how the flowers are arranged not just for aesthetic purposes but also for providing a stage where the audience members can actively see the arrangements and listen for the message in the life story. By using these metaphors Rev. Seino is able to construct the life story of the person and invite the audience to make sense of it all. If the deceased lived and died in Christ, the person's story is crafted as an invitation to accept the gospel. The person's life story is meaningful because the person was changed by Christ, and the presence of Christ provides a rationale for the gospel. It provides an explanation for why the person was changed and was fruitful. In this way, funeral participants are able to take the experiences of a person's life and merge them with what they hear at the funeral to create what Gilles Fauconnier and Mark Turner (2002) call "conceptual blending."

In the blending, an integral part of the message goes beyond the content to include the entire ambience of the surroundings: the shape of the ossuary, the arrangement of the flowers, the person's story, and the presence of the Savior in whom the person believed. This latter aspect of the funeral does not apply if the person was not a Christian. Nevertheless, even in such a case, those in attendance are invited to participate in the sense-making process. Through the process, attendees may understand the existence of the creator of life, the reality of the shortness of life, and the indispensable value of people whom God loves. The audience may not listen to the gospel directly but may receive a framework to construct meaning of the gospel into their life experience because of the context and the warm-hearted Christian response to life and death.

CULTURALLY APPROPRIATE MEMORIES IN COMMUNITY

Funerals in Japan are highly communal and designed to create a memory. In Robert McCauley and Thomas Lawson's terms, they create "high sensory pageantry" (2002, 51). Similarly, Tsuchiura Megumi Christ Church is highly communal and sensitive to traditional Japanese cultural practices. For example, Japanese funerals typically take place two or three days after the person's death. At the very end of the funeral, the family members and a few close friends of the deceased go to the crematory to pick up the bone ash. This is a sorrowful climax of the person's life and recognition of their death. After the service, memorial rites continue to take place on the forty-ninth day (seven weeks) after the person's death, then again at one year, three years, and seven years after the death. Despite regional variation, this pattern of date arrangement is important for the bereaved family members as it enables the living in different places to reunite and share their memories of the deceased.

According to Rev. Seino, the bone ash of important family members has a special ability to draw other family members together, in order to share their special memories of the deceased. In Japan, many people visit the ossuary or cemetery and honor their loved ones during Bon (annual ancestor memorial), a lunar celebration usually in July or August. At Tsuchiura church, this annual memorial service is held on Easter Sunday, allowing the audience to remember the deceased one with eternal hope in Christ. For most Japanese people, continuing the life from ancestor to descendant by keeping memories alive is highly valued. Doing so by continuing to participate in ongoing rituals in front of the ash is particularly significant. Bone ash is culturally and historically conditioned as a means to pass on the person's narrative and thereby help descendants maintain their own identity. Likewise, people who grew up in the culture and are conditioned by the value system recognize the drawing force of the ash and appreciate a tangible repository for the memories of their loved ones.

For significant ministry in Japan, Japanese churches cannot ignore this drawing force or the value system associated with it. Unfortunately, the majority of Japanese churches have not paid sufficient attention to the bone ashes of the deceased or the associated rituals. The spiritual condition of living people, especially in evangelical circles, is seen as more important than bone ash. This assessment and attitude toward the ash are grounded in the value system in Western evangelical Christianity, which members of the Japanese church need to evaluate critically. However, this set of repeated funeral rituals is important for constructing a framework for the story of one's own personal life. For most Japanese people, their identity is tied to the memory of their ancestors. Missiologically, this funeral rite holds great significance.

Examples of Funerals Held in the Ossuary

Consider these two stories of people who passed away and had funeral services at Tsuchiura church.

For a Non-Believer, With Dignity

First, we read about a nonbeliever whose daughter is a Tsuchiura church member. In agreement with her mother, the daughter asked Rev. Seino to conduct her father's funeral. In the funeral service, the flower arrangement vividly told the story of the man's life. Rev. Seino asked the flower arranger to draw a pasture and a mountain on the left side of the altar, and a bookshelf on the right side. This expressed how the deceased was born and raised in a mountainous village, became a scholar of geography, and served as the chairman of the Japanese Geographical Society.

In order to know how to arrange the flowers for the altar, Rev. Seino carefully listened to the bereaved wife and daughter. The very act of listening carefully and sensitively was a great support to the family in their mourning process. It also enabled the flower arrangers to tell the story with dignity. Even though the deceased was not a Christian, in the funeral service Rev. Seino sought to show how God's general grace was evidenced in his life and contributed to the quality of his family's well-being. Rev. Seino carefully performed the funeral to console the bereaved family and relatives. Many relatives from the man's hometown were deeply impressed by the way the church conducted the funeral.

This artistic flower arrangement was not just superficial ornamentation; rather it reflected the consoling heart of the funeral attendants and posture of the church toward the family. Even though the funeral may become a financial burden for the family (adding up to thousands of dollars), those who attend usually bring consolation gifts that help reduce the expense. The bereaved wife, in this case, decided to attend Sunday worship with her daughter. According to Rev. Seino, many who have attended such funerals have become Christians in his church. Even though Christian funerals for non-Christians are rare in Japan, Rev. Seino and the church are positive about reaching their community through their church's funeral services. Dignity for all is essential.

For a Believer: Christian Grace

The second story reflects God's grace for a Christian widow who was born in Osaka, lived in the Tottori Prefecture, and finally moved to Tsuchiura, where she died. Because she lived in three different places, Rev. Seino had flowers arranged in three large flowerpots, representing her life story. Each flower block contained a cross design, suggesting that Christ was the center of her life during her time in each of these three places. Rev. Seino prepared the eulogy referencing Scripture that supported her time in each of the three places. In so doing, Rev. Seino presented the special grace of God evidenced in the three places where she had lived. This eulogy and the flower arrangement allowed those who attended the funeral to share meaningful memories of her from each of the places she had lived.

The funeral commemorated not only her life but also the Word of God in her life, which supported, directed, and revitalized her as well as those who loved her. In line with Japanese custom, the woman's bereaved family met approximately seven weeks after the funeral and also met together during Bon, thereby drawing everyone together to retell the stories and maintain the memories of their beloved ancestor. These ongoing services provided a significant opportunity for those attending to encounter the gospel that transformed the life of their deceased loved one.

THE IMPORTANCE OF METAPHOR IN THE SENSE-MAKING PROCESS

Why is ritual significant for transmitting the gospel? To deal with this question, we have to reconsider the nature of the sense-making process. If the gospel is conceptually fixed, then receptors of the gospel are not invited to the sense-making process that allows them to make a decision regarding the message. However, study on metaphor may provide perspectives for understanding how people actively construct meaning. In order to let receptors contextualize the gospel message, we need to allow them to construct the meaning of the gospel for themselves. A study of the nature of understanding sheds light on the issue of why ritual is significant for the receptors' participation in the sense–making process. As Shaw and Van Engen have suggested, in order to avoid "twisted truth [what they call 'hocus pocus'] we need to consider the receptor's hermeneutic process" (2003, 114–25). This study is part of such a consideration.

In this discussion I use cognitive studies to focus attention on metaphor. Contemporary scholars of linguistic philosophy, including Paul Ricoeur (1979), George Lakoff and Mark Johnson (1980, 1999), and Fauconnier and Turner (2002), have focused on the cognitive dimension of metaphor in the role of meaning construction.

Metaphor as Cognitive Process

Metaphor has long been viewed as a figurative means for communication of ideas in a creative way. Lakoff and Johnson (1980) suggested that metaphor goes beyond representing meaning to reflect meaning creation. They maintain that human language should not be viewed simply as a system that represents reality, but rather as a conceptual process between external reality and the internal cognitive process (Fiumara 1995). In this approach, metaphor is not just a rhetorical or poetical expression, but more importantly is an indispensable means for human cognitive processing (Johnson 1987, 35–44; see also Turner 1987, 11; Lakoff 1993). This cognitive approach emphasizes the need for gospel recipients to make sense of the gospel message in light of their socioreligious experience. This insight is significant for contextualizing Christianity in Japan. Using this sense-making process encourages receptors to actively think of the gospel as God's intent for their lives.

Through the funeral, Rev. Seino creates a means for others to connect Christian values to Japanese life as reflected in the mourner's experience at the "ash church."

Metaphoric Mapping and Conceptual Blending

In the actual sense-making process, the human mind involves what Johnson (1987) and Lakoff (1987a; 1987b; 1993) call "metaphoric mapping" (or projection). It is a process by which certain image schemas are applied to constructing meaningful conceptual understandings in different domains of experience. Turner (1987) suggests that one of the major areas in everyday experience that provides rich sources for metaphoric mapping is kinship (or domestic) experience (cf. Sweetser 1995). The issue when mapping a complex set of symbols relating to the Japanese death ritual consists of multiple schematic and tacit knowledge, which Lakoff calls "polysemy generalization" (1993, 209). Think of the way human beings grow up and interact in a family. Various phenomena can be understood through people's concepts of kinship and family relationships.

Mapping ancestral relationships for the Japanese is to equate their kin with experience. In life, people express their relationship in terms of their genealogical position and give honor to that position by engaging in rituals. These rituals help them connect the generations of deceased in that family line with their living descendants. But the interaction between those who are part of that genealogy is what characterizes their behavior and symbolizes the relationship. When Rev. Seino listens to those experiences that demonstrate the loving relationship experienced by the family members, he can map those relationships in his eulogy in such a way that people not only remember their relationships in life but extend them into death through memory. By inviting family members back to celebrate the auspicious days by viewing the bone ash, he encourages them to enjoy their memories of the living and share their stories so that the deceased is not forgotten. To do so at the ossuary further creates a context of memory that adds blessing and value for the family and keeps them coming back.

Furthermore, since in most cases the process of metaphoric mapping is not simply a one-to-one correspondence, Fauconnier and Turner (2002) suggest that the phenomenon is seen as conceptual blending rather than simple mapping. Using the notion of mental space, they suggest that when the metaphor is understood, information from multiple domains or experiences is blended. Thus, when participating in ritual, people are invited to a space where many kinds of conceptual blending take place. In the process, participants are not passive but active in the sense-making process. In other words, Rev. Seino utilizes culturally relevant imagery to communicate an important message. The atmosphere created by the entrance, chapel, and place for keeping bone ash at the ossuary provides a context for the event that honors the deceased: displaying the flowers, telling the person's story, and inviting people to enjoy their memories. When all these domains coalesce, the audience can feel at home as the presenter of the ritual (the pastor or messenger) blends something new for the audience—a gospel message that makes sense.

RITUAL AS A LOCUS WHERE PARTICIPANTS DISCOVER THE GOSPEL

The study of the sense-making process in human cognition needs to address the study of ritual. Since my presentation is limited, I do not discuss here the anthropological issues regarding rituals that Shaw has already presented in chapter 1. Suffice it to say, structural analysis by Arnold van Gennep, Edmund Leach, and others are significant for analyzing common structures in ritual. My study, however, focuses more on meaning construction rather than culturally constructed meaning or tacit structure discovered through analysis of a symbolic system. In other words, my focus is more on the cognitive sense-making process than on the symbolic system used to make sense.

Ritual as Context for Creating Meaning

The basic premise I argue here is that ritual involves both symbol and metaphor and that attitude toward ritual impacts the way to transmit the gospel message. Ritual is not just a symbol in which a conventionalized meaning system is encoded. Rather, ritual provides context, or locus, where participants actively engage in creating meaning through mapping schematized imagery onto a new domain of experience. In the Old Testament, the Passover meal is a ritual through which participants construct meaning about who they are, where they are from, who the ruler is, the judge, and eventually, the savior. The Passover ritual involved conceptual blending of visible, tangible practice and unseen reality. It also provided a framework for the sense-making process. Participants were active in the sense-making process, thereby creating meaning and personal relevance. However, ritual can become a conventionalized symbolic system in which meaning is fossilized and not open to active metaphoric mapping or new conceptual blending, thus making the practice vague and impersonal. If this is the case, the participation of the ritual could be reduced to either passive repetition of old meaning or even meaningless repetition in a contemporary situation much like McCauley and Lawson's Type 1 rituals, where mindless repetition creates a "tedium effect" (2002, 51). If this is the case, ritual is no longer a locus where participants are invited to create new meaning through the experience.

In Japan, the negative attitude of the Protestant church (especially the conservative Protestant church) toward local ritual pushed missionaries away from engaging with those rituals. Therefore, conservative Protestants remain skeptical about ritual practice in Japanese culture. In their minds, the domains for ritual are closely tied to pagan beliefs, like, for example, anything to do with ancestors. At the same time, these churches are not positively engaging in Christian rituals that relate to Japanese life experience because of their negative view of ritual as a closed symbolic system. As a result, evangelism in the Japanese conservative Protestant church focuses on transmitting what they consider a "culture-free" gospel. But as Newbigin suggested, such a culture-free gospel is, in fact, conditioned by Western culture. Therefore, an unnecessary conflict may occur in receptors with a Japanese understanding of Western symbols. This creates what Shaw calls, in chapter 1, a "worldview clash."

In contrast, if ritual is a locus of the sense-making process, participants are viewed not only as receptors of a conventionalized meaning system but also as active participants who create their own meaning. In this case, the receptor of the gospel is not just a receptor but an interpreter of the meaning or even the author of a story in which one's origin, present situation, and future can be discovered and expressed. Ritual may provide participants a framework for meaning construction.

According to Fauconnier and Turner (2002), ritual performance provides a mental space where information from multiple domains can be blended for creating meaning. Such blends are the very essence of rituals, as they state:

> Even though rituals are constrained by social purposes, new meaning can arise inadvertently. This is a remarkable property of human cognition. An artificial intelligence program runs strictly according to its script, but human rituals, which seem highly scripted, depend on blends, and emergent meaning is always part of the blending process. The ritual takes place embedded in the full richness of human life, and the principle of emergent meaning can always recruit from that richness. (Fauconnier and Turner 2002, 86)

As they suggest, rituals provide rich opportunity for participants to create new meaning through various metaphoric processes.

Ritual as Locus of Communal Sense-Making

Ritual is a communal event with varying levels of occurrence. Ritual invites participants to sense-making activity. Ritual experience can encourage participants not only to create a meaningful world but also to belong to the world created through the sense-making process; as a result, ritual can be both a locus for individual sense-making and a locus of community building for many individuals who experience the ritual together, what Victor Turner called *communitas* (1969: 96, 97). The participants are those who are invited to participate in a specific metaphoric process through which a specific meaningful world is created and a specific community is formed.

The rituals in the Pisgah ossuary and the church chapel provide various communal sense-making opportunities for those who attend a funeral. The way the flowers are arranged provides a framework for understanding important aspects of the deceased's life, including where the person came from, what the person did, and so on. In addition, the way the funeral is conducted with the deceased's bone ashes provides relatives and friends an opportunity for communal sense-making. Japanese people construct and deepen familial relationship through the various domains contributing to honoring the deceased by properly caring for their bone ashes. The ashes link the invisible deceased person with the individual's visible remains.

Furthermore, the communal ritual related to bone ashes provides funeral attendees time and space to commemorate the life of the deceased.

In the ritual, the attendants actively construct meaning using something they already know, namely their memory of the deceased person. Even though the meaning of a deceased person's life is mystical, the bone ash ritual may provide the environment for making sense of the deceased's life.

If the deceased was a Christian, understanding the person's life requires incorporating the gospel. Without including the special grace of God or the gospel, constructing the meaning of the Christian's life is difficult. If the gospel is not incorporated, funeral attendees will not construct a hopeful meaning regarding the Christian's passing. Thus, the deceased's Christianity can be used as a vital source for non-Christians to map new meaning that involves the hope-filled gospel. The memory of the deceased person involves structurally organized bodily experiences, which are internalized through repetition and are communally shared, especially among relatives and friends as they engage in postfuneral rituals.

Thus, those who do not understand the meaning can still be active in the sense-making process. They are not just passive receptors, but rather active creators of meaning. In the sense-making process, all are welcomed to the community as persons who are creators of meaning regarding their identity, their origin, and their community. In so doing, people may construct their social, religious, and psychological identity with others. Metaphoric mapping allows people to create new meaning using schematized knowledge tacitly developed through repeated kinesthetic experience shared with important others.

CONCLUSION

In this chapter I have argued that transmitting a culture-free gospel does not fully allow the receptors to participate in the sense-making process. The content of the gospel has already been decided by somebody who may not share the receptors' socioreligious experience. In such cases, the gospel may be misunderstood or may not reach to receptors' hearts due to perceived irrelevance. As a result, receptors may not be challenged to repent and accept God's grace. Therefore, we ask, "How can we communicate the gospel in such a way that Japanese receptors are invited to the sense-making process and the receptors are challenged to repent and believe in Jesus Christ?" My argument has been that the use of culturally laden ritual may encourage receptors to be active in the sense-making process, and thereby open up creative ways to include them in making appropriate inferences about the gospel.

The study of metaphor in cognitive semantics gives insight for understanding ritual as a locus of the sense-making process. This process incorporates four basic insights developed by cognitive semanticists. First, rituals are part of receptors' daily bodily experience, such as putting food into their mouths, falling on their knees, lighting a candle in the darkness, and even arranging flowers.

Second, rituals provide participants with a schematized image, which functions as a framework for understanding seemingly unrelated items. The complexity of the imagery may vary, as images consist of concrete and simple structures—for example, up-down, inside-outside, and so on. Some other schematic images may carry more complex meanings, especially those images that consist of a story with certain imagery, such as the Passover narrative. In the case of the funeral at the ash church, the flower arrangement on both sides of the altar suggests the physical expressions as well as the spiritual aspects of the person's life. Participants are able to use culturally appropriate structures as a framework for understanding the meaning of the deceased's life.

Third, metaphorical mapping uses source domains for creating new meaning. The story presented in a ritual tends to be simplified (or schematized) and mapped to other domains of experience. In the funeral, a believer's life story is portrayed with flowers and other items that symbolize the deceased's life narrative. The life itself can be used as a source domain to construct meaning that observers can apply to their own lives. If the deceased went through severe disease before dying, yet never lost hope in Christ, then the story presented in the death ritual becomes a source to be mapped onto the message from the Bible. This, in turn, can affect how people think about their own lives and their physical and spiritual relationships. William Burrows addresses this "hybridity" in chapter 2.

Fourth, the metaphorical process of conceptual blending provides an important aspect for mission. The receptors of the gospel are not just receptors of a message but author of their own life stories, into which the gospel enters and brings completion. The receptors actively construct meaning for their lives, and in many cases, the ash ritual can provide a framework for that meaning. In the process of meaning construction at the funeral, participants are actively engaged in a sense-making process with the gospel that may provide a future possibility to construct a person's own life story.

Through conceptual blending, repeated participation in an important ritual may create a framework for discovering the gospel. In such conceptual blending, the meaningful metaphorical process may occur for constructing meaning regarding who people are, where they come from, and to what degree they are part of the spiritual existence that reflects relationship to God and to each other. Without the gospel story, people cannot construct their own meaningful life story.

If Japanese Christians are to seriously consider the importance of ritual for constructing meaning, we should better understand the relationship between ritual and the human mind. We need a culturally contextual model for the Japanese in order to construct the meaning of the gospel through participating in rituals that reflect biblical intent. As Rev. Seino developed the death ritual as a locus of the communal sense-making process, ritual can open other aspects of Japanese life as well.

Historically, the Japanese treated Christianity as just another religion. After the March 2011 triple disaster (earthquake, tsunami, and nuclear threat), the Japanese people are more sensitive toward the importance of familial, communal, and social bonds, which are often represented by ritual and ceremony. The present context offers Japanese Christians an opportunity to bring human care and understanding into line with Japanese expectations about physical and spiritual relationships as reflected by biblical relevance and meaningful expression. Thus, the Japanese people need to move beyond religious understanding and connect their spiritual and physical relationships to the reality of God's desire to live inside their context—to come alongside them. This brings Christianity into the immediacy of Japanese life (and death) as Rev. Seino has done at the Tsuchiura Megumi Christ Church.

More than ever before, there is an urgency for thinking ontologically/theologically as well as phenomenologically/missiologically about Japanese ritual. How the Japanese people connect to God and their fellow Japanese people is what they must consider. More than a foreign religion, Christianity must be blended into a Japanese conceptualization of expression that appreciates their story and connects it with God's story, which may be bridged by the story of their ancestors—those whose bone ashes symbolize their lived story and reflect a humble reality of sense-making.

11

Household Spirituality in a Messianic Jewish Context

Shabbat as a Ritual of Renewal

Stuart Dauermann

You only need to go as far as the nearest Starbucks to discover that most people have abandoned ritual like a half-empty cup of coffee. Just ask around and people will tell you, "I don't believe in organized religion and all that ritual stuff. But I like to think of myself as spiritual." People are grabbing personal spirituality while relegating ritual and "organized religion" to the status of stodgy old relatives fit only to be politely ignored. Ironically, just about everyone in that Starbucks would admit to craving a deeper encounter with the Transcendent, a greater experience with the Force, or a handshake with their Higher Power. Some would speak of long-ago friends or relatives whose spirituality they envy. And many will leave that Starbucks to go somewhere to practice various forms of martial arts or meditative disciplines at centers promising enhanced spirituality at a reduced price—"this month only." Others will make their way to the nearest bookstore to thumb through the latest book revealing hitherto undiscovered secrets to making the Universe do our bidding. If conditions were right, most would admit to being spiritually thirsty. And in our day they try to find some sort of personalized half-caff mocha fudge latte spirituality with whipped cream and a spritz of maple syrup to help them get through their long dark night of the soul. But truly, the solution to their dilemma lies elsewhere. They are going to have to retrieve that discarded ritual cup of joe.

In this chapter I explore the pathway to spiritual revitalization and a deeper encounter with the transcendent superhuman beings Shaw speaks of for everyone in that Starbucks coffeehouse, and particularly for the Jews there. I begin by retrieving that discarded cup of ritual. It is from this cup that life-giving water should be drunk, bringing renewal with which the merchandisers of pop spirituality cannot begin to compete. I speak here especially of household spirituality for Jews, like myself, who believe in

Jesus as Messiah and who are determined to preserve Jewish continuity. I argue that reclaiming ritual can and should renew spirituality and relationships both within and beyond the House of Israel.

THE ROOTS OF HOUSEHOLD RITUAL: ALIGNING OUR TODAY WITH OUR YESTERDAYS AND TOMORROWS

Three Christian anthropologists, Paul Hiebert, Dan Shaw, and Tite Tiénou, included the "way things used to be" in the Older Testament institution of rituals in an earlier volume (1999). In chapter 1 of this book, Shaw demonstrates that God with us began in the Garden of Eden and follows all the way through human existence on earth. Thus, the Eden beginning is where everything finishes at the end as well:

> Then I saw a new heaven and a new earth, for the first heaven and the first earth had passed away, and the sea was no more. And I saw the holy city, new Jerusalem, coming down out of heaven from God, prepared as a bride adorned for her husband. And I heard a loud voice from the throne saying, "Behold, the dwelling place of God is with man. He will dwell with them, and they will be his people, and God himself will be with them as their God." (Rev 21:1–3)

Just as in the Edenic beginning, so at the end, God will dwell in the midst of all people, and death and sin will be no more. This expectation appears throughout the Bible, perhaps best expressed as "My dwelling place shall be with them, and I will be their God, and they shall be my people" (Ezek 37:27). As in Revelation 10:11 and 17:15, the Greek text in Revelation 21:3 speaks of *laoi* (peoples), as in "they will be his *peoples*." The plural translation, though rare, is preferred here, thus preserving the particularity and diversity of humankind. This is God's dream, and this is our destiny—the way things were, will be, and ought to be now.

For the Jewish people, not only in the beginning and at the end, but also in the midst of time, the dwelling place is the locus of encounter with the God whom we honor. Exodus 25:8 states the purpose of the building of the Tabernacle in these terms: "Let them make for me a sanctuary that I may dwell in their midst." Earlier, in the Song at the Red Sea (Exod 15:16–17), the people are spoken of as those whom God has purchased, whom he will bring in and plant on his holy mountain, "the place, O Lord, which you have made for your abode." This is not the Mishkan/Tabernacle, a moveable tent, but the Temple, the Bet HaMikdash. In 1 Kings 8, Solomon not only dedicates the Temple but contemplates this theological conundrum: "where exactly is the dwelling place of God?"

The prophets also, especially Isaiah, Zechariah, and Ezekiel; the Newer Testament writers; and Jewish tradition have long grappled with Solomon's question. Does God dwell in the Temple? Yes. Does he not also dwell in the universe, which he has created by his will? Again, yes. Is he not greater than the universe and all the created order? Yes again. And in the Newer Testament, we ask and answer in the affirmative that God dwelt in Messiah, and that he also inhabits his people, individually and corporately. All answers are in the affirmative, the entire picture is both-and, holistic. Clearly, the juxtaposition of dwelling place and divine–human encounter is richly rooted in the entirety of biblical revelation. And although Christian mystic theologian A. W. Tozer could write of "Man [*sic*]: The Dwelling Place of God," Jewish practice sets its sights elsewhere.

God dwelling among his people foreshadows for us the genius of Jewish life and the thrust of this essay. With both the Tabernacle and Temples gone, Judaism sees the home as the dwelling place where God is honored and where lives that honor him are shaped and nurtured. Jewish religious discourse terms the home a Mikdash M'at (a little holy sanctuary). This is the center, the microcosm from which blessing flows to the macrocosm of life. The home is the holy of holies, and the blessing it nurtures spiritual renewal.

SPIRITUAL RENEWAL AS A FAMILY AFFAIR: HOUSEHOLDS HONORING GOD IN EVERY CONTEXT, TIME, AND RELATIONSHIP OF LIFE

While the central question of conservative Christians is, "What must I do to be saved?" the core Jewish question is, "In our relationships with humankind and the created order, how shall we best honor the God of our ancestors, obeying his commands in the situations before us?" You will notice that this statement is in the first-person plural, because in religious thought and action, the Jew is always part of a people. Our tradition reminds us, "All Israel is responsible for one another" (TB Shevuot 39a). Following God means walking together in the ancient paths (Jer 6:16), that is, "in paths of righteousness for His name's sake" (Ps 23:3). And while walking, even running in these paths requires discipline and exertion, these are for Jews the disciplines of renewal, touching eternity in the midst of time.

Abraham Joshua Heschel helps us understand our task by reminding us that "Judaism is the architecture of time" (1951, 8). There is holy time and mundane time, and honoring God requires us to respect the difference. In order to understand what God's commandments require of us, it helps to array these commands along an axis of time. And as a householder knows what he or she ought to be doing depending upon the time of day, the time of the week, and the season of the year, so Jews, as members of the household of God, are constantly aware of this question: "What time is it?" because our responsibilities are linked to the architecture of time.

This axis of time intersects with an axis of context—where and with whom events happen. Faithful Jews must also factor this into consideration. For example, some commandments are only in force in the Holy

Land, the Land of Israel. This demonstrates *where*. Other commands are conditioned by *with whom*. For example, one should behave differently with one's spouse than with other members of the opposite sex. And religious Jewish women will not be in a closed room with a nonrelative member of the opposite sex, but could freely do so with a crowd of siblings or other relatives. Paul's controversy with Peter at Antioch was not about what Peter was eating, but with whom. The truth of the gospel about which Paul was incensed was that Gentiles, with whom Jews formerly could not eat, were now, in Christ, likewise the people of God. Paul's gospel had done nothing less than restructure fundamental spiritual reality. The Judeo-Christian world has not yet come to terms with the implications of this revolution.

The routes of ritual take us from time to time, from place to place, from relationship to relationship, from context to context. Thus, in order to understand Jewish ritual life, *where*, *when*, and *with whom* things happen must be kept in mind. All of this proceeds from a network of assumptions, latent in the Torah but developed through time in Jewish life: we are members of the family of God, and our households are the home base where the righteousness that honors our heavenly Father is to be structured, lived out, and cultivated. My intent in this chapter is to make this clear and to encourage my people to awaken to the glorious privilege of their homes being the holy of holies where God and his people are meant to dwell together in love.

We can see this in the *Shema*, the quintessential Jewish faith declaration found in Deuteronomy 6:4–9 and recited twice a day:

> Sh'ma, Yisra'el! *Adonai* Eloheinu, *Adonai* echad [Hear, Isra'el! *Adonai* our God, *Adonai* is one]; and you are to love *Adonai* your God with all your heart, all your being and all your resources. These words, which I am ordering you today, are to be on your heart; and you are to teach them carefully to your children. You are to talk about them when you sit at home, when you are traveling on the road, when you lie down and when you get up. Tie them on your hand as a sign, put them at the front of a headband around your forehead, and write them on the door-frames of your house and on your gates. (Complete Jewish Bible)

"To your children," *with whom*; "when you sit at home, when you are traveling on the road," *where*; "when you lie down and when you get up," *when*. And we write these commands "on the door-frames of our houses and on our gates" as a reminder of *where* God's commands should be carried out for the purpose of governing our lives at home, at our home base. This further ties in with the biblical metaphor of one's "going out and coming in" (cf. Num 27:17; Deut 31:2; 1 Sam 8:20; and many others), encompassing the totality of life. We are meant to take this household holiness out with us into the world at large.

Finally we are enjoined to "bind them on [our] hand as a sign" and "put them at the front of a headband around [our] forehead," symbolic locations for guiding both action and thought. In all we think, in all we do, in every differentiated context, relationship, time, and place, we are to love Adonai our God with all our heart, with all our soul, and with all our might. These are the commitments in which Jewish life is meant to instruct, shape, and renew us.

SHABBAT RITUALS AND DISTRIBUTING KAVOD: HONORING GOD IN ALL OF LIFE

The love for God to which the *Shema* calls us is not an emotion. Rather, the call to love Adonai with all our heart, soul, and mind is a call to give God proper honor. This is covenant language related to the so-called Suzerain-Vassal Treaty of Esarhaddon (seventh century BC) and other documents of the ancient Near East, especially Hittite vassal treaties, upon which the structure of Deuteronomy was modeled. This "love" is actually proper honor, proper respect, and, in accord with the etymology of the Hebrew word *kavod* (proper weight).

Mark S. Smith and Tikva Frymer-Kensky along with Frank Moore Cross remind us that formal treaties in the Old Testament borrow family terms such as "father" and "son" from vassal treaties, and "brother" from parity treaties. Cross put it succinctly: "The language of covenant, kinship-in-law, is taken from the language of kinship, kinship-in-flesh" (1998, 11). Notice the direction: legal categories of covenant are derived from familial realities, not vice versa. So we can see that households are not simply an arena where honor and covenantal relationship are worked out. Rather, the household is the matrix, the womb, in which these realities are generated, where we learn all about covenant and kavod—that is, honor.

In Scripture we are told to "Give *Adonai* his due, you who are godly; give *Adonai* his due of glory [*kavod*] and strength; give *Adonai* the glory [*kavod*] due his name; worship *Adonai* in holy splendor" (Ps 29:1–2 CJB).

On the one hand Adonai has intrinsic kavod (weightiness of being), but on the other hand we are to worship him by acknowledging the supremacy of His Being—his kavod.

Preparations for Shabbat

Religious Jews do their shopping for the finest of foods earlier in the week, attempting to be done by Thursday, because Shabbat is likened to a queen whom we receive into our homes. Just as one would serve a queen the best of food, so we honor Shabbat by the kinds of food we eat and how it is prepared. As a queen receives greater honor than her subjects, so Shabbat is honored above all days. It should go without saying that nonkosher foods are not to be eaten, especially on Shabbat! God has permitted Jews to eat some foods, and others he has forbidden.

Even the way permitted animal foods are killed is prescribed by tradition. Animals must be healthy, and not specifically forbidden, such as pork. When the animal is killed, it must be with a sharp blade without any nicks, and in one smooth stroke. This concern for the well-being of animals is also a matter of kavod, in this case, *kavod hab'riot* (proper respect for living things).

And there are some modes of serving food that are forbidden, for example, serving milk and meat together (as often repeated in Torah: do not boil a kid in its mother's milk [Exod 23:19]), or eating meat too soon after having had a dairy product. These dietary laws demonstrate to all who look on that we honor God and distribute kavod in how we respond to the mandates from the written Torah (termed *d'oraita*) as well as those from the so-called traditions (*d'rabbanan*). This is but one of the ways in which ritual life distributes and acknowledges honor where honor is due.

Another is in preparing the house for Shabbat. In traditional Jewish homes, the house is especially cleaned prior to Shabbat. This again is in preparation for receiving the Sabbath Queen, sent to us by the Holy One, Blessed be He. Only the very best will do. We also bathe especially and dress up for Shabbat, all signs of respect. And as for the candlesticks, wine cups, and other implements we use during Shabbat, we bring out the very best we can afford. This is because Shabbat isn't just any other day; it is the holiest day of the week, deserving of special kavod.

Welcoming Shabbat

There is not room here to discuss the liturgy of prayers done at the synagogue prior to the Shabbat meal, and also after the Shabbat meal. But one prayer should be noted especially for its distribution of kavod. The prayer is called *L'cha* (Come, my beloved). It is a song encouraging the people of Israel to assemble ourselves to greet the Sabbath Queen, who comes as a bride. The chorus reads, "Come, my Beloved, to greet the bride; let us welcome the Sabbath," with the verses resplendently summarizing Israel's prophetic destiny. This is theology in song.

One may readily see from all of this that despite Israel's long history of suffering and exile, our people's love for God was kept alive and nurtured by rituals of glorification whereby we remembered our history with God, anticipated our vindication by him, and thanked him for his mercies. Honoring God through remembering God's role in Jewish history, praising him for his greatness, and celebrating Shabbat in the synagogue as well as in the household all relate to McCauley and Lawson's development of high sensory pageantry (2002, 43), thereby demonstrating kavod as both a vertical relationship reflecting honor and glory to God, while also celebrating established horizontal relationships.

Household Shabbat

The family returns from synagogue to find the table set. What awaits them is a time of worship, celebration, and family joy. Let's look briefly at the home Shabbat service, seeing it as eleven steps, with Step 4 having two parts. Throughout we notice a pageantry of differentiation and elevation through ritualized behaviors.

Step 1: Hadlekat Nerot—Yiddish, Bentschen Licht (Lighting the Candles)

It is customary to light two candles, although some families light one candle for each family member. The two candles stand for the two verbs attached to Shabbat in the Ten Commandments: "observe" and "remember." It is also customary for the woman of the house to light the candles, then to cover her eyes and say this candle blessing aloud: *Baruch attah Ado-nai, Elo-henu melech ha'olam, asher kid'shanu b'mitvotav, v'tzivanu l'hadlik ner shel Shabbat* ("Blessed are you Lord our God, king of the universe, who has set us apart through his commandments, and commanded us to light the Shabbat candles). After the woman of the house has said this, with her eyes still covered, it is customary for her to pray a silent prayer for her family, after which she uncovers her eyes to see the Shabbat candles.

The reason the woman of the house first lights the candles, then covers her eyes while saying the blessing, is because making a fire—or lighting candles—is considered "work" and should not be done on Shabbat. Our tradition discerned thirty-nine categories of activity that can be classified as "work," which we are to cease doing in order to honor Shabbat. Making a fire is one of those forbidden activities. One must remember, though, that in Jewish life such blessings (called *b'rachot*) are always said before the associated act. But since Shabbat will begin in the home the moment the woman says the blessing over lighted candles, were she to say the blessing first and then light the candles, she would be starting Shabbat by desecrating it. For this reason, she first lights the candles, and then covers her eyes so as not to see the flame while saying the blessing. Then, after saying the blessing she opens her eyes and there is the light, as if she had followed custom and said the blessing first and then done the act. This, too, is a matter of kavod. One wants to show proper respect for the Sabbath by not desecrating it, and even by taking a convoluted path to avoid such desecration.

Step 2: Birkat HaYeladim (Blessed Are the Children of the House)

The father certainly, and likely both parents, place their hands on the heads of their sons and bless them, that they might be blessed offspring like the sons of Joseph whom Jacob blessed: *Y'simcha Elohim k'Efraim u-k'Menasseh* (May G-d make you like Efraim and Menasseh). Then the daughters are blessed, with the parents' hands on their heads, that they might become like Sarah, Rivka, Rachel, and Leah, the matriarchs of Israel:

Y'simeich Elohim k'Sarah, Rivka, Rakhel, v'Leah (May G-d make you like Sarah, Rivka, Rakhel, and Leah).

Here, honor is bestowed on the children: they are being blessed by the father of the house, receiving a patriarchal blessing, and in many homes by both parents, thereby reflecting generational legacy. This is a very holy ritual, a time for expressing God-given parental authority, thus honoring the parents and bestowing blessing on the children, honoring God as well as family members.

Then all children are blessed with the Aaronic Benediction, in Hebrew if possible, or Hebrew and English.

Step 3: Shalom Aleichem (A Song of Blessing)

This is a sixteenth-century Shabbat song welcoming angels who, tradition says, join us at synagogue on Friday night and come home to spend Shabbat with us. There are a number of lovely melodies to this very imaginative and beautiful piece, which enables giving proper kavod to angels who, pious tradition says, come to join us at the table—again, distributing honor, appropriate to whom honor is due.

Step 4a: Eishit Chayyil (Bless the Woman of the House)

Next, the father of the house sings Proverbs 31, or perhaps reads it. I have seen the father and the children together sing this song, which celebrates the virtues, hard work, and indispensability of the woman of the house. Yet again, this is the bestowal of proper honor, through which, above all, God the architect of life is honored.

Step 4b: Ashrei Ha-Ish (Blessed Is the Man of the House) (Optional)

In our days of egalitarianism, in some households it is traditional to similarly bless the father of the household by reading Psalm 112 as a tribute to him, again in any comfortable combination of Hebrew and English.

Step 5: Kiddush (Sanctifying the Day)

As the wife initiated Shabbat in her home by lighting the candles with an appropriate blessing, so the head of the house says a prayer that declares the holiness of the day and the rationale for its holiness. The melodies are quite beautiful, and these brief few minutes have the warm familiarity for Jews that hearing the Christmas story from Luke's Gospel might have for Christians on Christmas day. The husband stands, holding a cup of wine in his hand, and sings the following in Hebrew:

> And there was evening and there was morning, a sixth day. The heavens and the earth were finished, the whole host of them. And on the seventh day God ended his work which he had made and he

rested on the seventh day from all his work which he had made. And God blessed the seventh day, and sanctified it because in it he had rested from all his work which God had created and done. [This recitation from Gen 1:21–2:2 commemorates the completion of God's creative work, and establishing Shabbat as holy.]

Blessed are You, Lord, our God, King of the Universe, who creates the fruit of the vine—Amen [This blessing over the wine ritually acknowledges the holiness of the occasion].

Blessed are You, Lord, our God, King of the Universe, who sanctifies us with his commandments, and has been pleased with us. You have willingly and lovingly given us Your holy Shabbat as an inheritance, in memory of creation. The Shabbat is the first among our holy days, and a remembrance of our exodus from Egypt. Indeed, You have chosen us and made us holy among all peoples and have willingly and lovingly given us Your holy Shabbat for an inheritance. Blessed are You, who sanctifies the Shabbat—Amen. [Much kavod is distributed: on God, on gathered human beings, on Shabbat, and on the memories epitomized for us by deliverance from Egypt. We are slaves no longer.]

In all these prayers God is honored, loved, adored, and thanked. Other things are treated as special, too—Shabbat, the mother of the house, the father, the children, all of this to the honor and glory of God. Acknowledging God in this way invokes an atmosphere of kavod on those who are fulfilling their roles in God's created order by participating in Shabbat.

Step 6: Netilat Yadaim (Ritual Hand Washing)

The blessing over the wine that precedes this step, and the blessing over the bread that follows this step, are regarded in Jewish life as a single act of blessing the meal we are about to eat. In order to preserve that unity, we do not engage in conversation at this point, but do a ceremonial hand washing as yet another act of preparing for the meal, which is regarded as a holy occasion deserving of appropriate preparation. Using a special vessel we pour water twice over each hand up to the wrist, beginning with the left and alternating hands.

This is the washing of hands of which we read in the Gospels. Of course it has nothing to do with removing dirt. Rather, we are a kingdom of priests and a holy nation, and the bread we are about to eat and the meal to follow are looked upon as a sacrificial meal (although of course not an atoning sacrifice), and the table is regarded as an altar. Therefore, since we are priests around the altar partaking of these sacrifices, we do as the priests and Levites: we first wash our hands. After that, we return to the table. The meal is about to begin.

Step 7: Motzi (Blessing the Bread)

At this time the head of the house—male if there is one, otherwise female—takes the two loaves of *Challah* (braided Shabbat egg-bread) that have been prepared and says over them the brief blessing we call "the Motzi." It is customary to eat the bread dipped in salt, since the meal is looked upon as a holy sacrifice of praise and thanksgiving, and all sacrifices in the Temple were seasoned with salt.

Could anything elevate this meal more than to regard it as a sacred meal eaten around the altar in the temple? No. Much kavod, much honor, is being bestowed here on the home, on the event, on Shabbat, because of the goodness of God—may his name be praised.

Step 8: Aruchat Shabbat (The Sabbath Meal)

Here, the family simply eats. The meal will be the best of which the home is capable. Much talk goes on around the table, about family matters, about the week. But arguments and negativity are excluded, as that would be disrespectful of Shabbat.

Step 9: Zemirot (Traditional Shabbat Table Songs)

It is traditional to sing songs at the table, all of them about Shabbat, about God, about the blessedness of being God's people. Some of these songs are centuries old, both Scripture songs and exalted religious poetry. Over the years, every home develops its own repertoire of songs and favorite melodies. The songs are sung a capella.

Step 10: D'var Torah (Holy Teaching)

A special treat at the meal is a brief lesson, usually from the Scripture readings associated with the particular Shabbat. This lesson is usually given by the head of the household, traditionally a male, the father or grandfather, but not necessarily so. In traditional Jewish homes the passages are from the Torah (Pentateuch), and associated with Haftarah (prophetic readings). Messianic Jews also include a reading from the Gospels or elsewhere in the Newer Testament. The lesson is short—not much more than a pregnant idea. These ideas symbolically give birth to stimulating discussion around the table, and it is the discussion which is especially cherished.

Step 11: Birkat HaMazon (The After-the-Meal Blessing)

The Torah reminds us, "When you have eaten and are satisfied, you shall bless *Adonai* your God for the good land which He gave you" (Deut 8:10). This is why, at the end of the meal, we say these wonderful blessings to thank him for all his goodness to us. These blessings provide a marvelous sketch of our Jewish world of thought, imagination, remembrance, and hope. Just prior to the Birkat HaMazon, we transition by singing Psalm 126, Shir Hama'alot (Song of Ascents), expressing the Jewish hope of return to Zion following our final national redemption. Birkat HaMazon itself is made up of four blessings. The first three blessings are regarded as required *d'oraita* (by written law) and the fourth *d'rabbanan* (by oral tradition):

- A blessing of thanks for the food
- A blessing of thanks for the Land of Israel
- A blessing of thanks for Jerusalem
- A blessing of thanks for God's goodness

After these blessings, other brief blessings are sung, each beginning with the word *Harachaman* (the Merciful One). Requests for God's compassion on the household, on Jerusalem, on God's people, on the world, and more follow. On Shabbat night it is difficult to know whether you have just had a service or a meal. The answer, of course, is that you have had both, and both are worth coming back for more.

Messianic Jews and the Lord of the Sabbath

As is clear from my earlier comments, some Messianic Jews believe in adhering closely to the cultural traditions of our ancestors. But what about the Messiah? What about Jesus? Where is he in all of this? We see him throughout, the often unacknowledged Lord of the Sabbath and the living Torah—the embodiment and perfect expression of the holiness to which our texts and tradition call us.

We make his presence explicit in our Shabbat observance in various ways, most commonly through our *divrei Torah*, our holy teachings around the Shabbat table. We commonly interpret whatever texts we are discussing through the lens of the teachings and example, the *Halacha* and *Aggadah* of Jesus and the apostles.

Another way his presence is made explicit, whereby we properly acknowledge his glory, is through our *z'mirot*, our Shabbat table songs. Here is one I wrote myself, based on Matthew 10. It is titled, "The Lord of the Sabbath Is Here."

The Lord of the Sabbath is here
And 'til that day when the stars pass away
No greater than he shall appear
The Lord of the Sabbath is here

Moses was faithful in all of God's house
He spoke holy words that he heard from his mouth
He promised another, God's ultimate choice
Whom Israel must honor,
Sh'ma hear his voice, hear his voice

A greater than Moses is here
A greater than Moses is here
And 'til that day when the stars pass away
No greater than He shall appear
A greater than Moses is here

King Shlomo's was mighty through God's holy hand
His wisdom was famous throughout all the land
The Queen of the South came to see and she cried.
"The half was not told me, you're such a wise guy,
A wise guy!"

A greater than Shlomo is here. . . .

Jonah was buried for three days it's true
Until the great fish spat him out good as new
Yeshua was dead in the depths of the earth.
Then the Lord raised him up the first fruits of new birth
Of new birth

A greater than Jonah is here. . . .

One day in wheatfield they picked heads of grain
Some people cried out, "It's shabbat, that's a sin!"
Yeshua replied, "Don't you know, *kohannim* [priests]
Can work on shabbat with their consciences clean
Really clean?"

The Lord of the Sabbath is here
The Lord of the Sabbath is here
And 'til that day when the stars pass away
No greater than he shall appear
The Lord of the Sabbath is here

Another way we commonly express our faith as believers in Yeshua is through slight additions to the Jewish liturgy. However, since our movement is so new, these additions have not been standardized; they range from the bold and innovative to the cautious and minimalist.

Havdalah, The Ritual at the End of Shabbat

Shabbat began with the lighting of the candles and the ceremony called *Kiddush* (the sanctification of the day). Everything that followed has been holy time set apart for God. Those hours are not simply hours for avoiding the thirty-nine categories of activity prohibited during Shabbat. These are hours of family contact, without televisions, iPads, computers, cars, or smartphones to impede a day of relationship, of holy study, of worship with others at the synagogue, of receiving life as given us by God and not as our own pet project. It is a time for giving appropriate kavod to each other, to Jewish traditions, to our people, and of course, supremely to Adonai. But we must also think of gearing up for the other six days, the workdays of the week. To bring Shabbat to an end twenty-five hours after it began so as to return to ordinary time, we have a ceremony called Havdalah (separation).

Havdalah is short and evocative, using a glass of wine, a spice box, and a braided candle. The wine symbolizes the joy of Shabbat and is a means of thanking God for a day of celebration. The spices symbolize the fragrance of the day, the lingering sense of its holiness now departing for another week of waiting. The multiwicked candle reminds us of the first day of creation when God created the greater light to rule the day, the lesser light to rule the night, and also the stars. It is a time for saying good-bye to Shabbat and saying hello to the created world and our work in it. Our prayer highlights the distinctions:

> Blessed are You, Lord our God, King of the Universe, who separates the holy from the mundane, light from darkness, Israel from the nations, the seventh day of rest from the six days of work. Blessed are You, Lord, who distinguishes the holy from the mundane.

Clearly, Jewish ritual life concerns itself with different kinds of time and with obeying God in every differentiated context, relationship, and place. Certainly this prayer reminds us of such differentiations.

THE OTHER SIX DAYS

"The teaching of Judaism is the theology of the common deed. God is concerned with everydayness, with the trivialities of life" (Heschel 1963, 102). Judaism insists that life is not lived in generalities but in the details of life, making it imperative that we understand the specifics of God's commands. All of this is necessary if we are to live our lives in answer to the Jewish question, "In our relationships with humankind and the created order, how shall we best honor the God of our ancestors obeying his commands in the situations before us?" Paul's question on the Damascus Road was a very Jewish one, and it is also our question: What would you have me do? What God wants is a disciplined life centered on the great commandment, our relationship with God, and its corollary, our relationships with others. It is to these "disciplines" that I now turn.

Halacha (Our Prescribed Walk)

Happily, our tradition has given us centuries of discussion, *halacha* (a prescribed walk). These specifics that Jews should follow reflect centuries of winnowed discussion of how God's commands are to be interpreted and lived out. These ideals are illustrated with *aggadah* (accounts of lives). These examples of conduct, and anecdotes told by and about ancient

Jewish exemplars, are regarded as living interpretations of how we should respond rightly to God's commandments. The apostle Paul spoke in similar terms. It was not enough that he had given his disciples their marching orders. They needed *aggadah*, stories of others who had trodden this path. They needed mentoring from worthy mentors. Beyond his didactic teaching, Paul holds out to the Philippians the example of Jesus, of his own life, and the lives of Timothy and Epaphroditus, calling them to "honor such men." The writer of the Epistle to the Hebrews reminds us, "Remember your leaders, those who spoke to you the Word of God. Consider the outcome of their way of life, and imitate their faith" (13:7), and in the eleventh chapter names nineteen individuals and various categories of unnamed others.

Limmud Torah (Holy Study)

The path of obedience to the 613 commandments discerned in the Older Testament becomes clearer as we form habits of studying the Bible and other holy texts. So important is sacred study that the tradition records this discussion:

> R. Tarfon and the Elders were once reclining in the upper story of Nithza's house, in Lydda, when this question was raised before them: Is study greater, or practice? R. Tarfon answered, saying: Practice is greater. R. Akiba answered, saying: Study is greater, for it leads to practice. Then they all answered and said: Study is greater, for it leads to action. (TB Kiddushin 40b)

Therefore, holy study is a foundational ritual of Jewish life.

Tefillah (Daily Prayer)

A second such daily discipline is *tefillah* (prayer). Figure 11-1 depicts the structure of the morning prayers said by tradition-honoring Jews. By praying these prayers we "suit up," so to speak, reminding ourselves of our identity as part of a covenant people with specific responsibilities and privileges. However, in such prayer we Messianic Jews express not only our union with our people Israel, but also our union with Israel's Messiah, Yeshua, who is present in all aspects of faithful Jewish life. In his divinity and in union with the Father, Yeshua is the embodiment of the holiness that Torah extols. He exemplifies both *halacha* (our prescribed walk) and *aggadah* (the balanced realization of a holy life). In praying our prayers we experience a dual unity—our unity with all Israel and the covenants given to them, and union with our risen Messiah.

In the accompanying figure, I give the basic structure of Jewish daily morning prayer. Although it is considered meritorious to pray at the synagogue in the morning with other Jews at the start of the day, most Jews who pray the liturgy in the morning do so at home, in their Mikdash M'at (little holy sanctuary).

One of the values of this kind of prayer is that such a regimen situates us in our identity as members of the Jewish people, part of that kingdom of priests constituting a holy nation. The prayers remind us of who God is by retelling what he has done and what he will do. In the process we are reconnected, not only to the past, but also to ourselves as members of his people, all of which anticipates what is to come. This, of course, has great power in conditioning our conduct throughout the day—grounding our behavior in God's will and presence.

Through the Spirit we aspire to increasingly reflect Yeshua's perfect embodiment of the righteousness required by God's commands, with him, in him, and through him, loving Adonai our God with all our heart, soul, and might, and our neighbors as ourselves, while faithfully honoring our unity with the wider Jewish past, present, and future. Mark Kinzer develops this in much greater detail in his exploration of our unity with Messiah and with Israel in the context of Jewish prayer in general, and the *Shema* in particular (2011, 62–87).

Figure 11-1: Structure of Jewish Morning Prayer

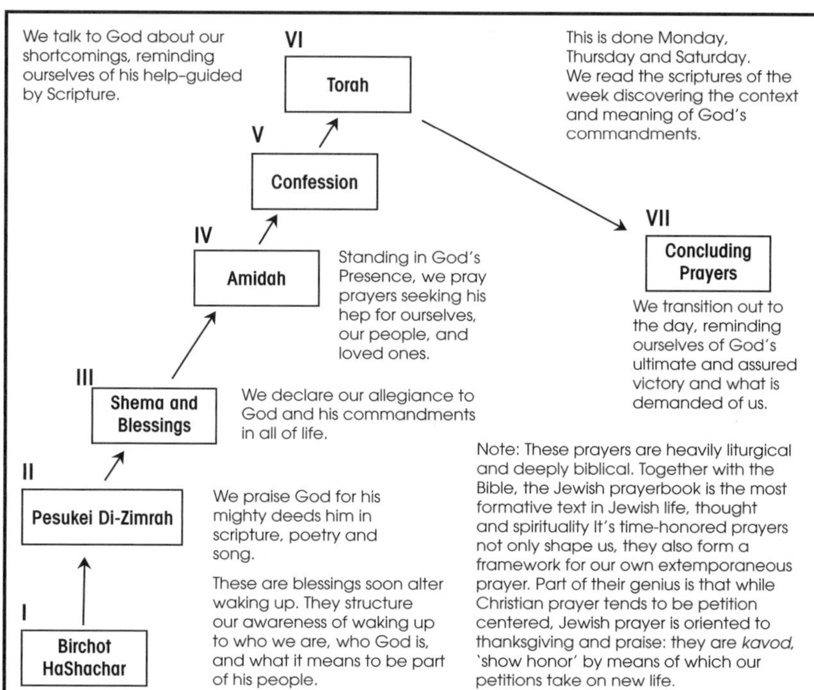

Kashrut (Holy Eating)

A third discipline for Jews is *kashrut* (holy eating). The first sin of humankind involved eating what had been forbidden. It then stands to reason that a faithful Jewish relationship with God involves obedient attention to what we may or may not eat. Eating is perhaps the most personal act we perform on a daily basis. Therefore, by prescribing what his people may eat, God is reminding us of who he is. By following his directives in the matter, we give him kavod. By adhering to these strictures, we actualize our unity with all Israel as a kingdom of priests and a holy nation, acknowledging the God of Israel to be our Supreme LORD, and ourselves his servants.

B'rachot (Holy Mindfulness)

A fourth daily discipline concerns *b'rakhot/b'rakha* (blessings). Today, many are intrigued by the Buddhist practice of mindfulness. However, this Jewish practice predates the Buddha and is enshrined in saying blessings of three kinds: (1) blessings over various types of enjoyment, including eating, drinking, and inhaling fragrances, with different blessings for different kinds of food and drink; (2) blessings recited before the fulfillment of a ritual commandment such as candle lighting, hand washing, studying, and so on; and (3) blessings of praise and thanks (which include the numerous blessings of the liturgy and the Birkat HaMazon (grace after meals). There are also blessings for various special occasions—happy, sad, usual, and extraordinary, such as deliverance from danger, seeing a long-lost friend, hearing bad news, seeing a person of great Torah learning, seeing a person of great secular learning, seeing someone congenitally disfigured, or seeing a rainbow.

While some *berakhot* are recited spontaneously as occasions arise, others are recited as part of daily liturgical prayer. Our tradition expects us to say at least one hundred such blessings a day, challenging us to find one hundred occasions to bless God for his goodness to all his children. This is a wonderful idea for Jews and anyone else. And this is blessed mindfulness. All of these blessings, of whatever kind, serve to elevate awareness or mindfulness of our relationship to God and to other human beings, and of the kavod to which each is entitled. On the other hand, our tradition frowns on mindless ritualism. Saying these blessings in their related circumstances forces us to pay attention to what is happening around us and to what we are doing. In the midst of life, we offer praise to God, in all things giving to Adonai the kavod due his name: "For from him and through him and to him are all things. To him be the glory [the kavod] forever. Amen" (Rom 11:36).

CONCLUSION

One might well consider all of Jewish ritual life as a modality for the distribution of appropriate honor—treating God, people, and things with proper weight, taking into account diversities of identity, relationship, and context. Indeed, it is as we give proper weight to the relationships and events of our lives that we best give kavod—honor, glory—to God, acknowledging the supreme weightiness of his being. What must not be missed is how Judaism combats monotony and sameness of life. Through the distribution of kavod we remind ourselves that not all people, not all things, not all places are the same. Each differs in its intrinsic and attributed kavod. Even different times differ in the kavod accorded to them. And by holy mindfulness, we give to each experience the attention it uniquely deserves.

The anchor of this differentiation is the weekly observance of Shabbat. The great Hebrew philosopher Ahad Ha'am (1856–1927), whose birth name was Asher Ginsberg, was an influential Zionist although not a religious Jew. One of his most famous quotes is, "It may be said without exaggeration that more than the Jewish People have kept the Shabbat, the Shabbat has kept the Jewish People." Even an agnostic like Ahad Ha'am held Shabbat to be the source of renewal for the Jewish people, an ever flowing stream of renewal.

Shabbat remains the marked day in the midst of every seven, the day that gives every other its character by virtue of the distance between them. And Shabbat is ineluctably different, forever protecting Jews from Macbeth's "tomorrow, and tomorrow, and tomorrow, [creeping in] its petty pace from day to day." And from his "tale, told by an idiot, full of sound and fury, signifying nothing." Judaism's passion for differentiation of persons, places, things, and time, ritually marked and protected, each accorded its appropriate kavod, is an ever renewing stream for those who will but pause to drink.

This is a far better drink than any might find in the Starbucks where we began. It is the drink of life in all its richness, its differentiation, in anticipation of that Day when "we all, with unveiled face, beholding the glory of the Lord, are being transformed into the same image from one degree of glory to another. For this comes from the Lord who is the Spirit" (2 Cor 3:18).

With Focus on Context

12

The Smudge Ceremony

Inspiring Faith in Indigenous North Americans

Cheryl Bear

My name is Cheryl Bear. I am an Indigenous woman from the Nadleh Whut'en community of the Dakelh People and am from the Bear Clan. The Dakelh of northern British Columbia were formerly known as the Carrier Nation, given that name in the 1800s by French fur traders who said our people were capable of carrying heavy loads for long distances. Our name for ourselves is Dakelh, which means "the people who travel on the water."

In this chapter I explore the smudge ceremony common among Indigenous people in North America. I also include an overview of Native experience as it pertains to ceremony and ritual. I intend to show how the smudge ceremony can be used as a Christian ritual in order to increase one's devotion to God. Because I believe ceremonies are not for God but for humans, I explore the deep meaningfulness of the smudge ceremony to inspire Christian faith among First Nation believers.

Throughout the chapter I use the term "Indigenous" (with an uppercase "I") because there are several ways to speak of native groups in Canada. "First Nations" refers specifically to Inuit and Metis, who, though distinct, have affinity with one another. The word "indigenous" in general is defined as "of the land." I use "Indigenous" as a generic term for Native American people from both Canada and the United States whose beliefs and values reflect their understanding of the land and all their surroundings, including the spiritual aspects of the world in which they live. These traditions are handed down by the elders. When an Indigenous person uses the term "elder," it refers to a person who is usually over fifty years of age.

Non-Native people might consider this a derogatory term because of the focus on age. However, Indigenous people use the term "elder" as a title of honor. In fact, a picture of wisdom would be a circle of elders.

BACKGROUND

The smudge is a cleansing or purification ceremony. Indigenous peoples have varied cleansing ceremonies; some involve washing in a river at dawn, dipping several times, and others involve pain being inflicted upon the body. Cleansing ceremonies are as unique as the Nations that practice them. Many Indigenous communities across the United States and Canada have adopted the smudge tradition as a cleansing ceremony, even though it is not a part of their own stories and traditions. This is perhaps because it is a rather modest ritual that is easily adapted and serves as a recognizable adaptation of particular experiences across the North American continent.

For example, in my Nadleh Whut'en community, there is disagreement between elders. Some say the smudge is not part of our culture, and others say it was a part of our culture long ago. However, the young people who use it demonstrate their appreciation of Native culture and its usefulness as a ceremony that demonstrates the value of an Indigenous cleansing ritual.

Although many cleansing ceremonies and rituals are found among the Indigenous peoples of North America, I focus on the smudge ceremony. Traditional Indigenous people (which is to say, those who follow traditional Native beliefs and values) use the smudge ceremony to cleanse the body, soul, and spirit. While some non-Indigenous Christian leaders consider this ritual syncretistic—an impermissible blending of two opposing belief systems and worldviews—I see it as demonstrating the value of Indigenous traditions, cleansing and bringing a sweet smell to God (Ps 141:2). In this chapter, I embark on a journey to discover how the smudge ceremony can be utilized and seen as hybridity rather than syncretism, as a positive rather than a negative. I do this by considering Indigenous expressions within the smudging ceremony and its value for articulating devotion to God using scriptural comparisons.

In chapter 2 William Burrows calls this process "hybridity" and distinguishes it from syncretism, which he views as an external critique on traditional practices made by people with a Eurocentric perspective of Christianity. The common view is that such practices are far from "proper" Christian experience. For Indigenous North American Christians, ceremonies such as the smudge are understood as reflecting their belief that they are a people recognizing their Creator and living in ways that were given to them from the beginning.

Regarding syncretism, Dan Shaw, in his introductory chapter, draws on the insights of third-generation missionary Paul Hiebert and his view that Scripture should be the standard related to ritual and ceremony. Hiebert noted two inappropriate approaches leading to syncretism: "denial and condemnation of old beliefs and practices" and "uncritical acceptance of old beliefs and practices" (Hiebert 1987, 106). The first avenue to syncretism resulted in driving practices underground—continuing to rely on the power of their old practices. The second approach often resulted in a confusing integration of outside behavior patterns with existing beliefs and practices without any critique leading to altering the behavior. For Hiebert, critical contextualization was the missiological fix (1987, 110; see also Shaw, chapter 1).

Christians from Europe and North America have largely forgotten that their Christianity has been contextualized over many centuries. They seem unaware that the Indigenous peoples of North America need to contextualize the gospel for themselves. Although it may seem harsh to say so, missionaries did not allow contextualization to occur in North America and have driven it underground in Latin America among the Indigenous and mestizo populations. Sadly the history of Christianity in Latin America, Canada, and the United States has a similar history with regard to Indigenous people—a history of colonization, both physical and cultural.

The United States and Canada first tried to solve the "Indian problem" by attempting to eradicate the Indigenous population. One of the ways of colonizing their minds and cultures was to initiate Indian boarding schools (in Canada, these schools were called residential schools). The goal of these schools was to kill the Indian in the child according to Richard Pratt, an advocate of using such schools to "Americanize" Native Americans. In a major report on these schools, Pratt (1892) wrote,

> A great general [William Tecumseh Sherman] once said that the only good Indian is a dead one, and that high sanction of his destruction has been an enormous factor in promoting Indian massacres. In a sense, I agree with the sentiment, but only in this: that all the Indian there is in the race should be dead. Kill the Indian in him, and save the man.

One school promotion stated, "Send us the Indian children and after two years the only thing left that is Indian will be the color of his skin."

This was the policy of both the Canadian and US governments. Unfortunately, the day-to-day operations were given to the church, which decided that everything in Native culture was evil. So this precious gospel, which we long to share with a broken world, was never given as a gift to Indigenous people but used as a weapon or a tool of assimilation.

A few years ago a group of Native leaders from across Canada was invited to meet with Paul Martin, former prime minister of Canada. He knew about the history of colonization in which the church played a devastating part, and he asked, "After all this history, why are you even Christians?" Good question. Our answer is that the story of Jesus is much older than our encounter with Europeans, as Richard Twiss makes clear in his excellent volume on Native American expressions of the Jesus way (2015). Twiss's book *Rescuing the Gospel from the Cowboys* helps us understand how the Holy Spirit is introducing new ideas of being both Native and "Christian" while walking with Jesus.

My concern in this chapter—after so much pain—is, how do we communicate the gospel to a people who have never heard it as good news? The gospel has become a part of this history of the ancient wounds of colonization. Incorporating the smudge ceremony as an act of devotion to God is one of the ways we can communicate the precious story of Jesus.

INDIGENOUS SPIRITUAL EXPERIENCE

Indigenous peoples see the world differently than non-Indigenous people. We do not only see the physical world of matter but also experience the spirit realm as very real, present, and functioning alongside our physical reality. It seems that many Indigenous people have a foot in both worlds. The monotheistic view of a great Creator is a foundational Indigenous understanding of spiritual reality. Every North American Indigenous ceremony and value begins with Creator. Indigenous people also have respect for humans, the earth, animals, and plants. These things are not seen as something to be dominated. The Indigenous view is that we have an interdependent relationship with the plants, animals, and earth (including air, land, and water), and thus we must relate to them in humility. The idea of stewardship is common among Indigenous people and is even found in many of our creation stories.

At this point it is important to say a few words about Indigenous ceremonies and rituals. First, they are a normal part of Indigenous thought and spiritual expression. They often revolve around cleansing the body, soul, and spirit. They point to our need to have an advocate or outside help to approach Creator to cleanse us.

Following Shaw, I am using the term "ceremony" in contrast to ritual, because most of the cleansing ceremonies involve community. Sometimes the cleansing is for the land or for a living space, but most often for people. Cleansing is needed for land or living space when something bad has happened or because there is a bad feeling, evil presence, or supernatural event. Cleansing for people as individuals or groups is an ongoing process and can take place daily.

Indigenous Prayer

The role of ceremony is perfectly illustrated by an experience I had in 2003. "I know how you Christians pray. Now I'm going to show you how I pray." A Dakelh chief spoke these words to the outreach team I led to the Dakelh community that summer. Ten of us happily drove up the mountain where we were scheduled to meet and learn from the chief. We stopped along the road, and the chief found some natural coal that he had us press on our foreheads as he explained, "It is a sign of respect to the mountain." I could not help being reminded of a passage in Isaiah:

> At the sound of their voices the doorposts and thresholds shook and the temple was filled with smoke. "Woe to me!" I cried. "I am ruined! For I am a man of unclean lips, and I live among a people of unclean lips, and my eyes have seen the King, the LORD Almighty." Then one of the seraphs flew to me with a live coal in his hand, which he had taken with tongs from the altar. With it he touched my mouth and said, "See, this has touched your lips; your guilt is taken away and your sin atoned for." (6:4–7)

We parked the car and walked a ways into the bush, where we found stones placed around what looked like a well-used campfire. Without a word the chief collected branches from five different trees and made a small fire, which mostly produced smoke. Then he explained that we were going to walk over the fire three times. As we did so, we would leave our troubles there. Whatever was bothering us, whatever was causing us grief, we were to leave, he said, and "the smoke will carry our troubles to Creator," which reminded me of Psalm 142:2: "Accept my prayer as incense offered to you, and my upraised hands as an evening offering." Having been raised in a Christian home, and despite my beautiful Dakelh heritage, I had heard it said that everything Native was not from God. This made me cautiously suspicious of the chief. Yet my missiological studies caused me to hush my strict, evangelical stream of thought and give the chief space to teach us.

Just as we were about to step over the smoldering fire, the chief said, "We need to pray," and at that moment a female Native elder walked out of the forest into our clearing. My outreach team members and I were quite shocked to see her approach until the chief said, "Oh, hi Mum." He introduced her to our team, and it turned out she knew my late grandpa, Alec George, and spoke well of him. She said she was there to gather medicines, and I bristled, worried she was a medicine woman. I had been warned about this in the various churches I had attended growing up and by many non-Indigenous and Indigenous Christians who were distrustful of Indigenous culture. I learned, however, that she used her herbs to help people, traded her medicines for blankets (never for money), and as a well-known healer was respected throughout the Dakelh community.

Then the chief asked his mother to pray for us. I braced myself, not knowing what to expect. She started praying, "Oh heavenly Father, we ask you to fill us with your Holy Spirit. . . . Let this smoke cleanse us . . . and we ask all of this in the precious name of Jesus." We were all in tears. We walked across the ceremonial fire, and the smoke carried our troubles to Creator. I was more than a little healed that day, and I left a great burden on that mountain. It was good, a very good day.

Indigenous Values

Every human being behaves in a certain way because of learned values. Values dictate behavior. The Indigenous belief in a benevolent creator affects the way we live. Indigenous people have specific values that determine their actions at home and in community. Prominent among Indigenous values are humility, honor, respect, family, healthy relationships, speech, leadership, elders, silence, and humor. Indigenous people talk often about honor and respect. First we must show honor to our creator. This is a common way of being for all First Nation communities I have visited. Every powwow, potlatch, memorial, and even political gatherings are opened with prayer from an elder or spiritual leader.

One of the ways we show honor to Creator is to show respect to everything. Respect is a strong value among Indigenous groups, which the elders pass on to young people. Indigenous children learn by watching the elders. Traditionally, if an Indigenous person does not agree with non-Native ways or is offended by something they see, rather than confront the issue directly, they will simply withdraw from the situation. These are the very old ways. Today, however, we have to defend our land and our rights and cannot simply withdraw anymore.

Indigenous people value relationships over agenda. Showing up on time is not a high value for Native peoples. Promptness is not a priority because the relationship takes precedence. If you ask, "When does the meeting start?" The answer will be, "When everyone shows up."

I have said that silence is also a value of Native peoples. In the past, Indigenous people were often considered slow or stupid because they did not answer questions quickly. If a Native person takes a long time to respond during a discussion, the person is demonstrating the effects of careful listening. Native people often pause in the middle of their dialogue, not because they are finished, but because they are carefully considering their next thought. This is the best method of discussion and the reason that Indigenous people tend to be great orators. Some non-Native speakers believe many words equate wisdom, while Native people choose words carefully and speak slowly so that every word is heard and understood.

Perhaps the most misunderstood value of Indigenous people is their recognition of leadership. The cultural attitude of white Canadians and Americans toward leadership is very different from those of Indigenous people. In non-Native settings, individuals who take initiative are most admired. Indigenous people differ not because they are unable to take the initiative, but because they wait to be recognized. If, in a meeting, someone calls out, "Someone open in prayer," the Native leader will not step forward because the Native value is to wait and be recognized. A Native leader may well step out and begin praying in such a setting, but only because they have been forced to adopt a foreign value in order to succeed in a non-Native world. This is a form of cultural assimilation. I have been challenged regarding this value. How can Indigenous people succeed since they will be consistently overlooked because non-Native values predominate? I now encourage our Native leaders to lean into our cultural values and ways of being.

This plays out in beautiful ways. There was an ordination service for Julia Lucas from the Nuxalk Nation in British Columbia. All of the hereditary chiefs were invited. As I was preparing at the front of the hall, someone came to me and told me that the hereditary chiefs had arrived. I said, "Let me go and find them." I went to the back of the hall and found them there. I said, "Why do I always find the chiefs in the back row?" And they laughed.

The answer is they were waiting to be recognized. In a non-Native setting, the leadership value of waiting to be recognized can be self-esteem-crushing, but in reality, it is a beautiful way of being. It is also very biblical, as we are reminded in Luke 14:7–11: "When you are invited, take the lowest place, so that when your host comes, he will say to you, 'Friend, move up to a better place.' Then you will be honored in the presence of all your fellow guests" (v. 10)

Indigenous people place a high value on elders, and the symbol of wisdom is a circle of elders. This is also why one of the descriptive names for Creator is "Grandfather." It is not that prayer is directed to an ancestor, but rather it is assigning Creator a description similar to "ancient one." Indigenous elders are rarely, if ever, found in a home for the aged; instead, they are cared for in their own homes and die in their own beds surrounded by family. Those fortunate enough to be grandparents know how precious it is to have a grandchild. Grandparents have an old love, a perspective that can only be understood by elders. They know the precious value of a grandchild's life. In this same way, Native people understand Creator—one who has the ancient love, understanding, and the perspective of a grandfather.

Still another Indigenous value is to not be proud. Pride evidenced by arrogance and conceit is generally unacceptable. Being proud of one's nationality, sports team, of being a veteran, or a particular accomplishment is good and right. The differentiating factor is pride taking on the shape of arrogance and conceit. In Native culture, no one can get away with being proud in the sense of arrogance. To deal with pride we use humor to help the offender learn humility through teasing.

Native humor is quite surprising because it comes out of nowhere and is so funny. Most Indigenous people have a great sense of humor and love to laugh. Humor is a large and significant part of Native life. It is used often to relieve tension. During the Niisga Treaty talks with the Canadian government, the more tense the negotiation, the more laughter was heard. My grandpa and other elders from Nadleh Whut'en would sometimes laugh at a joke in our Dakelh language. Interestingly, when we asked, "What's so funny?" they would reply, "It's only funny in Dakelh."

THE INDIGENOUS CONCEPT OF CREATOR

Where does the Indigenous concept of Creator come from? Why does every single Indigenous people group in Canada have a story of Creator? For many years I heard Christian leaders (both Indigenous and non-Indigenous) compare our stories of Creator to false gods. They said that our stories are not from the Bible and therefore were not valid. However, our stories are based on oral tradition, which has strong validation when compared with biblical stories. Most of the Bible is based on oral tradition.

Our stories tell of a benevolent Creator who started everything, made everything, watches over everything, hears and answers our prayers, who cares and deserves our highest respect. These stories would seem to rise from the pages of the Old Testament. I have found nothing in our Native stories about Creator that contradicts a biblical understanding of God. This belief in Creator is where Indigenous values come from; it is the foundation of our values and way of being. Our way of being reflects a life lived before Creator.

There are two ways Creator is made known to humankind: general and special revelation. These are commonly accepted doctrinal truths. General revelation refers to God being made known through Creation. Special revelation tells us that Creator is made known perfectly through the work and person of Jesus Christ. This outlook finds confirmation in Romans 1:20: "For ever since the world was created, people have seen the earth and sky. Through everything God made, they can clearly see his invisible qualities—his eternal power and divine nature. So they have no excuse for not knowing God." Most Euro-American and Canadian believers lean toward science and away from a notion of Creator revealed in nature. Most Indigenous people, on the other hand, start with a clear understanding of the sort of general revelation of which St. Paul speaks.

Lizette Hall, one of the elders of my Dakelh nation, wrote a book called *The Carrier, My People* (1992). In this book she described Creator's name as "The Being up on High." Hall states that her elders would sometimes shorten it by saying, "The Up on High." Hall did not write the actual Dakelh version of this name, only the English translation. Not until I met her did I learn the actual Dakelh word for "The Up on High," but I will not spell it out, following the example of my elder. As an Indigenous author I would like to honor both our elders and Creator by not writing out the name in our language. Hall tells us how they showed respect, by not ever speaking the name of the Being up on High. Rather, if someone noticed a sign from Creator, they caught the attention of another person silently and motioned toward the sign. Even this way of showing respect to Creator is similar to the way the Hebrews did not name God, but instead used the Tetragrammaton, YHWH (the Hebrew name of God without the vowels). We now understand our Creator to be Yahweh (or Jehovah), who is called Lord in our English Bible, after the term Adonai, which is an acceptable term for YHWH.

Such demonstrations of the great respect our people have for Creator shows that we recognize the need for help in order to approach Creator. This is the foundation of all our First Nation ceremonies. The purpose of all our rituals is to make us ceremonially clean in order to approach and pray to Creator. In some communities, regrettably, this tradition has been lost. Instead the cleansing ceremony becomes simply a rite performed to obtain cleansing, and some contemporary cleansing ceremonies sometimes do not even mention Creator. When one talks to elders about these matters, they are adamant that all our ceremonies are founded on Creator.

One of the descriptive Indigenous names of Creator is the "Great Mystery." The incarnation of Jesus, to Native people, means that Jesus has come into their world to reveal Creator, not that Creator revealed Jesus. Jesus points to Creator. The way to receive a fuller understanding of Creator, especially for our Indigenous people, is through a life, a character, a person that depicts for humanity the essence of Creator. The full and complete disclosure was given to people—not just in nature, or in sayings and stories, nor perfectly in the Bible. Although the Bible is God's word, the Bible is not *the* revelation of God; it is the inspired record of the revelation (Bear-Barnetson 2013, 56). The complete revelation is Jesus.

My contextualized paraphrase of John 1:14 is, "The Word became flesh and blood and moved onto the Reservation"—a term that describes the land allotted to Indigenous people, which is very different from a traditional understanding of land made available for Indigenous use by Creator. I have found that the greatest thing one can say to Indigenous people is, "To know Jesus is to know Creator, to love Jesus is to love Creator, and to serve Jesus is to serve Creator for Jesus has perfectly revealed Creator." Recall what Jesus says in John 10:38b, "The Father is in me, and I in the Father."

Today Jesus walks onto the reservation through his body, the church. The Incarnation means that the church must be an Indigenous church. It means that the true Christian message must be an Indigenous message. It also means that one's worship must be Indigenous and authentic: worship, ceremony, values, instruments, methods, institutions, and life.

I said earlier that most Indigenous people in Canada and the United States have never heard the true gospel, because the gospel they first heard was indistinguishable from conquest, land acquisition, and "civilization." It is simply a fact that the first Europeans felt superior to the Indigenous people and had a geopolitical agenda that entailed assimilation or extermination of Indigenous people.

Today the gospel must be given as a gift, and the seed of the gospel must grow into Indigenous hearts and minds—people living on the land. God is at work among all people all over the world. Our job is sometimes to walk in and recognize the hand of Creator or the story of Jesus among a people.

ANCESTORS

Indigenous people in Canada often talk about ancestors. Some even talk about praying to or for ancestors. Burrows discusses this issue in chapter 2, differentiating between Catholics recognizing the presence of ancestors and the worship of ancestors. Paul Mantae Kim in his chapter on the ancestor rite in Korea affirms the need to recognize the presence of ancestors and how to give them honor, as does DomNwachukwu among the Igbo. Joshua Daimoi emphasizes the Melanesian focus on giving due respect and honor in contrast to worshiping the ancestors. The Indigenous people in Canada and the United States have no need to "worship" ancestors, because every Indigenous culture has the concept of a creator who alone they worship. At the same time, they also recognize the past reality of their ancestors as well as their ongoing ancestral presence.

As an Indigenous person I am not anxious about the term "ancestors." Terminology found in the New Testament should put most Christians at ease: "Therefore, since we are surrounded by such a great cloud of witnesses" (Heb 12:1–3). Most Christians understand the "cloud of witnesses" to mean the Christians who have died and are now in heaven, while Native people simply refer to "ancestors." There is an interesting interplay between the spirit world and our physical one, a Native elder in his seventies once said, "The prayers my mother prayed for me are still being answered today."

Indigenous people do not see the spirit world as far up and away. Rather, the spirit world is close, another dimension of existence running parallel with our physical reality. This is the same as the Christian concept of God's omnipresence. God is not my table or a tree. That is not how God is everywhere. God is separate and "above" creation. Indigenous people would probably say that God is alongside creation.

The concept of Creator is strong among our people across North America. A respected elder opens every gathering with prayer to the creator. The gathering does not have to be a spiritual meeting. I have attended political meetings where heads of state acquiesce to open a meeting with prayer. It is one of the most consistent beliefs and values among our Indigenous people in Canada and the United States.

ORAL HISTORY

As part of my journey, I have visited nearly six hundred of the approximately one thousand Indigenous communities in Canada and the United States. My hope is to retell the story of Jesus in an Indigenous way. In my travels I have asked elders to tell me their stories. These stories are our oral history. Oral tradition plays a large part in the Indigenous worldview. Our entire culture is based on our stories, our oral tradition, and that tradition includes many genre. Some stories are historical accounts, some are spiritual and moral stories, and others are simply good, fun stories.

Every Indigenous community I have visited has a concept of Creator embodied in its stories. When anthropologists ask for the name of Creator, Native people only give the English translation for the name because our elders tell us the name of Creator deserves great honor. They will not give away the name of Creator to people who, they believe, will not give it the proper place of respect. As I already noted, this is what Lizette Hall did; she simply gave the English translation of Creator's name, "Being up on High." She never wrote out the descriptive name in our language.

Divine Placement

Indigenous people know how to present themselves to an audience. One begins by stating their tribal affiliation (nation), where they are from (reservation), one's clan (if any), and a little about their family, but almost never what their occupation is. The sequence is very important for Native people. Our origin, land, and people define us, not our occupation, as I demonstrate in the opening of this chapter.

Divine placement theology may be defined as the reconciliation between the biblical record and traditional First Nations records of Creator's original placement of the people on the land and his intended purposes for them. Every First Nation has within its recorded history the concept of "People of the Land." The very name by which most nations identify themselves is usually translated as a variation of "The People" or "The People of the Land." Thus, every First Nation believes that Creator placed them exactly where they are. The first item on the Charter of the Assembly of First Nations states, "We the Chiefs of the Indian First Nations of Canada having declared that: *our people are the original peoples of this land having been put here by the Creator*" (Assembly of First Nations 2003).

Language

Language is identity, and language is very important to the Indigenous community, not only for ordinary communication, but also for telling stories. One of the good things the church has done is to translate the Bible into Native languages, thereby encouraging an appreciation for what God has said while also building strong local identity.

The late well-known author and speaker Richard Twiss (of the Lakota Sioux) tells the story of an elder who was asked, "Have you lived your whole life on the reservation?" The elder answered, "Not yet." Not only does this exemplify the difference between Native and non-Native, it also illustrates how the journey is often more important than the destination.

A new model is needed to reach First Nations people. On the one hand, if there are Native people currently in non-Native-style churches and they are satisfied, then let them stay. On the other hand, direct attention is required to reach Indigenous people who will never darken the doorway of a church because they have been taught that the church was only interested in assimilation and annihilation of local people. Indigenous people must own the gospel, which has never really happened in the life of the Indigenous church of North America. They have never been fully trusted. But now I discuss the smudge ceremony as one way in which an important dimension of the gospel can be imparted.

THE SMUDGE CEREMONY

Smudging, at its core, is a cleansing ceremony practiced by many Indigenous people in Canada and the United States. As explained by our elders, the ceremony is designed to allow the smoke to cleanse all whom it touches. Smoke from a campfire once drifted to me no matter where I sat. My uncle John said, "It's good when the smoke follows you." The idea was the smoke makes us clean, and Uncle John embedded this notion deeply in me.

Smudging involves the use of sage, bundled and tied with string or yarn and then dried—a process that takes time. If visiting another community, permission to harvest must be received from the residence community.

The smudge ceremony begins by lighting a bundle of dried sage. After lighting the bundle with a match and placing it in a large abalone shell, the fire is blown out and the smoke wafts out like incense. The smell of the smoke is pungent, and the aroma of the incense is a call to worship Creator. The ceremony involves a sense of intentionality—the need for repentance—and it doesn't just happen. It is a call to attention. The smoke reminds us of Creator's forgiveness.

Integral to the ceremony, an elder or spiritual leader waves the smoke toward the participants with a feather. While the elder is directing the smoke, participants use their hands to pull the smoke toward their face, head, heart, arms, body, legs, and feet, thus cleansing themselves with the smoke.

Incense, we know, is found in many nations and religions around the world. I remember when I was a child the strong scent of incense filled our Catholic church during certain ceremonies. Some Protestants find the use of incense to be too elaborate, but mention of it abounds in the Pentateuch, the Psalms, and the historical books. And there is a beautiful Scripture in Malachi, where God reminds the Jews that people all over the world honor Creator. When this Scripture was written, Indigenous people in North America were already performing cleansing ceremonies using sage, sweet grass, and cedar. "My Name will be great among the nations, from where the sun rises to where it sets. In every place incense and pure offerings will be brought to me, because my name will be great among the nations, says the Lord Almighty" (Mal 1:11).

Cleansing ceremonies point to our need for cleansing from sin—from the sins we have committed before God and the sins that have been perpetrated upon us. We know we need this cleansing. The beauty of the smudge ceremony lies first of all in the Indigenous person recognizing this great need to turn to Creator—the One who started everything, the One who made everything, the One who holds everything, the One who watches over us, the Great Spirit, the Great Mystery, the Being up on High.

All our North American Indigenous cleansing ceremonies point directly to Jesus. Jesus is the cleansing sacrifice. These ceremonies remind us that we need cleansing and we cannot just do this ceremony once and for all. We must do it every day, sometimes more than once a day because our best human efforts cannot eliminate sin. The ceremony reminds us that we are cleansed and forgiven. Even the best of us so often forget the grace of God. Ceremony grounds us in the grace of God and a dependence on that grace. It brings back to memory God's faithfulness and love. As we participate in ceremony daily, we symbolically receive this gift of grace. Ceremony is for humans. It helps us remember what God has done for us through Christ.

Jesus did not dismiss the meaning of the cleansing ceremonies found in the Old Testament, but rather he deepened them. As the Holman online Bible Dictionary notes, Christ obeyed the Law (Lev 14:2–32) by sending healed lepers to the priest for cleansing (Mt 8:4). Jesus lived his life following Jewish traditions and purification ceremonies.

The apostle Paul underwent a Jewish purification ceremony in order to be accepted by his peers, then known as the Judaizers, even though he was adamant that following Jesus, who was God in the flesh, meant Christians were no longer bound by the Law. Was his return to the Jewish purification ceremony syncretism? I think not, for the cleansing ceremonies throughout the Old Testament point to the human need for a savior. They all point to Jesus, who did not stop at merely obeying the Old Testament cleansing rituals and ceremonies. Instead, Jesus fulfilled them to the extent he himself became the cleansing sacrifice to fulfill all the cleansing ceremonies in the Old Testament: "If we confess our sins God will forgive our sins and cleanse us from all unrighteousness" (1 Jn 1:9). Accepting Jesus is the only way to receive ultimate cleansing and forgiveness, since in Jesus we have the perfect Lamb of God who takes away the sins of the world by his self-sacrifice, the ultimate cleansing sacrifice. Here in the giving of his life, Jesus ransoms us, pays that debt, takes it all, all the sin of the world. Smudging serves as a symbolic representation of the cleansing available because of Jesus's sacrifice. Again, quoting from Scripture:

> This is the message we have heard from him and declare to you: God is light; in him there is no darkness at all. If we claim to have fellowship with him and yet walk in the darkness, we lie and do not live out the truth. But if we walk in the light, as he is in the light, we have fellowship with one another, and the blood of Jesus, his Son, purifies us from all sin. If we claim to be without sin, we deceive ourselves and the truth is not in us. If we confess our sins, he is faithful and just and will forgive us our sins and purify us from all unrighteousness. If we claim we have not sinned, we make him out

to be a liar and his word is not in us. (1 Jn 1:5–10)

The smudge ceremony also reminds us that we are human. Saginaw Grant, a Sac and Fox Nation elder, prayed at the beginning of the Pasadena, California, powwow in 2006, "Creator, have pity on us for we are human." Most of us remember that we are human and need more reminders that we are forgiven. Why do we as Indigenous people believe we need cleansing? Where does this ceremony originate? Elders speak of our need to be cleansed from the things we have done as well as the things done to us. While the term "sin" is rarely used in our Indigenous context, it is acknowledged. The chief on that mountain told us a part of the Dakelh creation story. He spoke of Creator and said one day Creator is going to come back and look at how we have taken care of the land that was loaned to us. There is always a reckoning. In ancient Native communities, if someone committed a terrible act such as murder, that person was often banished. This is judgment, revealing a concept of separation from family and especially elders or the head of that person's household—the grandfather or grandmother—that is close to the Christian concept of hell, which is eternal separation from Creator.

LIMITATIONS OF RITUAL AND CEREMONY

The limitation of the Old Testament cleansing laws is that they need to be done regularly. By that account, we too sin and need forgiveness regularly. This is simply the human condition. This is also the limitation of our Indigenous cleansing ceremonies. Without Christ they simply point out what is wrong and provide a temporary covering. The smoke does not actually cleanse our soul or spirit. In fact, we know from scientific studies that some properties of the smoke can be harmful to our lungs. But something else is going on here. It is a spiritual act of faith that brings about a physical change and healing. This is the heart of the gospel: reconciliation with God and the healing of our spiritual, mental, physical, and emotional selves.

For Christians, Jesus is already the fulfillment of our ceremonies. He is the only one who can cleanse our soul and spirit through the power of the Holy Spirit. Our ceremonies are only our best efforts to honor Creator and to symbolize cleansing by receiving forgiveness and being healed.

I remember playing in the Nadleh River when I was a child. We found some clay (it is of some interest to me that Nadleh elders say the clay is good for cleansing) and proceeded to become clay monsters as we covered ourselves from head to toe and had a blast. Bath time later that day, however, was not so fun. No matter how hard I tried, I could not get the clay off by myself. It even stuck to the soap! I needed help. One of my parents had to scrub and clean off all that clay and, thankfully, even got the soap clean.

Without doubt, humanness taints our ceremonies. We cannot help it. Our selfishness, greed, lust, jealousy, and much more affect every aspect of our lives. Beautiful ceremonies, given by Creator, can quickly become mucky. But does that mean we need to abandon all our ancient ceremonies? Or can we take these ceremonies as part of a grace-filled process of hybridity and create something that is deeply meaningful, Indigenous, and honoring to Christ, as Shaw suggests?

We can apply Burrows's concept of hybridity to the smudge ceremony, as we take two disparate ideas, the smudge ceremony and the Christian theological concepts of sanctification and justification, and blend them together into a new thing symbolizing a deeply, biblically rooted reality. Culture is not static. While many aspects of culture are consistent and easily transferable cross-culturally, some variables are not so easily grasped, and much discernment is necessary. Establishing how to understand them and ceremonially bring them into a different cultural world is the task of transformation. In this case the two "disparate ideas" can actually be closer to congruency than Euro-American Christian pioneers may have thought in earlier times. The burning of sage points to Christ, so why not focus the ceremony on the person and work of Jesus and think of the smoke symbolically representing Christ's forgiveness?

Ceremony is especially meaningful and may be largely lost on evangelicals because of Calvin's commitment to the "Word alone." I was born and raised a Catholic but then became involved in a Pentecostal church and had not been in a Catholic church for many years. While attending Regent College in Vancouver, BC, I gained a new appreciation for liturgy and spiritual traditions. So I attended our Catholic church at Nadleh, my Indigenous community. There I heard the priest say, "Your sins are forgiven." I did not remember ever hearing this statement before. It would be inappropriate in an evangelical setting, yet it sounded so beautiful. The priest's words flowed over me, and I received the forgiveness of Christ in a new way. I had heard most of my life that we are not to call anyone "Father" and that no one can stand in the place of Christ over us. But there in the little church where I had been baptized as a baby, I heard Jesus, and he spoke through our beloved Catholic priest, Father James, who is loved by everyone in Nadleh.

For too many years non-Native people have held the gospel over the Indigenous people with superiority. There has been and still exists a great reluctance to walk alongside Indigenous people, to experience their culture and values. The truth, however, is that Indigenous people have great knowledge of the spiritual realm and the power of Creator. Indigenous people are beautiful, spiritual, and full of wisdom to share with everyone. Non-Native people are all the poorer for not listening to the Indigenous voice. All you need to do is ask, even as I was invited to contribute to this book—and I'm grateful for the privilege of giving voice to our Indigenous people.

13

Ancestors as a Bridge for Understanding Jesus

A Case Study of Sentanian Biblical Theologizing

Joshua Kurung Daimoi

I belong to the Melanesian ethnic people—inhabitants of the West Papua, Papua New Guinea, Solomon Islands, Vanuatu, New Caledonia, and Fiji. My roots lie among the Sentanians who live along the edges of Lake Sentani, southwest of Jayapura, the capital of West Papua, the easternmost province of Indonesia.

At my birth, I was named Kurung after my grandfather, an act that identified me with my primal religion and ancestors. When I inherited my grandfather's name I became intimately one with him, and our lives merged. My grandfather represents my history, my belief, and my future inheritance. My grandfather is my guardian throughout my life. As long as I do my best to honor and care for him, his spirit will protect me and provide for me. In conferring my grandfather's name on me, my parents brought me into a covenant relationship with him, an ongoing relationship that Jon Davies calls "a covenant of mutual relationship between the living and the dead" (1994, 13).

Apart from my ancestral name, Kurung, I inherited our clan name, Daimoi, which identifies us with our original forefather. Thus, my clan name takes me deep into the very roots of my being. Although I had no personal involvement in the belief and practices of the primal faith, I learned much about it from listening to and observing what my parents and my people did. Our people practiced the primal religionist faith as part of honoring and maintaining relationship with our ancestors.

For centuries Melanesians have lived under the influence of ancestral spirits. Although Jesus Christ has been proclaimed in Melanesia for over one hundred years, the ancestral spirits continue to dominate the lives of the people. One common point of unity among all Oceanic peoples is our primal religionist orientation and the fact that we were among the last people groups to be evangelized (Trompf 1988). As primal religionists, we hold deep respect for our ancestors. As the last peoples to be evangelized, we struggle to understand how Christianity can be meaningfully related to our primal beliefs—more specifically, how does Christianity relate to our ancestors who have such a strong influence on our lives?

Many Melanesians continue to see Christianity as a white people's religion. Should the two belief systems, one with its core in the ancestors and the other centered in Jesus Christ, coexist or should one give way to the other? To answer that question, I see the priesthood of Jesus, as presented in the Epistle to the Hebrews, providing a meaningful understanding of the relationship between Jesus and the Melanesian ancestors. Hebrews is a text full of problems for people who think only in contemporary terms. In what follows, however, I hope to show that for Melanesians the Epistle to the Hebrews can provide the basis for inserting the ancestors into God's plan of salvation and for understanding the work of Jesus.

SENTANI HOLISTIC UNITY

The world of the Sentanians, as their history reveals, is an interrelationship of animate and inanimate, visible and invisible, living and dead, human and nonhuman. The Sentanian world exists in pairs: fathers and mothers, the living and the living-dead, jungles and waters, land and sky, what is above our world and what is below. These dualities are an interrelated, interdependent whole. Thus the community exists not just in pairs, but in unity, or as one holistic universe—a cosmology that unites the human world, the world above the earth, and the spirit world into an integrated whole, much as DomNwachukwu presents for the Igbo. In Paul Hiebert's terms, the "middle zone" spills into the transempirical as well as the empirical; the middle zone is full.

I identify with William Burrows's biblical-theological premise concerning Abraham and God's election of Israel as a covenantal relationship that becomes a source of blessing and a cause for judgment in making God known to all peoples including the Sentanians. I find in the New Testament Epistle to the Hebrews a clear revelation of both our present covenantal relationship and our future to be manifested in the eschatological return of Jesus Christ. Within Hebrews I see the plan of the ages revealed concerning Jesus. This specifically gives hope to the Sentanians and, more generally, Melanesians in their belief in and response to their ancestors.

The Sentanian leadership structure is hereditary in nature. The *kose* (created order) symbolizes this hereditary leadership structure and the blessing associated with it. The *ondoporo kabang* (supreme leader) is the apex of Sentanian leadership structure. The ondoporo kabang is the community's *yopa-yangpa* (son of the village; the roof) or *naribuna-waribunapa* (son of the life-giving water). The names symbolize the status of the ondoporo kabang as the political and spiritual leader of his people. The position of the ondoporo kabang is one sanctioned by the ancestral spirits.

As I show here, for Christianity to be meaningful for Sentanians, Jesus being God's firstborn needs to be presented as the ondoporo kabang. As their supreme leader, Jesus is therefore responsible for their well-being and the spiritual replacement of their ancestors on whom the people depended for all their needs.

Jesus, through his coming and death on the cross, fully adopts Melanesian identity with their ancestors as the fulfillment of all history: "In the past God spoke to our forefathers through the prophets at many times and in various ways, but in these last days He has spoken to us by his Son" (Heb 1:1–2). The history of the ancestors extends as far back as the primordial time to Adam and Eve, that is to say, the entirety of human history. Jesus provides full meaning to the Melanesian concept of *taim bipo* (long ago time) or *taim bilong tumbuna* (the [mythic] time of the ancestors) and becomes the focal point of Melanesian history.

This sense of history takes us into the Melanesian concept of time, which begins and ends with the ancestors. Biblically, time begins and ends with Jesus, thereby bringing Melanesian ancestors into the biblical view of time. Thus, when the writer to the Hebrews says, "But in these last days he [God] has spoken to us by his Son" (1:2), it means that the coming of Jesus marks the end of time, including the end of the ancestral time.

The concept of space, as a way of salvation for Melanesians, like history and time, is influenced by the issue of relationship, for the environment in which Melanesians live is religious, and everything in it contributes to the life of the community. Space for Melanesians is both concrete and personal. The well-being of the community and the richness of its resources directly relate to the people's relationship with their ancestors. Space is important to Melanesians because of its significance to their beliefs (Tuza 1987, 246). Sharing of space with the ancestors provides the people with security and continuity of life, a further expression of the Melanesian "search for salvation" (Strelan 1977).

For Melanesians, instead of looking to their ancestors for the meaning of history and time, they must now look to Jesus. Instead of keeping their ancestors perpetually before them, they must now keep their eyes fixed on Jesus. Instead of looking to their ancestors for protection, provision, and prosperity, they must now look to Jesus alone. Instead of worshiping and honoring their ancestors, all Melanesians must now worship and honor Jesus exclusively.

These statements do not, however, remove the importance of honor and respect Melanesians must have for their ancestors. As Paul Mantae Kim points out for Koreans, Melanesians can continue to honor the ancestors for who they were and what they achieved, and more especially to remember them as members of their respective families. But in so far as saving faith and worship are concerned, Melanesians are to look to Jesus and worship him alone. The phrase "in these last days" represents the time between incarnation and consummation, both of which carry special significance for Melanesians. Incarnation speaks of identification and substitution resulting in full adoption by faith, and consummation speaks of renewal and glorification. By definition, Jesus is the great ancestor, as well as the living ancestor, the alpha and omega, beginning and end, for Sentanians as well as the Hebrews, and indeed all those who put their faith in Christ.

THE EPISTLE TO THE HEBREWS

Melanesians honor and respect their ancestors as custodians of their past, present, and future. The Epistle to the Hebrews does the same with the ancestors of the Christian faith. They are referred to as "our forefathers"—in other words, "ancestors." Although these ancestors are dead, they continue to have a strong link with the new generation of men and women of faith, because these ancestors were the people to whom and through whom God spoke. This biblical truth complements what Melanesians held on to for generations before the coming of Christianity. This is to say, Melanesian ancestors and biblical ancestors were and are custodians of community faith.

What is of great interest to me is the way the Epistle to the Hebrews places Jesus in the context of the ancestors in Hebrews 1:1–2. In my judgment, Hebrews does this because the writer wants readers to see Jesus as an ancestor of their community. Jesus is presented in the context of faithful ancestors like Abraham, Moses, Joshua, Aaron, David, and all those listed in Hebrews 11. Melanesians need to see these biblical or Jewish ancestors as their ancestors, for three reasons:

- Melanesians have welcomed Christianity into their way of life.
- Through the concepts of "dual citizenship" and "an adoptive past," these biblical ancestors become part of the "new kith and kin" of Melanesians.
- The Melanesian practice of the *papamama* (parents or parental) family relationship makes these biblical ancestors also the Melanesian *papamama*.

The faithful ancestors mentioned in Hebrews spoke about Christ who was coming into the world. Thus, when Hebrews presents Jesus at the beginning in relation to the ancestors, the author makes two important claims about Jesus: Jesus is the one the biblical ancestors spoke about, and Jesus is the faithful ancestor.

The Death of Jesus

The death of Jesus is the climax of the demolition of the power of Satan, the strong man, together with the power and the fear of death. Death disarmed of its power means deliverance from the power of sin, which controls death, and the power of the law, which controls sin. Jesus conquered the cosmic powers by defeating the powers of Satan, death, sin, and the law. By way of summary, the apostle Paul states, "The sting of death is sin, and the power of sin is the law. But thanks be to God! He gives us the victory through our Lord Jesus Christ" (1 Cor 15:56–57).

As the merciful and faithful high priest, Jesus guards and protects his descendants through his intercessory ministry (Heb 7:25). The high priestly ministry of Jesus shows his deep personal and eternal love and care for those who have come to faith in him through his atoning sacrificial death. The sacrifice Jesus made two thousand years ago would be meaningless without his high-priestly follow-up ministry. God the Father has placed Jesus at his right hand as high priest (8:1) in order to attend to the needs of all descendants through all of time.

The victory of Jesus over Satan and his forces is presented in Colossians 2:15 as a public spectacle for all to see. A public display of victory is an open invitation to the enemy to strike back whenever he can. Jesus has completely defeated Satan, sin, and death, yet their presence and influence are keenly felt everywhere today. Through his death and priestly ministry Jesus challenges Melanesians to place themselves under his guardianship as their victorious ancestor-warrior throughout their journey in life.

Apart from the belief in the existence of life beyond death and the belief in a supreme being, the experiences that people went through in times of extremity, their dreams, and their ancestral myths prepared Melanesians for the coming of Christianity. Dreams took the people on journeys out of this world into the world of the spirits. In dreams, the people saw realities that were out of this world. They knew them to be real but did not know how to take hold of them. The people also had some ancestral myths that told them of people with light red skins who would come to them with something new to give to them.

Although Melanesians were prepared for the coming of Christianity, in many places the people still persist with their ancestral practices. For many Melanesians, being a Christian is understood as belonging to a denomination, adopting a certain way of life, and adhering to and practicing a new set of rituals. The process of pacification that forced the people to stop practicing cannibalism, sorcery, witchcraft, and magic encouraged many of the people to see the changing of these customs as the way to be a Christian.

Christ was sacrificed once and for all to take away the sins of many people, and he will appear a second time, not to bear sin, but to bring salvation to those who are waiting for him (Heb 9:28). Melanesians carried out sacrifices to establish good relationships with their ancestors. Animals were killed at designated places where the men of the community entered into communion with their ancestors, as Kuman illustrates in his discussion of the Simbu pig-kill and associating it with the Eucharist.

One-Blood

The concept of one-blood or *wanblut* (blood relative) in Tok Pisin provides Melanesians with a strong sense of identification with each other (Strathern 1972). The Epistle to the Hebrews compares the blood of Jesus with that of Abel, "to Jesus the Mediator of a new covenant and to the sprinkled blood that speaks a better word than the blood of Abel" (12:24). In identifying the blood of Jesus with the blood of Abel, Hebrews restores the relationship between Abel, the innocent, and his brother Cain, the transgressor. The broken relationship between Cain and Abel is a symbol of the broken relationship between members of the human race. Jesus the mediator and high priest shed his blood to restore both humanity and humanity's relationship with God. The incarnation brought Jesus into "one-bloodedness" with all humanity (Heb 2:1–18). Earthly restoration in Christ symbolizes eternal restoration in the heavenly world with God, through faith in Jesus and his finished work on the cross.

The Priesthood Changes

To make the universal priesthood effective, God changed the law governing the priesthood (Heb 7:12). This change of priesthood places Jesus outside the confines of the Jewish nationalistic priesthood represented by the Levitical system, and outside the realm of the tribal priests of the Judaic tribe into which Jesus was born (Heb 7:14). Jesus's priesthood is based on "the power of an indestructible life" (Heb 7:16). Jesus is the true universal priest. He is the true priest of every nation, tribe, clan, and family (Rev 7:9).

The priesthood of Jesus Christ makes Christianity a living religion in that the resurrected Jesus is the living high priest enthroned in heaven, interceding for his people. Christ's living priesthood, based on the power of "an indestructible life," not only transferred the Aaronic priesthood to that of the order of Melchizedek, it also brought an end to the law that governed the Aaronic priesthood based on rituals, sacrifices, laws, and regulations (Heb 7:12).

The writer of Hebrews sees the Aaronic priesthood as being superseded and fulfilled in the Melchizedek-like high priesthood of Christ Jesus. The incarnation and Jesus's priestly ministry belong to "the time of the new [eschatological] order," and "in these last days he has spoken to us by his Son" (Heb 1:2). The time of the new order inaugurated the new covenant, and made obsolete the time of the former order—the old covenant—"and what is obsolete and aging will soon disappear" (Heb 8:13). For

Melanesians, the powerful implication is they can no longer hold on to their old traditions without carefully relating and understanding these traditions with reference to the high-priestly ministry of Jesus.

Jesus as the Ancestor-Priest

The Epistle to the Hebrews presents Jesus as the Son of God within the community of ancestors. Being the creator and possessor of all things, his line of ancestry reaches beyond Abraham back to Adam—the father of all humanity. Although Adam is not mentioned in Hebrews, he is one among those who received God's revelation, just as had Abel, Enoch, Noah, and Abraham. Furthermore, being the Son of God, descended from heaven (Heb 1:3), Jesus's origin reaches beyond this world into the world of ancestral figures. He is, therefore, at once, of this world and out of this world. He is a citizen of this world and of heaven simultaneously.

In relation to Abraham, Jesus is the promised seed (Heb 11:19), and in that verse we see the figure of Christ whom God raised from the dead, prefigured in Isaac. So when we see Jesus being the promised seed of Abraham, we see him both as the ancestor and the high priest of Adam and Abraham. Jesus, therefore, is at once the ancestor and the high priest of all ancestors.

We have good reasons to regard Jesus as our ancestor and the high priest par excellence. Among them are the following:

- Jesus's humanity made him a member of the human community—brother of the brothers (Heb 2:11).
- Jesus alone can bring the people to glory; as the ancestor, Jesus is the leader and trailblazer of the community (Heb 2:10).
- Jesus is the embodiment of power and wisdom that Melanesians sought to obtain—a wholeness of life.
- Jesus achieved for the community what no other human ancestor has been able to achieve. Jesus died as a human being to purify the community from all its sins (1:3).
- Jesus's substitutionary death qualified him to be the ancestor of the community and its high priest. Melanesians revere and enlist the aid of the ancestors on the basis of their exemplary life, as those who have fulfilled the *lo* (law) of their ancestors (12:2).

In Melanesian society, the demonic power of sin is exhibited in the practices of sorcery, magic, witchcraft, and the worship of and communication with the dead. The ancestors as elders and leaders of the community in their time carried out ritualistic practices in order to deal with the consequences of breaking customary law. Melanesians can understand Jesus Christ as the ancestor–high priest who removes the taint of sin and its consequences from human culture, on the basis of his sinless nature and his sacrifice as a substitute for humanity.

Jesus as the Purification for Sin

The Hebrews writer presents the position and the lordship of Jesus at the wish of the Father: "Your throne, O God, will last forever and ever, and righteousness will be the scepter of Your kingdom" (1:8). Here we see how God the Father takes the initiative to install Jesus his Son as coequal or coruler with him. The idea of corulership is implied in 1:8 but becomes more explicit in 1:9 in the statement, "Therefore God, your God, has set you above your companions by anointing you with the oil of joy."

The context of these two texts suggests that the statements contained in them have a retrospective view of the Son's accomplished work for the purification of human sin. In other words, we are to understand these statements in the context of the Son's resurrection. Following this hermeneutical key, we can understand the relationship between the Son and the angels. Note that Hebrews 1:5 quotes Psalm 2:7 to demonstrate Jesus's superiority over the angels. This superiority was not present during the earthly ministry when Jesus was, for a little while, made lower than the angels (Heb 2:9). But now he is crowned with glory and honor because of his sacrificial suffering and death. Thus, Jesus was raised higher than the angels after he learned obedience through what He suffered—that is, precisely at the resurrection.

Jesus as the Community Head

In the Sentanian community, a man was accorded the highest honor when he took the head of an enemy warrior, especially if he happened to be the firstborn son of the leader. Such an act of bravery called for immediate marriage if he was a bachelor. The whole community would sing his praise and call his bride blessed because her groom made her the envy of all other young women in the community. The entire community would celebrate the victory for days, because not only had the warrior-groom achieved something great but also because his bravery was believed to have won the approval and blessing of his ancestral spirits. For this reason, the living and dead joined in celebration, because the firstborn of the leader was considered *yopa-yangpa* (the son of the village roof). Therefore the firstborn son of the village head is considered both the foundation and the pinnacle, the "roof" of the community. The *yopa-yangpa* is also known as the *waribuna-naribunapa* (the son of the life-giving water-spirit). This term stems from the world of the spirits. The waribuna-naribunapa identifies yopa-yangpa as the agent of the life-giving water-spirit, the agent of peace and prosperity. Furthermore, the home of the *ondoporo* (leader) is the resting place, a safe haven for friends and foes alike. The ondoporo is the mediator of all the people. Even if an enemy of the people enters his house, his people must lay down their weapons, since they cannot fight with or kill the enemy under the protection of their ondoporo.

Hebrews not only presents Jesus, God's firstborn, as king, but also as the bridegroom. The words quoted in 1:9 come from Psalm 45:6–7, which depicts the wedding day of the king where the king is set above all his companions and anointed with the oil of gladness. Hebrews applies the message directly to Jesus, who reigns supreme over all the kings of the earth. And no earthly king could have achieved what Jesus achieved for all humanity. Jesus conquered Satan (the greatest enemy of humanity, who brought sin into the world) and controlled death by dying on the cross (Heb 2:14–15).

If we relate this to the developing reflections of the Sentanians, Jesus could be conceived, typologically, as the supreme warrior, conqueror, and epitome of the Sentanian community, the culmination of all the *kosero* and ondoporo, the apex of all Sentanian ancestors—in other words, the true yopa-yangpa.

Therefore, according to the categories of Sentanian culture, Jesus is the Sentanian ondoporo kabang (supreme high priest)—the only way for Sentanians and, by extension all Melanesians, to come to God, the one who has defeated Satan and who has power over death. In assenting to the New Covenant in Christ, Melanesians no longer need to fear death, nor do they have to look to their dead ancestors to help them. Jesus is their supreme life-giving Spirit, their source of living water. As the people's leader, Jesus offered himself as their sacrifice to bring them into the family of God, under one roof, as their leader and protector.

Hebrews 7:14 presents Jesus as a Jewish ancestor through his birth into the tribe of Judah. Since we have already identified Abraham, the Jewish ancestor, as a Melanesian ancestor, and since Jesus is an ancestor of the Jewish tribe represented by Abraham, Melanesians can also see Jesus as their ancestor. Once again, there is a complementary relationship between the Melanesian and biblical attitudes toward the ancestors.

CHALLENGES MELANESIANS FACE

While Christianity and the Melanesian ancestral heritage share many things in common, Christianity is, and will continue to be, a challenge to the Melanesian culture. As Melanesians continue in their faith journey in Christ, they face a number of challenges. Having embraced Christianity as the Melanesian way of life, what should Melanesians now do about their relationship with the ancestors?

In keeping the focus on Jesus, Sentanians in particular and Melanesians in general must wrestle with historical reality as well as biblical and cultural reality:

- Jesus is not a Sentanian.
- The social structure under which Jesus was born and lived did not have a *kose* (historical leadership) system as do the Sentanians.
- Every effort must be taken to avoid making Jesus what he is not intended to be.

- Whatever cultural identity we assign to Jesus, it will not fully explain everything about him.

In my opinion, although these difficulties are real and need to be addressed, the problems they pose should not stop the attempt to make Jesus relevant by using Sentanian/Melanesian categories. I have addressed these difficulties in my discussion of the Epistle to the Hebrews above, contextualizing the eternal within the contingencies of time and space and thereby creating a hybrid, a new understanding of leadership, identity, and the person of Jesus Christ. I now turn to look at these same issues from a Melanesian perspective.

Meeting God as a Person

Anthropology as a discipline has helped Christian missionaries understand other cultures in order to communicate the gospel effectively. It has also broadened and deepened my appreciation for my own culture. Nevertheless, even though I believe that creation and culture point us to the existence and power of God, of which the Melanesian ancestors were conscious, I maintain that they were unable to find the person of God. Jesus, of course, affirmed the Bible as the book in which human beings will find the truth about him, as we see when he helped two of his disciples understand the events of their day: "Beginning with Moses and all the prophets, he explained to them what was said in all the Scriptures concerning himself" (Lk 24:27).

The Bible is a critical book for Melanesians. The Bible transcends cultural limitations, helping people understand who God is and what he has done in Jesus to bring the people back to God. Whether Melanesians could have developed true knowledge of God without missionaries and the Bible is a challenging question. But to imply that the knowledge of anthropology and culture is sufficient for people to know God, as I believe Ennio Mantovani implies, is wrong and misleading (2000, 37). Such thinking can lead Melanesians to believe their cultures can save them without God's disclosure of Jesus as revealed in the Bible. In this regard, the Epistle to the Hebrews assures the community that Jesus is absolutely reliable and sufficient. Hebrews uses the word "better" thirteen times to drive home the fact that Jesus will take better care of them than their ancestors or past mediators. This message is important for Melanesians as they seek to know God.

Where Are the Ancestors?

As their new ancestor and mediator, Jesus challenges Melanesians to trust in him for all their needs: physical and spiritual, community and individual. But if Jesus is the only person we can fully trust, then what about our ancestors, whom we experience to be a continuing part of our communities? What do we do about them and their needs? Burrows addresses these same questions.

His Melanesian students helped him understand that "those who had gone to be with God were also still within the village community as a source of blessing and wisdom" (see chapter 2, this volume). The impact of *gutpela sindaun* (the good life / salvation) is also crucial for Burrows and his students.

The answer, then, is that all believers, including the believing ancestors, are in the presence of God. As the Simbu erect the Bolim spirit house on the festival ground as a focal point of festivity during the pig-kill, and my Sentani people consider those who come under the protection of *yopa-yangpa*, we can say that Melanesians come under the care of Jesus (3:6). The house in Hebrews 12:22–24 is called "the heavenly Jerusalem, the city of the living God" (12:22). The house is further identified as "the church of the firstborn, whose names are written in heaven" (12:23). The members of this household include the believers to whom the book was sent, spoken of as "you have come" (12:22). The statement "you have come" would, by extension, include present-day believers, wherever they live.

This house is one united community of heaven and earth. The ancestors are mentioned here as "the spirits of righteous ones made perfect." These people are all in the past, the now-dead believing men and women of the Old Testament, our ancestors of faith—some of whom are mentioned in Hebrews 11. Today, this group would include New Testament believers and all the believers of the world who have died and are referred to as "a great cloud of witnesses" (Heb 12:1).

This is new information for Melanesians. Melanesians need Christianity to make clear to them where their ancestors are. They are not in the "skull" caves as the Baktaman believe, or in the spirit houses of the Sepik region, or beyond the treetops of the Samo. Those ancestors who believed in God are in heaven with him. They have gone "to Jesus the Mediator of a new covenant" (12:24a). The point here is that wherever the ancestors are, Jesus is among them and rules over them as the Son of the most high God, the *naribuna-waribunapa* (son of the life-giving water).

Melanesians can continue to remember their ancestors as they have done in the past. They can thank God for the faith, the commitment, and the achievements of their ancestors, and, together with their believing ancestors, worship God through Jesus Christ and look to him for strength and direction in life. Melanesian belief is centered in the ancestors being alive after death, as confirmed by the teaching of the Bible focused on Jesus Christ as the living ancestor in whose presence the believing ancestors are today. The ancestors are with Jesus, who died for their salvation.

The Question of the Ancestors' Salvation

Melanesians understand *gutpela sindaun* (human well-being / salvation) in relation to their ancestors. Traditionally, Melanesians viewed their ancestors as providers of *gutpela sindaun* (quality of life). I maintain that Melanesians looked to their ancestors and expected them to provide gutpela sindaun. They looked to the ancestors for this well-being because, in Melanesian thinking, salvation is related to the concepts of time, space, and history, all of which are directly related to the ancestors.

The opposite of gutpela sindaun is *i stap long hevi* (having problems). In the mind of the people, sickness, drought, and death are all problems associated with the activities of spirit beings. When something bad happens to an individual or in the community, the first question that comes to mind is, "Who did it?" For Melanesians who continually live with spirit consciousness, sicknesses and all kinds of ill fortune are associated with the activities of ancestral and other spirits. Today, when the Sentanian priest burns coconut husks for a sick person before the person goes to the hospital, the priest asks the ancestral spirit to watch over the sick one and to protect that person from other spirits and powers, thus ensuring that the sick person will receive gutpela sindaun. The Melanesian understanding of salvation is closely related to the biblical idea of deliverance or freedom from want, hurt, or starvation (for more, see Loeliger 1979, 134–45). The challenge for Melanesians, as well as others in faith communities around the world where ancestors are a relational part of the community, is the fate of their ancestors who died without knowledge of Jesus as the only one to bring salvation (Ac 4:12).

Issues of Faith

Faith is a way of life for the Melanesians. To speak of ancestral beliefs and practices is to speak about Melanesians having faith or believing in their ancestors who formulated the way of life for their people. Melanesian religion and belief, based on ancestral heritage, emphasized earning merits with the ancestors. This faith was based on keeping ancestral rules and regulations. The people had to follow the ancestral *lo* in order to experience gutpela sindaun. The term *lo* in Melanesian Tok Pisin is used to name the traditional ethical and religious code of behavior obligatory for the community and rooted in the teachings of the ancestors.

The Christian message missionaries brought is also about faith for living in this world and in the world of the dead. This message complements the Melanesian concept of faith and adds to our understanding of relationship with God through Jesus Christ, while expanding our awareness of our relationship with Jesus. Faith in Christ brings people into a spiritual father-child relationship with God. To explain this according to the Sentanian culture, it means being born under the kose of Jesus, being born into his house—the home of Jesus, the ondoporo kabang. To be born into Jesus's home is to be born into the family of God.

Issues of the Environment

Melanesians see the environment as containing the nonhuman and the human (including both the living and the dead), as well as good and bad spirits. The operational word for this holistic community is "relationship" (Ole 1990, 33–41). The traditional Melanesian community and the present-day Melanesian "Christian" community are built on relational living, "a living dialogue between man and nature in his total existence" (Tuza 1978, 247). The environment to which the community belongs was created or acquired by the ancestors as an inheritance for their descendants. There is a living dialogue with the life force that binds the human, the nonhuman, and the spirit communities into relationship with each other—a three-dimensional interrelationship reflected in the cosmos. The ancestors, as part of the human community, control the environment as *ol papa bilong graun* (owners of the environment), and environment is the community's living supermarket. A good relationship with the ancestors means the gardens will produce well, the jungles will be full of game, and the waters will teem with fish. The environment provides Melanesians with bridges to cross over from their world into the world of the Bible, from the physical to the spiritual, from the transient to the eternal, from longing to reality, from their ancestors to Jesus Christ.

GOOD NEWS AND THE TRUTHS

The believing ancestors are in heaven in the presence of God and Jesus Christ. They are in heaven because of their faith in the new covenant Jesus established through his death. This is new and exciting news about the ancestors that Christianity has opened up for Melanesians to know and understand. The believing ancestors have not moved from the *sope* (spirit house) into the church. They have moved from their transient earthly dwelling into the heavenly new Jerusalem, forever united with the Blessed Trinity, the Father, the Holy Spirit, and Jesus Christ.

A further truth to be learned from the Epistle to the Hebrews is that those who are identified as "the spirits of the righteous made perfect" (12:23) are not just the believing ancestors, they are all believers, both young and old from all over the world. The strong implication is that they are the innumerable multitudes from every nation, tribe, people, and language (Rev 7:9). But this new truth could not encompass all peoples, because local religions were often limited to one's own tribe. This universal truth was not available until Jesus came. Today, Jesus challenges Melanesians to include all other members of the human community, who are in God's care and must be seen as kin. The way to become a member of this earthly/heavenly community is through faith in Jesus, who died to save all.

Jesus as Mediator

The context of Hebrews 12:22–24 presents Jesus as the mediator of the living and the dead. The work of Jesus removes the need for other mediators, be they angels or human ancestors. Yes, the believing ancestors are in heaven in the presence of God. This was part of the promise Jesus made to his disciples prior to his death, "In My Father's house are many rooms; if it were not so, I would have told you. I am going to prepare a place for you. And if I go and prepare a place for you, I will come back and take you to be with me so that you also may be where I am" (Jn 14:2–3). Now that the believing ancestors are in heaven in the care of God the Father and Jesus Christ his Son, we are able to answer the question, "What should Melanesians do about their ancestors, and how should they remember them?"

Without fear, Melanesians should honor and remember their ancestors who have gone to be with Jesus. Since the living believers on earth celebrate their birthdays, it is equally good for families to celebrate the birthdays of those who are with Jesus, as Kim encourages Koreans to do. The church in Melanesia should think of setting aside one Sunday in the calendar to remember the dead in the same way that fathers and mothers are remembered. This action would be a healthy recognition of the preparatory work of the Spirit in each culture. It would also be a powerful reminder of the dead and provide a further opportunity to thank Jesus for what he did, by caring for the living dead under his roof.

Jesus as Cosmic Ancestor

The first three verses of the prologue of Hebrews clearly set out the uniqueness of Jesus, whom Melanesians can easily understand as our cosmic ancestor. The time for searching is over. God has revealed himself in a human body in the person of Jesus. This truth challenges Melanesians to enter into a personal relationship with God through Jesus Christ. The Supreme Being existed before all time, and Melanesians were conscious of his existence but had no way to know him in a personal way. Melanesians looked to their ancestors for life and well-being, and it would not be out of place to substitute "Word" in John's prologue with "ancestor." Thus, the prologue would read, "In the beginning was the ancestor, and the ancestor was with God, and the ancestor was God. He was with God in the beginning" (Jn 1:1–2 [amended]).

The Epistle to the Hebrews presents the death of Jesus in the context of cosmic warfare, with humanity on one side (2:6–8) and the forces of evil on the other (2:14–15). The battle has been fought and Jesus has been crowned with glory and honor (Heb 2:9). Jesus is the supreme ancestor-warrior, the one who singlehandedly conquered the enemy. The battle he won is for the salvation of the whole world. Jesus is the originator of human salvation. Brothers belong to the same house; they are members of the same family, born of the same father, possessing the same family characteristics, sharing one blood. Together they live under the same *kose* (created order), the same cosmos that Jesus created. Hebrews brings humanity into the kose of Jesus, "Both the one who makes people holy and those who are made holy are of the same family. So Jesus is not ashamed to call them brothers and sisters" (Heb 2:11). This is a new truth for Melanesians. Jesus became a blood brother of human beings so that he could originate and give birth to a fresh, new community: the community of holy brothers and sisters.

Jesus became a human being in order to fight the archenemy of all people: Satan, who controlled death and made the people live in lifelong bondage to the fear of death. The Melanesian concept of community is cosmic, a holistic community of humans, nonhuman entities, and spirits. The battle Jesus fought, therefore, is a cosmic battle, not simply to defeat the enemy, but in doing so to bring the entire cosmos into its proper relationship with its maker. Melanesians, to be sure, were once ignorant of the battle that had been fought and won on their behalf. Christians brought this news nearly two thousand years after the battle was fought and won through Jesus's death and resurrection.

This is very crucial new information for Melanesians. The battle between Jesus and the devil needs to be built into the story of Melanesian ancestral heritage. Jesus, the eponymous ancestor of the Melanesians, has conquered the devil in order to establish a new Melanesian community. This understanding is close to being the central pillar of the Christian faith, and it is codified in the preamble of the 1976 National Constitution of Papua New Guinea: "We the people of Papua New Guinea . . . pledge ourselves to guard and pass on to those who come after us our noble traditions and the Christian principles that are ours now" (PNG Constitution).

The gospel allows the living to honor and remember their ancestors, but not to worship them. Much of the ancestors' legacy is compatible with the gospel and should be used to explain and grow Christian faith and life in Melanesia. The gospel message needs to be carefully interpreted by using appropriate cultural bridges to make Christianity meaningful to Melanesians. The Melanesian ancestral heritage is a way of life, as is Bible-based Christianity. Together they have much to contribute to each other. The incarnation of Jesus Christ tells us that God takes human culture seriously and uses it to make his will and love known. This is what I believe hybridity is about, and I am grateful for the insights Burrows brings.

However, Jesus is more than an ancestor. Jesus is different from the ancestors because he is uniquely the Son of God and offers human beings eternal life, which the ancestors cannot provide. God the Father has placed Jesus his Son as God and king once for all to rule with justice from the throne of grace. The ancestors and the living members of the community are dependent on Jesus for eternal life and their day-to-day necessities of life. The new life that Jesus offers comes from God. No human ancestors could offer eternal life to their descendants. No human ancestors could accomplish what Jesus achieved for human salvation or be accorded such a high and honorable position as God has bestowed only on Jesus, his Son.

CONCLUSION

In spite of shortcomings, many missionaries did their work with a strong commitment and loyalty to the God who sent them to Melanesia. Many of them took the culture of the people seriously. They learned and spoke the language of the people; they translated the Scriptures, preached the gospel, and brought the people to true faith in God. The existence of Christianity in Papua New Guinea, where over 90 percent of the population claims to belong to some Christian group, is a credit to their hard work. Christianity, firmly rooted in Jesus of Nazareth, the Son of God, has become the faith of Melanesians. The urgent task for today is to faithfully incorporate Scripture into the Melanesian culture—to theologize. I have used the Epistle to the Hebrews to develop a biblical understanding of ancestors for a Melanesian context.

Instead of going to the extremes either of throwing away or retaining everything in our culture (both a sure path to syncretism), we should keep what is useful and discard what is harmful. We must evaluate the cultural in light of the biblical and seek to transform society based on that critique. In the introduction to this chapter I asked if the traditional belief system with its core in the ancestors can coexist with a belief system centered in Jesus Christ. I have argued that Melanesians can maintain their faith in Jesus Christ by combining "the Word, as Scripture, and the Word as revealed in the truths of culture [to] determine Christian truth for a given people" (Gilliland 1989, 10). As a Christian Melanesian, I need to decide how Jesus Christ fits into my culture and my relationship with my ancestors. The Epistle to the Hebrews, with its focus on Jesus being better than all other manifestations in the cosmos, points the way for Jesus to provide a house of faith that accommodates my ancestors as well as making me who I am.

I have presented how our ancestral heritage prepared us for the full truth to be revealed in Jesus Christ. What Melanesians expected their ancestors to do for them has found its ultimate fulfillment in Jesus the Son of God. Melanesians can therefore honor and remember their ancestors for who they were and what they did, but they must look to Jesus alone as the author and finisher of their faith. Faith in Jesus Christ demands total trust in him to provide for all their needs. There is a real and helpful relationship between the Melanesian ancestral spirits and the gospel. This truth allows Melanesians to move with cultural integrity and continuity from dependence on their ancestors to faith in Jesus Christ.

14

A House for God to Live In

Indian Manifestations That Reflect Old Testament Expressions

John Sanjeevakumar Gupta

Nearly two thousand years ago, a woman met a stranger at a well. As they conversed, she concluded he must be a Jewish teacher. Then she asked him a question, one that had been asked and debated over the ages, one that has divided believers over the centuries, creating movements, uprisings, and even wars:

> Our ancestors worshiped on this mountain, but you Jews claim that the place where we must worship is in Jerusalem. Who is right? The master replied, "A time is coming and has now come when the true worshipers will worship the Father in the spirit and in truth, for they are the kind of worshipers the Father seeks. God is spirit, and his worshipers must worship in the Spirit and in truth." (Jn 4:19–23)

In effect, she was asking, "Teacher, who has the God thing right?" This question is still with us, especially in places where people worship differently and cultural norms seem to clash with Western beliefs and interpretations of Scripture. How do Christians thread the needle of worshiping in spirit and truth when cultural differences enter the picture?

A HOUSE FOR GOD TO LIVE IN

Sitting on a platform in Andhra Pradesh, I watched as the Banjara marched into the church that our American construction team had just built, solemnly singing,

> I will enter into his gates with thanksgiving in my heart,
> I will enter into his courts with praise
> I will say that this is the day that the Lord has made
> I will rejoice for he has made me glad.

Then I heard someone say, "Do it the Banjara way," and the room burst into celebration. Young girls started to whirl around in place, their bright dresses of red, black, and white billowing around them. The mirrored glass and embroidery reflected the light. They stomped out a rhythm with the silver bells on their feet, and the crowd clapped to the beat. For some of the Westerners, the spectacle was overwhelming; our non-Pentecostal team members wondered if this behavior was acceptable in the sanctuary. We clearly had a different perspective of the event. The Westerners thought they had come to dedicate a church. The Banjara, on the other hand, were welcoming God into a new home.

The Banjaras are considered descendants of the Roma of Europe who migrated through Afghanistan to India twenty-three hundred years ago. Many of them were goat and cattle herders; some were traveling merchants. Like the gypsies in Europe, they wandered across the country leading life on their own terms and conditions. They spoke their own language and stayed away from outsiders. They would set up portable camps outside villages. They built no permanent structures, traveling in groups with their gods and idols, setting up places of worship as they traveled—reminiscent of the people Abraham encountered long ago.

In recent years, shrinking land for free grazing, the expansion of railroads and highways, and growing urbanization forced them into communities to build more permanent living structures and even schools for their children (Burman 2010). As they settled down they were evangelized, and a project to translate the Scriptures into their language was started.

A common definition of "success" in the Western church-planting movement is the completion of a building constructed with a cross at the peak of the roof. It is the establishment of Christ's presence in the community. Too often, this church-building practice simply provides funding for the existing Christians. The Banjaras did something different. They had not built a place for people to gather; they had built a place for God to live.

I was the fourth and last speaker scheduled that day. As I listened to the village elders speak of the history of their people and how they arrived at their new settlement, I felt a check in my spirit. I call that sinking feeling my "not *that* sermon, John" moment. I had prepared a good sermon about how this structure was just a building, and they, the Banjara believers, were the church. As I continued to observe the goings-on, however, I knew my sermon had no relevance to their reality. I scrambled through the concordance in the back of my Bible, then I realized the Banjara did not even have the full Bible translated into their language yet. As is common, Bible translators started in the New Testament and hadn't finished the Old Testament.

As I pondered what to say, a banner flapped in the wind behind me. It carried a verse from Leviticus in Telegu. Roughly translated, the three sentences read, "And I will dwell among you. I will be your God, and you will be my tribe."

I took my text from that banner. It was clear the Banjaras understood the significance of what was happening that day. Although they had no churches in their cultural experience, they gathered as a community around campfires, from times immemorial, to celebrate and to ask their god for good roads ahead and for green fields in which their herds could graze and multiply. From their perspective, they needed a home for God to live among them. Without a Bible in their own language, they understood the concept of "Emmanuel" God setting up living quarters with them. In these three sentences, these uneducated and mostly illiterate Banjara expressed their relationship with the divine. They sought to honor God by setting up a place for deity to dwell among them. Their desire was that God would honor them by choosing to live with them.

Based on that text, I told them the story of Israel wandering through the desert. I spoke to them of a people with no place to call home, observing that they spoke a unique language, followed their own laws, and married only within their own people. I told them of how they made a great tent and carried it with them, along with the Ark of the Covenant, as they journeyed through the desert. I spoke of how God's presence filled the tabernacle. I continued the story of the tribes entering the land that would eventually become their own. When the day arrived, I said, they desired to build a permanent home for their God. I could see the Banjara understanding. Amazed, they learned that the Scriptures spoke of people just like them, and they realized they had done the same thing.

In the West, churches are dedicated places for Christians to gather. Buildings are built to accommodate the Christians. In stark contrast to Western societies that glorify individuality, the Jews and other biblical societies (as well as many peoples around the world today) understood what it meant to belong to a family, a clan, a tribe. They understood the benefits of belonging and the demands of loyalty. The Banjara got it and identified with their biblical forebears. The welcoming celebration continued for several days, for God had, after all, decided to live among the Banjaras.

TRANSITIONING FROM MISSION TO CHURCH IN INDIA

In the following discussion, I highlight three issues that affect the understanding of Indian rituals and ceremonies. First, many of the rituals and ceremonies described here are not Christian, Hindu, or Muslim. They are Indian—expressions of culture, practices of beliefs already old when Jesus was born, older than the church and the Western Enlightenment. Not surprisingly, these Indian cultural practices run almost parallel to those of ancient Israel. Many exist in almost identical form in the Old Testament (explaining why Indians can find relevance and understanding in Old Testament passages).

Even though millions of Indians today are thankful for the missionaries who left their homes and countries to proclaim the gospel in obedience to their understanding of the Great Commission, we must admit that their limited knowledge of Indian culture fostered misunderstandings and mistakes now taking much time and effort to correct. Perhaps this was inevitable. As Dan Shaw points out in chapter 1, missionaries came from churches that had long been secure in their dogmatic heritage, and it was difficult for them to conceive of how God might view cultural differences in a way other than their Euro-American upbringing was able to understand. Like the early Christians in the Jerusalem community, the missionaries' expectation was that Indian Christians would naturally become Western in culture, lifestyle, and thought as they adapted to Christian beliefs and values.

The second issue is the nature of ritual as practiced by the people for whom it is meaningful. Even if some of these rituals are considered Hindu because they are performed in a Hindu temple or along with Hindu worship, we must consider the purpose driving the act and not the act itself. Simply stated, if people approach the divine in a way they have been taught or know, then only God can determine the attitude of their heart. Abraham was a worshiper of many gods when he first came into relationship with Jehovah. As Shaw points out in chapter 1: the objective is to establish "religious expressions that Christians and non-Christians within a society will recognize as reasonable adaptations of their cultural expressions . . . we are dealing here with a process that appropriates a need for discernment and listens to the Holy Spirit through Scripture."

The third issue of importance reflects on concerns Bill Burrows raises in chapter 2. If failure to carry out a ritual or ceremony brings alienation and discomfort within a society, people will find a way to perform traditional ceremonies and rituals to suit their need. Whether authorities in the church approve them or not is inconsequential if people make no sense of introduced substitutes, especially if those authorities are merely following the customs of founding missionary organizations. On the other hand, a broadening relationship with God brings an adaptation of ritual to conform to core Christian beliefs and traditions, as several of the chapters in this book illustrate.

Allow me to tell a family story. Many years ago, my parents purchased a newer car. As I went to the garage to inspect the acquisition, I noticed the remnants of a broken egg on the floor, so I asked our Hindu driver about the mess. He told me it was to keep evil spirits away. My father would not let him sacrifice a chicken, so he broke an egg, considering it a symbol of a chicken. From his point of view, his responsibility was to protect the car and the family for whom he drove. My father's objections were irrelevant. A few years later, my parents bought another car, but this time I did not see the eggshells. When I inquired, the driver pointed to a small cross he had painted on the front bumper. "We are Christians now," he said, "and Jesus is more powerful than the spirits." The practice was the same, but adapted to the knowledge of a new faith context.

Evaluating external changes alone fails to recognize the evolution of a growing understanding of beliefs and appropriate adjustment in practice inspired by the Holy Spirit. Was the practice just a transfer of superstition? Perhaps. But the driver knew in whom he now believed and wanted to adjust accordingly; the new God was greater than the gods of the past. He had made a stronger statement of faith than the less than perfect practice. Recognizing an evolving understanding of faith is rarely instantaneous because it must compete with thousands of years of culturally established practice.

MAKING IT REAL, MAKING IT RELEVANT

For more than twenty years, India Outreach Teaching Teams served several Christian organizations equipping village missionaries and pastors. This organization is a ministry started in 1990 to train and equip teams serving for short terms in India. Teams included members skilled in construction, computer technology, music and drama, medicine, and pastoral training. After a few years, the pastoral training teams began adopting an approach to encourage pastors to break away from Western theological education patterns in order to promote patterns of faith in harmony with the local cultural context and value systems. The teams were primarily American pastors and professors, armed with elaborate "what every pastor or missionary should know" curriculums. Their Indian students were in awe of the lessons and took notes as if the presentations were directly from God.

One evening, a student approached me. "Uncle," he said, "you should be teaching our classes."

"Why?" I inquired.

"Because, you are teaching things important to us and telling stories we understand." *Great!* I thought sardonically; just this afternoon I was criticized by the leader of the teaching team for barely getting to Moses, while my peers in the other classes were already crossing the Jordan. The students loved my stories adapted to their cultural context, but I couldn't get through the required lesson plan for the day, let alone delve into the theological implications of the events. I argued that if they learned to study the Bible with their own cultural experiences, they might understand the untouched bullet points by themselves. The team leader, however, told me it was my responsibility to complete the curriculum.

A Visit with My Mentor

As we continued to explore the issue of relevancy, I visited my mentor, a retired professor who was spending his retirement years training and mentoring Indian missionaries to work among unreached people groups. For him, being a mentor is to ask questions. Often these questions forced me to journey down paths challenging my faith and my well-defined beliefs.

"Tell me, nephew," he asked, "do you feel the Bible contains everything there is to know about God?" Before I could say yes, he continued, "or do you think it contains a specific message of a plan for the redemption of humankind, as portrayed by its authors and interpreters that followed?" I should have known it was a trick question. "Do you believe God can choose to convey power, knowledge, and understanding not expounded in the book you so firmly believe in?" As this conversation continued, I realized I was about to get my well-established categories placed in a classical tandoori oven. "Your Western education defined answers before you have all the questions. You defined God, the acts of God, and 'systematized' everything in perfect boxes you can defend and justify." He had started, and I knew this would be a long afternoon. My mentor then went back to the reason I had come to visit.

> You asked me to review your curriculum, to assist you in making the material relevant for our people. I am happy to do this because I understand your desire, but I am concerned your curriculum carries with it the same bias Western theology imposes. If you continue with it, the only right answers will be those answers that are right from a Western perspective. In your system, however, if an event is not explained by science, computed mathematically, or resolved with logic, it is myth, folklore, or superstition. You know our people, especially the villagers with whom these pastors interact. They are uneducated, often illiterate, and tradition-bound. Is it possible God might communicate with them in dreams, visions, and miracles? Might there be individuals who need to understand with something more than hearing or reading? Is it possible God might communicate a message in supernatural terms? Our people always followed the God of their ancestors, until they confront a God whom they consider more powerful. Then they follow the customs of their ancestors to approach and please the new God.

As I pondered his words, I recalled another such event. I was teaching a group of pastors in Chennai. Part of the introduction to our class was having students introduce themselves and tell the class how they became Christians. I was distracted until something I heard startled me. "I became a Christian when God raised my sister from the dead," one of the pastors said. In spite of everything I knew and had experienced, this was a category killer. *There must have been some kind of mistake*, I thought. *She was probably just unconscious*. But that little voice inside of me said, "That's what some people said about me, too."

As I questioned the pastor, it was clear the whole village considered her dead, and they had prepared her body for cremation. As the ceremonies went on, two men walked into the village and asked if they could pray for the girl. Everyone assumed they were going to bless her soul in the future life, and there was no harm in getting the blessings of an additional god. When the two men emerged shortly thereafter, walking with the young girl, everyone wanted to know about the God who raises the dead.

When I asked this pastor in my class, "What happened then?" he exclaimed, "The whole village became Christian!" astonished I would ask such a question. Over the years, I have heard many stories of people being raised from the dead, healed of incurable sickness, barren women giving birth. In almost every case, the outcome is families and villages acknowledging Christ's power and local ministries resulting.

Aunty interrupted our discussions with tiffin and tea. I was grateful for the break. I had too much to absorb. Later, as I prepared to leave, Uncle stood up, removed his shoes, and prepared to pray for me, after which he would then dispatch me with his blessings, as was our tradition. Before he started praying, he stopped and said,

> Nephew, I have one more story to tell you. I know you know this story because it is about the night our fathers met. It was late at night, and there was a loud pounding at our door. A young man was standing there demanding to know how to become a Christian. It seemed odd this was a matter of such urgency, but my father was an Anglican priest, ministering over the only church in the community.
>
> My father recognized him as the son of the leading Hindu family in the community. Remembering instructions from the diocese on procedures for Hindu conversions, my father explained to the young man that becoming a Christian was not that simple. He would have to learn the Lord's Prayer, the Apostles' Creed, take catechism classes, and be baptized before he could become a Christian. The young man looked at him, almost in tears and asked, "If I die tonight, how will I obtain salvation?" My father, the priest, was taken aback. No one had ever asked him this question. He looked at the passion and conviction in the young man's eyes. Finally, he asked the altar boy to bring him holy water from the church. When he got the water, he sprinkled the water on the young man's head and renamed him Paul. Your father's life changed that night. You may not realize it, but my father's life changed that night also. That night, he laid down his rulebooks and rituals and everything he had been taught.

As "Uncle" prayed to bless me, he quoted Acts 9:17: "Ananias went to the house and entered it. Placing his hands on Saul, he said, 'Brother Saul, the Lord Jesus, who appeared to you on the road as you were coming here, has sent me so that you may see again and be filled with the Holy Spirit.'" He observed that, like Saul, I was highly educated, and I needed the scales to fall off my eyes so that I could see the people of India as God saw them.

Developing a New Curriculum

In our determination to make our curriculum relevant to the culture of the Indian people, we recruited two ministry leaders—Dr. Balaji Valadarajan and Rev. Solomon Raj (actual names used with permission)—to assist us with the project and to test our conclusions. Balaji was a convert from a staunch Hindu background. He considered our invitation skeptically. "Who were these people who used a logo with a Hindu temple instead of a church or a cross?" he inquired. I told him our hope was that, over time, every church in India would reflect Christ but in the context of a Hindu perspective, including architecture and style of worship.

Solomon was an Indian responsible for the South India leadership of one of the nation's largest Indigenous Christian ministries. His growing concern was that Indians continued getting the subconscious message suggesting that good Christians were foreigners. Greeting-card depictions of all white angels, Jesus with his arms around blond children, works of art showing the disciples and even Jesus as white—all reflected Christianity as a religion where white people had special status in the sight of God.

Gradually we all agreed to develop a revised curriculum using the bedrock definition of salvation expressed in Acts 2:21: "And everyone who calls on the name of the Lord will be saved" just as they are—no preconditions, no creeds to learn, no practices to change, no rules to follow. We would allow people to use their ability to interpret the Scriptures in their own understanding and context. We would rely solely on the Holy Spirit to bring about change in their minds and hearts. We would encourage them to focus on teaching as Jesus did. The audiences Jesus spoke to were farmers, shepherds, and fishermen. He used parables relevant to their everyday lives. Among our principles and goals were to motivate and encourage people to:

- Interpret and pass on the Bible in a manner relevant to their cultural context, as opposed to a Western perspective.
- Live in their communities as members of those communities, following the practices and customs of their neighbors, and not live apart as some separate, marginalized sect.
- Understand that God looked at the attitude of their hearts and not at their acts. Their acts were reflections of the change in their hearts.
- Recognize that the mission of the church is proclaiming the good news to the unreached 80 percent of their villages, and not to simply gather more Christians to make a bigger church.

We soon learned these objectives were easier to write than implement. Each of us came with our own doctrinal biases about requirements for being a Christian. We had to journey together back to the beginnings of the New Testament church to understand the challenges that new Christians faced in modern-day India. In spite of Christ's teachings about God looking into the heart, people demand internal change as evidenced by external behavior. Perhaps because we cannot read another's heart, we demand proof in the form of compliance with rules measured and judged.

When the apostle Paul started taking the gospel to the Gentiles, he created a cultural crisis among Jewish Christ followers, for the early church primarily comprised Jewish converts, a homogenous group who spoke the same language, followed the same dietary practices, and kept the same religious rituals. When the Gentiles began coming to faith, the Jews attempted to require that the Gentiles become like Jews in order to become Christian.

What Western missionaries in India did amounted to the same thing. The only example they had of "good Christians" were themselves and the practices of their home churches. They demanded compliance, and many Indian converts eagerly complied to prove their loyalty to Christ as the white man's God by adopting these same practices.

Balaji was disturbed about what we suggested. "It took a lot of change of habits to establish myself in the Christian community as a proper Christian. Now you want me to tell others all this was unnecessary?" Remembering when he first became a Christian, Balaji continued,

> The list of things I had to do and could not do was overwhelming. If I wanted to be a "good" Christian, I could no longer go to the temple with my mother, who was still a Hindu. It hurt her very much. I could no longer put a *bindi* dot on my forehead symbolizing the cosmos and indicate I had done *puja*—morning worship. I could not bow and touch the feet of my elders, who considered this omission a sign of disrespect. I could not join in family festivals and go on pilgrimages with them. They did not see my behavior as positive. They saw it as the loss of a son. My seminary training reinforced abandoning these traditional practices. It marginalized me from my friends and family.

Solomon pondered, "The first objection we get will be on 'leaving it to the Holy Spirit.' What if they get it wrong? We will be dealing with hundreds of Christians creating *sonthum*—a personal theology." A PhD student doing research with us countered,

> In reality, all biblical interpretation is subject to the cultural filter of the reader and contains a personal element. Is the issue or concern here really that we only value "the truth of God" as interpreted by Western theologians? The earliest theologians, the Disciples of Christ and the apostle Paul, were Jews from a culture not dissimilar to India even today. Is it better to have foreigners who know nothing of this culture imposing their theological interpretations on Indian villagers whose lived experience is much closer to that of biblical times?

Sadly, the strongest challenge for Christianity is seeking to flourish within the Hindu community and to enjoy peace with Hindu social issues and customs in the Indian church itself. Educated in seminaries still dominated by Western theology, Indian church leaders perpetuate the problem. Not discussed is the reality that these Christian practices are the ways the missionaries taught the Indians. Not discussed is the reality that the missionaries did not understand most of our customs and practices and simply forbade anything not explained from a Western viewpoint. In fact, they marginalized converts away from their cultural identity and forced secularization identifying with the West and the religion missionaries brought.

APPROACHING HYBRIDITY

In chapter 2 Burrows presents the concept of hybridity by saying, "Hybrids result when genetically diverse plants are crossed to form a new plant. . . . Religious hybrids inevitably result when a religion is carried across a cultural boundary and adopted by the people in that milieu." Pushing the concept further, often plants from the same root evolve and adapt to the local soil mixture, the weather, and environmental conditions. The same is true socially as well as in religious expressions. The gospel finds room for germination under varying conditions, in turn resulting in different but viable expressions.

An Indian Wedding in North Carolina

Over the years I have had the privilege of officiating at a number of American weddings. While "tying the knot" is an American phrase to symbolize a wedding, knots are rarely tied. A simple band and the words, "With this ring, I thee wed," is the closest it gets. It is a very personal and individual commitment between two people. Indian weddings are very different affairs. Even today, in many instances, marriages are arranged by the families using a process that involves approvals by family elders, priests, and sometimes even the community. The bride and groom often seem incidental to the process.

Not long ago, my responsibility was to negotiate what seemed like an impossible task between an American bride and the groom's Indian family. The bride and her family did not understand or appreciate the groom's family intruding in arrangements that in American tradition are the choices of the children; on the other side, the groom's family was wondering what kind of family allowed their daughter to make all the decisions. The bride's family prepared for an event that sent their children off to live individual lives, while the groom's family struggled with the prospect of accepting a culturally clueless child as a daughter in their house with all the privileges this entailed.

In Indian weddings, tying the knot is real and is still part of the traditional ceremony. The critical ritual during the ceremony involves the tying of the *thali*, a gold pendant bearing a design unique to the groom's family on a gold chain with a gold cord at each end. Interspersed between the covenants and blessings, the groom places the chain around the bride's neck and fastens it with three knots. The first knot binds the bride to her husband, the second to his family, and the third to his faith. If this ritual sounds familiar, it is similar to what we read in the Book of Ruth: "Where you go I will go; where you lodge, I will lodge; your people shall be my people and your God my God" (1:16). My negotiations reminded me of my struggle to assist Indian village pastors as they sought to remain genuinely tied to biblical truth while making those truths relevant to their people.

Biblical Concerns vs. Cultural Values

An Indian bride is not just married to her husband; she is married to her husband's family and to his faith. During the ceremony, the family places bangles and anklets on her. Her responsibilities involve upholding the honor of her husband's family, and her husband's family determines her status. Historically, Western missionaries seemed to accept the tying of the thali as a substitute for a ring, since it was not visible because most women wear the thali under their clothes. Their greater problem came with the wearing of the *tilakam*, the dot a married Indian woman wears on her forehead. They assumed that since it did not follow Western cultural norms, it must be Hindu—and therefore forbidden. In reality, the wearing of the tilakam is not Hindu; it is Indian. It could be considered Hindu because of the ceremony it follows, but it is separate from the worship of Hindu gods.

Each morning after a married woman rises, she washes, after which the first act she does is to perform *puja* (worship). She bows to the god, rings a bell, lights a lamp, and expresses her desires to the god. The second act performed is placing a mark on her forehead to acknowledge her submission to her husband's authority and acceptance of his protection. In Tamil, *kanavan kunn kunda devam*—her husband is the god she sees with her eyes. This mark also defines her status in her husband's household, and she will wear it until she is widowed. Her husband and his family expect this. Following the missionaries' and the church's injunction against the tilakam, Indian Christian women find themselves torn between their culture and their faith. Some wear it at home and then remove it when they go to church, and it is more than an individual problem. Instead, it is a problem between the wife and the husband's family; for them it represents a statement that she is unwilling to submit to her husband's authority, or—even worse—that her husband is dead to her, another instance of cultural alienation.

Complicating this issue, many Pentecostal churches insist that their women wear white saris in church after they are baptized, although in India only widows wear white. In one instance, we had a Hindu husband arrive at his wife's baptism visibly upset and threatening to remove the thali around her neck, as he practically screamed, "I'm alive, I'm alive." He was not objecting to her becoming a Christian but to her wearing white while he was alive, and she lived in his house. Many such so-called Christian prohibitions not only go against Indian culture but are not rooted in Scripture or—even worse—distort Scripture. Movements to adopt Indian customs among Christians are not new in India. Unfortunately, many of them are sidelined by the church as a watering down of Christian beliefs, and their leaders considered members of an eccentric fringe.

Issues of Faith: How Will They Tell Christians from Hindus?

It is difficult for older Christians, especially those (like Balaji) who have paid a significant price for converting from Hinduism, to consider the relative value of culture-based options. They wonder how to tell the Christians and Hindus apart if they follow local, often Hindu-induced customs. My great-grandmother was burned in a haystack for her husband's conversion. My father was put out of his home with only the clothes on his back. Many others face expulsion not just from their families but from their communities. They deal with discrimination in school admissions and even the loss of subsidized food ration cards. They are openly persecuted by Hindu militants. Many are killed, their homes and churches burned, while the government does little to protect them. For them, Christianity has become a badge of honor.

This is a sensitive issue because many of the older Christians are today's leaders of the church and elders in their community. Loyalty to one's faith is a matter of personal honor. At the height of persecutions in 1999 I saw thousands of Christian men, women, and children in Orissa, willing to be burned out, beaten, and even killed for their faith. To suggest that those who suffered for their faith should forgive people who seek to adopt Indian traditions such as presented here seems to be a display of total ignorance coming from people who have not had to deal with these cultural symbols personally.

We debated, over many cups of tea and dinners, the issue of standing up for our faith. I was reminded of Peter's betrayal of Jesus (Jn 18:15). In spite of his denial, Jesus restored him (Jn 21:15), and he was eventually crucified for being a follower of Christ. Persecution for faith remains rare in Western culture today, which is not true in India and countries in the Middle East. Anger and prejudice run deep. It is easy to advocate grace, but difficult for those who have paid the price. Only the Holy Spirit brings about real inner illumination and change. Christian students must stand against evil practices, such as selling children to pay off family debt, abusing and beating wives, not providing for family needs, or believing a husband is the god a wife sees with her own eyes. The contrast between evil practices and Christian behavior is obvious. So when we confront people with their culturally appropriate responsibilities, contrasting what their conscience tells them to do with what they know is wrong (Ac 2:14–16), we account for culturally conditioned expressions of potential identity with Christ. We provide refuge and support for individuals who choose to stand and be known as Christians who fulfill Hindu expectations—living life to the full (Jn 10:10).

Encouraging Pastors to Teach as Jesus Did

In preparing this new approach to our curriculum for Indian missionaries and pastors, we focused on the methods Jesus used when teaching in his day. He was a master at understanding his audience. He taught the principles of God's kingdom in terms his audience understood. He taught in parables about shepherds and farmers, marriage ceremonies, and everyday events in their lives.

Take, for example, the life of a Kurumaa shepherd. He scarcely sleeps at home. Instead, he sleeps wherever his sheep sleep, getting up early to separate his sheep from those of other shepherds. He takes care of the sick sheep, and he knows each one by name. It is obvious why such people relate immediately to the parable of the Good Shepherd in John's Gospel (10:1–16) without elaborate explanations. His story is their story. Balaji now takes this teaching even further.

> If the only sacrifice God desires is worship, then everything else we do—whether it be Hindu, Christian, or Muslim—is ritual and ceremony in an attempt to express our desire to relate to and experience the divine. It is important for us to understand these practices and help focus them to an understanding of the true God. Using the apostle Paul's example at Athens in Acts 17, Luke shows how Paul used the altar to the unknown god as an opportunity to direct people's devout behavior to knowledge of a risen Lord. He lauded their attempts and then preached the gospel.

As we progress further in this approach, we are constantly challenged with the fear of syncretism. Church elders see their role as maintaining the purity of the faith. Those of us attempting to be relevant must walk a fine line between showing respect for the elders and questioning established Christian assumptions. We must convince the leaders that we are not preaching a new gospel, just trying to find ways to let God's truth reach the unreached. We must convince them we are not preaching an "all roads lead to Rome" message, helping them, instead, understand that, with the right attitude, any road leads to the knowledge of the true God and to honor and worship God in ways that make sense to the people.

When we rewrote our curriculum to help village pastors and their congregations understand the stories of the Old Testament and develop an understanding of God building relationships, we realized that even though the message resonates with their culture, many of our sponsors would prefer we deal with the New Testament. Our belief, however, was that teaching the New Testament before gaining an understanding of the Old Testament in India creates "religion" instead of a relationship with God. Much of the New Testament teaching makes little sense without the background of the Old Testament. Furthermore, the Old Testament background is essential for a culture similar in many ways to the patriarchal culture of the Old Testament.

The Results of Hybridity

We wondered what our students would do with the new approach and freedom of expression we gave them. When they returned the next year, we listened to their reports. As teachers, we listened for two milestones.

First, we listened for the reaction and responses received from their Hindu communities. The stories are too many to list. When the pastors opened the church doors to the community to serve Christians and Hindus alike, with no expectation of conversion, the Hindus came. Many came in the same manner they go to the temple. They came to obtain blessings for their children to do well in exams, and to offer prayers for prosperity for their families. They came for many reasons, but most importantly, they came! In many instances, they stood in line for prayer. They brought food and offerings. They even stayed long enough to hear of God's love. The pastors required no commitment from them to return. As their prayers were answered, they came back to the church. They came back when there was disruption in their families and when their other alternatives failed. Not required to participate in the service, they could just observe.

When one village priest objected to the Hindus going into the church building, the pastor relocated the service outside, under a tree. In a few months, the Hindu priest invited him to have his service in the courtyard in front of the temple. He eventually considered the "Christian God" to have real power because he saw people healed.

The second marker we listened for was growth in the pastors themselves. We expected that most of the pastors would report on the growth of their churches, but instead they reported on the greater community they served. Not counting bodies as measures of success, they focused on greater harvest fields. A few pastors were still hesitant about all the interaction with Hindus. Some expressions of genuine Christian practices, though misguided, die slowly. One pastor explained that he refused bananas offered him on Tuesdays because on that day the Hindus went to the temple, and he did not want his family partaking of food offered to idols for fear evil spirits would possess them. Even before one of our teachers responded, the other students offered quotes from the New Testament story of Peter's vision, interaction with Cornelius, and instruction on eating unclean meats (Ac 10:1–48). They told him that rejecting the offering meant missing a great opportunity to minister to the Hindus. The pastors grew beyond our expectations.

Stories of Hindus receiving the gospel are too numerous to count even if anecdotal. A young Hindu woman told how, as a Hindu, she went to temple with her mother every week because it was important to her father. She also told how her mother went to church with her every week. Then the young woman pulled out a Bible, opened to the inside cover, and showed us what she had written: "Jesus is my favorite God."

People seek the light on their own if leaders shift the barriers, erected by missionaries and their followers, from a focus on culture to matters of faith. Is it better for people to search for truth while living in obedience to their parents, or to have them renounce their past and their families and adopt foreign ways that make no sense to them? We carry the burden of imparting the biblical message delivered in a specific time and context in one culture, interpreted by another, and then passed on to a third. In the process, much is lost and much added from the values and cultures of the intermediating societies. Significant evidence suggests that the message of the gospel brought to India by the apostle Thomas in the first century thrived and grew because it accepted and adopted the culture of the Indian people. Encouraging this process today is our challenge.

CONCLUSION

In closing, I should comment on the impact a change in perspective has on ministry in India. Our focus was not on deconstructing Christianity; it was on enculturating biblical principles in our South Indian environment—an environment that just happened to be much closer to the cultural reality of people in biblical times than the missionaries who brought the Bible to us realized.

First, Western Christians must understand it is not the correctness of the theology, traditional Western practices, or the exact phraseology of the missionary culture that brings people into relationship with God. Rather, it is the *substance* of the message. My father became a Christian because of a single sentence spoken by an unknown street preacher, who said, "Jesus Christ came to save sinners." For a young man burdened with feelings of guilt for an unrighteous life that every other religion condemned, a message about a God who came to save sinners moved his heart to embrace Jesus.

Second, left to the Holy Spirit, Christian faith in India will inevitably appear different from Christianity in other societies. This is not to contradict the truth of the gospel of Jesus Christ, the same yesterday, today, and forever (Heb 13:8). Rather it is to recognize cultural distinctions and connect biblical truth with any local context in which the Holy Spirit is allowed to bring transformation.

I attended a Christian festival a few years ago. Part of the celebration was a performance of Barathnatyam, an Indian dance tradition expressing stories and feelings with facial, hand, and body movements. The young lady performing wrote the lyrics.

We, your creation,
We are like the individual petals on the flowers of the garlands
 we place on your neck to worship you, mighty God,
You are the light in the oil lamps we burn every night.

At this Christian gathering, the expression and similarities to puja were metaphorical but clear, and the expression was beautiful. This young woman took the symbolism of her Hindu upbringing and translated it to an expression of worship to the one true God. No Western hymn expresses the feelings of her heart or communicates the same message to those around her.

Just as William Carey started the age of modern mission when he arrived in India in 1793, we are at the beginning of an age of new missiological understanding. A day will come when mission is recognized as proclaiming a gospel that resonates with people's interests and concerns. Effective mission allows the Holy Spirit to create, within those who are reached, images of Christ acceptable to canons of correctness, within their own cultural milieu (Rom 8:29).

When I left the Banjara village after the church dedication, I was a changed person who had learned more than I had preached. The people who built a house for God did not fail in their understanding of the purpose for the church structure. Rather, they expressed a far deeper meaning in their worship, and in doing so, embodied a relationship with the God they understood. The word "Emmanuel" now brings a new realization to my life: God dwelling in the midst of God's people, wherever they are found.

Epilogue

A key question in the anthropology of Christianity literature is "what difference does Christianity make?" (Haynes 2014, S357). The contributing authors to this book make clear that Christianity (as expressed by the incarnation and presented throughout the Bible) makes a difference only when grounded in the beliefs and values of a particular people living in a specific time and place. What's more, their expressions of those beliefs and values reflect the rituals and ceremonies people already know and understand as genuine worship of God.

This epilogue is more reflective than informative, celebrating what we have learned from the contributors in helping us understand what is important to them and to their people. They sought to help us appreciate our commonality in worshiping the one true God. But each in their own way reflects their specific expression of their innermost being to the superhuman being they rely upon to provide the care and well-being they so desire in this life as they prepare for the life to come.

REFLECTING ON HYBRIDITY

In 1995 Dan Shaw was invited to participate in an anthropology workshop sponsored by Wycliffe Bible Translators (WBT) in Guatemala. He was delighted and looked forward to visiting the birthplace of WBT in the village of San Antonio Aguascalientes. In the course of the workshop, Dan was asked if he would like to visit a highlands Guatemala shrine, the famous Iglesia de Santo Tomás at Chichikastenango. It was Holy Week, and he jumped at the opportunity. Traveling there was an experience in itself, as they were forced to make frequent detours through small towns where people blocked off the main street for Holy Week celebrations similar to Segura-Guzman's tale of El Baile de la Yegüita. On arrival at Chichikastenango, Dan took in the main square, teeming with crowds of pilgrims from throughout Guatemala and neighboring countries. These worshipers were celebrating Holy Week in a traditional style that harked back to earlier centuries of Indigenous religious expression as well as Spanish influence. They made their way up the long stairway to the main entrance, looking back on a sea of humanity and forward into the gloom of the cathedral's interior.

Once his eyes adjusted to the candlelit church, Dan was quickly drawn to a multiplicity of activities taking place simultaneously. Priests were busy—baptizing infants, marrying a couple in a small side chapel, and receiving confessions while the pews filled in anticipation of the next Mass. As Dan made his way down the center aisle, he nearly stumbled over a small raised platform constructed in the middle of the walkway. On it were brightly glowing candles and smoking incense, and in the center sat a *curandero* assisting a parishioner. As he looked up the aisle, toward the altar there was a small platform about every fifteen feet, occupied with people waiting for the assistance of a traditional healer.

As a Protestant missionary and Bible translator, Dan was shocked by the apparent syncretism; traditional shamans in the context of clearly Catholic activity and expectations, applying their Indigenous expertise under the obvious sanction of the priest who blessed all in his path while walking down the aisle swinging his thurible. As an anthropologist, however, he was fascinated by the juxtaposition of religious symbols and the effect on all who had gathered. Priests were clearly ministering to people's spiritual needs, as exemplified by all the religiously appropriate activity both inside and outside the cathedral. The shamans, in turn, were similarly assisting people in need. And everything was under the blessing symbolized by the smoke of the waving censor all shrouded in the glow of thousands of candles. Was this a sacrilegious, so-called Christo-paganism of gross proportions, or a legitimate hybridity of Catholic and traditional religious articulation experienced by people in highland Guatemala?

As the subtitle of this book suggests, we are in the midst of a paradigm shift that asks this very question. What Shaw came to realize in the intervening years is what Burrows and his Catholic friends recognized much sooner than most Protestants: syncretism in local contexts was happening regardless of outside theological input, and the way people express their religious experience reflects their interpretation of what they hear in light of their culturally subsumed expectations. Anything outside their experience will be viewed as foreign and irrelevant, not to mention unnecessary. Our hypothesis subsumes that God relates directly to a people's assumptions of spirituality. Inasmuch as God's intention is for people's benefit as they worship God, and their behavioral expectations are impacted by local ritual and ceremony that has traditionally made sense to them, those practices will dominate their expressions of worship. A people's familiar practices demonstrate their desire to survive in what is often perceived as a hostile world. Therefore, people want to give honor to and worship a God who cares for their well-being, as most contributors to this book have noted.

Perhaps the best historical study of how missionary communication in Latin America was subsumed into local cultural categories is *St. Martin de Porres: The "Little Stories" and the Semiotics of Culture* by the late Alex García-Rivera (1995). In a careful study of historical documents and their deeper meanings, García-Rivera shows how the mestizos of Peru accepted Christianity as delivered by the friars who accompanied the conquistadors, but did so in ways that resisted the Spaniards' colonial and imperial project. One clear lesson of our book is that people insert the Christian message into their specific ongoing, religious, and cultural history. There is, in other words, a blending process that we call "hybridity" in every acceptance of the gospel.

We have come to recognize that hybridity is a blending, but it is not a "dangerous syncretism" so often decried by those who believe a synthesis is the goal. If, as we explained in the first two chapters, appreciating hybridity is an attempt to understand how people conceptualize God, then their relationship with the cosmos directly impacts their appreciation of God's intent for them (as DomNwuchukwu demonstrates in chapter 9). We must, then, encourage local people to bring Scripture into their lives and evaluate their religious experience in light of what God has said. Doing so is far more advantageous for them than anything introduced from the outside. A conscious evaluation of their experience in light of Scripture is essential to determine what, for them, is relevant and appropriate as they develop their relationship with God. Avoiding dangerous syncretism is a matter of avoiding foreign influence and allowing the Holy Spirit to guide and enlighten everyone involved.

The criteria for assessment, then, are from a biblical perspective with regard to local practice, not merely from another cultural perspective that judges from outside the context, no matter how well-meaning. Dan's experience at Chichikastenango demonstrated how quick he was to push the syncretism button and condemn this mixture of Catholic religious expressions and traditional healing practices. It was immediately negative and, from his perspective, contrary to God's intention. However, if one views all this through the prism of hybridity, it must be recognized as a cross-fertilization process that blends disparate experience into a new and vibrant recognition of God's presence. The result in Chichikastenango was an intermixture of beliefs and practices that were clearly meaningful to all involved—relating the God of the universe to the immediacy of human life. In the chapters of this book, each author demonstrates the value of hybrid thinking as we all reject the negativity of syncretism and seek to understand more fully how God interacts with needy people in a postcolonial world.

As a Catholic, Bill hastens to observe that when Evangelical and Pentecostal missionaries began to appear on the scene, many millions of Latin Americans appreciated the liberation those Catholics felt when Jesus was more clearly at the center of their preaching and when they were encouraged to give themselves over to the Spirit whose presence and power they felt. Bill also recalls words spoken in conversation with his friend the late William Cook, a respected Protestant interpreter of religious life in Latin America: "Many of my evangelical brethren," he said, "don't realize how near their converts feel to the Blessed Mother Mary and the saints. The final chapter in their religious history was not written when they became Pentecostals." We have come to realize that those who think of themselves as missionaries, bringing good news to people who follow other religious ways, do not have the final word.

Is there need for a process of discernment to ensure that hybridization leads toward an ever-deeper appropriation of the gospel under the guidance of the Holy Spirit? Certainly. But the criteria for this discernment must be biblical and not merely the result of another culture's own religiocultural, gene-splicing hybridity—all the more so when the mission-sending church may well have a completely undeserved sense of superiority when it comes to appropriating the gospel.

WHAT WE LEARNED

Each chapter in this book takes its author's perspective of people in a particular context and weaves a story of scriptural relevance in light of local belief and practice. Through these authors' experiences we have traveled from the highlands of Papua New Guinea to the plains of the Niger delta, from New Zealand marae to densely populated Korea and Japan—from a northwestern North America coast smudging ceremony to Jamaican mountain shaman and Central American mythology, from Lake Sentani in West Papua to urban Messianic Jewish homes celebrating Shabbat, and from Indian gypsies dedicating a house for God to Armenian Orthodox use of all five senses. All are appropriate to experiencing God. We have seen the immense impact that ancestors have on understanding people and their relationships. With Lawson and McCauley, we have struggled with the relevance of Type 1 (repetitive) and Type 2 (sensory pageantry) rituals and ceremonies and appreciated the importance of food, both as central to ritual and for binding people together in reconciliation. We have seen time collapse in mythology, where the past enters the present, which, in turn, presages the future. Ancient rituals become meaningful in contemporary contexts, while religious experience, held sacred by one people group, may be recognized as hegemonic and irrelevant by others. Is this controversial? Absolutely! But it also demonstrates a reflective and meaningful recognition of local value that brings new understanding of "superhuman agents," and more particularly, an omniscient, caring God.

Here then are some of the trends and insights from these distinct reflections on the role of traditional rituals in Christian worship, and how such awareness raises questions relating to the contrast between dangerous syncretism and necessary hybridity.

Incarnation

First and foremost, our authors reveal the difference Christianity makes in the way people live in the here and now. The response, however, is not because they follow the precepts introduced by outsiders as a "religion," but because they recognize their interaction is with the God of the universe who has already joined with them. In this sense, Christianity is a relationship people have with God, not merely a religion. God, not Christianity, is universal. Every chapter resounds with an awareness that incarnation is critical to effective spiritual interaction because it directs the focus of worship to a God who is present and cares about human needs and concerns.

This imminence of spiritual presence brings awareness that the God who missionaries told people about was already known to them. The names may vary, but the spiritual presence and power to make a difference is well integrated into human spiritual understanding all around the world. Their theological reflection is directly associated with explicit cultural and spiritual identity (more than religion per se) that redirects their acceptance of God. As Sanneh has famously noted, the missionaries brought the Bible and translated it so that people could appreciate in new ways the God they already knew (1989, passim).

Worship

Contrary to missionary negativity toward Indigenous spirituality and related practices, the Bible taught people what of their beliefs and practices they needed to adjust in order to effectively give honor to and appropriately respond to God. The Bible gave them Jesus, who lived out God's expression in a particular time and place in ways that could be meaningfully translated into any context. The Bible introduced them to the Holy Spirit, who provides the power to turn their prayers into substantive reality, contrary to the negative spiritual forces that also dominate their lives. Such is the message of DonNwachukwu's chapter, detailing the need for the Igbo to engage in Indigenous worship styles that reflect their cultural heritage over what missionaries introduced. This same notion dominates all the chapters in the "Focus on Context" sections of both parts one and two: Koreans recognizing their connection to God through their departed ancestors, who pass that understanding on to each generation; Armenians who hark back to their "pagan" roots to appreciate the Scripture in light of the prayers of the saints; and Sentanians recognizing Jesus as an archetypal leader who became the Great Ancestor as they read the Epistle to the Hebrews.

Ancestors

Another unmistakable message for us in the West is the prominence of ancestors. Without prompting, almost every author connects ritual and ceremony to some aspect of their physical, social, and spiritual heritage in the form of their ancestors: mythology for highland Costa Ricans and Jamaicans, lowland Sentanians, and Messianic Jews; ceremonial reenactment for the Simbu, Japanese, Armenians, Costa Ricans, and Indigenous North Americans; restoration of lost heritage and identity for Māori, Maroons, and Koreans. Clearly, local categories contribute to theological processing in ways that are far more meaningful than outside categories. Indeed, unless deemed relevant by local people, outside categories are not processed or are only associated with an already well-formed, foreign religion, as in the case of the Japanese view of Christianity.

Cultural Expression in Context—Relevance

Furthermore, we learn not to confuse culture and religion. Indian expressions of worship are clearly reflected by Hindu, Muslim, and Christian worshipers alike; the focus is on their Indian-ness, not the religious identity to which they ascribe. When properly appropriated, cultural expressions of worship should reflect recognizable elements associated with giving honor to God, not a religious expression taught by outsiders. As people associate their worship with their cultural identity, they will own the experience, they will understand it, and they will be able to pass it on to others in their own context while encouraging people of other cultural identities to do the same, as DomNwachukwu, Obasare, Gupta, and Dauermann all noted. Moreover, every chapter highlights the value of using culturally recognizable symbols for relevant worship, reflecting positively on McCauley and Lawson's hypothesis (2002) that expressions of high emotional impact reflect local agency (highlighting active spiritual application) over and against repetitive expressions that stress patience (emphasizing passivity). Dan's current research, supported by a John Templeton Foundation grant, lends support to the cognitive value of such local approaches (Barrett and Shaw 2015).

Cleansing before, during, or after worship serves as an example of cultural diversity despite religious identity. Among Indigenous North Americans, cleansing serves as the primary rationale for smudging rituals. For the Simbu, killing pigs prior to the main pig-kill cleanses the land and signals their resolve. Messianic Jews, like their predecessors, cleanse their homes as well as their minds and bodies, reflecting on God's instructions while preparing for Shabbat. It is not just another day; it is a day deserving of special kavod—honor.

God's Grace

How people approach the Almighty is crucial to what they receive. If the focus is on manipulating spiritual power for people's benefit, they have not understood God's intentions toward the creation. Rather, especially in Dan's view, the Bible makes it clear that people should humbly acknowledge God's omniscience and grace. Christianity must be a recognition of the one whom Christians worship, not the manifold expressions of their worship. Bill, on the other hand, remains more pragmatic about the activity of the spirits of the dead and believes that the ages-old Catholic intuition that various agencies are at work in the world and not all are Satanic is worthy of careful consideration. Both of us are clear that the God of Abraham, Isaac, and Jacob does not demand the same ritual expressions from all.

Rather Scripture places a high value on humility, honor, and respect as reflected in the particularity of worship (Mic 6:8). As Obasare demonstrates, manipulating spiritual power for one's benefit often turns dangerous. What Christianity heralds is the presence of Creator, whose grace is sufficient for all and who desires the worship of created ones. This theme emerges in most chapters and reflects on issues of globalization in the twenty-first century. The focus is on valid expressions of Christianity in context, a reflection on how people interpret biblical principles for themselves, not on one-size-fits-all practice. Such diversity is commensurate with biblical teaching and should be encouraged wherever "two or three are gathered" in Christ's name (Mt 18:20).

Christian Identity

Most authors in this compendium note that following the missionaries' approach to Christianity led to people's marginalization in their own cultures and feeling inferior to mainstream Christianity as reflected by the contexts from which missionaries came. Certainly this was the case among the Indigenous North American populations, while the Maroons, the Igbo, Messianic Jews, and people all across India reflect symptoms of being less than the missionaries hoped for. But when such peoples realize their equality with missionary-sending societies, the resultant hybridity both reflects a new thing and is part of a centuries-old process. Something as simple as eating the right foods at the right time can reduce marginalization.

Food, for example, is strategic, from its reflection on partaking in the Lord's table to sharing those strategic symbols with all who partake, a fact central to Kuman's argument. Food frequently features in reconciliation as people resolve their differences and recognize their oneness in Christ, as Haami makes clear in his Aotearoa case study. Reconciliation in the human realm is reflective of what Christ has done to enable human beings to be in relationship with God. As Daimoi makes clear for the Sentanians, recognizing Christ as the *ondoporo kabang*—the son of life-giving water—creates a bond between them and God; a relationship between humans and their creator is the spectacular result. Reconciliation, not alienation, is the message of the entire Bible and resonates through all of human enterprise. It is reflected in the way an Igbo elder uses his *ofo* staff, it dictates how food is displayed on an ancestral table in a Korean home, and it anticipates the display of flowers reflecting the relationship between a deceased Japanese and Jesus Christ.

Cultural Symbols

Time and space are other aspects of culture that dominate the pages of this book: mythical time reflective of the *tambuna* (ancient Melanesians who departed long ago, but still maintain order); the way time collapses as the people of Nicoya recite the myth, dance the story of *yegüita*, and bring its reality into the present; the necessity to recite one's lineage before entering the hallowed ground of a Māori marae, signals the role of ancestors as well as their contemporary descendants. Without this protocol, there can be no relationship, for relationship reflects heritage, a deep lineality that creates identity and gives understanding to those who acknowledge each other through the *hongi*, a symbol of greeting that has deep spiritual significance—the exchange of each other's breath.

Throughout the book, cultural symbols abound and produce a depth of relevance for each context, thereby demonstrating extensive ethnographic awareness. What these authors have done is briefly give insight to those who do not share their understanding, so that all who are part of the conversation—the other authors of this book and those who read it—can begin to appreciate the breadth of implications expressed herein. The expressions are specific to each Indigenous community. The principles, however, apply to any context and enable readers to approach each socioreligious environment with a new appreciation of God's presence. Such recognition will, we hope, free those who serve as message bearers to focus on the relevance of Christ in that place—what it means to those who hear the "word of the Lord" and recognize God in their context in the person of Jesus Christ. That is the message these authors give us.

Faith

Our message is to focus on faith as an outgrowth of a living trust in God, as opposed to focusing on religious behavior or practice. Faith is crucial to divining how people perceive God and connect God to their lives. This point comes out in each chapter. People living out their faith in all the ambiguities of life results in expressions of Christianity that reflect to God and to a watching population, as well as to a vibrant church in the society, what it means to be Christian. In short, faith expresses itself in ways that make sense to people who reflect their understanding of God back into their lifestyle and experience God as people who happen to be Christian.

Throughout the book, the authors, in their own way, affirm that Christianity makes a difference in the lives of their people because of God's presence among them. Incarnation is the theological watchword. God has come to real people in the context of their lives, and they in turn appropriately acknowledge God's presence through culturally meaningful worship—a hybrid resulting from what they already know, combined with the recognition of "Emmanuel."

FINAL WORDS

We, the two editors of this volume, began our careers in very different places. Across the years, our border crossings have brought us into contact with a wide variety of experiences and people who have affected our view of ourselves, our understanding of spirituality, and our appreciation for the other.

The essays in this volume show that belief in and experience with the excluded middle impinges on the lives of men and women in many parts of the world. By contrast, Max Weber spoke of the *Entzauberung* (disenchantment; lit., demiraclizing) of both religion and the world as a key defining characteristic of modern, bureaucratic, highly differentiated societies (Weber 1964, passim; see esp. 246–76). Weber's thesis has proved durable as a descriptor and predictor in Western culture, where religion has increasingly been pushed out of the public sphere and, to a very great extent, has enforced the exclusion of the ontological middle realm of spirits, at least in elite circles that dominate the press and the great universities. Yet this secularized segment is a relatively small portion of the world's population, as the authors of this book demonstrate.

Predicting the future of religious expression is difficult. What is clear, however, is the persistence of belief in and claims of middle-realm experience that has often been excluded from consideration. As long as ancestors and other spiritual presences are integral to societies' religious expressions, they will be integral to people's understanding of Christianity and demand a place in the rituals and symbols that Christians use to express their place in the cosmos.

Our objective throughout this book has been to bring hybridity into relief as both necessary and relevant to local development of spirituality in all its varied, even sometimes exotic, but always appropriate manifestations. People have a natural propensity to go with their instincts based on their assumptions about how things naturally are—what everyone knows, except that not everyone (especially outsiders) intuitively knows what is going on and therefore must be ready to pay attention to how people think and act. This requires learning from those we seek to reach. Simply instructing people how to practice their spirituality based on how others have always done it will only produce artificial, split-level syncretism. Allowing the tender prompting of the Holy Spirit to bring local reflection, assessment, and practical adjustment provides for the application of already understood ritual and ceremony to the reality of worshiping God in all his glory. This forms a hybrid that grows organically where it is planted and avoids dangerous syncretism.

The resulting variety of worship patterns reflects not only on how people do church, but also on how ancestors are given due respect and shamans adjust their practices to reflect the prompting of God's Spirit rather than manipulating local spiritual power. Sprinkling pigs' blood in the highlands of PNG is reflective of the Passover lamb's blood placed on doorposts and now eulogized in the Eucharist, bringing our Lord's table into high relief. Recapturing the spirit of cooperation assumed by expectant Māori at Waitangi, but often thwarted by the British and their descendants, now brings spiritually energized reconciliation to all people in Aotearoa.

These varied expressions are presented by the contributors, each closely involved in their development with deep understanding and humble appreciation for how they express hybridity of traditional and Christian principles within their respective cognitive environments. To that end, we herald these attempts to recognize God's presence and anticipate the impact such involvement will have. These expressions, developed and lived out "with respectful humility while maintaining a good conscience" (1 Pet 3:16), highlight the importance of allowing people to relate Christian faith directly into the spiritually focused assumptions of the society in order to give an answer for the "hope that is within them" (1 Pet 3:15). Hybridic inculturation rather than marginalization will be the contextualized result.

Yet our focus here is not on the diverse or exotic aspects of religious expression. Rather we desire to emphasize God's creativity by making human beings in God's own image. The human commonality expressed through this variety of spiritual expressions is the basis for appreciating incarnation. The metatheology that Paul Hiebert (1988) desired comes out in the overarching, even if often unconscious, ontological awareness that God intends good for all people and desires to have them eventually live with him in a place prepared by the creator of the universe (Jn 1:1–4), on one hand, while coming to live among us (Jn 1:9–11, 14) on the other. This commonality of Christian expression is not modeled on conformity and repetitious expressions of the tedium effect, but rather stimulated by the life-changing power of the Holy Spirit ministering to people in the particularity of their socioreligious expectations. Only then will people recognize both their own identity and their place within the context of the larger Catholic Church (in the universal sense). Only then will they know who they are in Christ, as they stand shoulder to shoulder with their sisters and brothers worshiping at the throne of the Lamb.

References

Achebe, Chinua. 1959. *Things Fall Apart*. Greenwich, CT: Fawcett.

———. 1964. *Arrow of God*. Oxford: Heinemann Educational Books.

Adeyemo, T. 1979. *Salvation in African Tradition*. Nairobi: Evangel Publishing House.

Adogame, A. 2004. "Engaging the Rhetoric of Spiritual Warfare: The Public Face of Aladura in Diaspora." *Journal of Religion in Africa* 34, no. 4: 493–522.

Akao, J. O. 1986. "Is the Mission of the Church Still Understood in Western Terms?" In *The State of Christian Theology in Nigeria, 1980–81*, ed. Mercy Oduyoye, 6 Ibadan, Nigeria: Daystar Press.

Anderson, Alan. 2005. "Pentecostal and Charismatic Theology." In *The Modern Theologians*, ed. David F. Ford, 589–607. Malden, MA: Blackwell Publishing.

Anjewac'i, Xosrov. 1991. *Commentary on the Divine Liturgy*. Trans. with an Introduction by S. Peter Cowe. New York: St. Vartan Press. Church of America.

Appiah, S. K. 2003. "The Quest of African Identity." *Exchange* 32, no. 1: 54–65.

Arbuckle, Gerald A. 2010. *Culture, Inculturation, and Theologians: A Postmodern Critique*. Collegeville, MN: Liturgical Press.

Arinze, Francis. 1970. *Sacrifice in Ibo Traditional Religion*. Ibadan, Nigeria: Ibadan University Press.

Arzoumanian, Z. 2014. *The Church of Armenia*. Burbank, CA: Western Diocese of the Armenian Church in North America.

Assembly of First Nations. 2003. *Charter of the Assembly of First Nations*. www.afn.ca.

Bae, Young Dong. 2002. "A View of Ancestors in Traditional Ancestral Rites." *Comparative Folklore* 23: 283–312.

Barrett, Justin L. 2011. *Cognitive Science, Religion, and Theology: From Human Minds to Divine Minds*. Templeton Science and Religion Series. West Conshohocken, PA: Templeton Press.

Barrett, Justin L., and R. Daniel Shaw. 2015. *Recruiting Field Data for CSR Questions: Pilot Phase—ID: 59142*. Research Grant from the John Templeton Foundation.

Bartholomew, Craig G., and Michael W. Goheen. 2004. *The Drama of Scripture: Finding Our Place in the Biblical Story*. Grand Rapids: Baker Academic.

Basden, George Thomas. 1966. *Niger Ibos*. New York: Barnes & Noble.

Bavinck, Johan H. 1960. *An Introduction to the Science of Missions*. Philadelphia: Presbyterian and Reformed Publishing Co.

———. 1964. *An Introduction to the Science of Missions*. Philadelphia: Presbyterian and Reformed Publishing Company.

Bear-Barnetson, Cheryl. 2013. *Introduction to First Nations Ministry*. Cleveland, TN: Cherohala Press.

Bede, the Venerable. 1907. *Bede's Ecclesiastical History of Britain*. Edited and translated by A. M. Sellar. London: George Bell and Sons. (Original MS not extant, thought to date to eighth century AD.)

Bediako, Kwame. 1992. *Theology and Identity: The Impact of Culture upon Christian Thought in the Second Century and in Modern Africa*. Oxford: Regnum Books.

Belich, James. 1998. *The New Zealand Wars*. Auckland, NZ: Penguin.

Benedict, Ruth. 1934. *Patterns of Culture*. Boston: Houghton.

Bhabha, Homi K. 1985. "Signs Taken for Wonders: Questions of Ambivalence and Authority under a Tree outside Delhi, May 1817." *Critical Inquiry* 12, no. 1: 144–65.

———. 1994. *The Location of Culture*. London: Routledge.

Boadt, Lawrence. 1984. *Reading the Old Testament*. New York: Paulist Press. (Second edition published 2004.)

Boff, Leonardo. 1989. *Faith on the Edge: Religion and the Marginalized Existence*. San Francisco: Harper & Row.

Boyajian, T. 2011. *Living the Armenian Church Year*. New York: Diocese of the Armenian Church of America (Eastern).

Bradshaw, Bruce. 1993. *Bridging the Gap*. Monrovia, CA: MARC.

Bradshaw, Paul E. 2002. *The Search for the Origins of Christian Worship: Sources and Methods for the Study of Early Liturgy*. 2nd ed. Oxford: Oxford University Press.

———. 2004. *Eucharistic Origins*. Oxford: Oxford University Press.

Brathwaite, Edward Kamau. 1977. *Nanny, Sam Sharpe, and the Struggle for a People's Liberation*. Kingston, Jamaica: Agout Press.

Brown, Colin. 1984. *Miracles and the Critical Mind*. Grand Rapids: Eerdmans.

Buber, M. 2000. *I and Thou*. Translated by Ronald Gregor Smith. New York: Scribner Classics.

Bulatao, Jaime C. 1966. *Split-Level Christianity*. Manila: Anteneo de Manila.

Burman, J. J. Roy. 2010. *Ethnography of a Denotified Tribe: The Laman Banjara*. New Delhi: Mittal Publications.

Burrows, William R. 2007. "Roman Catholic Church." In *Encyclopedia of Missions and Missionaries*, ed. Jon Bonk, 389–94. New York: Routledge.

———. 2010. "The Importance of Liturgy in Ecclesial Mission Animation." *Missiology* 38 (January): 37–49.

Calvin, John. 1960. *Institutes of the Christian Religion*. 2 vols. Edited by John T. McNeill. Translated by Ford Lewis Battles. Philadelphia: Westminster. (Original editions: 1536 in Latin; 1541 in French).

Carey, Bev. 1997. *Maroon Story: The Authentic and Original History of Jamaica, 1490–1880*. Kingston, Jamaica: Agout Press.

Casel, Odo. 1962. *The Mystery of Christian Worship and Other Writings*. London: Darton, Longman and Todd.

Catechism of the Catholic Church. 2000. Revised ed. Rome: Editrice Vaticana; Stratford, NSW, Australia: St. Paul's Publications.

Catholic Encyclopedia, The. 1912. Volume 14. Online edition, ed. Charles G. Hermann et al. http://www.newadvent.org.

Cha, Eun Jung. 1999. "The Establishment of Korean Protestant Rituals and Cultural Conflicts." *Korean Christianity and History* 10: 103–36.

Chesterton, Gilbert Keith. 2011. *Orthodoxy*. Hollywood, FL: Wilder Publications (Original edition, 1908).

Cho, Hyun. 2012. "Catholics May Exceed Protestantism in 2015." *Hangyeore Daily News Paper*, November 21, www.hani.co.kr.

Choi, Gil Sung. 1983. "A Study of Korean Ancestral Worship." *Korean Anthropology* 15: 81–92.

Chomsky, Noam. 1957. *Syntactic Structures*. The Hague: Mouton.

Clanet, M. C. 1990. *L' Interculturel: Introduction aux Approches Interculturelles en Éducation et en Sciences Humaines*. Toulouse, France: Presses Universitaires du Mirail.

Consedine, Robert, and Joanna Consedine. 2001. *Healing Our History: The Challenge of the Treaty of Waitangi*. Auckland, NZ: Penguin Books.

Cowan, James. 1995. *The New Zealand Wars and the Pioneering Period*. Volume 1. Wellington, NZ: R. E. Owen, Government Printer.

Cross, Frank Moore. 1988. *From Epic to Canon: History and Literature in Ancient Israel*. Baltimore: Johns Hopkins University Press.

Dauermann, Stuart. 2009. *The Rabbi as a Surrogate Priest*. Eugene, OR: Pickwick Publications.

Davie, Grace. 2000. *Religion in Modern Europe: A Memory Mutates*. Oxford: Oxford University Press.

Davies, Jon, ed. 1994. *Ritual and Remembrance: Responses to Death in Human Societies*. Sheffield: Sheffield Academic Press.

Derby, Mark. 2013. "Hakaraia Mahika—Prophet of Peace or Son of Satan." Paper delivered to New Zealand Historical Association biennial conference, University of Otago, November 20–22, 2013.

Devrishian, D. V. 2013. *Variables of the Divine Liturgy: Proper to Sundays and Special Feast Days and Church Knowledge*. Burbank, CA: Western Diocese of the Armenian Church in North America.

DomNwachukwu, Chinaka S. 1999. "Spiritual Power in Africa: Insights from the African Independent Churches of Lagos Nigeria." PhD dissertation, Fuller Theological Seminary, Pasadena, CA.

———. 2010. *An Introduction to Multicultural Education: From Theory to Practice*. Lanham, MD: Rowman and Littlefield.

DomNwachukwu, Chinaka S., & H. Lee. 2014. *Multiculturalism: A Shalom Motif for the Christian Community*. Eugene, OR: Wipf & Stock.

DomNwachukwu, P. N. 2000. *Authentic African Christianity: An Intercultural Model for the Igbo*. New York, NY: Peter Lang.

Dyrness, William. 2013. *Senses of Devotion: Interfaith Aesthetics in Buddhist and Muslim Communities*. Eugene, OR: Cascade Books.

Enuwosa, Joseph. 2005. "African Cultural Hermeneutics: Interpreting the New Testament in a Cultural Context." *Black Theology: An International Journal* 3, no. 1: 86–96.

Eriksen, Thomas Hylland. 2010. *Small Places, Big Issues: An Introduction to Social and Cultural Anthropology*. 3rd ed. London: Pluto Press.

Fauconnier, Gilles. 1985. *Menial Space*. Cambridge, MA: MIT Press. (Second edition: New York: Cambridge University Press, 1994.)

Fauconnier, Gilles, and Mark Turner. 2002. *The Way We Think: Conceptual Blending and the Mind's Hidden Complexities*. New York: Basic Books.

Fishbane, Michael. 1987. *Judaism: Revelation and Tradition*. New York: Harper and Row. Quoted in Ericka Meitner, "The Mezzuzah: American Judaism and Constructions of Domestic Sacred Space." In *American Sanctuary: Understanding Sacred Spaces*, ed. Louis P. Nelson, 182–202. Bloomington: Indiana University Press, 2006.

Fisher, Robert B. 1998. *West African Religious Traditions: Focus on the Akan of Ghana*. Maryknoll, NY: Orbis Books.

Fiumara, Gemma Corradi. 1995. *The Metaphoric Process: Connections between Language and Life*. London: Routledge.

Frazer, James G. 1894. *The Golden Bough*. 2 vols. London: Macmillan.

Frymer-Kensky, Tikva. 2002. *Reading the Women of the Bible: A New Interpretation of Their Stories*. New York: Schocken.

García-Rivera, Alex. 1995. *St. Martin de Porres: The "Little Stories" and the Semiotics of Culture*. Faith and Cultures Series. Maryknoll, NY: Orbis Books.

Gerhart, Mary, and Allan Melvin Russell. 1984. *Metaphoric Process: The Creation of Scientific and Religious Understanding*. Fort Worth: Texas Christian University Press.

Gerrish, B. A. 1982. "The Word of God and the Words of Scripture: Luther and Calvin on Biblical Authority." In Gerrish, *The Old Protestantism and the New: Essays on the Reformation Heritage*, 51–68. Chicago: University of Chicago Press.

Gilliland, Dean S. 1989. *The Word among Us: Contextualizing Theology for Mission Today*. Dallas: Word.

Gladwell, Malcolm. 2002. *The Tipping Point: How Little Things Can Make a Big Difference*. Bolson: Little Brown.

Goodenough, Ward H. 1956. "Componential Analysis and the Study of Meaning." *Language* 32: 195–216.

———. 1965. "Rethinking Status and Role: Toward a General Model of the Cultural Organization of Social Relationships." In *The Relevance of Models for Social Anthropology*, ed. Michael Banton, 1–24. London: Tavistock.

Grant, Robert M. 1963. *A Historical Introduction to the New Testament*. London: Collins, Fontana Library.

Gutiérrez, Gustavo. 1973. *A Theology of Liberation*. Maryknoll, NY: Orbis Books.

Gutt, Ernst-August. 2005. "On the Significance of the Cognitive Core of Translation." *The Translator* 11, no. 1: 25–49.

Guzie, T. W. 1974. *Jesus and the Eucharist*. New York: Paulist Press.

Haami, Bradford. 2012. "Report on Maori-British Reconciliation Journey from Westminster to Aotearoa." Unpublished paper.

———. 2013. *Hohou-rongo: Making Peace*. M. Bradford Haami.

———. 2016. *The River of the Water of Life: A Biography of Ihaka "Ike" Samuels*. Aotearoa, NZ: Ike Samuels Whānau.

Hall, Edward T. 1959. *The Silent Language*. New York: Doubleday.

Hall, Lizette. 1992. *The Carrier, My People*. Cloverdale, BC: Friesen Printers.

Hammond, Peter. 1964. *Cultural and Social Anthropology: Selected Readings*. New York: Macmillan.

Hansin University Theological Institute. 2005. *A Research on Cultural Consciousness of Korean People: Focus on the Changes of Family Culture*. Seoul: Hanulbooks.

Haynes, Naomi. 2014. "Affordances and Audiences: Finding the Difference Christianity Makes." In *The Anthropology of Christianity: Unity, Diversity, New Directions*, ed. Joel Robbins and Naomi Haynes, S357–S365. Wenner-Gren Symbolium Series, *Current Anthropology* 15 (Supplement 10).

Heschel, Abraham Joshua. 1951. *The Sabbath: Its Meaning for Modern Man*. New York: Farrar, Straus and Giroux.

———. 1963. *The Insecurity of Freedom*. New York: First Noonday Press.

———. 1976. *God in Search of Man*. New York: Macmillan / Farrar, Straus and Giroux.

Hicks, D., ed. 2010. *Ritual and Belief Readings in the Anthropology of Religion*. Lanham, MD: AltaMira Press.

Hiebert, Paul G. 1978. "Conversion, Culture, and Cognitive Categories." *Gospel in Context* 1 (October): 24-29.

———. 1982. "The Flaw of the Excluded Middle." *Missiology* 10, no. 1 (January): 35–47.

———. 1985. *Anthropological Insights for Missionaries*. Grand Rapids: Baker.

———. 1987. "Critical Contextualization." *International Bulletin of Missionary Research* 11, no. 3: 104–12.

———. 1988. "Metatheology: The Step beyond Contextualization." In *Reflection and Projection: Missiology at the Threshold of 2001*, ed.

Hans Kasdorf and Klaus Müller, 383–95. Bad Liebenzell: Verlag der Liebenzeller Mission.

———. 1991. "Checks against Syncretism." *Christianity Today* 35, no. 2: 39–40.

———. 1994. *Anthropological Reflections on Missiological Issues*. Grand Rapids: Baker.

———. 1999a. *The Missiological Implications of Epistemological Shifts: Affirming Truth in a Modern/Postmodern World*. Harrisburg, PA: Trinity.

———. 1999b. "Cultural Differences and the Communication of the Gospel." *Perspectives on the World Christian Movement*, 3rd ed., ed. Ralph Winter and Stephen Hawthorne, 373–83. Pasadena, CA: William Carey Library.

———. 2008. *Transforming Worldviews: An Anthropological Understanding of How People Change*. Grand Rapids: Baker Academic.

———. 2009. *The Gospel in Human Contexts: Anthropological Explorations for Contemporary Missions*. Grand Rapids: Baker.

Hiebert, Paul G., R. Daniel Shaw, and Tite Tiénou. 1999. *Understanding Folk Religion: A Christian Response to Popular Beliefs and Practices*. Grand Rapids: Baker.

Hill, Harriet S. 2003. *The Role of Context in Bible Translation: Enlarging the Mutual Cognitive Environment*. Dissertation, Fuller Graduate School of Intercultural Studies, Pasadena, CA.

———. 2006. *The Bible at Cultural Crossroads: From Translation to Communication*. Manchester, UK: St. Jerome Publishing.

Hillary, M. 1995. *Interculturation Theology of the Jerusalem Council in Acts 15: An Inspiration for the Igbo Church Today*. New York: Peter Lang.

Idowu, E. B. 1973. *African Traditional Religion: A Definition*. London: SCM.

Ilogu, Edmund. 1974. *Christianity and Ibo Culture*. Leiden, The Netherlands: E. J. Brill.

Imasogie, Osadolor. 1982. *African Traditional Religion*. Ibadan, Nigeria: University Press.

Jacobs, Adrian. 2006. "A History of Slaughter: Embracing Our Martyrdom at the Margins of Encounter." *Journal of the North American Institute for Indigenous Theological Studies* 4: 123–25.

Janelli, Roger L., and Dawnhee Im. 1982. *Ancestor Worship and Korean Society*. Stanford, CA: Stanford University Press.

Johnson, Mark. 1987. *The Body in the Mind: The Bodily Basis of Meaning, Imagination, and Reason*. Chicago: University of Chicago Press.

Jules-Rosette, Benetta W. 1991. "Tradition and Continuity in African Religions: The Case of New Religious Movements." In *African Traditional Religion in Contemporary Society*, ed. Jacob K. Olupona, 149–165. New York: Paragon House.

Kaloustian, S. 1964. *Saints and Sacraments*. New York: Diocese of the Armenian Church of North America.

Kang, Byungyul. 2001. "Legitimate to Be Divorced from a Wife Who Rejected the Ancestral Rite Based on Her Christian Faith." Korean Journalist Club, January 2, www.kjc24.com.

Kang, Wi Jo. 1988. "Ancestor Worship from the Perspective of Family Life." In *Ancestor Worship and Christianity in Korea*, ed. Lee Jung Young, 73–81. Lampeter, UK: Edwin Mellen Press.

Karmeian, M., ed. 2010. *Welcome to the Armenian Church: Essentials about the Armenian Church Faith, Religious Culture, and Traditions from Ancient Times to Present*. Burbank, CA: Western Diocesan Press.

Kilage, Ignatius. 1980. *My Mother Calls Me Yaltep*. Oxford: Oxford University Press.

Kim, Jae Deuk, Park Moon Su, and Park Il Young. 2004. *A Study on the Sociocultural Influence of the Korean Catholic Church during the Twentieth Century*. Seoul: Hanwool Academy.

Kim, Kwanguk. 1986. "Ancestral Worship and the Principle of Social Structure." *Korean Anthropology* 18: 109–28.

Kim, Mantae. 2010. "A Comparative Missiological Study of Sinhalese Buddhists and Sinhalese Christian Attitudes toward the Puberty Ritual." *Missiology* 38, no. 4: 411–30.

———. 2011. *The Puberty Ritual in Sri Lanka: A Comparative Exploration of Perceptions and Attitudes between Buddhists and Christians*. American University Series. New York: Peter Lang.

Kim, Miyoung. 2005. "Confucian Lifetime Rituals That Seek Relational Order." In *Religion and Lifetime Rituals*, ed. Korean Association for Research on Religion and Folklore, 55–80. Seoul: Minsokwon.

———. 2007. "Changes in Ancestral Rites and the Continuance of Identity: With a Special Reference to the An Dong Province." *Historical Folklore* 25: 270–99.

Kim, Youngjin. 2011. "A Christian Dilemma: Should the Ancestral Rite Be Practiced?" *Christianity Today*, January 26, www.christiantoday.co.kr.

Kim, Young Soon. 2001. "Ancestral Rites and Ritual Structure." *Historical Folklore* 13: 92–123.

Kim, Young Soo. 2005. "A Historical and Folkloric Approach to Korean Catholicism and Ancestral Rites." In *Religion and Ancestral Rites*, ed. Pyun Moo Young, 311–36. Seoul: Minsokwon.

Kinzer, Mark S. 2011. *Israel's Messiah and the People of God: A Vision for Messianic Jewish Covenant Fidelity*. Eugene, OR: Cascade Books.

Knight, James. 1979. "Bona Gene: The Pig-Kill Festival of Numai (Simbu Province)—Tradition and Change." In *Powers, Plumes, and Piglets: Phenomena of Melanesian Religion*, ed. Norman C. Habel, 173–93. Bedford Park: Australian Association for the Study of Religion.

Ko, Sukpyo. 2013. "Traditional Culture of New Year's Day and Christian Culture." Christian Broadcasting System, February 7, www.christian.nocutnews.co.kr.

Korean Ministerial Sociology Institute. 2006. "Korean Religiosity Shown in Converts from Protestantism to Catholicism." www.cainchon.or.kr/web/board/board_view.aspx.

Korean Presbyterian Education Department. 1993. *Standard Handbook for Ceremonies*. Seoul: Korean Presbyterian Assembly.

Kraft, Charles H. 2002. *Confronting Powerless Christianity: Evangelicals and the Missing Dimension*. Grand Rapids: Chosen Books.

———. 2005. *Christianity in Culture: A Study in Biblical Theologizing in Cross-Cultural Perspective*. 2nd ed. Maryknoll, NY: Orbis Books.

Kwesi, D. A. 1970. *An Introduction to the History and Religion of Israel*. London: Longman & Todd.

Kyakas, Alome, and Polly Wiessner. 1992. *From Inside the Women's House: Enga Women's Lives and Traditions*. Buranda, Queensland: Robert Brown & Associates.

Kyoungdong Church Home Ceremony Research. 1995. *Christian Home Ceremony Handbook*. Seoul: Papyrus.

Lakoff, George. 1987a. "Cognitive Model and Prototype Theory." In *Concepts and Conceptual Development: Ecological and Intellectual Factors in Categorization*, ed. Ulrich Neisser, 63–100. Cambridge: Cambridge University Press.

———. 1987b. *Women, Fire, and Dangerous Things: What Categories Reveal about the Mind*. Chicago: University of Chicago Press.

———. 1993. "The Contemporary Theory of Metaphor." In *Metaphor and Thought*. 2nd ed., ed. Andrew Ortony, 202–51. Cambridge: Cambridge University Press.

Lakoff, George, and Mark Johnson. 1980. *Metaphors We Live By*. Chicago: University of Chicago Press.

———. 1999. *Philosophy in the Flesh: The Embodied Mind and Its Challenge to Western Thought*. New York, Basic Books.

Lakoff, George, and Mark Turner. 1989. *More Than Cool Reason*. Chicago: University of Chicago Press.

Laudin, Larry. 1996. *Beyond Positivism and Relativism: Theory, Method, and Evidence*. Boulder, CO: Westview Press.

Lawler, Ronald, Donald W. Wuerl, and Thomas Comerford Lawler. 1976. *The Teaching of Christ: A Catholic Catechism for Adults*. Huntington, IN: Our Sunday Visitor.

Lawson, E. Thomas, and Robert N. McCauley. 1990. *Rethinking Religion: Connecting Cognition and Culture*. Cambridge: Cambridge University Press.

Leach, E. R. 1964. *Political Systems of Highland Burma*. Boston, MA: Beacon Press.

Lee, JungYoung. 1988. "Ancestor Worship: From a Theological Perspective." In *Ancestor Worship and Christianity in Korea*, ed. Lee Jung Young, 83–91. Lampeter, UK: Edwin Mellen Press.

Lee, Peter. 2016. "Hybridity as a Missiological Concept: Exploring Identity and Mission in a Globalizing World." Presentation at ASM Conference, St. Paul, MN, June 17–19.

Loeliger, Carl. 1979. "Biblical Concept of Salvation." In *Christ in Melanesia*, ed. James Knight, 135–45. Goroka, PNG: Melanesian Institute.

Lonergan, Bernard J. F. 1957. *Insight: A Study of Human Understanding*. New York: Philosophical Library.

———. 1972. *Method in Theology*. New York: Herder & Herder.

Lowe, Chuck. 2001. *Honoring God and Family: A Christian Response to Idol Food in Chinese Popular Religion*. Bangalore: Theological Book Trust.

Luther, Martin. 1957. *Christian Liberty*. Edited by Harold J. Grimm. Philadelphia: Fortress.

Luzbetak, Louis J. 1954. "The Socioreligious Significance of a New Guinea Pig Festival." *Anthropological Quarterly* 27: 59–80, 102–28.

———. 1988. *The Church and Cultures: New Perspectives in Missiological Anthropology*. Maryknoll, NY: Orbis Books.

MacCormac, Earl R. 1985. *A Cognitive Theory of Metaphor*. Cambridge, MA: MIT Press.

Magesa, Laurenti. 1997. *African Religion: The Moral Traditions of Abundant Life*. Maryknoll, NY: Orbis Books.

Malakyan, P. G. 2013. "Leadership Models in Armenia: Historical and Contemporary Perspectives." *SAGE Open* (April–July): 1–11.

Malinowski, Bronislaw. 1935. *Coral Gardens and Their Magic*. London: Allen and Unwin.

Man, Ronald E. 2012. "Lessons from Global Worship." *Evangelical Review of Theology* 36, no. 3, 214–30.

Manookian, A. 1986. *The Armenian Church Feasts*. Glendale, CA: New Hye.

Mantovani, Ennio. 1977. "A Fundamental Melanesian Religion." In *Point No. 1: Christ in Melanesia—Exploring Theological Issues*, 154–65. Goroka, PNG: Melanesian Institute.

———. 1984. "Celebrations of Cosmic Renewal." In *An Introduction to Melanesian Religions*, 147–68. Goroka, PNG: Melanesian Institute.

———. 2000. *Divine Revelation and the Religions of PNG: A Missiological Manual*. Goroka, PNG: Melanesian Institute.

———. 2009. "Dema as Religious Symbol in Papua New Guinea." In *Religion and Retributive Logic*, ed. Carole Cusack and Chris Hartney, 80–99. Leiden, The Netherlands: Brill.

———. 2014. *The Dema and the Christ: My Engagement and Inner Dialogue with the Cultures and Religions of Melanesia*. Siegburg, Germany: Studia Instituti Missiologici Societatis Verbi Divini, No. 101.

Mantovani, Ennio, and Mary N. MacDonald. 1982. "God's Word and Ancestor's Response." In *Occasional Papers of the Melanesian Institute, 1: Christ the Life of Papua New Guinea*. Goroka, PNG: Melanesian Institute.

Mateos, Juan. 1972. *Beyond Conventional Christianity*. Translated by Kathleen England. Manila: East Asian Pastoral Institute.

May, John D'Arcy, ed. 1985. *Point 8. Living Theology in Melanesia: A Reader*. Goroka, PNG: Melanesian Institute.

Mbiti, John. 1975a. *Introduction to African Religion*. Oxford: Heinemann Educational Publishers.

———. 1975b. *The Prayers of African Religion*. Maryknoll, NY: Orbis Books.

McCauley, Robert N., and E. Thomas Lawson. 2002. *Bringing Ritual to Mind: Psychological Foundations of Cultural Forms*. Cambridge: Cambridge University Press.

McCulloch, Allison. 2014. "A Man and His Mana." *The Listener Magazine*, June 14.

Mead, Hirini Moko. 2003. *Tikanga Maori: Living by Maori Values*. Wellington, NZ: Huia Publishers.

Metge, Joan. 2004. *Rautahi, The Maori of New Zealand*. Grand Rapids: Baker Books.

Ministerial Sociology Institute. 2006. "Korean Religiosity Shown in Converts from Protestantism to Catholicism." May 4, www.cainchon.or.kr.

Moon, Paul. 2001. *Hone HekeNgaPuhi Warrior*. Northland, NZ: David Ling Publishing.

Moro, Pamela, and James Myers, ed. 2012. *Magic, Witchcraft and Religion: A Reader in the Anthropology of Religion*. 9th ed. New York: McGraw Hill.

Mulago, Vincent. 1991. "Traditional African Religion and Christianity." In *African Traditional Religion in Contemporary Society*, ed. Jacob K. Olupona, 119–34. New York: Paragon House.

Mullenax, Nancy A. 1992. "Native of Her Land: Costa Rica's Virgin of Los Angeles." *Journal of Latin American Lore* 18: 3–13. Summer–Winter.

NationMaster.com. n.d. Armenia Religion Statistics. www.NationMaster.com.

Neisser, Ulrich. 1976. *Cognition and Reality: Principles and Implications of Cognitive Psychology*. San Francisco: W. H. Freeman and Company.

Nersoyan, H. 1970. *Divine Liturgy of the Armenian Apostolic Orthodox Church*. Bronx, NY: John XXIII Center.

Newbigin, Lesslie. 1984. *Foolishness to the Greeks: The Gospel and Western Culture*. Grand Rapids: Eerdmans.

———. 1995. *The Open Secret: An Introduction to the Theology of Mission*. Grand Rapids: Eerdmans. (Original edition: 1978.)

Newman, Keith. 2014. "Get Over It or Get On with It? Unfinished Business in Our Own Backyard." Auckland, NZ: Mission Koru.

Nicholson, Lori. 2015. "Encountering the Divine: A Tamil View of Experiencing God." PhD Dissertation, Fuller Graduate School of Intercultural Studies. Pasadena, CA.

Nida, Eugene A., and Charles R. Taber. 1981. *The Theory and Practice of Translation*. 2nd ed. Leiden, The Netherlands: E. J. Brill. (Original edition: 1969.)

Niebuhr, H. Richard. 1951. *Christ and Culture*. New York: Harper.

Niebuhr, Reinhold. 1952. *The Irony of American History*. New York: Scribner.

Nilles, John. 1977. "Simbu Ancestors and Christian Worship." *Catalyst* 7, no. 1: 63–90.

Nkwoka, A. O. 2006. "The Challenge of Nigerian Pentecostal Theology and the Perspicuity of Scripture." In *Study of Religion in Southern Africa*, ed. Johannes A. Smit and P. Pratap Kumar, 115–27. Boston: Brill.

Noth, Martin. 1960. "The 'Re-Presentation' of the Old Testament Proclamation." In *Essays in Old Testament Hermeneutics*, ed. C. Westermann, 76–88. Richmond, VA: John Knox Press.

Obasare, Emmanuel O. 2005. *Implications of Jamaican Maroon Understanding of Ancestors: An Interpretation*. PhD Dissertation, Fuller Graduate School of Intercultural Studies. Pasadena, CA.

Ok, Sung Deuk. 2005. "Korean Protestantism and Ancestral Rites." In *Religion and Ancestral Rites*, ed. Pyun Moo Young, 208–59. Seoul: Minsokwon.

Ole, Ronnie Tom. 1990. "Making Sense of the Oneness of Life: A Melanesian Christian View on Creation." *Melanesian Journal of Theology* 6, no. 2: 33–41.

Oluwola, C. 1993. *African Traditional Religion and the Christian Faith*. Ibadan, Nigeria: Africa Christian Press.

One Hot Mama. 2006, February 3. Powwows.com, http://forums.powwows.com.

Onwuegbuchulam, Damian Eze. 2008. *The Eucharist as Orikonso*. Frankfurt: Peter Lang.

Oosthuizen, C. G. 1979. *Afro-Christian Religions*. Leiden, The Netherlands: Brill.

Ormanian, M. 1955. *The Church of Armenia*. Burbank, CA: Western Diocesan Press.

———. 2000. *The Church of Armenia*. Montreal, Quebec: Armenian Holy Apostolic Church Canadian Diocese.

Orobator, Agbonkhianmeghe E. 2008. *Theology Brewed in an African Pot*. Maryknoll, NY: Orbis Books.

O'Sullivan, Dominic. 2005. *Faith, Politics, and Reconciliation: Catholicism and the Politics of Indigeneity*. Wellington, NZ: Huia Publishers.

Paden, William E. 1988. *Religious Worlds: A Comparative Study of Religion.* Boston: Beacon Press.

Pailin, David. 1990. *The Anthropological Character of Theology: Conditioning Theological Understanding.* Cambridge: Cambridge University Press.

PNG Constitution. n.d. www.wipo.int.

Pike, Kenneth L. 1967. Chapter 2: Etic and Emic Standpoints for the Description of Behavior. In *Language in Relation to a Unified Theory of the Structure of Human Behavior.* The Hague, Netherlands: Mouton: 37–47.

Pinnock, Clark. 1992. *A Wideness in God's Mercy: The Finality of Jesus Christ in a World of Religions.* Grand Rapids: Zondervan.

Pratt, Richard H. 1892. *Official Report of the Nineteenth Annual Conference of Charities and Correction*: 46–59. (Reprinted in Richard H. Pratt, "The Advantages of Mingling Indians with Whites," *Americanizing the American Indians: Writings by the "Friends of the Indian," 1880–1900* [Cambridge: Harvard University Press, 1973]: 260–71.)

Price, Richard. 1996. *Maroon Societies: Rebel Slave Communities in the Americas.* 3rd ed. Baltimore: Johns Hopkins University Press.

Rappaport, Roy A. 1999. *Ritual and Religion in the Making of Humanity.* Cambridge: Cambridge University Press.

Reese, Alistair. 2006. "Are You Listening? The Voice of Waitaha: A Forgotten People." Unpublished master's thesis for University of Waikato, New Zealand.

Reisman, Bernard. 1975. "The *Havurah:* An Approach to Humanizing Jewish Organizational Life." *Journal of Jewish Community Service* 52, no. 2: 202–9.

Richard, H. L. 2011. "All Things Are Yours." *Mission Frontiers*, May–June.

Ricoeur, Paul. 1976. *Interpretation Theory: Discourse and the Surplus of Meaning.* Fort Worth: Texas Christian University Press.

———. 1979. "The Metaphorical Process as Cognition, Imagination, and Feeling." In *On Metaphor*, ed. Sheldon Sacks, 141–57. Chicago: University of Chicago Press.

Ritual Table and Food Arrangement in the Korean Ancestral Rite. n.d. k.daum.net.

Robbins, Joel. 2004. *Becoming Sinners: Christianity and Moral Torment in a Papua New Guinea Society.* Berkeley: University of California Press.

Robbins, Joel and Naomi Haynes, eds. 2014. "The Anthropology of Christianity: Unity, Diversity, New Directions," *Current Anthropology* 55, Supp. 10. Wenner Gren Foundation for Anthropological Research. Chicago, IL: University of Chicago Press.

Rosch, Eleanor. 1977. "Human Categorization." In *Studies in Cross-Cultural Psychology*, vol. 1, ed. Neil Warren, 1–49. New York: Academic Press.

Russell, James C. 1994. *The Germanization of Early Medieval Christianity: A Sociohistorical Approach to Religious Transformation.* New York: Oxford University Press.

Rynkiewich, Michael. 2004. *Cultures and Languages of Papua New Guinea: The Story of the Origins, Migrations, and Settlement of Melanesian Peoples, Languages, and Cultures.* Goroka, PNG: Melanesian Institute.

Sam, D. L., and J. W. Berry. 2006. *Acculturation Psychology.* Cambridge, MA: Cambridge University Press.

Samuelian, T. J. 2001. *St. Grigor Narekatsi: Speaking with God from the Depths of the Heart.* Yerevan, Armenia: Vem Press.

Sanneh, Lamin. 1989. *Translating the Message: The Missionary Impact on Culture.* Maryknoll, NY: Orbis Books.

———. 2012. *Summoned from the Margins: Homecoming of an African.* Grand Rapids: Eerdmans.

Saroyan, W. 1936. "The Armenian and the Armenian." In *Inhale & Exhale.* New York: Random House.

Schaefer, Alfons. 1981. "Christianised Ritual Pig-Killing." *Catalyst* 11: 213–23, no. 4.

Schattauer, Thomas H. 2011. "God's Mission and the Christian Assembly: The Search for an Alternative Practice of Worship." *Journal of Theology* 50, no. 2: 143–53.

Schreiter, Robert. 1985. *Constructing Local Theologies.* Maryknoll, NY: Orbis Books.

———. 1998. *Reconciliation.* Maryknoll, NY: Orbis Books.

Seino, Katsuhiko. 2011. *Kirisutokyo Souseibunnka wo Motomete: Seisyo teki Tukagire no Riron to Jissen* [Toward Christian funeral culture: A theory and practice of biblical rite of passage]. Tsuchiura, Ibaraki: Ibaraki Publishing Center.

Shaw, R. Daniel. 1988. *Transculturation: The Cultural Factor in Translation and Other Communication Tasks.* Pasadena, CA: William Carey Library.

———. 1990. *Kandila: Samo Ceremonialism and Interpersonal Relationships.* Ann Arbor: University of Michigan Press.

———. 2009. "A Samo Theology of Mediumship: A Case Study of Local Theologizing and Global Reflection." In *Religion and Retributive Logic: Essays in Honour of Professor Gary W. Trompf*, ed. Carole Cusack and Chris Hartney, 65–79. Leiden, The Netherlands: Brill.

———. 2010. "Beyond Contextualization: Toward a Twenty-First-Century Model for Enabling Mission." *International Bulletin of Missionary Research* 34, no. 4: 208–15.

———. 2016. "The Cognitive Nature of Ritual." Presentation at ASM Conference, St. Paul, MN, June 17–19.

Shaw, R. Daniel, and Charles E. Van Engen. 2003. *Communicating God's Word in a Complex World: God's Truth or Hocus Pocus?* Oxford: Rowman & Littlefield.

Shaw, Ryan S. 2006. *Waking the Giant: The Resurging Student Mission Movement*. Pasadena, CA: William Carey Library.

Smith, Mark S. 2007. "'Your People Shall Be My People': Family and Covenant in Ruth 1:16–17." *Catholic Biblical Quarterly* 69, April.

Snyder, Howard. 2011. *The Ecology of Sin and Grace: Overcoming the Divorce between Earth and Heaven*. Eugene, OR: Cascade Books.

Somé, Malidoma Patrice. 1994. *Of Water and the Spirit. Ritual, Magic, and Initiation in the Life of an African Shaman*. New York: Penguin Group.

Sperber, Dan, and Deirdre Wilson. 1986. *Relevance: Communication and Cognition*. Cambridge, MA: Harvard University Press. (Reprint: 1995.)

Steinsaltz, Adin. 2012–15. *Koren Talmud Bavli*. Hebrew/English ed. Jerusalem: Shefa Foundation.

Strathern, Andrew J. 1972. *One Father, One Blood: Descent and Group Structure among the Melpa People*. London: Tavistock.

Strelan, John. 1977. *The Search for Salvation: Studies in the History and Theology of Cargo Cults*. Adelaide, South Australia: Lutheran Publishing House.

Sweetser, Eve. 1995. "Metaphor, Mythology, and Everyday Language." *Journal of Pragmatics* 24, no. 6: 585–93.

Tate, Henare Arekatera. 2010. "He Tirohanga Anganuikietahikaupapahohonumotewhakapono Māori: Towards Some Foundations of a Systematic Maori Theology." Unpublished dissertation, Melbourne College of Divinity.

Taylor, Charles. 2007. *A Secular Age*. Cambridge: Belknap Press of Harvard University Press.

TeAoHou The New World. 1956. No. 16, National Library of New Zealand, http://teaohou.natlib.govt.nz.

Thomson, R. W. 2001. *The Teaching of Saint Gregory*. New Rochelle, NY: St. Nersess Armenian Seminary.

Titiev, Mischa. 1960. "A Fresh Approach to the Problem of Magic and Religion." *Southwest Journal of Anthropology* 16, no. 3: 292–98.

ToVaninara, Caspar. 1985. "Melanesian Stepping-Stones for the Preaching of the Kingdom." In *Point 8, Living Theology in Melanesia: A Reader*, ed. John D'Arcy May, 132–71. Goroka, PNG: Melanesian Institute.

Tracy, David. 1987. *Plurality and Ambiguity: Hermeneutics, Religion, Hope*. San Francisco: Harper & Row.

Treaty FAQs. 2014. Ministry for Culture and Heritage, http://www.nzhistory.net.nz.

Treaty of Waitangi Timeline. 2004. In *The Treaty of Waitangi Information Programme*, State Services Commission. Wellington, NZ.

Trompf, Garry W. 1981. "Oral Sources and the Study of Religious History in Papua New Guinea." In *Oral Tradition in Melanesia*, ed. Donald Denoon and Roderic Lacey, 151–74. The University of Papua New Guinea and the Institute of Papua New Guinea Studies.

———. 1988. "Salvation and Primal Religion." In *The Idea of Salvation*. ed. D. W. Dockrill and R. G. Tanner. 207–31. Prudentia, Supp. No. 1988, University of Auckland.

Trompf, Garry W., ed. 1987. *The Gospel Is Not Western*. Maryknoll, NY: Orbis Books.

Turner, Mark. 1987. *Death Is the Mother of Beauty: Mind, Metaphor, Criticism*. Chicago: University of Chicago Press.

Turner, Mark, and Gilles Fauconnier. 1995. "Conceptual Integration and Formal Experience." *Metaphor and Symbolic Activity* 10, no. 3: 183–204.

Turner, Victor. 1969. *The Ritual Process*. Harmondworth, UK: Penguin Books.

———. 1970. *Forest of Symbols: Aspects of Nembu Ritual*. Ithaca, NY: Cornell University Press.

Tuza, Esau. 1978. "A Melanesian Cosmological Process." *Catalyst* 8: 244–58, no. 4.

Twiss, Richard. 2015. *Rescuing the Gospel from the Cowboys*. Downers Grove, IL: IVP Books.

Tylor, Edward B. 1871. *Primitive Culture*. 2 vols. London: Murray.

Van Engen, Charles E. 1996. *Mission on the Way: Issues in Mission Theology*. Grand Rapids: Baker.

van Gennep, Arnold. 1960. *The Rites of Passage*. Translated by M. B. Visedom and G. L. Caffee. Chicago: University of Chicago Press. (Original edition: *Les rites de passage* [Paris: Picard, 1909].)

Vatican Council II. 1965a. *Ad Gentes* (*Decree on the Church's Missionary Activity*). In *Vatican Council II,* 2 vols., vol. 1, *The Conciliar and Postconciliar Documents*, ed. Austin Flannery, 803–62. Northport, NY: Costello Publishing Company. [Published 1992.]

Vatican Council II. 1965b. *Gaudium et Spes* (*Pastoral Constitution on the Church in the Modern World*). In *Vatican Council II,* 2 vols., vol. 1, *The Conciliar and Postconciliar Documents*, ed. Austin Flannery, 903–1001. Northport, NY: Costello Publishing Co. [Published 1992.]

Vatican Council II. 1965c. *Lumen Gentium* (*Dogmatic Constitution on the Church*). In *Vatican Council II*, 2 vols., vol. 1, *The Conciliar and Postconciliar Documents*, ed. Austin Flannery, 350–426. Northport, NY: Costello Publishing Company. [Published 1992.]

Volf, Miroslav. 1989. "Materiality of Salvation: An Investigation in the Soteriologies of Liberation and Pentecostal Theologies." *Journal of Ecumenical Studies* 26, no. 3: 447–67.

Von Rad, Gerhard. 1965. *The Theology of the Old Testament*. Vol. 2, *Theology of Israel's Prophetic Traditions*. Translated by D. M. G. Stalker. Edinburgh: Oliver and Boyd.

Wainwright, Geoffrey, and Karen B. Westerfield Tucker, eds. 2005. *The Oxford History of Christian Worship*. New York: Oxford University Press.

Waitangi Tribunal Official Website. n.d. http://www.justice.govt.nz.

Walls, Andrew F. 1996. "The Translation Principle in Christian History." In *The Missionary Movement in Christian History: Studies in the Transmission of Faith*, 26–42. Maryknoll, NY: Orbis Books.

Weber, Max. 1964. *The Sociology of Religion*. Translated by Ephraim Fischoff. Boston: Beacon Press. [Translated from 4th ed. *Religionsoziologie* (1956). First German edition, 1922.]

Weerakoon, Kamal. 2016. "Towards a Theology of Culturally Hybrid Missionality, with Special Reference to 1 Corinthians 9." Presentation at ASM Conference, St. Paul, MN, June 17–19.

Wheelwright, Philip. 1962. *Metaphor and Reality*. Bloomington: Indiana University Press.

Williams, Herbert. 1957. *A Dictionary of the Maori Language*. 6th ed. Wellington, NZ: R. E. Owen, Government Printer.

Willowbank Report. 1978. "Consultation on Gospel and Culture." Lausanne Occasional Papers No. 2. Wheaton, IL: Lausanne Committee for World Evangelization.

Wright, N.T. 2005. *The Last Word: Beyond the Bible Wars to a New Understanding of the Authority of Scripture*. New York: HarperCollins.

———. 2008. *Surprised by Hope: Rethinking Heaven, the Resurrection, and the Mission of the Church*. New York. HarperOne.

———. 2009. *Paul in Fresh Perspective*. Minneapolis: Fortress Press.

Wuthnow, Robert. 1999. *Growing Up Religious: Christians and Jews and Their Journeys of Faith*. Boston: Beacon.

Yoon, Duk. 2005. "A Comparative Study of Traditional Ancestral Rites Table Arrangement and Practice." *Comparative Folklore* 28: 329–63, www.korea4expats.com.

Zahan, Dominique. 2000. "Some Reflections on African Spirituality." In *African Spirituality*, ed. Jacob K. Olupona, 3–25. New York: Crossroad.

Zahniser, A. H. Mathias. 1994a. "Between Proclamation and Dialogue: An Elenctic Approach to Cross-Cultural Witness." Class Lecture MW-605, Fall semester. Asbury Theological Seminary, Wilmore, KY.

———. 1994b. "Close Encounters of the Vulnerable Kind: Christian Dialogical Proclamation among Muslims." *Asbury Theological Journal* 49, no. 1: 71–78.

———. 1997. *Symbol and Ceremony: Making Disciples across Cultures*. Monrovia, CA: MARC.

Zips, Werner. 1999. *Black Rebels: African Caribbean Freedom Fighters in Jamaica*. Kingston, Jamaica: Ian Randle Publishers.

Zocca, Franco. 1997. "God's Salvific Presence outside Christianity: A Roman Catholic Perspective." Occasional Papers of the Melanesian Institute, No. 10. Goroka, PNG: Melanesian Institute.

Zocca, Franco, ed. 2009. "Sanguma in Paradise: Sorcery, Witchcraft, and Christianity in Papua New Guinea." *Point No. 33*. Goroka, PNG: Melanesian Institute.

Index

Previously Published in The American Society of Missiology Series

1. *Protestant Pioneers in Korea*, Everett Nichols Hunt Jr.
2. *Catholic Politics in China and Korea*, Eric O. Hanson
3. *From the Rising of the Sun: Christians and Society in Contempory Japan*, James M. Phillips
4. *Meaning across Cultures*, Eugene A. Nida and William D. Reyburn
5. *The Island Churches of the Pacific*, Charles W. Forman
6. *Henry Venn: Missionary Statesman*, Wilbert R. Shenk
7. *No Other Name?Christianity and Other World Religions*, Paul F. Knitter
8. *Toward a New Age in Christian Theology*, Richard Henry Drummond
9 *The Expectation of the Poor: Latin American Base Ecclesial Communities in Protest*, Guillermo Cook
10. *Eastern Orthodox Mission Theology Today*, James J. Stamoolis
11. *Confucius, the Buddha, and Christ: A History of the Gospel in China*, Ralph R. Covell
12. *The Church and Cultures: New Perspectives in Missiological Anthropology*, Louis J. Luzbetak, SVD
13. *Translating the Message: The Missionary Impact on Culture*, Lamin Sanneh
14. *An African Tree of Life*, Thomas G. Christensen
15. *Missions and Money: Affluence as a Western Missionary Problem . . . Revisited* (Second Edition), Jonathan J. Bonk
16. *Transforming Mission: Paradigm Shifts in Theology of Mission*, David J. Bosch
17. *Bread for the Journey: The Mission and Transformation of Mission*, Anthony J. Gittins, C.S.Sp.
18. *New Face of the Church in Latin America: Between Tradition and Change*, edited by Guillermo Cook
19. *Mission Legacies: Biographical Studies of Leaders of the Modern Missionary Movement*, edited by Gerald H. Anderson, Robert T. Coote, Norman A. Horner, and James M. Phillips
20. *Classic Texts in Mission and World Christianity*, edited by Norman E. Thomas
21. *Christian Mission: A Case Study Approach*, Alan Neely
22. *Understanding Spiritual Power: A Forgotten Dimension of Cross-Cultural Mission and Ministry*, Marguerite G. Kraft
23. *Missiological Education for the 21st Century: The Book, the Circle, and the Sandals*, edited by J. Dudley Woodberry, Charles Van Engen, and Edgar J. Elliston
24. *Dictionary of Mission: Theology, History, Perspectives*, edited by Karl Müller, SVD, Theo Sundermeier, Stephen B. Bevans, SVD, and Richard H. Bliese
25. *Earthen Vessels and Transcendent Power: American Presbyterians in China, 1837–1952*, G. Thompson Brown
26. *The Missionary Movement in American Catholic History*, Angelyn Dries, OSF
27. *Mission in the New Testament: An Evangelical Approach*, edited by William J. Larkin Jr. and Joel W. Williams
28. *Changing Frontiers of Mission*, Wilbert R. Shenk
29. *In the Light of the Word: Divine Word Missionaries of North America*, Ernest Brandewie

30. *Constants in Context: A Theology of Mission for Today*, Stephen B. Bevans, SVD, and Roger P. Schroeder, SVD
31. *Changing Tides: Latin America and World Mission Today*, Samuel Escobar
32. *Gospel Bearers, Gender Barriers: Missionary Women in the Twentieth Century*, edited by Dana L. Robert
33. *Church: Community for the Kingdom*, John Fuellenbach, SVD
34. *Mission in Acts: Ancient Narratives in Contemporary Context*, edited by Robert L. Gallagher and Paul Hertig
35. *A History of Christianity in Asia: Volume I, Beginnings to 1500*, Samuel Hugh Moffett
36. *A History of Christianity in Asia: Volume II, 1500–1900*, Samuel Hugh Moffett
37. *A Reader's Guide to Transforming Mission*, Stan Nussbaum
38. *The Evangelization of Slaves and Catholic Origins in Eastern Africa*, Paul V. Kollman, CSC
39. *Israel and the Nations: A Mission Theology of the Old Testament*, James Chukwuma Okoye, C.S.Sp.
40. *Women in Mission: From the New Testament to Today*, Susan E. Smith
41. *Reconstructing Christianity in China: K. H. Ting and the Chinese Church*, Philip L. Wickeri
42. *Translating the Message: The Missionary Impact on Culture* (second edition), Lamin Sanneh
43. *Landmark Essays in Mission and World Christianity*, edited by Robert L. Gallagher and Paul Hertig
44. *World Mission in the Wesleyan Spirit*, Darrell L. Whiteman and Gerald H. Anderson (published by Province House, Franklin, TN)
45. *Miracles, Missions, & American Pentecostalism*, Gary B. McGee
46. *The Gospel among the Nations: A Documentary History of Inculturation*, Robert A. Hunt
47. *Missions and Unity: Lessons from History, 1792–2010*, Norman E. Thomas (published by Wipf and Stock, Eugene, OR)
48. *Mission and Culture: The Louis J. Luzbetak Lectures*, edited by Stephen B. Bevans
49. *Comprehending Mission: The Questions, Methods, Themes, Problems, and Prospects of Missiology*, Stanley H. Skreslet
50. *Christian Mission among the Peoples of Asia*, Jonathan Y. Tan
51. *Sent Forth: African Missionary Work in the West*, Harvey C. Kwiyani
52. *Mangoes or Bananas: The Quest for an Authentic Asian Christian Theology*, Hwa Yung
53. *Contemporary Mission Theology: Engaging the Nations: Essays in Honor of Charles E. Van Engen*, edited by Robert L. Gallagher and Paul Hertig
54. *African Christian Leadership: Realities, Opportunities, and Impact*, edited by Kirimi Barine and Robert Priest
55. *Women Leaders in the Student Christian Movement: 1880–1920*, Thomas Russell
56. *Traditional Ritual as Christian Worship: Dangerous Syncretism or Necessary Hybridity?*, R. Daniel Shaw and William R. Burrows